DATE DUE

Demco No. 62-0549

AUDREY COHEN COLLEGE LIBRARY
75 Varick St. 12th Floor
New York, NY 10013

TRANSFORMING PRIVACY

**Praeger Series in
Transformational Politics and Political Science**

The Politics of Transformation: Local Activism in the Peace and Environmental Movements
Betty H. Zisk

The Latino Family and the Politics of Transformation
David T. Abalos

Mediation, Citizen Empowerment, and Transformational Politics
Edward W. Schwerin

Strategies of Transformation Toward a Multicultural Society: Fulfilling the Story of Democracy
David T. Abalos

Beyond Confrontation: Transforming the New World Order
Charles Hauss

Teaching Democracy by Being Democratic
Theodore L. Becker and Richard A. Couto, editors

TRANSFORMING PRIVACY
A TRANSPERSONAL PHILOSOPHY OF RIGHTS

Stefano Scoglio

Praeger Series in Transformational Politics and
Political Science
Theodore L. Becker, Series Adviser

Westport, Connecticut
London

Library of Congress Cataloging-in-Publication Data

Scoglio, Stefano.
   Transforming privacy : a transpersonal philosophy of rights / Stefano Scoglio.
      p.   cm.—(Praeger series in transformational politics and political science, ISSN 1061-5261)
   Includes bibliographical references and index.
   ISBN 0-275-95607-5 (alk. paper)
   1. Privacy, Right of—United States—History.   I. Title.
II. Series.
KF1262.S36   1998
342.73'0858—dc21   97-9180

British Library Cataloguing in Publication Data is available.

Copyright © 1998 by Stefano Scoglio

All rights reserved. No portion of this book may be reproduced, by any process or technique, without the express written consent of the publisher.

Library of Congress Catalog Card Number: 97-9180
ISBN: 0-275-95607-5
ISSN: 1061-5261

First published in 1998

Praeger Publishers, 88 Post Road West, Westport, CT 06881
An imprint of Greenwood Publishing Group, Inc.

Printed in the United States of America

The paper used in this book complies with the Permanent Paper Standard issued by the National Information Standards Organization (Z39.48-1984).

10 9 8 7 6 5 4 3 2 1

CONTENTS

Introduction: The Abysmal State of Privacy in the Age of Absolute
    Capitalism   1

Chapter 1   The Philosophy of Privacy   21

Chapter 2   Right to Privacy and Natural Law   53

Chapter 3   From Mill to Brandeis   77

Chapter 4   1937–1965: Between Two Constitutional Revolutions   125

Chapter 5   Abortion and the New Privacy Paradigm   153

Chapter 6   Brandeis, Douglas, and the Transpersonal Theory
    of Rights   187

Chapter 7   What to Do about Privacy?   225

Selected Bibliography   237

Index   243

TRANSFORMING PRIVACY

INTRODUCTION: THE ABYSMAL STATE OF PRIVACY IN THE AGE OF ABSOLUTE CAPITALISM

When we talk of the dreadful state of privacy today, we generally refer to the field of "informational privacy," that is, to the control over the disclosure of personal information. This is the area of privacy that is most visibly under attack. But informational privacy, in spite of the widespread habit of identifying it with privacy as a whole, is indeed only one aspect of privacy.[1] We can reasonably subdivide privacy into four main areas:

1. *Physical privacy*, which is traditionally related to the category of property, both through the idea that "a man's house is his castle" and through the idea that we have a sort of property over our bodies. The two must not be confused: Privacy is an independent value that the outer shell of property normally protects, but that sometimes—for instance, when the government claims the legitimate power to penetrate the proprietary shell through searches and seizures—reemerges in its full independence, as we shall see. This is the area that refers to the classical "habeas corpus."

2. *Decisional privacy*, which has emerged as an important aspect of privacy through the rights-revolution of the *Griswold-Roe* era and which refers to all that concerns decisions and choices of the person about his/her personal private actions. Generally this area is associated with the sphere of personality rights, the second of the three levels that will constitute our general conception of rights. We shall see that here too decisional privacy, although normally implicitly protected by personality rights, emerges, in specific situations, as an independent component of the right to privacy.

3. *Informational privacy*, which as we said concerns the control of information about

oneself. This area, which we are about to explore more in detail, is at the center of the current massive attack on privacy. Informational privacy, having to do with the knowledge that others have of an individual, is most directly related to the sphere of political privacy, which involves the freedom of and the control over individual expression and participation in the public realm. To be sure, informational privacy has a most visible impact on our economic relations, yet its reality is inherently political.

4. *Formational privacy*, which is the most essential dimension of privacy, although it is scarcely considered at all. It refers to privacy as interiority. It concerns all those activities, such as TV, advertising, and mass culture, that penetrate more or less unduly into people's mind. Penetrating the mind is indeed the ultimate goal also of the other forms of invasion of privacy. Creating a situation in which *minds can be left alone*, where culture and education foster a self-reflecting and critical interiority, is the fundamental end of the battle for privacy and for an ethically and spiritually sustainable society.

These four categories of privacy are the four aspects of a unitary concept of privacy as "withdrawal" that we will explore later. Here I would like only to stress the importance of a unitary concept of privacy. In fact, the complex nature of privacy has been the main **reductionistic** argument to claim that the right to privacy is an incoherent conglomerate of unrelated elements, an approach that stands in direct opposition to the **holistic** assertion of the fundamental unity underlying its different aspects. It has been mostly **holistic** thinkers who have tried to do something about the "death of privacy" in our times.[2]

The constant scrutiny of individuals and groups on the part of immense "private" and "public" bureaucracies, together with the progressive fusion of those bureaucracies into a Leviathanish superorganism, has steadily dissolved what was thought to be a clear distinction of private and public into an increasingly "total" system organized under the primacy of the economic dimension, which S. Wolin calls the "Economic Polity."[3] Like Aristotle's "polity," this too is a mix of oligarchy and democracy, but one in which a giant oligarchic distribution of wealth and power on a planetary level is associated with a formalistic political democracy and a "democratic" mass society and culture. Mass society has been chastised by J. S. Mill as the "tyranny of the majority," while others—for example, the Frankfurt School—have seen it as the product of a giant bureaucratic manipulation of needs and minds typical of late capitalism. In fact, it is probably both. It would be a mistake to think that the organization of needs and desires has active manipulators on the one hand and passive manipulated minds on the other. The reality is that the huge, planetary structuring of needs and desires through TV, advertising, education, and even social and political symbols is possible and keeps growing precisely because the "manipulated" minds do not play just a passive role. One wonders how "TV and advertising" can have changed our lives so radically, a fact that becomes intelligible only by introducing the element of active complicity from the powerful human mind. Indeed, the great system of capitalistic and consumeristic formation of the mind works

Introduction

by appealing to something that is already present within the human mind, that which we can call the consumeristic, competitive, and thus also fearful and aggressive "lower self," the same self that emerges as a social factor in Mill's "tyranny of the majority."[4]

Because we talk of capitalism repeatedly, we would do better to explain what we mean by it. By capitalism most people mean "market economy." It is a very neutral definition, one that reduces capitalism to an "objective" category that can then be modulated in liberalistic or social democratic terms. It is evident, though, that such a definition does not withstand the light of a more accurate analysis. The market economy has always existed, even in premodern and precapitalistic societies. If anything, capitalism is inherently antimarket. It uses the market only to open up space for its initial penetration, as it happened at the beginning within Europe, and between Europe and the rest of the world.[5] After that, its *monopolistic impulse* tends toward the suppression of the market and creates an oligopolistic economy in which the big monopolistic actors can temporarily coexist, also through the mediation of a government that increasingly falls under the direct control both of the global capitalistic system and of its main actors. What essentially defines capitalism is its inherent absolutistic impulse, its inner necessity, which characterizes at once the general process and the specific individuals and groups that reproduce it, to posit the unlimited maximization of wealth on the one side and of consumeristic choice on the other as the concrete absolute that should satisfy the human quest for fullness and totality. The essence of capitalism is the channeling, into the realm of material and technocultural expansion, of that absolute-impulse that belongs to the realm of the spirit and that from our spiritual depths moves every act of our existence. Capitalism is the self-destructive delusion that unconsciously attributes to nature and human society, in their material aspect, the ability to sustain absolutizations (unlimited economic growth, the worldwide monopolistic tendency of multinational corporations, total cultural conformity) that remain indifferent to the limits imposed by natural/social interdependence and relativity.[6] Let it be clear, then, that when we talk of capitalism we do not refer to "market economy," which is in fact an important value to be rescued from its capitalistic erosion, but to the power of a misdirected absolute-impulse.

Due to its impulse toward unlimited material expansion, capitalism is identifiable with social, economic, and technological Bigness, a category that was central to its critique by Justice Brandeis and Justice Douglas and that we can reinterpret as the ultimate horizon of the misdirected absolute-impulse. Given the impossibility to reach absoluteness within the world as matter, the next reachable level is that which Hegel called "bad infinity," the unlimited accumulation of finite things that never reaches true infinity but that can certainly reach the "big finite" or Bigness. Considering that the shift from knowledge of the finite to knowledge of the "big finite" characterizes also modern science, it is plausible to think of Bigness as "bad infinity," and thus primarily as the quintessential spiritual power that animates the planetary capitalistic machine.

Bigness presupposes a constant and growing externalization into the outer, because the outer is the dimension of finitude and also because it is only out of ourselves that we can search for the finitudes that feed into our misdirected absolute-impulse. Inside we may only find the traces of true infinity, the unlimitedness of thought, the symbolic expressions of eternal archetypes or the sudden feelings of our own original happiness and self-sufficiency, thus moving away from the painful and never-satisfied search for Bigness. There is thus a profound incompatibility between privacy and capitalistic Bigness, and that is why Brandeis, who understood this thoroughly, made the battle against Bigness and the battle for privacy the two sides of a unitary endeavor.

It is from the removal of privacy as spiritual self-reliance that derive all the other forms of privacy invasion, which are in different ways related to the fundamental goal of promoting the inner emergence of people's lower self, and thus of those lower needs and desires on which the global capitalistic economy thrives. Because Bigness is in the end a search for totality that lacks the unlimited openess and freedom of spirit, its processes acquire totalitarian traits. It is a grave mistake to identify totalitarianism with absoluteness, as spiritual absoluteness is indeed perfect freedom. Totalitarianism is essentially generated by a situation whereby the protective limits of relativity and reciprocity, naturally and socially indispensable, are crushed by a misdirected absolute-impulse. Concretely, this happens through the complete absorption of people's life, of work as well as leisure, in the industrial system of production/consumption, which destroys privacy by "discouraging the individual from reliance on his own resources and judgement," both because s/he is "always under observation ... by market researchers and pollsters who tell him what others prefer and what he too must therefore prefer," and because of a popular culture that produces a constant "invasion of experience by images."[7] Indeed, there is an organic link between different and sometimes unsuspected invasions of privacy in the global capitalistic society. Information is extracted from the private sphere

1. to produce images with which to invade the formational privacy of individuals (such as with the gossiping or model-proposing images of the rich and famous)
2. to better know which individuals can be stimulated, and how, in order to become their possessive-consumeristic selves
3. to make sure that people actually belong to the conforming but difficult category of lower-self persons who nevertheless do not fall into criminal behavior (criminal behavior of the powerful does not usually count, being generally integrated in the capitalistic project).

Through these different strategies of mind transformation, people can finally make the "right" decisions on private consumption and life-style. The process eventually ends at the very core of the capitalistic society, the material-sensuous self, which is now willingly ready to be invaded by all sorts of commodities, useless and harmful foods, fashionable and expensive clothes, ineludible cars,

Introduction 5

harmful drugs, and so on. When there is resistance to "freely" accept such an invasion, it may be necessary to legally and/or forcefully subdue decisional and physical privacy, as it happens when certain health practices are more or less forcefully imposed on people in the "general" interest (of the pharmaceutical industry), when certain foods are forced into school or university cafeteria according to "majoritarian" nutritional standards (mostly junk foods), or in the extreme case of a military dictatorship imposing the most-radical laissez-faire economic dogmas, as with the Pinochet Chilean junta teaming up with the so-called Chicago Boys. Again the process we have just described confirms that even the currently all-encompassing physical-economic dimension depends on what happens at the level of ethical and spiritual interiority, which means that even those mainly interested with economic and political justice should treat the disappearance of privacy as the central problem of our world.

Let us look, then, at how the loss of privacy is changing for the worse the various dimensions of our existence. Beyond the most-subtle and unexpected trespasses, including environmental pollution with its secret and deadly violation of our psychosomatic constitution,[8] it is the conflict between privacy and technology that has hit most vehemently the collective unconscious, as witnessed by the success of novels such as A. Huxley's *A Brave New World* and Orwell's *1984*, or of the cult movie *Blade Runner*, whose Replicants are the perfect incarnations of our secret fear of being turned into genetically engineered human robots. We are just at the beginning of the medical use of genetic engineering, and yet things are already getting quite scary, as doctors are beginning to play wizardry with our deepest biological privacy based on a scientific knowledge that is imperfect to say the least. What is even more worrisome at this point is the informational use of genetic testing. Genetic researchers are going around, these days, explaining everything away with genes, including all sorts of psychological conditions, as if human beings could be mechanistically reduced to their genes. The reality is that there are many individuals with similar genes and yet some get sick and others do not. Nevertheless, if the genetic ideology will win, and there are big economic interests that want it to win, we all may soon find ourselves targeted as "asymptomatically ill." In such a scenario, people not only could be stigmatized and marginalized, as it happens today with the seriously sick, because of seemingly defective genes, but we all may be forced to undergo "preventive" pharmacological treatment to avoid a sickness that possibly we would have never contracted and that we may instead very well contract due to the iatrogenic pharmacological side effects. Such a world would be paradise for the powerful pharmaceutical industry. Once again we can see how following a general model, the collecting of personal genetic information, which may become mandatory very soon, together with the formational work of promoting the genetic ideology, are the presupposition of what is most important for capitalism, the remunerative invasion of our decisional and physical privacy with commodities (in this case, drugs).[9]

The attack on genetic privacy is the newest frontier of the more general attack on medical privacy, a fundamental principle of that Hippocratic oath that doctors still recite. As reported by David Burnham, doctors themselves today acknowledge that "the principle of medical confidentiality described in medical codes of ethics and still believed in by patients no longer exists."[10] The collection and distribution of medical information has become a multimillion-dollar industry, and the Medical Information Bureau alone (the major specialized agency in the field) manages information on tens of millions of people. Almost everyone seems to have free access to private medical information, "among them employers, government agencies, credit bureaus, insurers, educational institutions, and the media." Sometimes the circulation of medical information is legitimate, but very often it is not, and Rothfeder shows how there is a thriving underground information industry, which is about to experience a boom with the advent of the Internet, which puts to the most illegitimate use easily obtained medical information. The circulation of personal medical information "has an enormous impact on people's life," affecting "decisions on whether they are hired or fired, whether they can secure business license and life insurance, whether they are permitted to drive cars, whether they are placed under police surveillance or labeled security risks, or even whether they get nominated for or elected to political office."[11] Just think to when medical information will incorporate genetic markers that will keep us out of a job or any other opportunity for no real reason. Of course something could be easily done to stop the uncontrolled circulation of medical information, simply by strictly forbidding doctors and hospitals to reveal medical data and severely sanctioning the violations. But there is a superior interest that will not allow for this, namely the "general interest" that corporations and institutions minimize risks and increase profits, even at the expense of those more important human values, such as respect and personal appreciation, that in the end are the true source even of economic success.

This last point emerges very clearly in reference to the problem of privacy in the workplace. According to Linowes, about 50 percent of all firms make use of medical records for the management of their employees. It is not at all clear that one's medical condition, let alone one's potential illness, should be considered relevant to one's professional destiny, unless in the case of serious illnesses directly interfering with the fulfillment of one's responsibilities. In any case, computerized information, including medical information, is often seriously flawed, and both Linowes and Rothfeder report exemplary horror stories of people not being hired, being fired, or being discriminated against on the ground of mistaken medical data.[12]

The use of computerized data for the hiring and the control of workers is producing radically damaging effects in the realm of work. The use of computerized technology to control workers during the performance of their work, and lately even to read and interfere with their e-mail, is creating hostility and tension between employers and employees, and a collapse of the sense of loyalty and belonging to the firm on the part of the workers that produces results, in terms of both productivity and quality, that are the very opposite of what com-

Introduction

puterized monitoring is supposed to achieve.[13] The computerization of the relationship between administration and workers undermines the most important ingredient of both administration and workmanship, namely *responsibility*. Managers delegate the responsibility of knowing and evaluating workers to less-intelligent and certainly less-sensitive machines, and workers, feeling the company's lack of trust in their ability to behave responsibly and loyally, are demoralized in their ability to spontaneously adhere to the interest of the firm and begin to behave irresponsibly not only as a means to strike back but also because they are unconsciously invited to think of themselves as untrustable and irresponsible. The loss of responsibility is probably the worst product of the wrong use of computers and data banks in our society, resulting in an abstraction of people from direct judgment and personal relationship. The same *abstraction from responsibility*, a general trait of modern liberal society, results from the widespread practice of hiring on the base of computerized data:

Employers are so caught up in the technology, the databases and other gadgetry at their disposal, that they forget what hiring is all about. It's really about being open to the person across the desk and going beyond the obvious, the surface, and seeing what's going on *inside the person* applying for a job—to make sure that he or she culturally, ethically and humanistically fits into the company's mandate and purpose.[14]

Employers use all sorts of data in their hiring procedures, from criminal to medical to credit records. Once again, such data are often marred with mistakes, the result being that some people not only are unjustly discriminated against but, unaware that they have not been hired due to incorrect information, continue to be excluded from the opportunity to work. The problem is really bigger than that, because the exclusion from working is now assured in the case of people with correct ''negative'' data: people who have commited some crime in the past, or have some bad credit situation due to poverty, or have contracted some socially shameful illness. In both cases, the risk is that of creating a ''national *caste system of unemployables.*''[15]

Personal and social irresponsibility as a result of the loss of privacy is also evident in the management of police activity. At the core of the use of computerized data for investigative and social control purposes stands what already in 1971 Arthur Miller called *''inferential relational retrieval,''* that is, the activity whereby computers reconstruct large pictures of individual and social activities starting from apparently insignificant and unrelated data.[16] This has grown to huge proportions due to the fusion of all private and public data banks into a gigantesque electronic Panopticon, a Panopticon that Bentham originally conceived only for prisons, but that is now expanding throughout society and, through the information highway of the Internet, to the whole planet.[17] Investigators know that ''few people, even criminals, can escape a data bank,''[18] and this new power against criminals seems to be the gift of data banking. But is it? More and more, the police make arrests based on hot-line information from computerized data banks that are managed both by the police departments of the various states and by the FBI, although there has been a growing trend toward the centralization of the system under the direct control of the FBI. A study has revealed that only 25.7 percent of the data that the FBI sends out to police officers is correct and accurate in accordance with the law and that in a single day of 1979 "17,340 Americans were subject to false arrest because the FBI computer incorrectly showed that they were wanted when the warrants in question had been cleared or vacated."[19]

A more fundamental problem is that, apart from the issue of the correctness of the data, a massive accumulation of data is really useless and ultimately counterproductive in fighting crime. Generally, the fact that one has been arrested in the past doesn't necessarily imply that s/he was a criminal then, let alone now, especially considering that in 30–40 percent of all arrests the case is generally dismissed before trial or at least before the question of guilt or innocence has been resolved. And then, as Burnham explains, "only a small portion of the millions of traumatic events logged yearly into the criminal history records involve what are now called career criminals ... The sad truth is that many of the murderers and rapists who terrorize the American people are not marauding strangers," but relatives, friends, and acquaintances turning violent because of exasperation, anger, lust, or alcohol. This is why, "[c]ontrary to popular belief and what the police sometimes contend, research indicates that very few arrests are the result of any kind of investigation at all."

But when investigation is needed, the complete reliance on computerized information "inhibits the development of traditional police skills of interviewing, interrogating and investigating."[20] This is a further example of how the attribution of enormous powers to outer tools and machines tends to compress and ultimately annihilate what counts most even in terms of efficiency and productivity, namely the intelligence and sensitivity of human interiority.

Again, less privacy equals deresponsibilization, but the process does not stop here, because less responsibility, generated by the loss of privacy, requires in turn more control from the outside and thus a further diminution of privacy, which continues lessening responsibility, and so on. We can define this as *"the vicious circle of privacy."* In concrete terms, this means for instance that the loss of the investigative skills of the police, together with the deresponsibilization regarding making choices about arrests, generates a higher level of arrests and a higher number of mistakes, resulting in a wider body of people marked as "criminal" and thus a wider need for social control through a larger and deeper violation of informational privacy. And there is more: Because the investigative power, relying on outer computerized data, is no longer an exclusive asset of the investigator, an ability belonging to his or her interiority, but an external tool more and more accessible to others, criminals too have begun to use it. The result is the appalling growth of computer crimes, where criminals are able to control and manipulate the computerized actions and choices of people and institutions to their advantage. The movie *The Net* was a frightening but quite realistic representation of the problem. While we are waiting for an unlikely perfect cryptographic mechanism, the growing absorption into the Internet of many ordinary economic and social functions such as buying, selling, banking, and so on, has created a situation where no one can feel totally secure even when doing such a simple thing as taking cash from a banking machine.[21] Meanwhile, the growth of computer crime creates in turn the need of further computerized control, resulting in an unending destructive spiral whose first victim is the constitutional guarantee against illegitimate searches.[22]

In fact, electronic control creates a situation of universal and preventive search that empties both the Fourth and the Fifth Amendments of all practical significance. Mass espionage is widely practiced with all sorts of electronic means. The National Security Agency has a very sophisticated spying apparatus: "The NSA's unique leverage on world events is based on its massive bank of what are believed to be the largest and most advanced computers now available to any bureaucracy on earth."[23] Telephone companies have widely adopted the practice of the so-called *pen register*, that is, the computerized memorization of data relative to telephone calls, which affords a detailed reconstruction of people's life-style and actions. Burnham in particular warns against the virtually unlimited and judicially uncontrolled access to such data enjoyed by the police.[24] The telephone becomes especially relevant as a privileged source of "transactional information," or information relating to commercial transactions. In the 1970s the multinational giant AT&T was accused of using the transactional information running through its telephone lines to spy on a small rival company. Some years later, an AT&T New England branch produced a study of various segments of the population, dividing the different social and ethnic groups on the base of their different ways of using the telephone (locations, times of callings, average duration of conversations, and so on). An ex-CIA expert in the field warns against the possibility of creating *transactional signatures*:

Let's say that one of our powerful federal agencies became worried about the activities of a group of people who share a common interest in stopping the country's involvement in some war or in halting the placement of some new missile system. The organization conducts a detailed study of how the members of the group . . . use the telephone. Then the federal agency instructs the computer to raise a flag any time a series of phone calls are made from a telephone that fits the transactional signature already established as common for members of the group.[25]

This "subtle and hard-to-detect form of mass surveillance," as Burnham defines it, is available to both governmental agencies and private corporations who use transactional control to improve and individualize their marketing ability. In fact, public institutions and private corporations often put their means at each other's disposal in order to pursue common political and economic goals, thus fostering an unprecedented integration of the supposedly separate private and public realms. For instance, the data bank giant TWR, whose activities should be limited to credit information, has in the past collaborated with the CIA to set up a system of satellite surveillance capable of producing astonishingly detailed pictures.[26]

The flow of information runs also from the "public" to the "private" sector. Governmental bureaucracies maintain more than 4 billion computerized records, seventeen for each American citizen. In 1978, the fifty American states distributed 10.1 million reports taken from juridical and penal records, and 2 million of these were given to public agencies and private corporations that have nothing to do with the legal system. And the uncontrolled collection and circulation of personal data concern all sorts of information—not only legal, but medical, transactional, financial, fiscal, and so on.

This evokes again the picture of a general Panopticon whereby everyone's action is constantly monitored, with the important difference that this postmodern Panopticon does not have one but *many all-seeing centers*, now further multiplied and disseminated by the Internet revolution. Let it be clear that despite what has been said, we are not blind toward the positive personal and political potentialities of technology, especially of computers. This is not the place to enter such a debate. However, it is quite clear that computers have greatly expanded the left-brain power of human beings, and that their educational and cultural potential, their ability to promote a wider and livelier diffusion of knowledge and, through the World Wide Web of the Internet, a planetary exchange of ideas, is indeed unprecedented. In the same vein, there is no doubt that these powers could greatly increase political participation and a more direct and decentralized democracy.[27] But we have seen that the risks for both liberty and ethical growth are equally unprecedented. Goethe said that everything that frees our spirit without giving us more control over ourselves is destined to destroy us. The great powers of the modern informational and computing technology need, if they are to be used in favor of rather than against human fulfillment, the control and self-control guaranteed by personalities endowed with a superior ethical and spiritual power. Yet, the current use of technology goes precisely in the opposite direction. The picture is even worse, because behind this totalitarian "vicious circle of privacy" lies the more benign but no less dangerous picture of the quiet and silent attack on formational privacy. In fact, *the attack on informational privacy is to be seen as preparing for and sustaining the parallel and ultimately more essential invasion of formational privacy*. At the center of the informational "vicious circle of privacy" stands thus the more fundamental goal of creating an unending *circle of vicious privacy,* to turn people's interiority, as much as it is possible (there remains always a considerable degree of human resistance), into those lower selves who live as consumeristic and money-making/money-spending machines (where the problem is not money, as it is not the "market economy" but the materially absolutist use of it.)[28]

Formational privacy, the protection of one's space for solitude, silence, and inner reflection, is at the very core of the privacy problem, because the possibility to transform the world into a more human place, where people are treated as ends rather than as productive and consumptive machines, depends on the rescuing of an adequate space for a deeper relationship with one's self. But even though there is a wide and big cry over the demise of informational privacy, the occupation of formational privacy on the part of advertising and mass media culture (which is often but a slightly different type of advertising), completed by a "modern" school education that merely covers, with the noble dress of "culture," the same fundamental truths of our productivistic/consumeristic society, is taken for granted as beneficial both to the economic performance of society and to the ability of the individual to fit into such a society. Most of the people who want to fight against the attack on informational privacy do not realize that the true and final end of such an attack is formational privacy and that without protecting the latter the fight for the former is doomed. We have already seen various examples of how the violation of informational privacy preludes and supports that of formational privacy, but the best example of all is that of *credit information*. The 1,200 credit agencies presently operating in the United States are part of five major companies, which concentrate in five megacomputers about 150 million files recording the personal credit history of each individual. Again, we find here the usual combination of both mistaken and apparently irrelevant data. Credit rates are often based on data, such as one's life-style and ideological orientations, that should remain totally irrelevant but are in fact extremely relevant from the point of view of fitting into the capitalistic market.[29] Moreover, about one-third of those who have been able to obtain access to the files of the various credit agencies have found serious mistakes in them. In one such case, the company involved, TWR, refused to rectify the mistakes until it was brought to court, where it was sentenced to both rectification and compensation. During the trial, TWR argued that the credit agency cannot take responsibility for the information it receives from the various sources contacted. Burnham comments that this "is a fascinating argument for a company that currently is selling 35 million credit reports each year to 24,000 subscribers." In fact, says Burnham, such a voluminous business is possible only because of the extreme velocity and inaccuracy of the information-gathering and -distributing process: "Quite obviously the largely automated system developed by TWR would not be able to function were the courts to force TWR to check the accuracy of the underlying reports it receives from subscribers about individual consumers."[30]

Why do we, as a society, authorize the existence of an information system inherently bound to be widely mistaken and to make discrimination rational? Because without credit information there would be no *credit economy*, which is essential to promote and sustain the irresponsible release of our appetitive self, on which our unlimited-growth economy rests. The credit economy tempts directly our appetitive self, and at the same time makes the temptations of advertising attainable. It severs the concrete link existing between expenses and wealth, promoting irresponsibility and an attitude of living above one's means that has now thoroughly infected our capitalistic debt-ridden nations. As such, the credit economy participates directly in the formational molding of our interiority, and credit information has become essential to protect the system from the very risks of irresponsible and illegal behavior, such as the nonrepayment of loans, that it itself promotes. But things do not stop here, as the huge amount of data collected by credit information agencies is more and more being sold and used to develop *micromarketing*, which, as it gives the possibility to direct both telemarketing calls and "junk mail" to the most-responsive persons, represents the best technique so far to accomplish the darkly alchemical work of raising to power the lower appetitive element within the human self. As Rothfeder explains, "Businesses increasingly shun mass-marketing techniques such as broad-based magazine, newspaper, and TV advertising in favor of *micromarketing*, which is predicated on knowing something about each consumer before deciding which ones to pitch to."

He then reports that in the last five years the sale of lists with names of potential consumers has increased "about tenfold," "while the number of names that are rented has grown ten to fifteen times": "No wonder that Americans receive sixty-three billion pieces of junk mail and twenty billion unsolicited telemarketing calls annually." Telephone companies, phonecard companies, credit card companies, and—most of all—credit information companies, are turning all the more to selling data for micromarketing, which is becoming by far the most profitable data business.[31] The basic end of buying data for micromarketing is, says Rothfeder, that of building "*psychographic profiles*" of individuals to see where their weak point lies in terms of availability to consumer temptations. This makes it again very clear that the treasure at stake in the battle over informational privacy is the human mind, and thus formational privacy.

But how to intervene in the subtle and legally refractory area of formational privacy? The real solution will only come from a deep cultural and spiritual transformation of our society. Only when cultural energies will not be spent so thoroughly on getting people to buy and consume and accumulate wealth will the need to penetrate and form the human mind return within acceptable limits, and only then will the need for a massive and potentially unlimited accumulation of data begin to recede. This of course does not mean that we just have to wait for such a radical transformation to happen, nor that our actions in favor of an independent ethical and spiritual interiority will have to be limited to a merely cultural battle. There are things that can be done legislatively and legally in order to protect formational privacy from the most-degrading forms of invasion of the mind on the part of TV, the media, and all forms of economic as well as cultural advertising. Here the primary legal point of reference is the *First Amendment*: If the current multifarious invasion of informational privacy makes a mere show of the Fourth and Fifth Amendments, *the silent but constant and pervasive invasion of formational privacy on the part of the media perverts the First Amendment's primary constitutional command to preserve and respect human interiority and its expressions.* Indeed the Founding Fathers knew very well, in putting freedom of religion and conscience at the very beginning of the Bill of Rights, the foundational value and the inherently spiritual quality of human interiority. When they derived freedom of expression from spiritual interiority in the very same First Amendment, they certainly had in mind something very different from the use that most contemporary media make of that Amendment, a use that degrades, through gossip and trash culture, the very interiority that the Amendment was born to defend. Reintegrating the true meaning and purpose of the First Amendment within the law is the very first task that is required in the battle for formational privacy. The parallel battle in favor of informational privacy, which is probably capable of gathering a wider and more immediate consensus, is very important not only in itself but also as an indirect form of protection of formational privacy, given that, as we have seen, without the use of personal data on individuals the ability of the "mind invaders" to do their work is greatly diminished. We shall see in the course of the book which are the most-important measures to be taken to protect and advance both formational and informational privacy.

But who are the "mind invaders"? The question itself is somewhat misleading, because it presupposes that there are certain people or powers that manipulate and victimize the great majority. We have seen that such a picture is only partially correct. To be sure, there are certain people and powers that are more active in the invasion of privacy. But the reality is that everyone tends to be involved in such an invasion and that we become accomplices of the invasion of our own mind every time we give in to the attraction to gossip, to trash culture, to the pornography and violence that are rampant in the media, to the models of glamorous life-style that pervade our mass culture. We are also directly responsible for the destruction of informational privacy. In the past, only large institutions could collect, organize, and distribute personal information. But the PC revolution, and now its expansion with the Internet, gives everyone who wants the opportunity to steal and even resell personal information. Rothfeder calls this the shift *from Big Brother to Little Sister*: not only is there a large and proliferating number of private and governmental agencies who independently collect personal information and then share this information among themselves, there are now a whole range of Internet services that make it very easy for people, "in the privacy of their own home," with "little fear of getting caught, of being embarassed publicly," to play Peeping Tom with everyone else's private life.[32] Here we see yet another aspect of privacy invasion, its being a primary economic good in itself. People spend good money to read and watch gossip of all kind, and they will spend money on the Internet to play the same gossiping game on their relatives, friends, acquaintances, and so on. It all fits in perfectly, although disastrously, because the market of gossip, besides being very remunerative in itself, is also the perfect educational tool to bring out that (worst) part of human beings that is so essential to the capitalistic market. It is along these lines that a neoutilitarian thinker such as Richard Posner has explicitly claimed the educational value of gossip.[33] To conclude on the current social dissemination of Big Brother, the reality is that there has never been a Big Brother, nor even the risk of it, because the model of contemporary capitalism has never essentially been one of manipulation but one of co-optation of people into the system by appealing to their appetitive, accumulative, and egoistic lower side. In this, the transpersonal poet and thinker Aldous Huxley has been much more prophetic and lucid than the more popular but less penetrating Orwell.[34] To be sure, there is a central power that drives the whole mechanism in which we all more or less participate, but it is not a central secret institution or alliance, although there are secret and centralizing agents. Even they are just embodiments of a fundamental power that is transcendental, of *capitalism as the corrupt spiritual power* that has been behind the modern unlimited growth economy and into which we all feed and participate by giving in to our lower selves. Precisely because the capitalistic power is one, although at once disseminated and innerly fragmented by the aggressive competition it promotes, it necessarily produces centralization. That is the reason for the existence of privileged agents, the most powerful and wealthy who identify more intimately with it, who make sure that the process of its social dissemination remains under its firm stronghold, keeping its values and goals at its center. This does not necessarily happen with full consciousness, as centralization is also the product of the inherent tendency of all bureaucracies and human institutions to bring things as much as possible under their control. Indeed, if the process of centralization were just a means to better sustain the interest of the predominant social and economic system, then it would be a most rational and efficient mechanism in terms of such interests. But we have seen how computerization and data banks are riddled with a very high degree of inefficacy and errors, and thus of social and economic irrationality. The best example of this, in reference to governmental bureaucracy, is the so-called *computer matching*, which is the comparison of different lists or files from the data banks of different administrations to discover duplication, fraud, and any other abuse especially in relation to welfare and social security programs. There is no doubt that this "most vicious invasion" of privacy, as Rothfeder calls it, with its generalized computer search into the lives of millions of people, only very few of whom can be seriously suspected, is a violation of the Fourth and Fifth Amendments. Yet it could be argued that computer matching helps to reduce frauds at the expense of the public, thus promoting the rationalization of the welfare system from the point of view of an efficient management and of a healthy economy. But in fact it is now quite clear that its costs far outweigh any benefits. The inevitable problem of the mistakes afflicting huge amounts of data that are difficult to control and update has resulted mostly in situations where "computer matching has wrongly identified alleged embezzlers of taxpayers' dollars, cases that have embarassed individuals and showered them in public and social humiliation."[35] Rothfeder also shows how the true reason behind computer matching is the ideological justification of welfare programs (being more efficient, they can be more socially acceptable), and thus of that Big Government that, as Brandeis was the first to point out, is the political-bureaucratic side of that illiberal and self-destructive Bigness that characterizes the civilization of capitalism.

Here we arrive at the core of the issue, because if the massive centralization of data into the public and private data banks of big institutions (the institutions of Bigness!) is not justified by efficiency and rationalization, then other interests are at stake. Besides the powerful economic interests of the information and computer industries, the other great interest is that of centralization itself. In other words, centralization is to be seen as a *tautological phenomenon*, having as its own goal and reason for existence the alteration of the distribution of power between central governmental institutions, be they "public" or "private," and local communities and independent individuals. This is done not only by private/public governmental and economic bureaucracies, as we have already seen, but also by the politicians who represent the interests of such a capitalistic Bigness. For instance, the detailed knowledge of the orientations of the different sectors of public opinion may allow politicians to address different speeches to different social groups, or to speak only to those who will vote, or even only to those who may vote for the government. This is a clear example of how informational centralization "tend[s] to undermine the democratic process."[36] But the democratic process is undermined in many other ways: through the emptying of the fundamental constitutional rights indicated in the First, Fourth, and Fifth Amendments; through the breakdown of the *separation of powers*, a constitutional pillar of American democracy, due to the increasing informational interpenetration and networking of the different branches of government; through the dissolution of the basic distinction between *particular* and *general interest*, which the informational interpenetration of governmental and nongovernmental institutions has deeply accelerated; and finally through the final overturning of the fundamental principle of *popular sovereignty*, due to the impossibility, for the fully surveilled and constantly inspected citizen, to control and know what public and private governmental institutions do, and ultimately to the totalitarian occupation of private interiority. Centralization is therefore efficient and rationalizing in a different sense. It generates situations that, by being very costly not only in human but also in economic terms, create that waste of public money on which the economy of Bigness and its dominant groups thrive. Most of all, it constructs a political scenario whereby the institutions of Bigness remain in control, so that the necessary processes of social and electronic decentralization will remain under the guidance of the capitalistic ideology and interests, thus wasting their inherent ability to promote real democracy, which is always ethically and spiritually grounded. Again, this is not a product of some secret conspiracy or alliance, but the natural convergence of different private and public actors, of private industrial/financial and public political/bureaucratic powers, around the shared values and interests of Bigness.

Centralization will become indispensable the more the democratic potentiality inherent in the electronic dissemination of informational and cultural power will manifest itself. The battle is not over yet, but whoever will win, it will not be a question of either/or, as any political and social system needs some point of balance between centralization and decentralization. The transpersonal and ecological project will tend to promote centralization at the level of principles and rights, and decentralization of the economic and political processes. The capitalistic project, on the other hand, is already at work in promoting a specific type of balance, whereby an informational and cultural dissemination in which everyone becomes a further point of irradiation of the consumeristic and wealth-maximizing project is sustained and controlled by the centralization in the hands of the institutions of Bigness. Indeed, even something as "democratic" as the Internet will require the increasing support and controlling power of big informational bureaucracies, which are most deeply representative of the capitalistic project not just for some accidental historical convergence but because of their inherent "capitalistic" impulse toward self-aggrandizement and bigness. This means that in the end, in spite of the inevitable tension between centralization and decentralization, and between their actors, they can both be perversely reconciled by becoming the two complementary if opposite faces of a unitary totalitarian process, totalitarian both in its invasion of formational privacy in order to enslave people to their lower selves and in its total occupation of both center and peripheries.

In fact, the capitalistic project, as a materialistic "mundanization" of the absolute impulse, depends on keeping deeply contradictory things together: the irrationality and irresponsibility of both individual consumers and self-interested economic powers taking advantage of the public waste of money, together with the tight calculative rationality that its wealth-maximizing economic model requires; the liberal and decentralizing "privatism," shielding individual irresponsibility and self-concern with the utilitarian will to subject every person to the "social" point of view of corporate wealth maximization, with its inherent push toward centralization and Bigness. It is a project that cannot endure precisely because the tension is never overcome, opposites are never transformed but only played against each other in order to obtain some kind of precarious balance. The articulation of the capitalistic power into the two opposite yet complementary forces of liberalism and utilitarianism manages to create such a precarious balance. The outcome of such a capitalistic dialectic of liberalism and utilitarianism is a forceful if quiet and inviting totalitarianism. It is not a totalitarianism of outer oppression but of inner and powerful seduction. Its field of conquest is not the "habeas corpus" but the "habeas mentem." It is a *totalitarianism of souls*, one that powerfully elicits the emergence of the lower self to produce minds willingly accepting to become consumeristic machines. Its liberal nature is something to be very thankful for, and it comes from its very root, from its liberal need to preserve and promote the private sphere of idiosyncratic consumption and the social activation of "free" individuals into the productive and consumptive expansion. That the freedom thus guaranteed has then been used also for genuine political and intellectual expression, as opposed to the special-interest politics of economic lobbies, is something that comes from other traditions or that survives as a contradictory republican element within liberal and utilitarian thought. The contemporary benign, liberal-utilitarian totalitarianism works through an appropriate blend of attacks on formational and informational privacy. Liberal culture, with its exaltation of irresponsible freedom and its prohibition of any acknowledgment that the essentially advertisement-oriented culture by which we are submerged is debased and morally wrong, leads the attack on the true object of conquest, formational privacy, an attack whose goal, in spite of all liberal declarations of neutrality, is the utilitarian "pleasure-through-wealth" maximization. In turn, the utilitarian and panoptical invasion and control of informational privacy are an invaluable support of that project, both in terms of its preparation for and improvement of the formational invasion and of its keeping in line the already colonized interiority, primarily through the so-called "chilling effect" on those who know that they are being controlled, or, when necessary, through more direct and forceful intervention, although the form that this utilitarian control assumes is preferably the more liberal one. The battle for privacy, as the shield of our ethical and spiritual interiority, is essential for transforming politics and society and for the overcoming of the liberal-utilitarian predicament in a way that, by asserting an ethical-spiritual individualism whereby persons learn to freely and spontaneously perceive the general will and communal good as their own, saves even the basic liberal and utilitarian values, namely free individuality and communal utility, from their own corruption.

NOTES

1. See, for instance, Alan Westin's definition, which first links privacy to the protection of personal information, and this is the element that has been mostly underlined by others, but then immediately adds a notion of privacy "as the voluntary and temporary *withdrawal* of a person from the general society through *physical* or *psychological* means, either in a state of solitude or small-group intimacy or, when among larger groups, in a condition of anonymity or reserve." A. Westin, *Privacy and Freedom* (New York: Athenaeum, 1967), p. 7.

2. J. M. Rosenberg, *The Death of Privacy* (N.Y.: Random House, 1969).

3. "Following Marx, we may call the new formation the political economy of capitalism.... 'The economy' represents the ontological principle of modernizing ideologies.... The name Economic Polity best captures the ontological/ideological assumption of an underlying reality to which ideally the society should be attuned." S. Wolin, "Democracy and the Welfare State," in *Political Theory* 15, 4 (November 1987): p. 471.

4. See J. S. Mill, *On Liberty* (1859); and M. Horkheimer and T. Adorno, "The Culture Industry: Enlightenment as Mass Deception," in *Dialectic of Enlightenment* (1944). The criticism of mass society is not based on some sort of elitism, as some "pluralists" claim. The core of mass societies is the loss of quality and personal meaning in the life of everyone: It is not a criticism of quantity but of a quantity that has no quality.

5. See I. Wallerstein, *The Modern World-System*, 2 vols. (Academic Press, 1974,

1980). Even the formation of capitalistic markets within Europe has been the product of a monopolistic warring effort, as explained in the work of Tilly. See Charles Tilly (ed.), *The Formation of National States in Western Europe* (Princeton, 1975).

6. There is something foolishly wise in the modern attempt to force nature to be unlimited, because nature is indeed unlimited in its power to generate and reproduce. But nature is so as *physis*, as the spiritual power of that *anima mundi* that the world essentially is, and it is only by cooperating with it through the respectful and loving knowledge of its essential being that we can hope to enjoy her unlimited generosity. But capitalism, precisely because of its radical fall from spirit into the absolutization of matter, can only ask nature to be a merely material source of materials. And because everyone gets what one asks for, to capitalism nature is simply a big material being, and material beings are by definition finite and mortal.

7. C. Lasch, *The Minimal Self* (New York: Norton & Co., 1984), pp. 27–28, note, and p. 19.

8. "The abuse or misuse of the environment, as sanctioned or encouraged by government, intrudes upon the individual zone of privacy. Obvious examples are noise and pollution. The use of pesticides is similarly obtrusive." ACLU working paper, "Civil Liberties and the Environment," quoted in E. Beardsley, "Privacy: Autonomy and Selective Disclosure," in R. Pennock and J. Chapman (eds.), *Nomos XIII: Privacy* (Atherton, 1971), pp. 58–59. For an interesting discussion of privacy violations due to overpopulation, crowding, overconsumption, garbage disposal, and so on, see E. Van Den Haag, *On Privacy*, in Pennock and Chapman, pp. 149–168.

9. See J. Rothfeder, *Privacy for Sale* (New York: Simon and Schuster, 1992), 187ff.

10. Dr. Siegler, in the *New England Journal of Medicine*, quoted by D. Burnham, *The Rise of the Computer State* (New York: Random House, 1983), p. 161.

11. Rothfeder, pp. 180–81.

12. For instance, according to Linowes, 58 percent of all firms subject their workers to drug testing. Apart from the important point that subjecting people to drug testing with no "probable cause" could be considered a constitutional violation and an offense to human dignity, drug testing is generally acknowledged to have a 5 percent error rate. Linowes reports that in one year about 5 million people were tested, which means that 5 percent of those tested have been unjustly accused of being drug consumers, and 16 percent of that 5 percent, that is approximately 40,000 people, have subsequently been fired! D. Linowes, *Privacy in America* (Urbana: University of Illinois Press, 1989), pp. 36–43, which quotes A. Trebach, *The Great Drug War* (1987).

13. Rothfeder, Ch.7.

14. Rothfeder, pp. 161–62 (quoting the employee counselor David Foerster). See also Linowes, pp. 23, 120.

15. Burnham, pp. 75–76. See also Rothfeder, p. 165.

16. A. Miller, *Assault on Privacy* (Ann Arbor: University of Michigan, 1971), A Mentor Book, New American Library, 1972, p. 57 and more generally pp. 36–69. See also A. Westin and M. A. Baker, *Databanks in a Free Society* (New York: Quadrangle, 1972).

17. On J. Bentham's *Panopticon* see Michel Foucault, *Discipline and Punish* (Penguin, 1977), pp. 200–5.

18. Rothfeder, p. 112, quoting Private Investigator Bob Lesnick.

19. Burnham, p. 74, and more generally, pp. 71–79.

20. Ibid., p. 70

21. Rothfeder, pp. 113–16.

22. Ibid., Ch.5 (for the growth of computer crime), p. 73 (on the violation of "reasonable search and seizure").

23. Burnham, pp. 120–42.

24. See Linowes, pp. 17–18; and Burnham, pp. 168–71.

25. Burnham, p. 62.

26. "The details of this TWR/CIA spy operation are of particular interest because of evidence that during the late 1960s and early 70s the CIA used computer-enhanced photographs taken from satellites to determine the crowd sizes and activities of a number of anti-war demonstrations and urban riots in the United States." Burnham, pp. 43–46.

27. For a "transformational" discussion of the expansion of democratic participation through electronic means see Christa Daryl Slaton, *The Televote Experiment: Expanding Citizen Participation in the Quantum Age* (New York: Praeger, 1991).

28. For an excellent overview of the spiritual origins and significance of money see *Parabola. The Magazine of Myth and Tradition* (Spring 1991): *Money*.

29. Linowes, pp. 129–31. Linowes mentions the case of a journalist whose application for an insurance policy was rejected because of a report from a credit agency describing him as a past anti-Vietnam war hippie, based on the gossip of a neighbor who didn't like him!

30. Burnham, pp. 43–46.

31. A general manager of TWR said to Rothfeder, "Two billion dollars a year is spent on direct marketing and $800 million is spent on credit reports . . . Who wouldn't want to move from our traditional business to that one?" Rothfeder, p. 97; for the previous quotations and for a discussion of micromarketing pp. 89ff.

32. Ibid., pp. 22–30.

33. R. Posner, "J. A. Sibley Lecture: The Right to Privacy," in *Georgia L.R.*, 12, 3, (1978), p. 396.

34. In terms of predictions, it seems to me that Huxley has been more insightful than Orwell. He saw very clearly how at the core of contemporary totalitarianism there was going to be the complacent consumeristic alienation of the masses, paired with the cultural marginalization, rather than the explicit repression, of alternative minorities, including the independent and questioning individual. For Huxley's transpersonalism, see *The Perennial Philosophy* (1946) (London: Grafton, 1985).

35. Rothfeder, p. 142, and for the previous quotations, pp. 139–41. See also Linowes, pp. 92–96, who basically confirms, with plenty of cases, the dangerous inefficiency of computer matching.

36. Burnham, pp. 88–89.

1
THE PHILOSOPHY OF PRIVACY

DEFINING PRIVACY

Given the growing confusion about what is privacy and how it should be legally protected, then a philosophical analysis of the concept of privacy would seem to be critical to the future of the right to privacy and American constitutional law, yet contemporary political philosophers have hardly entered the debate.[1] Even liberal theory has traditionally neglected the notion of privacy, and with good reason, because privacy was born to put more emphasis on solitude and introspection rather than on the central liberal value of freedom of choice and action.

The right to privacy has grown to include so many areas of individual rights that it has become difficult to define it as a unitary concept. Yet we shall see that a unitary although multilayered conception of privacy is not only possible but indispensable and that such a conception will be able to encompass many of the rights currently associated with the *right to privacy*, though excluding others from the direct realm of the right to privacy but not from the wider *principle of privacy*.

According to Ferdinand Schoeman, the fundamental requirements of a satisfactory definition of privacy (as of any other concept) are those of "distinctiveness" and "coherence": distinctiveness, to disentangle the concept from similar ones like autonomy, freedom, intimacy, secrecy, solitude, and so on; coherence, to show that privacy is a unitary concept that cannot be torn apart without losing something essential. Rejecting the views of those who define privacy normatively as a right or as a form of control, Schoeman proposes to understand privacy descriptively "as a *state* or *condition* of limited access to a person."[2] This allows, says Schoeman, for a clear distinction between descriptive and prescriptive, between the condition of privacy and its right. This is no doubt an important distinction, but it can be corrupted into dualism, a mistake that we should try to avoid, because even the most-advanced frontiers of the natural sciences are showing the impossibility to oppose description and prescription, the real and the rational, matter and mind.[3]

A good example of the absurdities that can be produced by a radical dualism of descriptive and prescriptive is offered by W. A. Parent's categorization of privacy definitions into five purely descriptive types,[4] with the result of placing under the same category E. Bloustein and R. Posner, who actually stand at the very antipodes of the privacy debate. Parent justifies his choice by saying that although Bloustein and Posner have radically different normative views of privacy, they both describe it in terms of "being let alone." But their opposite normative views produce two very different descriptive pictures of the condition of "being let alone." Precisely because he attributes to privacy a personalist and spiritual meaning, Bloustein describes "being let alone" in terms of an introspective solitude promoting a substantively moral autonomy. For Posner, on the other hand, "being let alone" is basically the condition of hiding personal information from others for economic reasons.[5]

However, the dualism of descriptive and prescriptive can also produce a normative type of reductionism. Privacy can be considered as a merely normative reality, a right completely dependent on the arbitrary choice of the entitled subject. But in this way privacy risks self-annihilation, because the holder of the right "may choose to have privacy or to give it up. To be non pre-emptive, privacy must not depend on choice."[6]

These two examples show how it is impossible to separate description from prescription, the factual from the normative view. In human history, as well as in human geography, privacy has been and is an indefinite number of conditions, and any attribution of a specific meaning to its concept cannot but be based on a normative choice regarding which condition best represents the essence underlying its indefinite scope. If we follow a fundamental principle of both Roman and Brandeisian jurisprudence, the "*ex facto oritus jus*," then the fact of privacy, insofar as it conforms to the value of its normative essence, though remaining descriptively a fact, reveals and shows the right of privacy as its original and inner content.

By overcoming the dualism of descriptive and prescriptive, we apprehend privacy simultaneously as a fact and as a right, as an empirical state defined by what is rightfully and intrinsically private, and as an "a priori" right concretely determined and limited by the empirical conditions in which it emerges and expresses itself. Only by being inscribed in and modulated by the fact, that is, by being a *natural right* in the proper sense, can the right of privacy become a truly fundamental right.

It is from this nondualistic point of view that we can evaluate the various definitions of privacy in light of a *holographic analysis*.[7] From a dualistic point of view distinctiveness and coherence are redundant concepts, because whatever distinguishes privacy from more or less similar concepts is precisely what makes it atomistically coherent with itself. To eliminate the redundancy, and the atomistic understanding of coherence that produces it, we must conceive of distinctiveness and coherence as the two dialectical faces of the same coin. Not to be reduced to self-cohesion, and thus to distinctiveness, the notion of coherence should be centered on the "with" that it contains (*co = together, with; haerere = stick, cleave*). With this new centering, the concept of privacy implies a fundamental "co-hering" of its distinct identity with the whole of concepts: Without losing its distinctiveness, privacy becomes essentially inclusive of ideas both complementary—as in the case of autonomy, intimacy, or solitude—and opposite, as with the concept of the public. Thus, at the very core of this holistic and dialectical analysis rests the *principle of integrity*, which discriminates between the conceptions of privacy that search for distinctiveness and coherence within the narrow limits of an atomistic identity and those that progressively widen the definitional horizons toward a more universally inclusive definition.

By applying our holographic analysis, we obtain three fundamental privacy paradigms. The first we call *possessivism*, because it identifies privacy with the narrow world of material and sensual/emotional goods understood as external properties. In so doing, this approach reduces privacy to a particular aspect of an all-encompassing right of property, and more specifically to the right of property over personal information, and then degrades it into a mere commodity, the commodity "information on oneself." In this way, privacy is completely subjected to the fundamental end of wealth maximization and to its implicit imposition to contract out and mobilize property. Indeed the fundamental right of this position, identifiable with *utilitarianism*, is only secondarily the right to property, being ultimately the *right to wealth*.

The second paradigm moves beyond possessivism to identify privacy with the private sphere of the body and its personal actions conceived in more or less atomistic terms. We have here a *privatism* that oscillates between a legalistic and a personalistic atomism. In the first case, privacy is reduced to a formalistic spatial sphere within which one is supposed to be able to have an unlimited possibility of arbitrary choices, an abstractly legalistic natural right that makes the individual "deontologically" immune from any consideration of individual and/or social goodness and utility. In the second case, we have an appeal to personal selfhood in more substantively ethical terms, mainly in reference to its concrete capacity for intimacy (friendship, eroticism, family life), and to its moral autonomy. But even this second approach conceives of moral autonomy as an abstract container of arbitrariness, being unable to truly overcome a purely atomistic deontology. This position is essentially identifiable with *liberalism*.

The third paradigm we can define as *ethical-spiritual privacy*, in that it conceives of privacy as the locus of an interiority, be it soul or mind, characterized by ethical and/or spiritual values that make the individual person inherently connected and responsive to a more or less universal public realm.

Inside this paradigm we find the *communitarians* on the one hand and the *transpersonalists* on the other. As for the communitarians, they do for the most part acknowledge the value of privacy as cultivating interiority and mental/spiritual life. The problem is that, in different ways, they all conceive of it as an inferior reality whose meaning and value can only be derived from some kind of public realm (political, religious, social, etc.), from its empirical and/or traditional structures and principles, although these may be inherently charged with some interpretation or other of universal ethical values.

It is only with "transpersonalism" that privacy acquires both a factual and normative self-subsistence, being identified as the inner condition of being perspectively inclusive of the whole cosmic community and of each particular community included within it. Privacy is seen as a withdrawal from one's mere particular being, be it one's living individuality or one's family, town, and nation, a withdrawal that implies a potential retrieval of one's infinite roots. Withdrawing into oneself, thus, far from being a negation of community, is here valued as the action that helps the individual to retrieve its universally communal essence and thus as the primary indispensable presupposition of one's aware and creative participation in the life of one's many communities. Only with transpersonalism does the notion of privacy acquire its widest denotation, thus satisfying the principle of integrity of our holographic analysis. In this sense, the transpersonal definition of privacy perfects at once both distinctiveness and co-herence (in the sense explained earlier), because, without losing its clearly defined distinctiveness, which we can temporarily establish as related to "withdrawing into oneself," it at once opens up to the prospective inclusion of the individual and cosmic other.

The three paradigms sketched here have an archetypal quality in that they express three basic modalities of human existence. In his VIII Letter, Plato says that there are three basic human realities, which are also three levels of (self)consciousness: money/body/soul. Money stands for all that in human life has to do with "external goods," or possessions; body stands for the person in her separate identity, perceived as a physical entity expressing a psychological personality; soul stands for the further dimension of a self-subsistent psychical interiority that participates of eternal realities and ethical principles, the body and its acquisitive impulses being what the soul becomes in time. The fact that money and body too are modalities of soul is reaffirmed by Plato through his other fundamental triad referring to the three types of soul: the *instinctual-acquisitive soul*, the inner side of the money and possessive reality; the *spirited-aesthetic soul*, the source on the one hand of the separative/warring mode of self-assertion and the childlike attraction to the most varied beautiful and colorful things, and on the other hand the seat of the romantic impulse toward a plenitude of feeling/love and toward beauty as a source of symbolic-mythical meanings of transcendence; the *ethical-spiritual soul*, the only one that lives *in time* without being *of time*, the only one to be a true soul, the other two being its mortal offsprings necessary to give inner sustenance to the two realities of body and property.[8] Let it be immediately clear that for Plato, the very source of all western transpersonal thought, it would be very wrong to conceive of money and body, as well as the appetitive and spirited souls, as something intrinsically evil or wrong. Given that the proper hierarchies are respected, that money and the money-soul be put into the service of bodily wellness, courage, and harmonious feelings, and these in turn be put in the service of mental and spiritual growth and under the power of the reasonable and ethical mind, both money and body, as well as appetites and the heart, are good and indispensable components, and presuppositions, of an integral way of being human. Problems arise when each of the lower dimensions claims primacy and power, disregarding the priority of ethical-spiritual growth. This is exactly what happens with *possessivism*, with its *utilitarian* reduction of human nature to the search for money or external goods, and with *privatism*, with its *liberal* reduction of human nature to a separative freedom of idiosyncratic enjoyments. Indeed, behind most of the antiprivacy arguments we will meet lurks Benthamite utilitarianism (e.g., J. Ely) and/or utilitarian positivism (e.g., Dean Prosser); whereas most theories that reduce privacy to a private sphere shielding an absolute right of free choice are still molded in the Lockean fashion (from Mill, in spite—and, as we shall see, because—of its at once utilitarian and transpersonal roots, to Dworkin, in spite of its pretended novelty). Philosophical fathers can of course be found also for the two remaining approaches, the communitarian, which is generally steeped in the Aristotelian or Aristotelian-Thomistic tradition, and the transpersonal, which, besides finding its roots in the Platonic tradition, reemerges in America in the trascendentalism of Emerson and Thoreau, and in the legal and political work of Brandeis and Douglas, who inherited the transcendental mind and infused it into the "invention" (Brandeis) and constitutional establishment (Douglas) of the right to privacy.

THE PHILOSOPHICAL BASES OF THE CONCEPTIONS OF PRIVACY

Because I have analyzed the philosophy of privacy elsewhere,[9] I will limit myself to sketching my main views regarding the four philosophical traditions indicated in the belief that this will help in understanding the various positions that have emerged in the context of the legal evolution of the right of privacy.

Utilitarianism, in its Benthamite version but also its many reformed versions that have been developed afterwards, is the quintessential political expression of empiricism; it is empiricism brought to its most-consistent conclusions in the field of political theory. Bentham writes, "Sense, which is the basis of every idea, is also the basis of every enjoyment, and unless man's whole nature be new modelled, so long as man remains man, the stock of sense ... never can increase."[10] As is well known, this reductionism results in the fundamental utilitarian principle, the maximization of pleasure and the minimization of pain, pleasure and pain being fully understood in purely sensistic and materialistic terms, as shown by Bentham's famous equalization of "pushpin" and "poetry" on the ground that, regardless of their presumed higher or lower quality, both produce a measurable amount of pleasurable stimulation of the senses. Reality, including human beings, is thus interpreted as a unitary continuum of sense-matter, and whatever is claimed to transcend such a level of reality is by Bentham discarded as metaphysics. The absolutization of the sense-matter dimension makes utilitarianism a radically monistic philosophy. But whereas the monism of the transpersonal tradition is intrinsically dialectical, inclusive of both vertical (essential/existential) and horizontal (self/other) duality, utilitarian monism leaves no room for any such duality. For instance, it is true that the utilitarian search for the maximization of pleasure seems to require a forceful desiring self. But the fact that such a desiring self has no legitimate choice to withdraw from wanting more and more sensual pleasure reveals how in the end the utilitarian self is no self at all, but only a modulation of the sense-matter continuum. Such a dissolution of selves into a radical hedonistic and materialistic monism has also its positive side: Bentham's insistence on the "greatest happiness of the greatest number," as well as his noble sensitivity for the suffering of all sentient beings, can be explained only in reference to the strong sense that all beings share a common and unitary sense-matter nature. Yet the solidaristic and ecological potential of such a posture is quickly disposed of by the "possessive egoism" intrinsic to such a nature. We know that the principle of pleasure maximization turns, in Benthamite utilitarianism, into the principle of "wealth maximization," on the presupposition that "money is the instrument of measuring the quantity of pain and pleasure."[11] Yet, when wealth grows beyond certain limits, it becomes too large to be directly enjoyable by the individual. In this case, the principle of the "greatest happiness of the greatest number" would suggest a redistribution of wealth, so that others could have more pleasure and the total of social pleasure would increase. Bentham considers such an argument, but concludes that without the security of the property acquired either through capital or labor remaining in the hands of the owner, there would be no more incentive to increase productivity, with the result that not only the individual but also society as a whole would suffer from what would amount to a limitation of the wealth-maximization impulse and process.[12] Indeed, in the context of utilitarian monism, which is totalitarian also insofar as it admits of no individual independence from the only legitimate sense-matter dimension, one cannot say that individuals are free to pursue wealth maximization, but in fact that they must, at once for themselves and for the general welfare. This is why Bentham banishes from legitimate behavior not only the "asceticism" of the "philosophic party," which preaches moderation and withdrawal from the allures of the senses, but even the "aristocratic" pursuit of idiosyncratic pleasures not justified by measurable effects on the senses (what he calls the "principle of sympathy and antipathy").[13] In Bentham there is no room for privacy, because there is no self to be searched beyond the sensual impulses that lead us into the public life of economics, sexuality, and political economy. In fact, the very private sphere that the liberal wants to maintain separate regardless of what happens inside it is for Bentham but one side of that unitary whole of life, public and private, inherently and thus legitimately governed by the same absolutistic ethics of wealth maximization.[14] The result is a radical reduction of privacy to an economic category, and we shall see many recurrent expressions of such a reductionism in the course of the legal history of the right of privacy.[15] Sometimes, utilitarian reductionism takes the form of legal positivism, as shown by Dean Prosser's famous attempt to bring privacy back into the precinct of property.[16] But the apparent neutrality of legal positivism cannot hide its substantive Benthamite view of things, also because Bentham's own legal positivism, the source of many attacks on the right to privacy, has been shown to be ultimately resting on his substantive and fundamental "principle of utility."[17]

Moving on now to liberalism, it too, at least in its Anglo-American version, is an empiricist political philosophy, and this is why, in spite of all the polemics between liberals and utilitarians, between rights-based deontologists and good-based consequentialists, liberalism and utilitarianism are brothers under the skin. Liberalism represents the dualistic version of empiricism, and although its dualism is not totally ineffective, being capable of temporarily and precariously creating a protective barrier for individual rights, in the end it only paves the way for the triumph of that utilitarian absolutism that lives in its own empiricistic depths. The only reality that empiricism recognizes is that of matter as perceivable by the senses and their technological expansions, that is, the interdependence of sense and matter. All that is perceivable by the sense is material, all that is material is finite, and all that is finite is by definition interdependent with some other finite reality. When the whole of reality is fully captured by interdependence, there can be no room for independence, no room for self-subsistence, and therefore no self, and this ultimately applies also to liberalism. We must be careful here not to confuse the no-self of empiricism, which annihilates the self in spite of the fact that it desperately needs it, with the no-self of the transpersonal tradition, as in Buddhism or Platonism, which does not deny the psychical and soul reality of the self but claims it to be only a partial and precarious reality, whose true nature is a spiritual infinity (the Good or Buddha-nature) transcending all particular definitions or selves.

The liberal tension of trying to establish a self within a context of full interdependence that does not allow it emerges with utter clarity in John Locke. Locke claims a direct link with the "Schooles," that is, with the Aristotelian-Thomistic tradition as represented by the "judicious Hooker." Yet he is the "inventor" of modern political empiricism, of a view of the world in which the self-subsistent realities and principles of the spiritual-ethical dimension lose the profound ontological and deeply felt status they previously had had. The Christian Locke transforms the world into a merely sense-matter reality, a place of endless sensuous desires and acquisitive actions. Ironically, Locke's genius (although we should probably say "shrewdness") is in his ability of presenting the radical autonomy of the atomistic and possessive world as wanted by God himself![18] This is done by Locke not only to earn recognition from a society that could have not openly accepted anything that would have sounded irreligious but also for less-instrumental reasons connected to the very nature of his political theory.

Acquisitive individualism[19] is not only historically but also logically inseparable from empiricism. If we are essentially infinite, as believed by transpersonalism, then we will not stop until we become aware of the infinity we forgetfully are. This we call the *absolute-impulse*, whose power is such that it will move us secretly from our unconscious depths even if we think of ourselves as essentially and insuperably finite, as empiricism teaches us to do. In fact, when we think of reality as purely finite, our moving toward infinity will express itself into a process of accumulating as much finitude as we can, unconsciously deluding ourselves that this will get as close as possible to the realization of our absoluteness. Through empiricism, we become acquisitive and ego-centered individuals who need to expand by continually "incorporating" things and beings that, by their autonomous and unpossessed existence, limit and thus deny our absoluteness. This is why empiricism is caught in an unsolvable contradiction between its world of full interdependence and its need to recognize the independent self that operates to incorporate all that for him is no-self. Whereas utilitarianism ultimately chooses the side of interdependence, producing a stifling monism that clashes against the rights and rebellion of individuality, liberalism chooses the side of individuality through the dualism of public and private, trying to confine interdependence within the public realm and independence within the private realm, even though its empiricism cannot offer any solid ontological support to private independence, which therefore remains a mere abstract ideal.

Locke understood this problem and tried to solve it by surreptitiously preserving notions of a spiritual and religious transcendence that would legitimate the autonomy of individuals from the public human realm. Thus, he argued against slavery by claiming that our life is God's property; claimed a right of the people to "appeal to Heaven" against tyranny; established a space somewhat free from the absolute interdependence of the sense-matter dimension by adding "ideas of reflection" above and beyond the ideas directly produced by sense-experiences, ideas of reflection that, as Locke says in the attempt of positing an independent interiority, "every man has wholly in himself." In the end, however, all such ideas reveal themselves to be a mere show, the product of the liberal will to give some kind of deontological ground to private autonomy. In fact, through a complicated turn of arguments that cannot be discussed here, Locke eventually betrays his spiritual intimations: He allows for slavery in certain circumstances, especially in the case of the western occupation of "primitive" lands such as America and Africa; the "appeal to heaven" is revealed to be but a deontological mask for the will of the majority; and finally, the independent interiority grounded on the "ideas of reflections" collapses back into the interdependence of the sense-matter continuum, when Locke explains that even the "ideas of reflections" are but a further elaboration of the material that the senses provide the mind with. Having no ontological ground, private autonomy remains an abstract value, a voluntaristic claim that constantly clashes against the inevitable requirements of interdependence. In this respect, liberalism has not changed a bit, as we shall see in various instances in the following chapters.

The problem with liberalism is only partially the fact that it leaves too much room to the arbitrary freedom of individuals, thus compromising the integrity of community. This is true insofar as its central value is not privacy, with its protection of an essentially and thus potentially spiritual and ethical interiority, but *privatism*, the upholding of a private sphere inside which individuals are supposed to be free to do whatever they want, even that which is unethical and socially or self-destructive (what is truly unethical is always destructive), as long as their actions do not harm the equal arbitrary liberty of others. We shall see how this view, best expressed in Mill's theory of harm but supporting in different ways the whole of modern liberalism, although it can be more easily accused of being destructive for the community and for the individual, is indeed deeply lacking in the very field that is considered almost an exclusive monopoly of liberalism, namely the protection of private autonomy. Precisely because private liberty is asserted abstractly and thus regardless of its interplay with communal and cosmic responsibility, in the end the liberal either must accept the unacceptable destructiveness and self-destructiveness of private arbitrariness or s/he must side with the repression of private arbitrariness by the community, as all liberals who have maintained some degree of reasonableness do. There is no third way, such as the one that shall be presented in this work, precisely because liberal dualism can only oppose individuality and community, so that the former is reduced to a communally irresponsible and unjudgeable liberty of action and choice, which in turn forces the community to be the mere agent of the external limitation of such a liberty. The liberal trick is that of maintaining a rhetorical notion whereby liberty is defined as absolute and inviolable (i.e., Dworkin's "rights as trumps") in spite of the acknowledged necessity that it be socially and legally curtailed, so that it can continue reproducing itself as it is, and this is essential for the perpetuation of the irresponsible utilitarian-consumeristic model, against the background of what is therefore an inevitably growing repression.[20] We saw in the Introduction that this creates a deep contradiction within the capitalistic partnership of liberalism and utilitarianism, a contradiction that can be temporarily solved through a deeper formational penetration of minds, to achieve the impossible dream to have acquisitive and consumeristic egoists who at the same time behave in accordance with the calculative and legal rationality of the utilitarian general interest.

Having identified liberalism with privatism, we can better understand my platonic claim that liberalism sets itself at the level of the spirited-emotional soul, in the same way in which utilitarianism expresses the acquisitive soul. This classification by soul-type is important because it supports an important tripartition that will accompany us throughout the book and that constitutes the ground of our theory of rights, the tripartition of property, personality, and privacy that we shall introduce in the next paragraph. Privatism is the upholding of the private sphere as a spatially enclosed place where the individual can decide freely about his/her aesthetic choices, his tastes in consumption, and more generally his self-care, and about his/her love and family life, that is, about things that deal with our emotional fulfillment (and with the "inner child," who needs family care and a colorful life of varied playthings). As we shall see, these are precisely the elements that characterize the intermediate dimension of personality, which stands above the merely possessive and acquisitive character of property but below the spiritual and ethical dimension of privacy. To say that utilitarianism stands at the level of property-wealth, and thus of the possessive-acquisitive soul, and liberalism stands at the level of personality, or of the spirited-emotional soul, is of course a generalization to be taken with a grain of salt. Every human being has a material as well as an emotional life, and of course we are not saying that the utilitarian does not have an emotional life, or that the liberal does not have an inner life. We are saying that the whole of the human experience is interpreted by the utilitarian through the lenses of sensual and financial acquisition. The liberal personality, in turn, puts at the core the "free finite personality" (to adjust a hegelian concept), placing the idiosyncracy of its tastes and its freedom of choice above wealth maximization.[21] Indeed, the liberal private sphere is supposed to protect equally the saint and the scoundrel, and in this respect liberalism is different from utilitarianism, because, at least in theory, it remains indifferent to what is going on inside the private sphere, whereas for the Benthamite neither the "ascetic" saint nor the idiosyncratic chooser are legitimate forms of human existence. The problem, as we mentioned earlier, is that the liberal psychology is not much different from that of utilitarianism, sharing with it the same empiricist roots, whereby the life of the hero or the saint becomes unintelligible and indeed laughable, so that the liberal private sphere, surrounded and then formationally penetrated by the consumeristic and egoistic culture that liberal relativism breeds, turns out to be for the most part a haven for the small scoundrels we all are when taken by our acquisitive and egoistic impulses.

To make sense of this last claim, we have to answer an objection that immediately arises: Is not the spirited-emotional soul the soul of the hero full of courageous spirit, the soul of the Platonic guardians? And if liberalism is based on a psychology of possessive and selfish impulses, how can it be characterized by a "spirited" soul? Liberalism is indeed deeply antiheroic. Historically it can be seen as the political philosophy of the "petty" bourgeoisie protective of its "small" private pleasures, as J. Shklar—among others—has rightly clarified.[22]

Yet, this antiheroic nature of liberalism does not erase completely its link with the emotional soul. When speaking of that soul, Plato says that it is like a child, and in the same way in which a child can be educated by a good or bad adult, so the emotional soul can place itself under the materialistic guide of the possessive-utilitarian soul or the spiritual guide of the transpersonal soul. The problem with liberalism is that its fundamental roots are much closer to utilitarianism, as we said, and so cannot escape its embrace. The result is that liberalism creates a split inside the spirited-emotional soul, keeping and developing only the emotional side, incorporating it in the acquisitive soul to form a new powerful force. Utilitarianism by itself, with its secularized puritan insistence on wealth maximization as a duty prevailing over any personal fancy, risks being too dry. People do not want money for its own sake, they want it to satisfy desires, and desires, differing from the instinctual, self-preserving, and fear-based needs of the acquisitive soul, are made of emotional stuff. What sustains our current global capitalistic society is precisely the unity of the liberal will to satisfy idiosyncratic desires and the utilitarian focus on the wealth-maximizing processes that present themselves as capable of giving concrete actualization to that satisfaction of desires. In this respect, utilitarianism and liberalism represent the two faces of a unique project, guided by an individual and collective psyche made up of two reciprocally reinforcing, although sometimes clashing, types of soul: the self-preserving and acquisitive soul on the one hand and the emotional yet no longer spirited soul of liberalism on the other. From a legal point of view, this produces a dependence of personality rights on the more fundamental right of property, which is indeed a *right to wealth*, given that in the modern dominant formulation property is valued only as a servant of wealth maximization. In the end, the liberal private sphere turns out to be precisely the place where the acquisitive, egoistic, and ultimately fearful-angry man flourishes, as it is shown, for instance, by the fact that in Rawlsian liberalism, for all its egalitarian and supposedly anti–wealth-maximization elements, the starting point remains the fact that every member of society wants as much as possible of primary goods. The result is that although the radical dualism of private and public established by the liberal private sphere can partially protect the individual, including the virtuous and cosmically responsible one, from public interference, it protects much more forcefully and significantly the utilitarian human being not only because of the utilitarian premises of liberal culture but also because of liberal relativism which, by preventing any possibility of ranking above and then promoting the more difficult path toward virtue, makes it possible for the easier acquiescence to socially and ecologically irresponsible pleasures to grow into social and political dominance.

Now we can begin to understand the impossible relationship between liberalism and the law. The liberal private sphere is the place of irresponsibility not as an accident, as something that happens in the course of individual growth toward responsible freedom, but as a basic value, given that the fundamental ethical value for liberalism is the impossibility to establish any ethical value as primary or superior. Liberalism is in itself the assertion of the part against the whole, it is the denial of the whole. How can it ground or even inspire the law, whose intrinsic purpose and essence is the promotion of the unity of part and whole, the guarantee that the individual will act in a universal and holistic way? Contrary to current common thinking, *the law has never been liberal*, as we shall see in the course of our historical exploration of American constitutional law, and less than ever during the privacy revolution of the 1960s. In the instances in which liberalism has been imported into the law, it has been only partially, only through an integration with some more communitarian theory, such as transpersonalism, as it has happened with some post-*Roe* judges like Blackmun and Brennan, or utilitarianism, as we shall see for instance in reference to the Legal Formalism of the second half of the nineteenth century. The latter is more natural, given the intrinsic unity that exists between liberalism and utilitarianism. Utilitarianism is, in its own way, very holistic, insofar as it wants every individual to be wholly subordinated to the global wealth-maximizing whole. In the utilitarian context, it makes sense to talk of a "general interest," of a "common good," as oppressive and self-destructive as it may be in the long run. When liberals talk of such notions, generally as realities to be "trumped" upon, they explicitly refer to the utilitarian version. And it is therefore to the utilitarian common good that they end up bowing to when their abstract "absolute" liberty collapses. Liberalism is in this sense inherently self-destructive, insofar as it fosters those utilitarian and capitalistic tendencies that inevitably crash in upon privacy, and eventually upon that liberty that is supposed to be its foundational value. It is no accident that in the liberal societies of today, where the rhetoric of privacy and freedom is at its highest ever, the condition of privacy, and consequently of liberty in its concrete rather than formal status, is sinking deeper and deeper into oblivion.

Moving on now to the third approach, the communitarian, we can say that historically communitarianism finds its roots in the Aristotelian-Thomistic tradition, which today presents itself in a nonreligious Aristotelian version (from Arendt to Sandel) and in a Christian-Aristotelian Thomism (e.g., MacIntyre). To summarize briefly a philosophical analysis that I have developed elsewhere,[23] let it suffice to say that both in Aristotle and in Thomas there is a radical dualism of spirit and matter, although spirit is placed above matter in a dualistic and separative way. Their doctrine stands in opposition to the so-called "emanationism" of the Platonic tradition, whereby matter itself is nothing but a denser state of spirit, so that material beings are essentially spiritual beings, and this applies most of all to humans, who are essentially and potentially self-conscious of their spiritual nature. In Aristotelianism, as well as in Thomism, human beings are half spirit and half matter, a "synolon" or whole innerly split into two fundamentally separate and irreconcilable parts. Each part lives according to its distinct rules and ways, although the autonomous material side is supposed to conform itself to the ethically higher spiritual dimension to which it is supposed to be analogous. In other words, the materialistic and utilitarian way of life is acknowledged as lower yet inevitable and natural given the irreversibly fallen nature of human beings, whereas its subordination to ethical-spiritual principles from above on the one hand has the merit of preventing a full materialistic corruption, but on the other hand potentially seals the materialistic way of life with a justification from above.[24] Both in Aristotle and in Thomas the spiritual and intellectual life maintains a higher status. But precisely because human spirit is irreversibly marked by the fall into matter, the spiritual and intellectual privacy of human beings is limited "from above," and it can know God or the archetypal ethical-spiritual forms only as something that stands outside of itself, even when, as in Thomas, it reaches the visionary and the mystical. Evil is thus placed into the very depths of human interiority, so that our good ethical-spiritual side must find support from an outside purer and uncompromised source. And because what characterizes the evilness of matter is precisely its finitude, its particularism, the salvific source must have a universal character, must represent the universality of the religious (Church) and/or political (State) community. On the other hand, privacy becomes the dimension in which humans can acknowledge and play out their lower acquisitive, sensual, and sexual nature, which, being essentially fallen, cannot be spiritually transformed but only circumscribed and limited by an ethical-spiritual dimension from above, as materially represented by community religious and ethical standards. On the religious side, this radical dualism of spirit and matter as the source of the dualism of private and public is best expressed by MacIntyre:

Surely in the eyes of God I am an individual prior and apart from my roles. This rejoinder embodies a misconception, which in part arises from a confusion between the Platonic notion of the soul and that of Catholic Christianity. . . . For the Catholic Christian, as earlier for the Aristotelian, the body and soul are not two linked substances. I am a body and my body is social, born to those parents in this community with a specific social identity . . . [then] I am also held to be a member of a heavenly, eternal community in which I also have a role, a community represented on earth by the Church.[25]

On the more political side, we can look at another modern thinker inspired by the Aristotelian tradition in order to see how privacy has no value apart from its being a function of public life, so that it can be even etymologically equated with "privation." For Arendt the meaning of privacy is derived from its Greek etymology, where "private" or "one's own" is "idion," so that the "idiot" is quintessentially s/he who is purely private. Apart from the fact that the Greeks certainly did not intend to identify privacy with idiocy,[26] there is more to this than just provocation. Human privacy is not, as it was for Plato and as it has been for Brandeis, the locus of a powerful "spiritual nature" whose cosmic universality shines even through the evil and fear and pain of being human but the cage of a spiritual sparkle irreversibly buried within the "idiocy" of matter and at best reduced to a rationalistic mind dependent and delimited by sensual finitude. This is why, being captured by outer extension, human interiority as the smallest of reality can overcome the evilness of particularity only by resting upon the more spatially and temporally universal realm of the public community. In Aristotle or Thomas, God himself has the quality of a public institution, of a father or judge that stands outside of and above us: God as a Supreme Person is very different from the Platonic and Buddhist God and Gods at once outside of and inside us. In Arendt and other nonreligious Aristotelians, only the human public community can rescue our individual poverty, by offering us the possibility of patriotic heroism or of "work" (as opposed to mere labor), both of which make us less ethereal, if not fully real, because it is through our acts or through our crafts that we can hope to achieve the immortal life that only a historical community can provide to finite beings like us.

Human life should therefore be as public as possible, and even the "nonprivative" traits of privacy that Arendt admits to are in the end constitutionally subordered and made dependent on the public. For Arendt, here too faithful to the Aristotelian tradition, family's privacy has the positive function of enclosing and hiding matters of birth and death, which, being related to the invisible and indeterminate surroundings of life in its inherent publicness, would have a destructive impact on the visibility and determinacy of public life. Here too privacy only serves the public and has no value in itself. The other area where privacy is important is the "life of the mind," the Aristotelian theoretical life. But in Arendt, as well as in Aristotle, there is a radical dualism of theoretical and practical, so that the life of the mind is enclosed in its own abstractness and becomes politically irrelevant, at least in terms of the direct participation of theoretical humans in politics. Besides, the privacy of the mental life is not even really private, because its sources do not spring from interiority, which is rather reduced to an arena in which the public discourses and writings of the academic and political community are reflected upon.[27] The Aristotelian stress on the life of the mind, as well as the Aristotelian-Thomistic stress on the spiritual inner life, is certainly important insofar as they create, especially in contrast with the modern empiricist indifference to any form of interiority, a certain space for privacy. But it is a limited space, a space eventually insecure, as it is inherently subordinated by the rules and traditions of the Church on the one hand and by some academic or scientific community and authority on the other. For many communitarians, intellectual freedom and privacy are indeed a very important value. However, the communitarian lack of understanding of the importance of privacy in itself, independent of any public pattern or function, is in itself dangerous because it fundamentally sustains, even if unconsciously, the current global attack on privacy.

We shall see in Chapter 3 how one contemporary communitarian, Michael Sandel, speaks out for privacy in terms that are more convincing and genuinely concerned than those of liberals; yet how he too in the end wants to keep privacy within narrow traditional limits whereby privacy has value only insofar as it promotes public participation and life. Even Ferdinand Schoeman, who has done good work in the name of privacy, falls into the communitarian pitfall. He begins by assigning privacy the function of "protecting individuals from the overreaching control of others," and this is certainly one of the functions of privacy. Yet privacy has a value in itself, not only as a negative barrier against the interference of others: The negative barrier is necessary to protect that which is positive and essential in privacy, namely ethical-spiritual interiority. Unfortunately there is no reference to this whatsoever in Schoeman, and in fact he eventually reduces privacy to "associational privacy," that is, to the privacy of individuals inside the many different associations that for him (probably rightly so) constitute a healthy community.[28] Now, associational privacy and more generally the privacy and the rights related to political participation are a very important element of any serious theory of rights. Yet, if the highest horizon is political privacy, if we stop before arriving at the privacy of individual interiority, associational privacy itself is left without solid ground and thus is made insecure, because political privacy is intelligible at all only if first we have a grasp of privacy as such (as we shall see more clearly in the next paragraph). In the same way in which utilitarianism stops at property and liberalism stops at personality, communitarianism reaches the dimension of privacy but stops at its "public" side, at its political aspect, being unable to satisfy our holistic criterion of analysis. Analogously communitarianism is characterized by a soul that, though sublimating the "spirited-emotional" soul into the transpersonal element, is unable to complete the process. As we have seen with Arendt, patriotic heroism is an essential component of the communitarian conception of the public life, together with the development of transpersonal feelings capable of elevating the particular individual into a universal perspective, be it political or religious. Indeed, faith-based religion is mainly a thing of the heart, as Hegel pointed out; and patriotism is also mainly an emotional state, which can become spirited when actively manifested. Thus, we can say that communitarianism is also centered on the "spirited-emotional" soul, but contrary to liberalism it brings that soul in contact with the higher rather than with the low, with the transpersonal soul, capable of universality and self-sacrifice, rather than with the instinctual-acquisitive soul, which is centered on fearful self-preservation. The problem is that communitarianism's knowledge of such a soul is only indirect. For the reasons explained earlier, due to the Aristotelian-Thomistic idea that our spiritual nature has essentially and irreversibly fallen into matter and interdependence, the experience of the transpersonal can only be mediated, it can never be introspective and thus truly spiritual. In communitarianism universality can only be experienced as something outside ourselves, something of which we are parts, rather than our deepest inner nature. Therefore, rather than *being* universality, we can only *feel* in awe in front of that *sublime* that transcends and encompasses us, be it God or Nation. The transpersonal soul is thus reduced to an intellectual understanding of universality that sustains and justifies the action of our spirited-emotional element. A good communitarian is s/he who participates in public life out of his feeling for the public interest. This is an absolutely crucial contribution, as most people participate and care for the public life not through and because of a direct perception of their inner universality but precisely through a proper education of feelings. But if the process stops here, if the reality of the enlightened spiritual interiority is erased from the picture, then public life itself is in danger, not only because it will have false leaders with no direct understanding of ethical and then political principles, but because its very inner essence vanishes with the fading away of privacy-interiority.

Rousseau makes a very clear and very important distinction between the "general will" (*volonté générale*) and "will of all" (*volonté de tous*). The latter refers to the will of the concrete community in its accidental condition: It may be the will of a majority or even a unanimous will, but this in itself does not guarantee its being a just and good will. A just and good will is not determined according to some substantively predetermined values but in accordance with *the substantive form of the Whole of Wholes*, and it is such an accord that makes it "general." *The general will as Whole of Wholes means that only that community is Whole whose end is the Wholeness of its parts, who become self-realized Wholes by learning to discover inside themselves their essential identity with the social and cosmic Whole of which they are parts.* As Rousseau explains, the general will is "indestructible," because it remains formally unaltered by any concrete wrong decision of the community, which is wrong precisely from such an indestructible, or "non separately a priori," point of view. Let it be clear that its stability does not mean rigidity, as the general will emerges each time as a different concrete answer, as the answer that is right for that specific situation insofar as it is the unfolding of the basic idea/reality of the Whole of Wholes. The "general will" has thus the same quality of "*non-separate independence*" that belongs to the categorical imperative in ethics and to Plato's Ideas or Forms, who are so inseparate from their concrete embodiments as to be in fact the body itself in its essential truth (in the same sense in which even Wittgenstein says that the body is the best picture of the soul); and yet it remains untouched by the corruption of the body, maintaining that archetypal independence of an original imprint that is the very precondition for the eternal rebirth of new bodies. We shall see how this idea of "nonseparate independence" plays a crucial role in our theory of privacy and rights, privacy being precisely the condition through which one can experience that inner independence from the social, political, and even ecological realm that nevertheless, when most genuine, knows itself as encompassing the whole world, not just through the experiential introjection of social habits and environmental interdependencies but as being more originally and fundamentally one with the spirit that unfolds as the world. And without the "nonseparate independence" of the general will, without the possibility of a self-subsistent critical standpoint from which to judge the will of the community, politics becomes corrupt and unable to transform itself, while political and social participation risks becoming the tool of injustice, as when the faithful soldier gives up his life due to a feeling for his country that nevertheless leads an unjust war.

With communitarians participation becomes an end in itself, and this means that the basic end of human life is that of being a part rather than a whole. Moving beyond communitarianism is necessary precisely to find the independent essence of the community itself, that essential and inner justice that is the very powerful, indeed indestructible support of any community. This is clarified by Plato's example of the "band of thieves," which, although based on evil, will survive only as long as it maintains harmony, and thus some measure of goodness, among its members. The recognition and valuation of such a *community's interiority* are essentially related to the recognition and valuation of personal interiority and privacy, because no community can last whose leaders are not endowed with a spiritually and ethically evolved interiority or whose members behave ethically only by habituation and/or coercion rather than through an inner spontaneous adherence to the ethical principle. The shift from participation to interiority, from publicity to spiritual privacy, is thus indispensable not just for individuals but for the community itself. It is important to understand that this transpersonal shift is not a denial but rather a more secure and solid affirmation of communitarian values. No one denies that communal and patriotic feelings, ethical habituation to the community mores, and political participation in the life of the community are indispensable pillars of any community. But they are so only if they foster the development of that private spiritual interiority that, being inseparable from the public interiority of the general will, elevates them into the plan of the just social, planetary, and ecological community guided by the reason of the Whole of Wholes. In so doing, communitarian values are secured beyond the cages of majoritarianism or traditionalism, while finding a much needed ground, one that is at once above any historical corruption and yet capable of penetrating history with the utmost transformational power.

It should be quite evident by now how a genuine *transformational* conception of politics[29] requires a transpersonal foundation giving spiritual privacy the primacy it deserves. Brandeis said that privacy is the "most comprehensive of rights," and we shall see how our own understanding of the right to privacy, and of rights in general, remains faithful to this view. But he also said that privacy is the right "most valued by civilized men," who tend to engulf themselves in outer competitive and possessive engagements, forgetting that inner being whose proper ordering and justice is the only true source of happiness both for the individual and for the community. The idea of justice as being an ethical ordering of the soul and simultaneously of *collective political souls* is the guiding thread of platonic politics, as every attentive reader of Plato's *Republic* can ascertain. Contrary to Aristotle and the ensuing communitarian tradition, platonists have always refused to legitimize a political will only because of its traditional or majoritarian justification and have always sought to form both leaders and citizens of a high moral and spiritual standard, in the conviction that only a "good man," a human being who has found wholeness within him/herself, can be a "good citizen," whereas "good citizenship" is all that a communitarian can consistently ask for. Therefore the transpersonalist approach to politics is more powerful and realistic, precisely because it consciously asserts the central place of privacy and spiritual-ethical interiority.

To want to transform the world without trans-forming souls is a delusion. That the world can change us for the good or for the bad from the outside in, there is no doubt. And this is why the surest way to change the world for the better is the way "from the inside out." If it wants to succeed, *transformational politics must also be transpersonal*, as the etymology itself makes clear: Transformation does not mean merely change but that *formation* that makes us *trans*-cend not only our current ways of being but more fundamentally our limited, competitive, and egoistic selves, in order to return to our perennial essence.

Some transformational theorists have in fact begun to underline in various ways the need to reunite politics and spirituality in the direction of an "ecological transpersonalism."[30] But we need to go further and to elaborate a transformational and transpersonal political theory capable of giving a new and central place to those fundamental and perennial values that every human being can respond to.[31] In order to do so, we need to draw inspiration from that Ageless Wisdom that includes eastern religions as well as the western inner and platonic tradition. From such a point of view, the "interdependence" of community is given its very important place, without forgetting, however, the spiritual and ethical independence that essentially defines individuality. The Buddha, like Socrates, valued very highly dialogue and community, but only if dialogue is *from and for* a perfected interiority.[32] That such Ageless Wisdom is not some abstract theory but a fruitful source of effective answers to concrete problems is shown by the legal and political thought of L. D. Brandeis and W. O. Douglas, who to such a tradition were connected through the genuine and platonic "ecological transpersonalism" of R. W. Emerson and H. Thoreau.

A REVOLUTION IN THE CONCEPT OF PRIVACY

All that we have said so far posits the need for a revolution in the concept of privacy. "Re-volution" is an astronomical concept that indicates the movement of celestial bodies (but it applies at all levels, down to the microcosm of the atom) circling around a reference point only to return to the starting point, to its beginning. The idea of a re-turn to the initial point, once applied to moral or social phenomena, indicates a re-turn to that perennial transpersonal essence of both person and community that is also the seed from which the moral and social life have sprouted and keep trans-forming themselves. Any movement, even the most dramatic one, that does not bring one closer to its deepest being has only the appearance of a revolution, being in fact an involution. Thus, a revolution in the concept of privacy is not just any *radical* transformation of it, but that transformation that reaches to its very *roots*, to what has always been its secret but most fundamental definition.

The definition of privacy that will emerge through our analysis of American law is revolutionary in the sense explained here. It is a definition that runs afoul

The Philosophy of Privacy

of the dominant liberal and/or utilitarian understanding and finds its roots within the American constitutional tradition, not in the merely traditionalist or majoritarian way, not by pointing only at the visible body of the constitutional experience, but by searching for the transformative powers integral in its very soul. *Spiritual individualism*, with its insistence on privacy and self-reliance as the foundation of political and cosmic responsibility, constitutes the best element that American history has offered to the world, not only through figures such as Emerson and Thoreau but going back to the very founding of the United States and its Constitution. There have been various unconvincing attempts to attribute Lockean origins to the work of the founding fathers, but in fact their sources were indeed many, including classical platonic thought and even modern Platonic thinkers such as Harrington, who played a prominent role and left deep transpersonal influences on the Constitution.[33] It is unlikely that the Founding Era could be linked as a unitary whole to one or another thinker. There were deep contrasts among the different lines of thought participating in the founding activity, and certainly it was the Jeffersonian current and tradition that embodied most directly and consciously the transpersonal inspiration. This is no place to enter into such a discussion. Let it suffice to say that the outcome of the oppositions and compromises among the different currents involved in the founding left many crucial transpersonal elements intact within the constitutional project and structure, and many a serious student has detected a powerful transpersonal ground, both Platonic and Pythagorean, to the whole of the American founding.[34]

This is nowhere as clear as in the American Bill of Rights, which in the deep unity of structure and content, form and substance, characterizing its original ten-amendments version, reveals a powerful transpersonal inspiration. The *revolutionary emergence of the right of privacy*, promoted by Brandeis, Douglas, and other important judges influenced by the Jeffersonian and Transcendentalist movements, has been its best expression and the main tool through which they were capable of keeping concretely alive the transpersonal essence of the law, that unwritten Constitution deeply inscribed into the substantive form of the written one. As pointed out very clearly by Harold Berman, both law and revolution grow together from the tree of spirituality and metaphysics.[35] We need therefore to explore very briefly the basic metaphysical presuppositions of our revolutionary definition of the law of privacy.

In describing reality as a whole, Plato says, "If the Being is to be produced from the One, that One cannot produce it but by being itself multiplicity."[36] This may seem a sort of obscure metaphysical riddle, but it is indeed quite simple and very concrete, although it must be very clear that Plato's statement, as well as the following explanation of his words, is *but a metaphorical myth or tale that portrays, in words that the ordinary human intellect can grasp, a reality that is utterly beyond language*. What Plato is saying, in a language that was that of the Greek youth trained in philosophical debate, is that the world or reality appears to us as "many," that is, as a multiplicity of things and beings.

This multiplicity is the dimension of *Existence*, whereby *Matter* cuts beings apart from each other, yet only apparently, because material existence, beyond the empiricist separative apprehension of things, is an infinite *interdependence* of particular and relative identities (the "co-dependent origination" of Buddhism) that transforms the initial multiplicity into a *unitary and whole Being*. By being such a cosmic unity, Existence can be said to contain within itself *Essence*, that is, Being as such. This is in fact what Essence means, being derived from *Esse*, latin for "to be" or "being." The universe as a harmonious and organized whole is possible not through interdependence, which in itself could be just the casual succession of attractions and repulsions among the infinite mass of things, but through the independent Logos or "general plan" that within the body of the universe lives in and as its governing Mind or *Nous*.[37] This "Cosmic Mind" (a crucial Emersonian concept, as we shall see) is also the source of the universal spiritual archetypes, called Ideas or Forms by Plato. They are the *Essences* of all particular realities and things, and these too, while being so much within existing things as to be the "things themselves" (which means that things are nothing but essences embodied and thus individualized through time and space), are fundamentally "independent" from the becoming of the things in their existence, in their being born and dying. Essence maintains with existence that relation of *nonseparate independence* discussed in the previous section. In line with the platonic and transpersonal claim about the identity of *macrocosm and microcosm*, the nonseparate independence of Essence applies both to the universe and the individual. This means that the individual has within him/herself, as his/her own essence, the universality, or oneness, that belongs to the realm of Essences and that in turn carries within itself the even deeper and ultimate Oneness that, as Plato says, is even beyond Being and Essence.

Plato says that Being is produced by the One, thus positing a reality more fundamental than that of Essence. This is reasonable. We have said that Being is most fundamentally the unity and wholeness of the universe (Essence) and of each being and thing within it (Essences) and is in this sense the Cosmic One. But the universe is a spatial and temporal reality and as such bound at least by two conditions, being in space and being in time. This means that the Oneness of the cosmos, its inherent Logos, is itself conditioned and limited, and that therefore there must logically be a reality that is outside of it, beyond its limits. This is one version of the famous problem of "infinite regression" and forces the mind to consider, at least by opposition, the reality of an absolutely unconditioned and thus truly unitary One. At this level, Plato's One, which is also the supremely Good, is that ineffable and ultimate reality that the Chinese call the Tao. For the human mind, this ultimate reality presents itself as an *Absence* of any determination, an emptiness that in reality, in a reality that the ordinary human mind cannot grasp, is the perfect presence and fullness from which everything springs *and in which everything is contained*. This last point is essential to our argument. From the platonic transpersonal point of view, as Plato says, "the One is itself multiplicity": The ultimate Oneness is not simply the source of Essence and through it of all Existence, but it itself unfolds as that Essence/Essences, which in turn unfolds as Existences. This means that the ultimate and divine One, far from being a separate and majestic Person, is present in the deepest marrow of each being and thing, it is in fact the "thing as such or in itself." The ultimate One is therefore *Spirit*, because only as spirit or "sacred wind" can It circulate freely all over the universe, and within its own innumerable souls and bodies. But it is also fundamentally Matter, because each one of us material beings is fundamentally It, and we are It without losing our finite precarious identities, precisely because those identities are truly the material unfolding of the most real One.

From all this we derive some conclusions that are central to transpersonal thought. Each thing in the universe is an embodiment of the One as Spirit, and Matter itself is nothing but Spirit "slowed down." This means that the basic rule of reality is that "the part is the whole, as the whole is the part," not only because of material interdependence but more deeply because each part is spiritually the Whole One. This is the true meaning of the notion of a *holographic identity* whereby any finite reality has infinite otherness in itself and as its own very self, precisely like a holographic film, any part of which, if cut out from the whole, reproduces that very whole.[38] The fact that we retrieve the fundamental principle of the *Whole of Wholes* not only in a piece of film but even more intensely at the level of biological and physiological matter, whereby holistic medical science has shown that each part of the body (the iris, the ear, the foot, etc.) reproduces the model of the whole body within itself, shows immediately that such a principle applies to all levels of reality, and that therefore it can be identified as the fundamental content of the cosmic Logos (at least insofar as our human intellect can understand it in its own terms).

This brings forth a paradoxical truth that is fundamental to understanding the human condition and its self-organization through law and politics. We call this truth the *paradox of equality and inequality*. There is a change in perspective when we move from the "view from existence" to a more essential vision. If we could look at things and persons through the divine eye of the One and its Mind/Essences, we would see the perfect equality of spirit and matter, of intelligence and rocks, more generally of all that from our point of view appears as above and below. Yet, this cannot erase the importance of distinguishing from above and below when we judge and act as mortals. From the point of view of existence, *mind takes precedence over matter*, because our ordinary perception is still unable to see matter as mind, and only the protection and promotion of a mental and spiritual life can generate an active intelligence capable of transvaluing matter, as much as possible, into the spirit it essentially is. It should be immediately clear how the precedence of mind over matter requires a different organization of rights whereby intellectual and potentially spiritual privacy cannot but play a predominant role.

Each human self not only is the Whole One in the unconscious way everything else is, including rocks and plants, but is also It in the active spiritual mode of self-awareness. This means that we can become aware of the absolute-impulse that secretly guides us, thereby transferring our search for fullness and completeness from the path of outer acquisition to that of inner growth. It also means that we can become, precisely because "essentially" although forgetfully we are already so, *morally autonomous*.

Ethics is in the end the ability to gladly and spontaneously accept the limits that interdependence imposes on us, as finite selves who want to become existentially and materially infinite, learning to live such existential limits as positive opportunities to grow toward our essential and inner infinity. But if we are essentially infinite, if our unconscious leads us from such a premise, we will be able to attend to the need for external limits only if sustained by a sense of inner and essential unlimitedness. *Privacy is the place to cultivate and experience, if only partially, the sense of our inner universality and wholeness, because privacy is withdrawal from one's particular conditions and attachments and thus toward our less conditioned and thus more universal self.* There are different ways of developing such a sense inside our mind, also because mind or soul, as we have seen, has itself different levels. Intellectually we can acknowledge both our material interdependence with all other beings and our moral faculty to develop an independent universal standpoint, and it is from both of these that spring our ethical judgment and action, our ability to act according to the "golden rule" or "categorical imperative" ("act in such a way that your action could become a universal maxim" or "do unto others what you would want others to do unto you"). It is here that privacy shows itself to be fundamental not only for the transpersonalist but also for the religious individual as well as the "secular humanist," because they too must be concerned with a true and spontaneous ability to judge and act ethically.

Religion comes from *re-ligo*, "to connect things," which expresses the idea of the cosmic interdependence of all things, and this is an experience that every human being, including those who would consider themselves "secular humanists," can and do experience. J. C. Raines, who declares himself to be a child of the 1960s, says that the "attack on privacy" is in the end an attempt to eliminate the *spiritual depth of human life*, the sensitivity of all human beings to the "*mysterium tremendum*," the terrifying and yet awe-inspiring mystery that human life is, and whose exploration helps us search for meaning beyond the narrow limits of our finite and egoistic existence.[39] Every religious person, unless s/he has reduced religious experience to the purely external participation into social church rituals, should have a deep interest in the promotion through privacy of mental and spiritual interiority.

The same applies to the "secular humanist," who often has the advantage of being unhindered by any metaphysical dogma or despiritualized ritual in his/her facing of the "ultimate mystery" of life. Even the secular humanist who is not interested in the exploration of inner spiritual transcendence, as long as s/he remains open to the idea that we are part of a mysterious and infinite cosmic whole and that such a belonging challenges us to a deeper moral and political

The Philosophy of Privacy

involvement (remember Kant's famous phrase: "the starry sky above me, the moral law inside me"), cannot avoid acknowledging the primacy of privacy in the human experience:

> Privacy is *communion*, passive and active, with our fellow beings when we are not physically in their presence. When in privacy, we talk to ourselves, we use the common speech, feel the preferences and aversions common to the race, and are then least personal because least self-regarding, for when we are alone we stand before no audience but man.

These beautiful words of Capuoya express the spiritual depth of *privacy as communion* in a way that is acceptable not only to the transpersonalist but to every human being, be s/he openly religious or not.[40]

It is therefore through an alliance among the different ways of appreciating true privacy, as opposed to liberal "privatism," that the battle for privacy can be won. The transpersonalist has a special interest in winning such a battle, because for him/her privacy has a deeper spiritual character, as the seat of "man's spiritual nature" (Brandeis).

To be sure, spiritual self-realization is not something easily attainable by ordinary human beings. Yet, such a state remains fundamental for all of us, because our own genuine ethical behavior rests on the intimations and intuitions of a deeper spiritual understanding. When we let ourselves flow into the peacefulness that is our deepest "private" interiority, in our dreams, visions, symbolic expressions, we all channel the universal and archetypal forms and meanings that come from the "realm of the Mothers" (Goethe), and that helps us not just to understand but also to feel and desire the happy way of responsible freedom, whereby we gladly accept to live as parts of the Whole precisely insofar as we find Wholeness, including the Whole of which we are parts, inside our limited selves.[41]

The idea of the community as a "Whole of Wholes" is the guiding thread that runs through transpersonal political theory. We define the idea of the "Whole of Wholes" through a concept that will return throughout the book, that of *substantive form*: As a general structural model with no reference to any content whatsoever, concrete contents being determined by the evolving embodiments of the "general will," it looks like an *empty form*; yet it is a form that has an immediate *substantive relevance and power*, because the communal Whole is bound by it to keep as its fundamental end the material and inner development of its members that will help them to recognize their Wholeness.

That privacy is communion, and thus true Wholeness, has already been said. But privacy is communion only essentially, only as the potential end of personal growth. In its most immediate form, privacy presents itself mainly as withdrawal. This is why from a legal point of view the element of withdrawal into interiority takes precedence: The law cannot intervene at the level of interiority to discriminate what is going on inside it (apart from very strict exceptions, as we shall see) and can only hope that the withdrawal of privacy will indeed produce communion and thus a compassionate and ethical behavior, a hope that is sustained by the awareness of the great power that true silence and inner reflection have on the human psyche.

Privacy as interiority is a very special and at the same time very problematic place from the point of view of the law, because it is at the threshold between empirical and essential reality. Because the law works within the realm of outer human experience, while possibly channeling the inner ethical and spiritual principles, privacy is a place to which the law remains generally external, but on which it depends both to be effective, because no law that has no inner approval from the citizens can work, and to draw the creative energy that makes it evolve in accordance with the formal-substantive principle of the Whole of Wholes. To understand this double nature of privacy from the point of view of the law, we need to focus on the tripartition of *empirical/existential/essential*, which reproduces at the level of material existence the fundamental metaphysical and ontological tripartition of One-Absence, Essence, and Existence as analyzed earlier, together with that paradox of equality/inequality, whereby essentially the three dimensions are one and the same yet without losing their difference, which existentially presents itself as the nondualistic inequality of nonseparate independence. The *empirical* reality and consciousness is our ordinary experience, whereby things and selves appear as fundamentally separate and in atomistic conflict among themselves. The *essential* reality and consciousness is of course that which we become when acknowledging ourselves as both interdependently and spiritually Whole. *Existential* reality and consciousness is the bridge between the two; it is that transformation of empirical consciousness and interiority that moves one person toward his/her own cosmic Essence, where *essential liberty* and *existential or universal responsibility* tend to coincide.

Such a coincidence brings with it the essential identity of *spiritual privacy* and *ethical action*, whereby ethical behavior emerges as ''contemplation in action,'' if by contemplation we understand to mean any form of the returning to our original and silent Absence of personal preferences, which only can generate the most responsible and just choices in each specific situation. But, as we said, law and politics deal with ordinary existence and in fact are born as answers to the shortcomings of such an existence, which oscillates between the empirical and the essential, therefore encompassing the unessential and irresponsible. Here, the hierarchical priority of contemplation and mind over action and matter is a must. It could be argued that contemplation itself, as well as the withdrawal into thinking, may be the formalistic shell of a bad and irresponsible interiority. But this is an insufficient argument, because a corrupted interiority, being unable to overcome its selfish attachments to externals, is bound to manifest itself into the outside world through atomistic, unethical, and eventually illegal actions, and it is at this level that the law can and should intervene. *However, as long as it remains within the realm of thought and mind, interiority maintains an important degree of independence from action, a measure of reflexivity in which genuine and responsible self-awareness may still develop.* Thus, the law should promote the privileged position of thought and interiority, and we shall see how this is practically done through the hierarchical tripartition of rights into the three categories of *privacy/personality/property.*

These three categories constitute a practical and existential continuum that moves from the external and externalizing dimension of property to the most inner dimension of privacy. Personality represents the intermediate stage between them: As "persona" (etymologically, "mask"), it refers to the relation of reciprocally external subjects, but it immediately implies that which it masks, the privacy of interiority. Consistent with the overall scheme, we shall see that this hierachical tripartition is simultaneously an essential unity, to the point of transvaluing property itself.

However, with the current predominance of empiricism, a conception of privacy has arisen that has nothing to do with the original notion of privacy and its right. Such a conception tends to flatten the hierarchy of the three existential dimensions, collapsing the nonseparate independence and priority of privacy down into the lower dimension of property, or at best of personality. This happens even to those most advanced liberal thinkers that tend to incorporate dialectical thinking. For instance, W. Weinstein compares the relation of public and private to an onion, each layer of the onion being private in relation to the outer layers, and public in relation to the inner ones.[42] This beautiful image perfectly visualizes the fact that life and experience rest on the relativity and interdependence of all things. Yet, if interdependence is left as the only dimension, privacy, which requires independence and self-subsistence, is clearly erased from the picture. A merely empirical dialectic cannot grasp the "in itself" of things and is thus incapable of ensuring the protection of privacy. Furthermore, by silencing the search for the private as such and in itself, it makes the very dialectics of private and public unintelligible. In other words, it is true that all things are interdependent, but in order to say that two things interdepend, we need first to know those things in themselves. If I keep defining private and public phenomena only in relation to each other, there must come a point where either I say what they are in themselves, or else, interdependence being the only "in itself" left, I could just invert meanings and names without changing the relation, so that whatever I was previously calling private I can now call public, and vice versa. The nominalism implicit in a merely empirical dialectic makes conventionalism the only ground for definition, with the result that privacy and its rights end up being defined by the very reality against which they are supposed to protect, the accidental and fleeting will of empirically public majorities and dominant cultural traditions.

To avoid such a positivistic surrender,[43] we need to define privacy in itself. Paraphrasing Plato, we would say that we cannot know privacy in its various and particular manifestations without knowing the absolutely private, the essential Idea or Form of privacy.[44] The apprehension of the Form itself is a task that transcends our discursive enterprise. But we can shed light on the essence of privacy, from within the limits of language, by developing an appropriate philosophical "tale" or myth in which the empirical relativity of Weinstein's definition can be integrated into a larger and multilayered view, structured along the three fundamental dimensions of empirical, existential, and essential.

Empirical privacy is defined in purely negative terms, as a mere difference. This is the relational definition of privacy given in Weinstein's metaphor of the onion, where private and public are defined only on the ground of their reciprocal difference, without any knowledge of their own identity. Here, privacy is an empty *withdrawal/forthcoming*, yet we do not know wherefrom and whereto one withdraws, nor whereto and wherefrom one comes forth. This is the "privacy as privatism" of empiricist political theory. Mere empirical privacy is that *private sphere* in which there is no distinction between interiority and exteriority, between introspection and watching TV, between withdrawing into one's property and into one's soul. Taken alone, the empirical understanding of privacy is not only quite useless, because it does not tell us anything about the nature and quality of the withdrawal/forthcoming process, but it is also dangerous, because it hinders the law from attaining its end, that growth toward individual Wholeness without which no "general will" and thus no true law can exist. Nevertheless, the empirical notion of privacy as withdrawal/forthcoming becomes very important when supplemented by a proper understanding of the further dimensions of privacy, especially because it stresses how—because the process of withdrawal/forthcoming happens everywhere also within personal and material relations—privacy, which in its elementary form is indeed withdrawal/forthcoming, is necessarily implied in the spheres of personality and property too, as we shall see in due course. Privacy as withdrawal/forthcoming emerges thus as the quintessence of individual rights, which in their most immediate form are indeed protective shields for the *private* individual in his/her "withdrawn" or presocial nature (the right to property is a right to "private" property). But precisely because withdrawal/forthcoming acquires any meaning at all only in relation to the more essential notion of privacy as interiority and eventually communion, the participation of the principle of privacy in the lower levels of personality and property brings with it also those more fundamental meanings, so that, for instance, property is transvalued into the material support for the ethical and spiritual development of the person and is therefore subjected to the limits and ways imposed by such a new and higher function.

The second level of definition, *existential privacy*, takes the empty and dualistic empirical process of withdrawal/forthcoming and gives it meaning by linking it to the higher reality of essences, that is, to *essential privacy*. The concept of essential privacy gives linguistic expression to the platonic form of privacy as a holographic encompassing of the cosmic and public whole. Essential privacy is thus the paradox of the *invisible unity* and *inner cosmic communion* of each part with the whole of reality, a paradox in which the movement of withdrawal/forthcoming is no longer necessary. Consequently, *existential privacy* is the inner withdrawal toward one's essential privacy, which is at the same time a forthcoming from there and into the outer world of political, personal, and proprietary relations. Of course, the inner dimension of existential privacy, still being an empirical condition, bridges toward but does not necessarily reach those essential depths that give us the strength to live outer relations at once with absolute liberty and full responsibility.

Existential privacy, as opposed to empirical privacy as the outer "private sphere," is therefore *interiority*, with its varying degrees of essential awareness. Thinking solitude is its quintessential and paradigmatic condition, although in fact any situation where the question of the integrity of one's interiority predominates, including situations staged in public settings, is to be treated in terms of privacy. From the legal and political point of view, existential privacy or interiority is privacy *tout-court*. It is the more defined scope of the "right of privacy," because the more general concept of privacy as withdrawal/forthcoming, in its being the basic ground of all rights, participates in the different levels of personality and property, thus losing its specificity. Therefore, from the point of view of the law, we must distinguish between a *right of privacy*, which refers more specifically to interiority, and a general *principle of privacy*. The latter penetrates the whole of rights by its reference to withdrawal/forthcoming, and because of its inherent link with privacy as inner communion, it also invests rights with higher ethical and spiritual meanings. In this sense, as we have seen in reference to property, the principle of privacy elevates the empty empirical withdrawal/forthcoming of rights into a withdrawal/forthcoming from and to our ethical-spiritual interiority, from and to our essential privacy. We shall see how the distinction of principle and right of privacy solves many of the legal problems related to the supposed "inflation" of the right of privacy without reducing but rather deepening its impact on the law.

Essential privacy is an immaterial reality that is difficult to ascertain empirically, whereas empirical privacy is by itself an indistinct and unintelligible withdrawal/forthcoming. Existential privacy, as their bridging link, includes both the materiality of the neutral-descriptive withdrawal/forthcoming and the normative-ethical endowment implicit in essential privacy. This normative element has important practical and descriptive implications, because it will allow us, through the medium of the principle of privacy, to order in a proper hierarchy the different levels of rights, namely property, personality, and privacy, and also to evaluate, in relation to each level of action, if the point has been reached in which it is no longer possible to warrant immunity from interference (something that is regulated by our principle of *existential harm*, as we shall see). In the course of our exploration of the history of the right to privacy in the United States we shall see how the idea of privacy as interiority is to be understood in a wide sense. Being at the threshold of spiritual and material, "implicit" and "explicit" (in Brandeis's words), privacy is also at the border of life and death: Before being born, and when we die, we are in a state of radical withdrawal from the human community; we are private in the most profound sense. This implies that all birth and death issues must be treated, both philosophically and legally, as privacy issues. Also, we have already seen how privacy as interiority applies not only to the individual person but also to the collective person each community is, and this is why we shall introduce the important concept of "public privacy," encompassing all questions and rights related to the political formation of the "general will," which stands in relation to the community as essential privacy stands to the individual. But it is time to begin our philosophical and historical voyage into the evolution of American constitutional law and rights, beginning with its true hero, Justice Brandeis.

NOTES

1. Besides the already classical discussion of privacy by H. Arendt, *The Human Condition* (University of Chicago Press, 1958) Ch. 1, more-recent philosophically relevant works on privacy include: F. Schoeman, *Philosophical Dimensions of Privacy* (Cambridge University Press, 1994); B. Moore, Jr., *Privacy: Studies in Social and Cultural History* (New York: M. E. Sharpe, 1984); P. Weiss, *Privacy* (Carbondale: University of Southern Illinois Press, 1984). Important chapters on privacy are included in S. Benn, *A Theory of Freedom* (Cambridge, 1988) and in N. Rosenblum, *Another Liberalism* (Harvard, 1987).

2. F. Schoeman, "Privacy: Philosophical Dimensions of the Literature," in *Philosophical Dimensions of Privacy*, pp. 2–5. For a critical discussion of privacy as control see J. Wagner DeCew, "The Scope of Privacy," in *Law and Philosophy*, 1986, pp. 166–67. For privacy as a "condition of being unobserved" see R. B. Hallborg, Jr., "Principles of Liberty and the Right to Privacy," in *Law and Philosophy* 5 (1986), p. 177.

3. Heisenberg's indeterminacy principle, one of the main tenets of quantum physics, shows that "there are no objective properties of nature independent of the human observer. Now this insight, which is one of the main parallels to mystical knowledge, implies that science can never be value free." F. Capra, "The Tao of Physics Revisited," in K. Wilber (ed.), *The Holographic Paradigm* (Boston: Shambhala, 1985), p. 228. For an excellent overview of the possible connections between politics and quantum physics see Theodore L. Becker (ed.), *Quantum Politics* (Praeger, 1991).

4. W. A. Parent, "Recent Work on the Concept of Privacy," in *Amer. Philos. Q.*, 20 (1983): 341–55. The five types are: a) being let alone; b) sexual autonomy; c) control of information about oneself; d) control over access to oneself; e) limitation of access to oneself.

5. E. Bloustein, "Privacy As an Aspect of Human Dignity: An Answer to Dean Prosser," in *New York Univ. L.R.*, 39 (1964): 962–1007; R. Posner, "An Economic Theory of Privacy," in *Regulation* (May/June 1978): 19–26.

6. R. Gavison, "Privacy and the Limits of Law," in F. Schoeman, p. 350.

7. The basic idea of the "holographic paradigm," which is a new name for a very ancient tenet, is that each part is essentially the whole, and thus contains in itself every other part as well. The hologram is the best representation of this idea precisely because even the smallest part of a holographic film is capable of reproducing the whole picture contained in the film. See K. Wilber.

8. The "eternity" of this soul does not necessarily imply a religious creed and is fully compatible with an atheist yet spiritual vision. Although Socrates speaks often of the immortality of the soul and of its rebirths, this could be interpreted through a Buddhist

understanding, as a mythical way of asserting that sentient beings have a spark of divinity and eternity inside (Buddha-nature), without implying that there actually is an individual soul that remains unaltered through its many wanderings. Indeed, both for Buddhism and Platonism, all that is personal, be it soul or God, is by definition not eternal, eternal being only a divine ultimate reality and its transpersonal thought-forms, which remain utterly ineffable.

9. See Stefano Scoglio, *Privacy, Rights and Natural Law*, Ph.D. thesis, University of Toronto, 1993, Part II.

10. J. Bentham, *UC cxlii. 200* (Bentham's manuscripts in University College, London Library, box 142, p. 200).

11. *Jeremy Bentham's Economic Writings*, ed. W. Stark, 3 vols., London, 1952–1954, I, p. 117.

12. See J. Bentham, *Principles of the Civil Code*, Part I, Ch. 2. In reality, Bentham's argument is not wholly ungrounded, because human beings, not necessarily for egoistic reasons, prefer to have a direct control over their property rather than putting it into the hands of unknown and not always trustable bureaucrats and politicians. But this is an argument that, rather than denying all redistributive claims, should encourage a more decentralized and participatory use of taxation funds, and a legislation exempting from taxation the wealth that people independently use for socially, ethically, and ecologically relevant purposes. For a criticism of Bentham's argument see C. B. MacPherson, *The Life and Times of Liberal Democracy* (Oxford, 1977, 1988), pp. 29–30.

13. J. Bentham, *Principles of Morals and Legislation*, Ch. II.

14. It would be too complex and long to show the passages through which Bentham arrives at such an annihilation of privacy. I have developed such an analysis more fully in my Ph.D. thesis, *Privacy, Rights and Natural Law*, University of Toronto, 1993, Chap. IV, § 6.

15. The current definition of privacy as a mere good to be bought and sold, promoted by Posner and his *Economic Analysis of the Law*, is the most radical brainchild of Benthamism. See R. Posner, "J. A. Sibley Lecture: The Right to Privacy," in *Georgia L.R.*, 12, no.3 (1978); R. Posner, *The Economics of Justice* (Harvard, 1981), Ch. 9–11.

16. W. Prosser, "Privacy: A Legal Analysis," in *Calif. L.R.*, 48 (1960):338–423.

17. See G. J. Postema, *Bentham and the Common Law Tradition* (Oxford, 1986).

18. I have developed this argument in my Ph.D. thesis, *Privacy, Rights and Natural Law*, Ch. 5, § 8.

19. "Acquisitive individualism" is a better definition of the modern capitalistic posture, which is not "possessive," precisely because its impulse to the unlimited accumulation and consumption of the world is opposite to the "conservationist" element implied in the notion of possession.

20. The most explicit and consistent upholding of the dualism of individual liberty and communal responsibility can be found in I. Berlin, "Two Concepts of Liberty," in *Four Essays on Liberty* (Oxford, 1969). On Dworkin's "rights as trumps" see *Taking Rights Seriously* (Harvard, 1978) for its original, and never really changed, formulation.

21. Liberals like Rawls and Dworkin claim to put equality, not liberty, above wealth maximization. But it is equality in the ability to choose idiosyncratically among "primary goods," so that liberal liberty maintains its foundational role. See J. Rawls, *A Theory of Justice* (Harvard, 1971); and R. Dworkin, "Is Wealth a Value?" in *Journal of Legal Studies* 9, 2, (1980):191, now in *A Matter of Principle* (Harvard, 1985), pp. 237–66.

22. See J. Shklar, *Ordinary Vices* (Harvard, 1984).

23. Scoglio, Ch. 6.

24. Locke's justification from above of the atomistic-possessive way of life is indeed a radicalization of a process that was already under way within Aristotelian Christianity (as Locke's constant appeal to the "judicious Hooker" confirms).

25. A. MacIntyre, *After Virtue* (Notre Dame, 1984) (1st ed., 1981), p. 263.

26. On this point see Arlene Saxonhouse, "Classical Greek Conceptions of Public and Private," in G. Gaus and S. Benn (eds.), *Public and Private in Social Life* (London: Croom Helm, 1983), pp. 363–84.

27. For H. Arendt's provocative referring of the notion of privacy to its ancient Greek etymology, "idion," whereby the "privacy of one's own . . . is idiotic by definition," see *The Human Condition* (University of Chicago Press, 1958), p. 38. But see also *The Life of the Mind*, 2 vols. (New York, 1978).

28. F. D. Schoeman, *Privacy and Social Freedom* (Cambridge University Press, 1992).

29. For two interesting and complementary approaches to transformational politics, see Ted Becker (ed.), *Quantum Politics* (Praeger, 1991), collecting various innovative approaches to politics and law; and Corinne McLaughlin and Gordon Davidson, *Spiritual Politics: Changing the World from the Inside Out* (New York: Ballantine Books, 1994).

30. We have already mentioned McLaughlin and Davidson, *Spiritual Politics*; in the same vein, see Mark Satin, *New Age Politics* (New York: Dell Publishing, 1978). See also Charlene Spretnak and Fritjof Capra, *Green Politics* (Santa Fe: Bear and Company, 1986).

31. A good book that goes in such a direction is Francis Moore Lappé, *Rediscovering American Values* (New York: Ballantine Books, 1989).

32. Often the western followers of Buddhism forget that in Buddhist cosmology Samsara, the realm of "co-dependent origination" or interdependence, is the apparent face of Nirvana, the absolute transcendence of no-self. Again, the Buddhist no-self is far from being a dissolution into a mushy cosmic interdependence. It is rather the overcoming of the necessarily interdependent self into a state of complete freedom, although inherently inclusive of cosmic interdependence and responsibility. See the identification of no-self with the "no-ego-self" or "true Self" in Masao Abe, *Zen and Western Thought* (Honolulu: University of Hawaii Press, 1985), pp. 7ff. The strong reliance of Buddhism on inner meditation proves indeed the centrality of spiritual privacy. In Platonism too, although there is a deep stress on dialogue as a spiritual way, there are clear indications that the way would be incomplete without the practice of spiritual privacy. The main principle of the various Socratic schools has always been "know thyself," and in the *Symposium* we find a Socrates involved in a deep meditative state.

33. For one last attempt to attribute a Lockean character to the Founding Era see Jerome Huyler, *Locke in America* (University Press of Kansas, 1995). I still consider more useful, on the question of the philosophical influences on the "founding fathers," the work of Bernard Bailyn, *The Ideological Origins of the American Revolution* (Harvard University Press, 1967).

34. Joseph Campbell talks of the transpersonal inspiration of the American revolution, underlining how the classical Platonic and Pythagorean themes were imported into the mind and work of the founding fathers through the mediation of Freemasonry. See J. Campbell (with B. Moyers), *The Power of Myth* (New York: Doubleday, 1988), pp. 24–30. A relatively unknown but excellent work on the classical Pythagorean influence on the American Constitution, and especially on its doctrine and practice of the division of powers, is that by Armand Delatte, *La Constitution des États-Unis et les Pythagoriciens*,

Bulletins de l'Académie Royale de Belgique, 5e série, t. 34, fasc. 6, 1948. See also A. Delatte, *Essai sur la Politique Pythagoricienne*, 1992, Slatkine Reprints, Geneva, 1979.

35. Harold Berman, *Law and Revolution. The Formation of the Western Legal Tradition* (Harvard, 1983).

36. *Parmenides*, 142e–143a. The whole dialogue is about the logical necessity of the paradoxical compenetration of Forms and One.

37. Remember John's Gospel: "In the beginning was God, and with God was Logos and God was the Logos."

38. There are many different new frontiers of science that concretely demonstrate the principle "the part is the whole." See for instance the notion of "fractals," in which each smaller detail of a whole figure reproduces the same design of the entire figure. See Robert Mandelbrot, *Gli oggetti frattali* (Torino: Einaudi 1987). The holographic paradigm in science has been developed mainly by two contemporary scientists, D. Bohm and K. Pribram. See D. Bohm, *Wholeness and the Implicate Order* (London: Ark, 1983); K. Pribram, *Languages of the Brain* (New Jersey: Prentice-Hall, 1971).

39. "Religion as the courage to be oneself, as the courage to transcend, surrenders to the established world of significance—Glamour, 'making it', 'doctor', all-American healthy-mindedness, and football-religion—as living spirit many would see dead." J. C. Raines, *Attack on Privacy* (Judson Press, 1974), Ch. V.

40. E. Capuoya, "On Privacy and Community," in Money and Stuber (eds.), *Small Comforts in Hard Times* (Columbia, 1977), p. 119.

41. For an intelligent "platonic" treatment of the important notion of "limited whole," and thus of the idea that even a limited being can be whole, see Iris Murdoch, *Metaphysics As a Guide to Morals* (Penguin, 1992).

42. W. L. Weinstein, "The Private and the Free: A Conceptual Inquiry," in J. Pennock and J. Chapman (eds.), *Privacy: Nomos XIII*, p. 34.

43. A reknowned jurist has written that, given the difficulty to define the concept of privacy, legal writers have limited themselves to "list the various rights comprised in this concept in the domestic legal systems of different States." J. Velu, "The European Convention on Human Rights and the Right to Respect for Private Life, the Home and Communications," in A. H. Robertson (ed.), *Privacy and Human Rights* (Manchester University Press, 1973).

44. The same, in reference to equality, is said by Socrates in the *Phaedo*, 74–75.

2
RIGHT TO PRIVACY AND NATURAL LAW

In the United States the history of political theory since the founding of the Republic has resided in the Supreme Court. The future of political theory probably lies there too.[1]

HOW A RIGHT IS (RE)BORN: PRIVACY AND COMMON LAW

Toward the end of the nineteenth century, the United States was in the midst of radical economic, social, and technological transformations that were threatening the reality of a right to privacy that had been a factual reality in no need of legal protection. The growth of agrarian and industrial oligopolies caused the disappearance of the "yeoman farmer" and thus of that "propertied privacy" that was supposed to materially foster and protect the development of personal and civic virtue; meanwhile the increasingly economic use of natural areas reduced the opportunities for that solitude in the womb of nature that H. D. Thoreau had presented in his *Walden* as a model of material self-sufficiency and spiritual self-realization.[2] The demographic explosion (between 1790 and 1890, the U.S. population grew from 4 million to 63 million people) brought with it the development of crowded urban areas in which privacy and solitude were becoming increasingly more rare. Such an erosion of privacy was accelerated by the explosion of new technological wonders as the telephone, the telegraph, the "fairly inexpensive portable cameras," and "sound recording devices."[3]

Newspapers were particularly aggressive in their use of photographic and recording devices, and it was in reference to that that Henry James forged the term *newspaperization*.[4]

It is at this point, in the year 1890, that Warren and Brandeis's article appeared.[5] The direct subject of the article was indeed newspaperization, because its immediate cause seems to have been Warren's reaction to the scandalmongering reports of some Boston newspapers on the social activities organized by his wife, but the substance of the article resonated so soundly with the general feeling of the time that the "popular intellectual press immediately greeted Warren's and Brandeis's concept of the right to privacy as an idea whose time had come."[6]

The subtitle of Warren and Brandeis's article was "The Implicit Made Explicit," to stress how a fundamental right of privacy had been implicitly present in the common law all along:

In very early times, the law gave a remedy only for physical interference with life and property... Later, there came a recognition of *man's spiritual nature*, of his feelings and his intellect... and now the right to life has come to mean the right to enjoy life—*the right to be let alone*; the right to liberty secures the exercise of extensive civil privileges; and the term "property" has grown to comprise every form of possession—intangible, as well as tangible.

However, for the two authors the legal recognition of the sacredness of the inner spiritual dimension could not be entrusted to an extended right of property and needed the support of an explicit and self-subsistent right to privacy. There were important reasons for this:

Instantaneous photographs and newspaper enterprises have invaded the sacred precincts of private and domestic life; and numerous mechanical devices threaten to make good the [biblical] prediction that "what is whispered in the closet shall be proclaimed from the housetops."

Gossip is no longer the resource of the idle and the vicious, but has become a trade.... When personal gossip attains the dignity of print, and crowds the space available for matters of real interest to the community, what wonder that the ignorant and thoughtless mistake its relative importance.... [Gossip is] appealing to that weak side of human nature which is never wholly cast down by the misfortunes and frailties of our neighbours.... Triviality destroys at once robustness of thought and delicacy of feeling.

The intensity and complexity of life, attendant upon advancing civilization, have rendered necessary some retreat from the world, and man, under the refining influence of culture has become more sensitive to publicity, so that solitude and privacy have become more essential to the individual.[7]

That privacy is an independent category in need of an independent right, say Warren and Brandeis, is shown by comparing it with the torts of *slander* and *libel*. The latter are instances of defamation and deal

> only with damage to reputation, with the injury done to the individual in his external relation to the community, by lowering him in the estimation of his fellows. . . . In short, the wrongs and correlative rights recognized by the law of slander and libel are in their nature *material* rather than *spiritual*. That branch of the law simply extends the protection surrounding physical property toward certain of the conditions necessary or helpful to worldly prosperity.[8]

The right to privacy, on the other hand, protects the spiritual nature of human beings, and the principle that supports it "is not in reality the principle of private property, but that of an *inviolate personality*." This is why the right to privacy is said to be "a part of the more general right to the immunity of the person—the right to one's personality."[9] Though technically an innovation, we have seen that the two authors considered the right to privacy implicit in the common law. For instance, Warren and Brandeis claimed

> Legal doctrines relating to infractions of what is ordinarily termed the common-law right to intellectual and artistic property are, it is believed, but instances and applications of a general right to privacy . . . [and this because] The common law secures to each individual the right of determining, ordinarily, to what extent his thoughts, sentiments, and emotions shall be communicated to others.

This right "may exist independently of any corporeal being," which means that the relation between private interiority, and the property that embodies it, is one of nonseparate independence, because whereas the value of privacy and individuality is the implicit essence of any rights of property, there is a point above which the notion of property is useless and that of privacy stands on its own. Nonseparate independent privacy can be reduced to property only

> so long as we have only to deal with the reproduction of literary and artistic compositions. . . . But where the value of the production is found not in the rights to take the profit arising from publication, but in the *peace of mind* or the relief afforded by the ability to prevent any publication at all, it is difficult to regard the right as one of property, in the common acceptation of the term.

This difference becomes clear when contrasting this common law right with the statutory copyright: "The statutory right is of no value, unless there is a publication; the common-law right is lost as soon as there is publication."[10]

At this point, Warren and Brandeis refer to a famous English precedent, *Prince Albert v Strange*, 1 McN. & G. 25 (1849), in which the Court declared unlawful not just the public reproduction of the etchings that Prince Albert and Queen Victoria had made for their own personal pleasure but even the publication of a literary description of such etchings. This case, say Warren and Brandeis, cannot be construed in terms of artistic or literary property, because there has not been any undue appropriation or reproduction. What is violated, then, is not the property of the materials incorporating the ideas nor the property of the ideas themselves, something that would have at least required the reproduction of the etchings. What is violated is instead the control over the manifestation and diffusion of one's ideas, and so ultimately over the disclosure of one's personality. It could be argued that there is no reason why the right of property, having been extended to include immaterial goods, could not include also the activities of self-disclosure. But in comparison to such a generalized extension of the concept of property, which Prosser and other utilitarian and/or positivistic jurists have in various forms solicited, the presumed "vagueness" and generality of the concept of privacy, which those same jurists present as a radical flaw, would pale. What is more, such a general possessive reductionism would erase the possibility to distinguish between proprietary values on the one hand and personality and privacy values on the other, with the result of a generalized commodification of actions, persons, and thought. This is why Warren and Brandeis supportively underlined the fact that Lord Cottenham, who presided over the case, concluded that "privacy is the right invaded."[11]

Having thus shown, through this and other related cases, that the common law did indeed recognize a right to privacy, at least in reference to the expression of one's ideas, Warren and Brandeis conclude: "If, then, the decisions indicate a general right to privacy for thoughts, emotions and sensations, these should receive protection, whether expressed in writings, or in conduct, in conversation, in attitudes or in facial expression."[12]

This shows that Brandeis had already in mind a wide conception of the right to privacy and that the 1890 article already contained the premises of the remarkable growth that the right to privacy was to enjoy in American common and constitutional law. It is because of the context of the article, focusing on the informational invasions of privacy by the press, that Warren and Brandeis entrusted the defense of privacy only to a tort action, an action that the subsequent developments in the common law of this century, after its first recognition in the *Pavesich* case, have barely changed.[13]

W. Prosser, in an article that has been considered no less important for the law of privacy than that of Warren and Brandeis,[14] has attacked the common-law right of privacy by claiming that it is but a muddle of four distinct torts with very little in common. Moreover, Prosser claimed that only two of those four torts would be consistent with the original definition given by Warren and Brandeis.[15]

Under the first of the four Prosserian torts, namely *"public disclosure of private facts,"* we find two famous cases: *Melvin v Reid*, known as the case of the "red kimono"[16]; and *Sidis v F-R Publish. Corp.*[17] Under the second tort, *"false light in the public eye,"* Prosser places a series of cases concerning the false attribution to someone of certain opinions or statements,[18] or the unauthorized use of someone's image to illustrate books or articles.[19] The most famous precedent, in this last category, is undoubtedly a case involving Lord Byron, who successfully brought a suit against the publication of a low-quality poem falsely attributed to his pen.[20] These first two torts are for Prosser the only ones compatible with Warren and Brandeis's definition.

Yet, Prosser cannot properly distinguish between the second and the third of his categories, "*appropriation*," which refers to the commercial exploitation of someone's name or image. If one were to adopt Prosser's point of view, many cases would be at once "false light" and "appropriation" cases, as shown by *Lord Byron*, a "false light" case where the falsifiers had also obvious profit-making or "appropriation" motives. This is explicitly confirmed by Prosser himself, who places the *Pavesich* case in both categories.[21] This quite clearly dismisses Prosser's claim that the various torts grouped under the concept of privacy have nothing or very little in common. More importantly, we can see how misleading is Prosser's pretension of excluding from Warren and Brandeis's definition cases such as *Lord Byron* and *Pavesich* insofar as they involve elements of the "appropriation" category, a category that was never part of Warren and Brandeis's right to privacy, or even of the common law right to privacy to begin with. Because "appropriation" has to do with the commercial use of name and image, Prosser links it with the very opposite of the right to privacy, the *right to publicity*, and presents *Roberson* as the paradigmatic example of such a right.

But this is a tricky move, because Ms. Roberson, like Pavesich and Lord Byron, was not claiming her share of the profits derived from publicity, wanting instead to stop the reduction of her "persona" to an object of advertising. Prosser unduly overlooks the viewpoint of the plaintiffs in the cases, the very viewpoint that Warren and Brandeis had established as essential to distinguish the right to privacy from the right to publicity.[22] The lack of coherence and unity is therefore in the mind of Prosser, not in the common law right to privacy as developed from the premises of Warren and Brandeis.

There would seem to be more substance in Prosser's claim that Warren and Brandeis "do not appear to have had in mind any such thing as intrusion upon the plaintiff's seclusion or solitude," being supposedly concerned only with the public disclosure of private information.[23] "*Intrusion*," the last of Prosser's categories, includes unauthorized "searches," which he considers mere instances of physical/proprietary "trespass," as well as "eavesdropping" through wiretapping and long-range microphones. Eavesdropping is especially significant, because it is not easily reducible to the traditional category of physical/proprietary trespass. But cases of eavesdropping have been very rare in the common law; only two have appeared until the 1960s.[24] According to Westin, this is due to various factors: Often the victims of eavesdropping are not even aware of it; bringing suit against eavesdropping is bound to turn more public what was supposed to remain private in the first place; the traditional doctrines of the common law are inadequate to evaluate injuries as "subtle" as being listened to without permission. A final factor, says Westin, may have been that "Warren and Brandeis had in mind private rather than official invasions of privacy."[25]

Although they referred explicitly only to nongovernmental invasions of privacy, such as those of the press, Warren and Brandeis clearly placed such "informational privacy" within the larger frame of a general right to privacy protecting against both private and public intruders. For instance, they wrote: "Under our system of government he [i.e., the individual] can never be compelled to express them [i.e., thoughts, sentiments and emotions]."[26] Here, the right to privacy is given the status of a general constitutional principle and therefore cannot but bind the government itself. This will be reconfirmed by Brandeis, the U.S. Supreme Court Justice, who, in his famous Dissenting Opinion in *Olmstead v United States* [277 U.S. 438 (1927)], asserted the illegitimacy of an unauthorized wiretapping on the part of the federal police by appealing precisely to that same right to privacy that he had creatively rediscovered almost forty years earlier. This consistency in the holistic understanding of privacy reveals how insubstantial is the claim that intrusion in one's solitude was not part of the notion of privacy as expounded in the 1890 article. In that article, as well as in *Olmstead*, Brandeis used *right to privacy* and *right to be let alone* as synonyms, concluding that "the protection afforded to thoughts, sentiments, and emotions, expressed through the medium of writing or of the arts, so far as it consists in preventing publication, is merely an instance of the enforcement of the more general right of the individual to be let alone."[27]

PRIVACY AND NATURAL LAW DURING THE LOCHNER ERA

The rights protected by the Fourth Amendment (searches and seizures) and by the Fifth Amendment (privilege against self-incrimination) have always been a major object of constitutional jurisprudence, which, during the Lochner era, did for the most part incorporate the common law principles, as shown by the U.S. Supreme Court's decision in *Boyd v United States*.[28] The government had accused Boyd of illicit smuggling, based on private documents that he had been forced to submit.

Justice Bradley, writing for the Court, rested the test of reasonableness[29] on common law principles establishing that the government had no right to search or seize the belongings of the accused, with the exception of stolen, illegally possessed, or contraband goods, or of goods already owned by, or forfeited to, the state. This was an argument from the Fourth Amendment, but Bradley appealed also to the Fifth, stating that the incriminating use of the accused's private documents is a form of forced self-incrimination. To strengthen his decision, he underlined the "intimate relation" existing between the two amendments, claiming that the "Fourth and Fifth Amendments run almost into each other." There have been two major interpretations of this claim: Some believe that Bradley "merely pointed to a significant overlap in the protection provided by the two amendments"[30]; others believed that he thought that the two Amendments taken separately could not afford the same amount of protection that they provide when taken together.[31]

Both readings seem insufficient.[32] Neither separation nor addition is here at stake, but rather the fact that both amendments, although the Fifth more explicitly and clearly, manifest the same implicit fundamental principle. That principle states that individual personality and conscience are the true object of constitutional protection and that material properties such as houses, closets, or documents are protected only insofar as they shield those fundamental realities. This principle was an integral part of Bradley's natural law approach, and it is quite significant that he rested the protection of the inner life of the person on similarly inner principles implicit in the constitutional text. In this sense, *Boyd* is the bridge connecting the natural law content of the traditional common law to Warren and Brandeis's article, written only four years later: "During the 17th and 18th centuries there evolved an American tradition of 'natural law', postulating that 'certain principles of right and justice ... are entitled to prevail of their own intrinsic excellence.'"[33]

But the development of *Legal Formalism* in the second half of the nineteenth century greatly distorted the natural law appeal to implicit and self-subsistent principles, turning them into abstract formulations hypostatizing the achieved triumph of oligopolistic capitalism: "For seventy or eighty years after the American Revolution the major direction of common law policy reflected the overthrow of eighteenth century precommercial and antidevelopmental common law values. . . . By around 1850 that transformation was largely complete."[34] Such a transformation constitutes for Horwitz the "emergence of an instrumental conception of the law" (Ch. 1), a utilitarian legal theory serving the interests of the new capitalism. He speaks of a "triumph of contract" (Ch. 6) that destroyed old forms of property and promoted the mobility of exchanges indispensable to a wealth-maximizing economy.

Legal relations that had once been conceived of as deriving from natural law or custom were increasingly subordinated to the disproportionate economic power of individuals and corporations that were allowed the right to "contract out" of many existing legal obligations. Law, once conceived of as protective, regulative, paternalistic and, above all, a paradigmatic expression of the moral sense of the community, had come to be thought of as facilitative of individual desires and as simply reflective of the existing organization of economic and political power.

This is certainly true, and Horwitz seems also quite correct in relating the emergence of *legal formalism* with the completion of this radical transformation. But Horwitz's lucid analysis, besides being pervaded by an excessive economism, is also mistaken in the assumption that legal formalism, with its utilitarian-capitalistic understanding of natural rights, was all-encompassing in relation to the natural law discourse of the time, as if the more genuine natural law tradition had suddenly vanished.

In the famous *Slaughter-House Cases*, the U.S. Supreme Court upheld a Louisiana statute granting a private corporation a twenty-five-year monopoly over the slaughterhouses of New Orleans. Tribe notices that the decision, which was part of the general trend favoring the growth of private oligopolies, was taken by "some of the same judges who endorsed natural law methods."[35] The case was discussed after the adoption of the Fourteenth Amendment, which imposed on the states a duty to endorse the same fundamental rights enjoyed by American citizens as members of the federal union. Because the amendment doesn't explicitly enumerate those rights, the Supreme Court has become the final arbiter over the *incorporation* of federal constitutional rights into the local level of government. The Fourteenth Amendment only mentions the fundamental and very general rights to life, liberty, and property, asserting that nobody can be deprived of such rights "without due process of law" (a clause already present in the Fifth). The meaning of the "due process" clause has been the object of a perennial controversy between those who want it to be the source of a merely technical and procedural control of legislation—and among them are to be included the extreme legal positivists who link such a formalistic control to the sole letter of the Constitution—and those who instead favor a *substantive due process*, whereby the validity of legislation is supposed to rest on broader and more fundamental "principles of liberty and justice" implicit in the written Constitution.[36] Substantive due process reintroduces into the law not only informal and unwritten legal sources, from legal doctrine, social customs, or even "current views of right and wrong which collectively have come to be accepted as a part of the established law of the land,"[37] but a full-fledged appeal to natural law principles. H. Berman explains why this is not accidental: " 'Due process of law' is a fourteenth-century English phrase meaning natural law."[38]

Nevertheless, in the *Slaughter-House cases*, the very same judges who approved of the natural law substantive due process "refused to employ the fourteenth amendment itself in order to scrutinize state legislation allegedly interfering with natural rights or common-law rights." The natural law rhetoric of the legal formalists was to be used only insofar as it did not clash with the wealth-maximizing ideology and interests of the emerging oligopolistic capitalism. But we cannot forget the vehement dissent of Field and Bradley, who, "both relying on the natural law tradition," claimed that the "monopoly created by Louisiana ... violated butchers' fundamental right under the fourteenth amendment to pursue their occupation."[39] Together with Bradley's decision in *Boyd*, this dissent shows that a more genuine natural law constitutional jurisprudence was still alive. Yet, there has been a widespread tendency to read the whole 1880–1937 period as thoroughly dominated by Legal Formalism, the only presumed exception being Justice Holmes's radical anti–natural law jurisprudence. This period is generally defined as the Lochner era. In *Lochner v New York*, the 1905 case after which the period is named, the majority of the Court decided that a New York statute, fixing a maximum of ten working hours for bakers, was violating the freedom of contract implicit in the right to liberty of the Fourteenth Amendment.[40] *Lochner* became the symbol of the Supreme Court's opposition to social legislation.[41] But Tribe rightly warns that the Lochner era

> should be so characterized only with great caution—and with a recognition that "*Lochnerizing*" has become so much an epithet that the very use of the label may obscure attempts at understanding. While the Supreme Court invalidated much state and federal legislation between 1897 and 1937, more statutes in fact withstood due process attack in this period than succumbed to it.[42]

The reality is that we need to distinguish the more general *substantive due process* from the *economic substantive due process* of *Lochner*, which resulted from a peculiar mix of formalistic natural law discourse and utilitarian social darwinism *à la* H. Spencer.[43] But this predominant *natural rights utilitarianism*, the first full-fledged legal expression of that capitalistic dialectic of liberalism and utilitarianism dominating today's global civilization, had to face the opposition of a more genuine natural law approach (only partly identifiable with a stable group of Justices), whose conception of substantive due process was incompatible with the Lochner ideology. Here, we need to return to Louis D. Brandeis, because the famous *Brandeis briefs* in *Muller v Oregon* [208 U.S. 412 (1908)] showed that substantive due process, if properly understood, is inherently conducive to results very different from those of *Lochner*.

After becoming one of the major corporate lawyers of the nation, Brandeis turned more and more to public and political life, with a genuine devotion to the common good and especially to the interests of the "little man." Without ever competing for public office, he quietly but steadily fought important battles for the rights of the individual and of the working people against the overpowering growth of capitalistic oligopolies. Those battles, first at the local level in Boston and then at the national level, contributed to the growth of his fame, and he was invested by the public opinion with the title of *People's Lawyer*, yet being discredited with the epithets of "socialist" and "communist" by his opponents.[44] Then, in 1908, Brandeis was asked to defend, in front of the U.S. Supreme Court, an Oregon law imposing a limit of ten working hours per day for women. Rather than opposing *Lochner*, Brandeis tried to overturn it from the inside by pulling down its abstract logic to facing the facts. He presented a massive set of scientific studies showing the noxious effects of overwork. It was not an exercise in empiricism, as some have claimed, but rather in empirically grounded reason, as Brandeis centered his argument around what he called "*the logic of facts*." He opposed his "logic of facts" to the "common knowledge," which is equivalent to "popular ignorance and fallacy," and asserted that the logic of facts, or *reason inherent in things*, can emerge only with the support of *all the facts*.[45]

It is from the point of view of this realistic and holistic reason that Brandeis, in a way that can surprise only those who mistake him for an empiricist, appealed directly to *Lochner*. Brandeis saw that in *Lochner*, notwithstanding its result, the Court recognized the power of the State to interfere with private contracts for reasons relating "to the safety, health, morals and general welfare of the public."[46] Even though *Muller* and similar decisions "appeared as exceptions to the rule," they were grounded on jurisprudential principles implicitly rooted in the natural law discourse and that had therefore been part of the legacy of the courts for a long time.[47]

Why then did "Lochnerism" become prevalent? Because, as the *Brandeis briefs* showed by contrast, the majority of the Justices were able to ordinarily pervert the fundamental principles of justice inherent in the legal tradition by abstracting them from the concrete environment that gives them life, without which there may be some abstract logic but not a "logic of facts." Brandeis explains this limit of the law of the time in his writings on the *living law*. He argues that the end of the Jeffersonian model of agrarian democracy, and the parallel growth of oligopolistic capitalism, radically changed the context of the law. Yet,

Courts continued to ignore newly arisen social needs. They applied complacently eighteenth-century conceptions of the liberty of the individual and of the sacredness of private property. Early nineteenth-century scientific half-truths like "The survival of the fittest," which, translated into practice, meant "The devil take the hindmost," were erected by judicial sanction into a moral law.

This illuminates why, says Brandeis, the popular respect for the Courts has greatly diminished. Yet, he believes that what "we need is not to displace the courts, but to make them efficient instruments of justice."[48] Precisely because "moral law" and "justice," as the true essence of the law, need to be constantly actualized within the dynamic context of life, Brandeis believed that the best remedy was to educate lawyers to learn from the facts. He was of course well aware of the economic and personal ties that most lawyers had with industrial and financial corporations, having himself been a prominent corporate lawyer. But he deemed such ties to be a historical accident, not at all intrinsic to the legal profession as such: "The leaders of the Bar, without any preconceived intent on their part, and rather as an incident to their professional standing, have, with rare exceptions, been ranged on the side of corporations."[49] As Socrates did when using crafts and professions as examples, Brandeis appealed to the intrinsic principles and values of the legal profession, distinguishing between the accidental behaviors of lawyers and the essential character of the law as law. Brandeis knew that the essence and spirit of the law, even though not fully actualized, do at least constitute a limit to the perverted lawfulness of injustice.

Even the staunchest representatives within the courts of capitalistic interests must justify their decisions in terms of "reasonableness," not just through an

Right to Privacy and Natural Law 63

instrumentally formal logic but also at least by a partial reference to the facts and thus to the reason inherent in the facts taken as a whole. Judicial reason can never fully separate itself from "justice," from the nonseparate independent moral and natural law that lives within the interdependent whole of reality.

Brandeis knew this, and this is why he believed that the widespread corruption of the law was due to the fact that lawyers lacked a holistic legal education and practice. Once upon a time, says Brandeis, the lawyer, who would later become a judge, lived in small communities, and being

a general practitioner, he was brought into contact with all phases of contemporary life. His education was not legal only; because his diversified clientage brought him, by the mere practice of his profession, an economic and social education. . . . [Furthermore] the same lawyer was apt to serve at one time or another both rich and poor . . . [and] every lawyer of ability took some part in political life. . . . The last fifty years have wrought a great change in professional life. Industrial development and the growth of cities have led to a high degree of specialization . . . not only in the nature and class of questions dealt with, but also specialization in the character of clientage. The term *corporation lawyer* is significant in this connection.[50]

The law loses its vitality due to the remoteness of the lawyers from the whole of life in all its aspects and interdependencies. In a deep sense, this means that the corruption of the law progresses insofar as the lawyer is unable to overcome his/her particularistic point of view and to integrate the whole in his/her partness. In the Brandeisian perspective, the attention to the whole of reality or facts doesn't just provide one with a mass of data but rather allows one to see through the interdependence of facts into the independence of their inner logic. As we shall see, for Brandeis, human beings can access that logic or Logos of things within their spiritual interiority as well as through outer holistic experiences.

Brandeis belongs to that transpersonal tradition that recognizes the fundamental unity underlying the polarity of mind and matter, rationality and reality, whole and part. It is from this point of view that he inherits and promotes a *homeorhetic natural law* approach,[51] whereby the self-subsistent and realistic principle of the Whole of Wholes is not frozen in abstract formulas but dynamically embodied in a progressive series of historical actualizations. This approach to natural law is the best possible interpretation of those fundamental legal principles that impregnated deeply if inconsistently the jurisprudence of the Lochner era, as based on the classical natural law conception of the "implied limitations on governments":

Each level and branch of government was thought to be confined to a sphere of authority defined by the nature and function of that level or branch and by the inherent rights of citizens. . . . [Therefore] governmental authority has implied limits which preserve private autonomy.[52]

The principle of the separation of powers and of their reciprocal checks and balances is at the very core of the American political system and constitutional tradition and goes back to that theory of the subordination of the sovereign to a higher law, which was typical of ancient and medieval natural lawyers.[53] For them, the separation of powers was supposed to promote the emergence, within the political context, of the fundamental unity on which it is grounded. Thus, in the American political system (as well as in most modern democracies), the separation of governmental powers rests on the monistic principle of popular sovereignty, whose primacy it is supposed to reinforce. In a genuine natural law approach, popular sovereignty can only refer to the true general will, that is, to that self-subsistent idea of the Whole of Wholes that always grounds the right decisions of the empirical political community and that stands in radical opposition to that merely empirical sovereignty that Rousseau defines as the "will of all."[54]

But there is a different, dualistic understanding of the principle of the separation of powers. Here popular sovereignty, rather than being the fundamental and unitary ground, is identified with one of the separate powers, namely the legislative power, which is supposed to play against the executive power of the monarch or of the government. This is the central idea of Locke's constitutional philosophy, which was meant to establish a radical dualism of State and Society. Yet, as Bailyn has shown, it is not the Lockian version that most influenced the founding of the American republic and constitution: "Most conspicuous in the writings of the revolutionary period was the heritage of classical antiquity." Rather, other English thinkers directly inspired by classical Platonic thought, such as Harrington and his followers, played a prominent role.[55] As to the specific theme of the separation of powers, the two most influential thinkers were probably Montesquieu and Blackstone.[56] Writes Montesquieu:

Here, therefore, is the fundamental constitution of the government of which we are speaking. As its legislative body is composed of two parts [that is, nobility and common people], the one will be chained to the other by their reciprocal faculty of vetoing. The two will be bound by the executive power [that is, the Monarch], which will itself be bound by the legislative power. *The form of these three powers should be rest or inaction.* But as they are constrained to move by the necessary motion of things, they will be forced to move in concert.[57]

The reciprocal limitation of the different powers is supposed to minimize the impact of narrow self-interest, so as to produce a synchronous and complementary action whereby each part, in its partness, rests immobile yet moves by the force of the whole ("in concert") and together with the movement of things. This implies that the identity of wholeness and partness is the force itself of things, and this is why parts must act, paradoxically, from the point of view of inaction, or contemplation of the inherent logic of things. Montesquieu was very clear about such logic of facts, which he identified with a universal natural and human reason of which positive laws and institutions are to be perspective incarnations.[58] Such a universal reason implied for him the recognition of the dialectical unity of opposites, especially of liberty and responsibility, rights and duties: "It is true that in democracies people seem to do what they want, but political liberty in no way consists in doing what one wants. In a state, that is in a society where there are laws, liberty can consist only in having the power to do what one should want to do and in no way being constrained to do what one should not want to do."[59]

This sentence alone is enough to show Montesquieu's remoteness from liberalism. The same is true of Blackstone, for whom the separation of powers is not an end to itself, as in Locke, but is meant to establish the dialectical unity of State and Society: "Thus every branch of our civil polity supports and is supported, regulates and is regulated, by the rest. . . . They mutually keep each other from exceeding their proper limits; *while the whole is prevented from separation.*"[60] With all the due differences between Montesquieu, Blackstone, and the classical natural lawyers, what characterizes them all in opposition to liberalism is a radically different understanding of the notion of limit or boundary: The limits that one experiences existentially are perceived as openings to the wholeness of one's interdependence and therefore to the independent reason inherent in that wholeness and in each of its parts, including oneself as a part. This larger and deeper understanding of oneself through the positive acceptance of one's existential limits is in direct opposition to the liberal notion of limit as a mere negative barrier, whereby the other becomes an obstacle for the self, and freedom is identified with the removal of that obstacle.[61] From this notion of limits springs the classical liberal idea of "negative liberty,"[62] which guarantees the dualism of private part and public whole by using the separation and delimitation of powers as a way of subordinating governmental action not to the common good but to the abstractly absolute immunity of the private sphere.

Legal Formalism is the direct offspring of this liberal/dualistic tradition, although it has radically corrected it by appealing to the utilitarian/monistic insistence on capitalistic maximization. The fusion of these two strands was possible, for the Court, due to their common reliance on the same materialistic premises. *Lochner* is the best example of the legalistic sanctioning of the absolute immunity of the private contractual sphere, whereby individuals are considered only in the abstract equality of their legal personality, without any reference to their different socioeconomic conditions and powers. Justice Peckam's majority opinion claimed to defend the equal right of both workers and entrepreneurs to choose their contracts, constructing the case around the deceiving opposition of (individual/social) liberty and (governmental) authority:

Therefore, when the State . . . has passed an act which seriously limits the right to labour or the right of contract in regard to their means of livelihood between persons who are *sui juris* (both employer and employee), it becomes of great importance to determine which shall prevail—the right of the individual to labour for such time as he may choose, or the right of the State to prevent the individual from labouring or from entering into any contract to labour, beyond a certain time.[63]

We can begin to understand the link between liberal legal formalism and utilitarian/capitalistic ideology, as the abstract legalism of rights is used to ensure a quasi-absolute "deontological" freedom to the capitalistic actors, in their monopolistic and socially oppressive drive. That wealth-maximizing and utilitarian concerns were the true core of the Supreme Court's natural rights discourse during the Lochner era has been made clear by Justice Holmes's famous dissenting remark: "The Fourteenth Amendment does not enact Mr. Herbert Spencer's Social Statics."[64] On the other hand, although a lot could be said about the Justices of the *Lochner* majority as being oligopolistic agents, they had nevertheless to work within a jurisprudential framework deeply influenced by the genuine natural law foundations of the American legal tradition.

D. Kennedy, a member of the *Critical Legal Studies* movement, admits to the relative autonomy of the judicial consciousness from class interests, although he doesn't go so far as to acknowledge the self-subsistent essence of the law that grounds and explains that relative autonomy.[65] According to Kennedy, the cornerstone idea of the formalistic legal consciousness was the dualistic separation of spheres, and in *Lochner*: "[B]oth the right [of the individual] and the power [of the state] are entitled to protection; each overrides and annihilates the other, and is in that sense absolute, but only within a "sphere" . . . They most certainly do not come across as conflicting 'interests' to be 'balanced.' " But this interpretive view does not seem to account for Peckam's acknowledgment of the State's power to interfere with the private contractual sphere in order to protect and promote public health, morality, security and welfare. Kennedy gets around the difficulty by saying that it is an "an accident of exposition."[66] The reality is that Peckam, having to develop a legal argument—that is, having to argue from the point of view of justice and the general interest—cannot completely disregard the wholeness and unity sustaining the duality of public and private. For instance, a main tool of the judicial review of the time was the means-ends analysis, directed at ascertaining the subsistence of "a 'real and substantial' relationship between a statute and its objectives." A merely procedural form of control would have been ineffective in guaranteeing that exclusion of the narrow self-interest of the governing powers, and so, due to its natural law origins and background,[67] the means-ends analysis was inserted into a more substantive "strict judicial assessment of legislative ends."[68]

Guaranteeing the universal and holistic form of legislation represents the fundamental goal and content of this "substantive" approach, which is thus *formal/ substantive*, because, rather than positing content-predetermined legal principles, it identifies the lawful and the good with the form of the Whole of Wholes, which is in itself empty of concrete determinations and therefore capable of innumerable historical "substantializations." That form, which implies the creative, simultaneous, and reciprocal integration of individuality and community, was the implicit framework within which Peckam and his colleagues had to work, so that the problem for them was how to reconcile such a framework at once with the liberal atomism underlying their conception of natural rights and with the utilitarian axiom of wealth maximization. The very contradictory mix of liberalism and utilitarianism provided them with the solution.

Within the liberal theory of the time, the answer to the problem of public interference in the private sphere was generally perceived to be something like Mill's *harm principle*, which posits that only perceivable physical or moral *harm to others* can justify such interference. In accordance with the atomistic notion of self that characterizes the empiricist tradition, Mill's principle denied that interference could be justified by self-harm. In the *Lochner* scenario, such an approach would have meant that the contractual will of the worker, formalistically abstracted from the material and social pressures constraining it, was to be left alone even if producing bad consequences for the worker himself. Although this was precisely the type of result that Peckam was looking for, he could not adopt the liberal harm principle in its pure form, again because the American legal tradition was providing him with a different, natural law harm principle, based on a dialectical understanding of actions as productive of individual and social effects at once.

Thus, the harm principle adopted by Peckam differs from that of Mill in that it cannot avoid accepting the social relevance of the ''harm to self'' and cannot therefore exclude the legitimacy of public interference with self-harmful actions. Indeed, for Peckam the governmental interference under review is illegitimate ''unless there be some fair ground, reasonable in and of itself, to say that there is material danger to the public health *or to the health of the employee*, if the hours of labour are not curtailed.''[69] This is the moment when utilitarian monism can make its fundamental contribution. Benthamite utilitarianism rejects the dualism of private and public and accepts the social relevance of the harm to self. The principle of sensistic and hedonistic utility, the ''greatest happiness for the greater number'' principle, defines the good and the harmful in equal terms for both private and public, integrating both private and public actions into a simultaneous movement toward a social wholeness based on capitalistic wealth maximization.[70]

In the utilitarian model, the maximization of the overall amount of wealth is paramount and gives full support to those proprietary and contractual public arrangements, as well as to private behaviors and motives, that make such maximization possible. Thus, the protection of the market from interferences that may reduce the opportunities for wealth maximization, such as limiting the working hours or cutting the levels of production and consumption, is considered to be in the general interest, at once private and public. In fact, from such a utilitarian point of view, the immunity from social legislation is in the interest of the workers themselves, based on the assumption that their toil and suffering is but a way toward the comfort and pleasures that higher levels of production and consumption make possible, at least in part, for them too. This is the very approach adopted by Peckam, whose main argument is that the "employee may desire to earn the extra money, which would arise from his working more than the prescribed time."[71] This posture is further reinforced by the Court's Spencerian view of the market as a darwinistic field of competition, whereby the best social forces are selected.

Through such a utilitarian characterization of the general interest, the Court is able to overcome the difficulty posed by the integration of the "harm to self" into the harm principle. Within the previous natural law point of view, it was the economic system that had to prove its goodness against the presumption that unbridled competition and possessive egoism, unlimited exploitation and self-exploitation of the human and natural resources, are intrinsically harmful and bad, so that even behaviors *omitting* to change such conditions become liable to legal interference. On the contrary, by identifying such a system of social and economic relations with the general interest, the *Lochner* jurisprudence generated *a reversal of the burden of proof* whereby any governmental regulation was made conditional to proving the specific harm and its seriousness. At times this was possible, as *Muller* and similar cases show, but it was very difficult, also because the harm to be proved had to be so serious as to be more than a mere "collateral" effect of the generally beneficial capitalistic market.[72]

Supporting such an approach was the empiricist presupposition that the general interest is but the sum of atomistic and quantitatively unequal interests pursued by naturally egoistic individuals. For the Court, "the only legitimate goal of government in general, and of the police power in particular, was to protect individual rights and otherwise to enhance the *total* public good . . . [c]onceived as an amalgam of 1) the aggregate welfare of individuals, and 2) conventional morality."[73] This utilitarian understanding of the social whole and its good made it possible for the Court to overturn from the inside the original natural law viewpoint. At the same time, the arithmetic character of the utilitarian common good gave the Court the possibility to reintegrate the liberal atomistic natural rights discourse into serving the capitalistic project of wealth maximization. In the end, the natural law substantive due process was maintained as the empty shell within which the liberal-atomistic rights to utilitarian wealth-maximizing property are turned into abstract absolutes.

But the contradictions that this complex synthesis necessarily implied left room for a more genuine substantive due process to flourish, which in *Lochner* emerged through the dissent of Justice Harlan. D. Kennedy, following the general tendency to read Legal Formalism as all-encompassing, claims that the "main point about Harlan's dissent is that it employs exactly the same conceptual structure as the majority opinion."[74] The truth is that Harlan used in the proper way those traditional natural law tests and tools that Legal Formalism had usurped and corrupted. That Harlan reached a conclusion opposite to that of the majority is not an inexplicable accident, as Kennedy thinks, but the necessary outcome of a genuinely homeorhetic apprehension of the natural law. Like Peckam, Harlan acknowledges the legitimacy of private autonomy by claiming that "the state, in the exercise of its powers, may not unduly interfere with the right of the citizens to enter into contracts that may be necessary and essential in the enjoyment of the inherent rights belonging to everyone." Together with the recognition of individual natural rights (the "inherent rights belonging to everyone"), there is a much more qualified definition of the contractual area immune from interference ("contracts... necessary and essential"). More extensively than Peckam, Harlan accepts governmental regulation of the private and interprivate or contractual sphere, although within the limits intrinsic to the governmental function: "The liberty secured by the Constitution ... does not import... an absolute right in each person to be at all times wholly freed from restraint. There are *manifold restraints* to which every person is necessarily subject *for the common good.*" The interfering power of the government is thus intrinsically bound to the common good, and the manifold presence of the common good, in its private/public nature, makes it impossible to presumptively exclude any a priori area of behaviors from possible governmental interventions. Harlan approvingly refers to the fact that the power and the interfering activity of the State "has doubtless greatly expanded in its application during the past century, owing to an enormous increase in the number of occupations which are dangerous, or so far detrimental, to the health of employees." Harlan uses the harm principle to unite private and public, not to separate them. Whereas for the majority harm can only be the result of a directly and positively causative action, for Harlan even omissive behavior that exploits the disadvantaged conditions impinging upon a contracting party are to be considered legally relevant harms, because even such disadvantages are the result of parallel or previous human actions and choices. Thus, the inequalities and disadvantages that the majority considers the natural results of the inherently beneficial capitalistic market are by Harlan deemed a constriction over human freedom and thus over the contractual market itself. That situation cannot be covered up by the legalistic fiction of the equality of the contractors:

It is plain that this statute was enacted in order to protect the physical well-being of those who work.... It may be that the statute had its origin, in part, in the belief that employers and employees in such establishments were not upon an equal footing, and that the necessities of the latter often compelled them to submit to such exactions as unduly taxed their strength.

Private autonomy is not an axiomatic presupposition but something to be constantly tested in the concrete realm of facts. Half of Harlan's dissent, which opened the way to the "Brandeis briefs," is devoted to the presentation of empirical data on the effects of overwork on one's health. In the realm of facts, the private and public are always interdependent, so that private autonomy is legitimate only when it positively accepts that interdependence by fostering the common good. Common good that, as opposed to that of the "natural rights utilitarians," implies everyone's equal right to both material self-sufficiency and spiritual self-realization, so that the resulting social obligation is not a mere duty not to harm others but, if the private wants to remain free from interferences, also to remove, as much as possible, the general economic and social conditions that hinder the implementation of such an equal right.

In this respect, the government that intervenes to remove those conditions not only fulfills a function inherent in its power but also substitutively performs a duty that belongs to the private actors involved to begin with. This is why Harlan restored the original distribution of the burden of proof corrupted by Peckam: "When the validity of a statute is questioned, the burden of proof, so to speak, is upon those who assert it to be unconstitutional." With this, Harlan anticipated the 1937 constitutional revolution.[75] But it would be a mistake to interpret the categorical nature of Harlan's statement as if it implied an unconditional judicial restraint. This is the position taken in *Lochner* by Holmes, who recognized "the right of a majority to embody their opinions in law."[76] Harlan abdicated neither to private nor to public powers and did not renounce the substantive review of legislative ends.

Following in Montesquieu's and Blackstone's footsteps, Harlan believed the end of the various governmental powers to be the same, their institutional differentiation and separation resting on the different ways and perspectives in which that same end, the public/private common good, is to be realized. This is why Harlan's judicial restraint did not involve ends as such but only the relationship of means to ends, that is, the determination of policies, which is to be left under the exclusive competence of the legislator: "Under our system of government the courts are not concerned with the wisdom or policy of legislation ... [and] must keep their hands off, leaving the legislature to meet the responsibility for unwise legislation." The judge cannot question a bad policy's assessment of means, but s/he can and must question bad or illegitimate ends. For Harlan, the test of ends consisted in ascertaining "what are the conditions under which the judiciary may declare ... regulations to be *in excess of legislative authority* and void." Harlan explains how that "excess" is to be ascertained when, quoting from *Mugler v Kansas* [123 U.S. 623, 661], he writes that the courts can interfere with legislation "only 'when that which the legislature has done comes within the rule that, if a statute purporting to have been enacted to protect the public health, the public morals, or the public safety has no *real or substantial relation to those objects*, or is, beyond all question, a plain, palpable invasion of *rights secured by the fundamental law*.' "[77] The courts have to make sure that the ends of governmental policies, efficient or inefficient as they may be, are the simultaneous promotion of public good (public health, morality, safety) and fundamental private rights, inclusive of both material (health) and spiritual/ethical (morals) wellness. The "excess" to which Harlan refers is not a mere stepping beyond some formalistic and/or literal limits, but a much more profound violation of the dialectical form of the common good. If in *Lochner* and in other cases involving the limitation of economic monopolies and the implementation of social legislation, Harlan sided with the government, he also opposed government when it tried to limit the civil freedom and spiritual privacy protected by the Fourth and Fifth Amendments.[78] In *Hurtado v California* (1884) Harlan explained that the "fundamental law" is not limited to the written Constitution, but it includes all those principles "expressly or *impliedly*" contained in it. Such implied principles were for Harlan to be derived from the common law tradition of England, which was deeply steeped in the larger European natural law jurisprudence. In later cases, he supplements his *Hurtado* notion of "implied principles" with explicit natural law notions of "natural justice" [*Monongahela B. Co. v United States*, 216 U.S. 177 (1910)], "natural equity" and "principle of universal right" [*Chicago, B & Q. Ry. Co. v Chicago*, 166 U.S. 226 (1897)]. Natural justice was for Harlan not a list of substantive commandments but rather a form of reasoning about the common good, and this is why the most crucial element of his jurisprudence came to be the "test of reasonableness."[79] The reason that stands at the core of that test, as we have seen, is the "logic of facts" itself, the reason inherent in things as dynamically actualized within the becoming of existence. Truly, Harlan was Brandeis's ancestor within the Supreme Court.[80]

NOTES

1. Theodore Lowi, *The End of Liberalism* (Norton and Co., 1969), p. 314.
2. T. O'Connor, "The Right to Privacy in Historical Perspective," 53 Mass. L.Q. 101 (1968): 104–9.
3. See D. Glancy, "The Invention of the Right to Privacy," in *Arizona L.R.* 21, no. 1 (1979): 7.
4. H. James, *The Reverberator* (MacMillan, 1888). See also the short stories *The Private Life* and *The Death of the Lion*. The first article dealing with the issue was by a famous journalist. See E. L. Godkin, "The Rights of the Citizen IV—To his own Reputation," 8 *Scribner's Magazine* 58 (July 1890).
5. L. D. Brandeis, and S. Warren, "The Right to Privacy. The Implicit Made Explicit," in *Harvard L.R.,* 4: (1890) 193–220, now in F. Schoeman, *Philosophical Dimensions of Privacy* (Cambridge, 1984), pp. 75–103. P. Freund, who was legal assistant to Brandeis, claims that "internal and other evidence indicates his dominant authorship." "Privacy: One Concept or Many," in R. Pennock and J. Chapman, *Privacy. Nomos XIII* (Atherton, 1971), pp. 182–98, p. 184.
6. Glancy, p. 6.
7. Brandeis and Warren, 75–77.
8. Ibid., pp. 82–83.
9. Ibid.
10. Ibid., pp. 78–79.
11. Ibid., p. 81.
12. Ibid., p. 82.
13. Since *Pavesich v New England Life Insurance Inc.*, 122 *Georgia* 190 (1905), the common-law right to privacy has undergone a great expansion, focusing almost exclusively on the control over the communication to others of one's thoughts, words, or images. Up to 1966 there have been 331 decisions on privacy, for the most part favorable

to its legal recognition. See H. Kalven, Jr., "Privacy in Tort Law," in *Law and Contemporary Problems* 31, 2 (1966): 326–41, 333. *Pavesich* was decided after *Roberson v Rochester Folding Box Co.* (1902), whereby the Court of Appeals of the State of New York refused to recognize a legal right to privacy, and two years after the State of New York's first statutory regulation of such a right. In *Pavesich*, a case still involving the conflict between privacy and commercial interests, the Supreme Court of Georgia established that not only was the right to privacy implicit in the common law, but that it directly derived from natural law and consequently also from the Constitution of the United States and the Constitution of Georgia. The modernity of the decision is remarkable. The Court referred to a theory of implicit rights that would characterize the constitutional recognition of the right to privacy in the 1960s, and in a time when the natural law discourse was mostly used in support of possessive and commercial capitalistic interests, the *Pavesich* Court defined a natural right to privacy in terms of a personalistic and spiritual individualism. On this, see M. C. Slough, *Privacy, Freedom and Responsibility*, p. 37.

14. See Wade, "Developing Trends in the Tort Action for Invasion of the Right to Privacy, in 16 *Va. Weekly Dicta Comp.* 7 (1965).

15. Prosser, "Privacy: A Legal Analysis," in *Calif. L.R.* 48 (1960), p. 106.

16. 112 *Cal. App. 285, 297 Pac.* 91 (1931). An ex-prostitute, acquitted in a murder trial, had later married, leading for many years an irreprehensible life. Afterwards, her story was turned into a movie in which her original name was used, and, because nobody knew about her past in her new environment, her reputation was shattered.

17. 113 *F. 2d 806 (2d Cir.)* (1940). The case involved an "enfant prodige" named Sidis who at age eleven had lectured on the fourth dimension in front of eminent mathematicians, and who later rejected completely his condition, choosing to lead an obscure life of low-paid jobs and unusual hobbies. The *New Yorker* magazine found Sidis and wrote an article on his story. "The effect upon Sidis was devastating and the article unquestionably contributed to his early death." Prosser, p. 112. However, Prosser defends the decision of the Court, unfavorable to Sidis, on the ground that Sidis's sensitivity was abnormal.

18. See, for example, *Hinish v Meyer & Frank Co.*, 166 Ore. 482, 113 P.2d 438 (1941). The name of the plaintiff was used, without his knowledge, to support a political petition that he, as a public employee, could not legally sign. In this category, Prosser inserts also the cases of falsely attributed books and articles.

19. See, for example, *Peay v Curtis Pub. Co.*, 78 Suppl. 305 (D.D.C. 1948), and *Martin v Johnson Pub. Co.*, 157 N.Y. S.2d 409 (Sup. Ct. 1956). Both cases concern the undue use of the plaintiff's image to illustrate articles referring to morally dubious activities.

20. *Lord Byron v Johnston*, 2 Mer. 29, 35 Eng. Rep. 851 (1816).

21. Prosser, endnotes #130, #157.

22. Recently the U.S. Supreme Court has given constitutional support to such a distinction in *Zacchini v Scripps-Howard Broadcasting Co.*, 53 L.Ed. 2d 965 (1977), p. 975.

23. Prosser, p. 107. For a similar view see H. Kalven, Jr., *Privacy in Tort Law*, p. 330.

24. *Rhodes v Graham*, 238 Ky. 225, 27 S.W.2d 46 (1931); *McDaniel v Atlanta Coca-Cola Bottling Co.*, 60 Ga.App. 92, 2 S.E.2d 810 (1939).

25. A. Westin, *Privacy and Freedom* (New York: Athenaeum, 1967), pp. 344–49.

26. Brandeis and Warren, p. 78.

27. Ibid., pp. 81–82.

28. 116 U.S. 616 (1886).

29. "The subpoena at issue in *Boyd* clearly satisfied the requirements of the fourth amendment warrant clause, thereby ending a modern courts' analysis, during the nineteenth century compliance with the warrant clause was both by itself sufficient to validate a search and seizure; the appellants' fourth amendment claim therefore required that the court also decide whether the seizure was *reasonable*." Note, *Formalism, Legal Realism and Constitutionally Protected Privacy under the Fourth and Fifth Amendments*, 90 Harvard L.R. 945, (1977), 952.

30. Ibid., pp. 955–56.

31. E.S. Corwin, "The Supreme Court's Construction of the Self-Incrimination Clause," in 29 *Mich.L.Rev.*, I, 1930, pp. 15–16.

32. Note, "Search and Seizure in the Supreme Court," 28 *U. Chi. L.R.*, 664 (1964), 669.

33. L. Tribe, *American Constitutional Law* (Foundation Press, 2d ed., 1988), p. 560, quoting Corwin, "The 'Higher Law' Background of American Constitutional Law," in 42 *Harvard L.R.* 149, 365 (1928–1929).

34. M. Horwitz, *The Transformation of American Law: 1780–1860* (Harvard, 1977), p. 253.

35. Tribe, p. 562.

36. This is the notion introduced by Justice Harlan in *Hurtado v California*, 110 U.S. 516 (1884), and accepted by the majority of the Court in *Palko v Connecticut*, 302 U.S. 319 (1937).

37. E. C. Smith and A. J. Zucher, *Dictionary of American Politics*, Barnes and Noble, 1955, p. 128, quoted in H. Abraham, *Freedom and the Court* (Oxford, 1988), p. 121.

38. H. Berman, *Law and Revolution* (Harvard, 1983), p. 12.

39. Tribe, pp. 562–63.

40. 198 U.S. 45 (1905).

41. Other cases similarly decided were: *Adkins v Childrens Hospital*, 261 U.S. 525 (1923), invalidating a statute establishing a minimum salary for working women; *Coppage v Kansas*, 236 U.S. 1 (1915), invalidating a law against the so-called "yellow dog contracts," which forced the hired worker to stay out of unions.

42. Tribe, p. 567.

43. On this see Tribe, p. 570.

44. For a detailed account of Brandeis's battles, and especially those against the monopolies New Haven Railway and United Shoe Machinery, see A. Mason, *Brandeis: A Free Man's Life* (Viking, 1946), pp. 96–241.

45. Quoted in Mason, *Brandeis*, pp. 249–50.

46. 198 U.S. 45 (1905), at 53.

47. L. Tribe, p. 569.

48. L. Brandeis, "The Living Law," in *The Curse of Bigness* (Viking, 1934), pp. 316–26.

49. L. Brandeis, "The Opportunity of the Law," address delivered May 4, 1905, at the Harvard Ethical Society, in *Business: A Profession* (1914) (New York: 1971 [repr.]) pp. 313–27, p. 322.

50. L. Brandeis, "The Living Law," p. 324.

51. The term "homeorhetic" was forged by the embryologist Waddington in alternative to homeostasis, and it indicates the maintenance of equilibrium through change.

52. Tribe, pp. 560ff.

53. Corwin refers back to Bartolo da Sassoferrato, John of Salisbury, Aquinas, Occam, and Nicholas of Cusa. Corwin, p. 166.

54. For Rousseau's distinction of general will ("volonté générale") and will of all ("volonté de tous"), see *Du Contrat Social*, esp. II, 3; IV, 1.

55. B. Bailyn, *The Ideological Origins of the American Revolution* (Harvard, 1967), 23.

56. For an account of the influence of Montesquieu on the American founding, see P. M. Spurlin, *Montesquieu in America: 1760–1801* (Octagon Books, 1969).

57. Montesquieu, *L'Esprit des Lois*, Livre XI, Ch. 6.

58. "Law in general is human reason insofar as it governs all the peoples of the earth; and the political and civil laws of each nation should only be the particular cases to which this human reason is applied." *L'Esprit des Lois*, Livre I, Ch. 3.

59. Ibid., Livre XI, Ch. 3.

60. Blackstone, *Commentaries on the Laws of England*, I, 2.

61. So Hobbes, who cannot be considered a liberal in the proper sense, but who shared the basic empiricist premises of liberalism, to which he did lend several crucial concepts, writes: "By Liberty is understood . . . the absence of externall [sic] Impediments." Law, and the limits it imposes, becomes thus the opposite of liberty. Though starting from this "liberal" definition of liberty, Hobbes's arguments proceed to demonstrate the identity of liberty and legal necessity. *Leviathan*, XIV and XXI.

62. See I. Berlin, "Two Concepts of Liberty," in *Four essays on Liberty* (Oxford, 1969), which essentially defends Hobbes's definition of liberty.

63. 198 U.S. 45 (1905), at 54.

64. For this, and all other quotations of Holmes in this section, see Holmes, "Dissenting Opinion," in *Lochner v New York*, 198 U.S. 45 (1905).

65. D. Kennedy, "Toward a Historical Understanding of Legal Consciousness: The Case of Classical Legal Thought," *Research in Law and Sociology* 3 (1980): 3–24. See also R. Unger, "The Critical Legal Studies Movement," *Harvard L.R.* 96 (1983): 561.

66. Kennedy, p. 11.

67. "The opposition which it discovers between the desire of the human governor and the reason of the law lies, indeed, at the foundation of the American interpretation of the doctrine of the separation of powers and so of the entire American system of constitutional law." Corwin, p. 156.

68. See Tribe, pp. 570ff.

69. 25 S.Ct. Report 545 (1904). Locke himself integrates the harm to self into his harm principle. But this, as we shall see, is one of those remnants of natural law theory in Lockean thought that later liberal thought has discarded.

70. We cannot discuss here this claim, which has been more thoroughly developed in my Ph.D. thesis, "Privacy, Rights and Natural Law," University of Toronto, 1993, Ch. 4, sec. 6.

71. 198 U.S. 45, at 52.

72. Thus, in *Coppage v Kansas*, another paradigmatic case of the period, though abstractly reasserting the principle that the freedom of contract can be limited to promote public welfare, the Court specified that limitations are not legitimate that try to correct those inequalities of contractual power "that are the normal and inevitable result" of the exercise of contractual rights. 236 U.S. 1 (1915), pp. 17–18.

73. Tribe, p. 571.

74. Kennedy, pp. 11–12.

75. "Harlan may have been in many respects a 'premature New Dealer.'" L. Filler, "John M. Harlan," in F. Israel and L. Friedman (eds.), *The Justice of the U.S. Supreme Court*, Vol. II (New York: Chelsea House), pp. 1281–1324, p. 1292.

76. Holmes, "Dissenting Opinion," 25 S.Ct.Rep., Oct.Term, 1904, at 546.

77. Harlan, "Dissenting Opinion," 25 S.Ct.Reporter, Oct.Term (1904), at 547–51.

78. For cases showing Harlan's "hatred of monopolies" (L. Filler, p. 1285), see *Northern Securities Co. v U.S.*, 193 U.S. 197 (1904), and *Standard Oil Company v United States*, 221 U.S. 1 (1911). For civil liberties cases see *Hurtado v California*, 110 U.S. 516 (1884), and *Twining v New Jersey*, 211 U.S. 78 (1908).

79. In *Lochner*, Harlan says: "We cannot say that the state has acted without reason." "Dissenting Opinion," at 550. On Harlan's understanding of judicial review as an "honest application of reason to law" see F. B. Clark, "The Constitutional Doctrines of Justice Harlan," in *Johns Hopkins Univ. Stud. in Hist. and Pol. Sci.*, 33 (1915), Vol. 4, Ch. 3, pp. 59–82.

80. Abraham points out that though being the two more frequent dissenters in the Supreme Court, Harlan and Holmes were not on good personal terms, and that Harlan was "closer to Louis Dembitz Brandeis." *Freedom and the Court* (New York: Oxford, 1988), p. 17.

3

FROM MILL TO BRANDEIS

J. S. MILL'S PRINCIPLE OF LIBERTY

The utilitarian/darwinistic outlook proves itself clear of any relation with the natural rights discourse in a third approach, that of Justice Holmes: "The name of Holmes' economic God was not property, which is reactionary, because static and concerned with vested interests. . . . It was Competition."[1] In an early article, Holmes accepts the presupposition that legislation "must tend in the long run to aid the survival of the fittest" and thinks that "in the last resort a man rightly prefers his own interest to that of his neighbours." In this fundamental respect, he is very close to those "natural rights utilitarians" he rejected as being too influenced by Spencer. In fact, he only criticized them for presenting in the monistic terms of the 'greatest happiness of the greatest number' what he considered the outcome of the dualistic opposition of class interests:

> The objection which we wish to express at the present time is, that this presupposes an identity of interests between the different parts of a community which does not exist in fact. . . . It is no sufficient condemnation of legislation that it favours one class at the expense of another; for much or all legislation does that; and none the less when the *bona fide* object is the greatest good of the greatest number.[2]

Elsewhere, he established a "proximate test of excellence for legislation," based on its "conformity to the wishes of the dominant power."[3] Due to such a complete abdication vis-à-vis the dominant classes, some have called Holmes a "totalitarian,"[4] but even those who have not gone that far have had to admit that he had scarce interest in the protection of individual rights, at least initially, as confirmed by the undoubtedly repressive standards he adopted in cases of freedom of expression before 1919.[5] He completely rejected the idea of natural or human rights and wrote to Laski: "You respect the rights of man—I don't."[6]

On the other hand, Holmes was somewhat concerned with the freedom of minorities. Already in the early article just quoted, he had hoped that while "the legislation should . . . modify itself in accordance with the will of the *de facto* supreme power in the community . . . the spread of an educated sympathy should reduce the sacrifice of minorities to the minimum."[7] The concern for minorities may have come to Holmes from both Spencer and J. S. Mill,[8] but Holmes was overall hostile to Spencer, and on the whole he was more essentially indebted to Mill's reintroduction of liberal dualism within monistic utilitarianism.

In 1919 Holmes wrote the Court opinion in *Schenck v United States*, claiming that the letters written by Schenk inviting people to refuse conscription as a violation of their constitutional rights, created a *"clear and present danger,"* apt to "bring about the substantive evils that Congress has a right to prevent."[9] At stake, in *Schenck* and similar cases, was the freedom of expression of civil disobedients and thus implicitly the privacy of their conscience. For Holmes, such a privacy was no less arbitrary than any other private opinion, so that the government had an equally arbitrary power to interfere with it. But because of his growing sensitivity toward minorities, Holmes modified his repressive "clear and present danger test," turning it into a tool for limited toleration. In his classic dissent in *Abraham v United States*, he wrote:

Nobody can suppose that the surreptitious publishing of a silly leaflet by an unknown man, without more, would present an immediate danger that its opinions would hinder the success of the Government arms. . . . *Persecution for the expression of opinions seems to me perfectly logical.* . . . But when men have realized that time has upset many fighting faiths, they may come to believe even more than they believe the very foundation of their own conduct that the ultimate good desired is better reached by *free trade in ideas*, that the best test of truth is the power of the thought to get itself accepted in the *competition of the market*.[10]

The notion that the persecution of opinion is both legitimate and logical is an expression of Holmes's social darwinism, but the conclusion of the paragraph and its rationale reveal the extent of Mill's influence upon him. The idea that truth is something established by a free trade in the *marketplace of ideas* derives directly from J. S. Mill's epistemological relativism (although there is in Mill a nonrelativistic side that is missing in Holmes).[11] Although the relativism implicit in "marketplace of ideas" seems to guarantee the legitimacy and toleration of all points of view, in fact, because its only test of truth is the opinion of the majority, in the end it may become quite oppressive for minorities, unless supplemented by further principles. Mill added to it a dualistic mediation whereby majorities are given the power to impose their understanding of truth, goodness, and utility within the public sphere but are denied that same power within the private sphere. In private, minorities and individuals are supposed to freely experiment with their lives, as long as they do not make themselves "a nuisance to other people." Mill's basic principle of liberty claims that "the only purpose for which power can be rightfully exercised over any member of a civilised community, against his will, is to prevent *harm to others*. His own good, either physical or moral, is not a sufficient warrant."[12] This is an overall principle covering both action and thought, and within thought both private opinion and its expression through speech. But as we said, opinions and speeches deserve immunity also because of epistemological fallibility: "We can never be sure that the opinion we are endeavouring to stifle is a false opinion.... Those who desire to suppress it, of course, deny its truth; but they are not infallible.... All silencing of discussion is an assumption of infallibility."[13] The fact that Mill appeals to epistemological fallibility, rather than to the unreality of any substantive truth, already shows that he cannot be properly considered an ethical relativist. Nevertheless, Mill's absolutist version of epistemological fallibility ("all silencing of discussion is an assumption of infallibility"), by making all judgments on the quality of different opinions concretely inapplicable and legally unenforceable, plays in practice the same role of a full-fledged ethical relativism.

However, behind this self-contained relativistic side, there is a substantively deontological side that emerges, for instance, when he asserts the partial and progressive attainability of truth immediately after claiming its epistemological indecipherability: "As mankind improves, the number of doctrines which are no longer disputed or doubted will be constantly on the increase: and the well being of mankind may almost be measured by the number and gravity of the truths which have reached the point of being uncontested."[14] The explicit claim that truth is bound to progressively emerge implies not only that there must already be some generally accepted truths but also that the truth that will one day be grasped by the whole humanity is, in and of itself, fully self-subsistent. That also means that it is at least likely for such truth to be already at least partially visible and thus already partially present in some opinion more than in others. Therefore, as Mill knew very well, it must be possible to distinguish between more and less truthful opinions, although of course such a possibility cannot and must not in itself justify the possibility of curtailing the freedom of expression. This denies the power of the fallibility argument, thus invalidating Mill's claim that speeches be equally and absolutely immune, and creating an insuperable contradiction, and in fact a radical aporia, between Mill's substantively deontological and relativistic sides.

Such a contradictory coexistence of opposites is a general methodological feature of Mill's thought. Mill claims to be a utilitarian. At the same time, he is widely considered a champion of liberalism.[15] But the most crucial tension within Millian thought is that between hedonistic/sensistic utilitarianism on the one hand and Platonic transpersonalism on the other.[16] It is this crucial tension that moves Mill to reintroduce liberal dualism within the stifling monism of Benthamite utilitarianism. Writes Mill:

> It is proper to state that I forego any advantage which could be derived to my argument from the idea of abstract right, as a thing independent of utility. I regard utility as the ultimate appeal on all ethical questions; but it must be utility in the largest sense, grounded on the *permanent interests* of man as a *progressive being*.[17]

Though rejecting the abstract deontology of liberalism, Mill cannot avoid deontology altogether. Even the purest consequentialist needs some independent criterion to evaluate consequences, and we know that the deontological standard of utilitarians is the maximization of sensuous pleasure and the minimization of sensory pain. Mill accepts such a standard, but his understanding of it is quite peculiar.

His reference to "utility in the largest sense" is a thinly veiled polemic against Bentham. The same can be said of his appeal to the "permanent interests of man," which implies the notion of a self-subsistent human nature larger and deeper than the mere impulse to sensuous pleasure, characterizing man/woman as a "progressive being" capable of perfecting him/herself toward higher and nobler pleasures. Writes Mill:

> It is quite compatible with the principle of utility to recognise the fact, that some *kinds* of pleasure are more desirable and more valuable than others. It would be absurd that . . . the estimation of pleasure should be supposed to depend on quantity alone. . . . [A truly utilitarian theory cannot but] assign to the pleasures of the intellect, of the feelings and imagination, and of the moral sentiments, a much higher value . . . than to those of mere sensation. . . . [Unfortunately] utilitarian writers in general have placed the superiority of mental over bodily pleasures . . . in their circumstantial advantages rather than in their *intrinsic nature*.

Mill's deontological upholding of the intrinsic value of interiority goes as far as claiming that the human essence subsists untouched even in the midst of unpleasant material and bodily conditions. Against Bentham's quantitative reduction and equalization of sensual, emotional, and intellectual pleasures, Mill wrote: "It is better to be a human being *dissatisfied* than a pig satisfied; better to be a Socrates *dissatisfied* than a fool satisfied." In referring explicitly to the Stoics, Mill even accepts the notion that true happiness may require the renunciation of sensuous pleasure and utility: "Paradoxical as the assertion may be, the conscious ability to do without happiness gives the best prospect of realising such happiness as is attainable. For nothing except that consciousness can raise a person above the chances of life." Happiness and utility are thus made to rest on an inner noetic and ethical development that verges on the spiritual, as inner spiritual fullness seems to be the best possible ground for a completely ethical life. And in fact, Mill praises self-renunciation as a saintly virtue: "[The] readiness to . . . serve the happiness of others by the absolute sacrifice of his own . . . is the highest virtue which can be found in man. . . . In the golden rule of Jesus of Nazareth we read the complete spirit of the ethics of utility."[18]

Besides Jesus and the Stoics, Mill also enlists Socrates among his direct predecessors.[19] But for various personal and intellectual reasons, Mill never quite made that connection the true core of his thought, trying instead to accommodate some of its main elements within the empiricist/utilitarian framework inherited from Bentham. Had he been faithful to his Platonist inspiration, he would have accepted a holographic understanding of the relation between virtue and utility, whereby true utility can only be generated by what is inherently virtuous, and true virtue can only foster the general utility.

Instead, when discussing virtue and utility, Mill states that virtue, which he explicitly relates to noetic and ethical development, is at the same time "a part" and a "means" to utility. Utility is said to be the only reality that is good in and for itself, whereas virtue/mind is valuable mainly insofar as it leads to it. We find in this the roots of what would later be called *rule utilitarianism*, according to which it is not always necessary or good to apply the principle of utility directly, being at times better to promote it indirectly through ordinary and traditional moral rules. On the other hand, by claiming that virtue is a part of utility, Mill makes virtue and utility at least partially coincide. He identifies the other part of utility with selfish and sensuous pleasures, and more explicitly with the "love of money, of power, or of fame." In fact, he describes the role of virtue in the definition of utility as similar to that of money, which from "being a means to happiness has come to be itself a principal ingredient of the individual's conception of happiness."

The result of this new definition of utility/happiness is quite astounding. In his deontological moment, Mill considered virtue an intrinsic and ultimate value. Thus, virtue is given the power to define utility completely, without the least participation of the "love of money, of power, or of fame," as utility is said to be increased by renouncing egoistic and sensuous pleasures, and thus by augmenting its opposite, virtue. But because in the end both of these elements equally constitute utility, the same power must be given to hedonistic egoism, with the consequence—logically inevitable, although Mill would have never accepted it—that utility can also be increased by renouncing noetic and selfless virtue! In other words, virtue/interiority and hedonism/egoism both play the equal role of essentially constitutive parts of utility, so that any increase of either one cannot but increase utility overall, even while diminishing the other, possibly to the point of annihilation. Mill adopts here a clearly contradictory pattern, which posits as coessences two mutually exclusive elements. It is a contradictory type of mediation, whereby the two opposites of virtue and egoism confront and limit each other externally without altering their original constitution, so that their reciprocally destructive tension remains. At the same time, this invites the return of Bentham's hedonistic relativism, whereby there is no difference between the virtuous and the selfish as long as it generates sensuous pleasure. This is why Mill has to restore the hierarchical priority of the virtuous/mental he had just abolished: "The love of money, of power, or of fame . . . may, and often do, render the individual *noxious to the other members* of the society to which he belongs, where there is nothing which makes him so much a blessing to them as the cultivation of the disinterested love of virtue." Thus, immediately upon denying it, Mill implicitly reestablishes virtue as the true essence of utility and thus of all pleasures:

And consequently, the utilitarian standard, while it tolerates and approves of those other acquired desires, *up to the point beyond which they would be more* injurious *to the general happiness than promotive of it*, enjoins and requires the cultivation of the love of virtue up to the greatest strength possible, as being above all things important to the general happiness.[20]

Virtue is not only said to constitute the most "important" component, but is in fact fully identified with utility, given that only with its growth there is a parallel growth of utility, and this "to the greatest strength possible," that is, without limits. The other component is merely tolerated, and only insofar as it does not become more injurious than promotive of the general happiness or utility. Virtue could never injure the general happiness/utility, precisely because in essence they thoroughly coincide, which means that hedonistic/egoistic behavior can be tolerated only insofar as it does not injure virtue, that is, as long as it itself retains a sufficient degree of virtuousness. Thus, Mill implicitly upholds the transpersonal notion that virtue/interiority is the essence and truth of the sensuous/egoistic element and of its lower forms of utility.

Yet again, the full development of such a notion would simply erase the previous attempt to establish a dualistic mediation between the virtuous/mental and the selfish/sensuous, as well as between deontology and empiricism. And so Mill inserts at the very core of his system the element that is supposed to make such a mediation possible, the notion of *self-regarding actions*. Actions that are selfish and nonvirtuous, and thus potentially noxious, are nevertheless "tolerated" as long as they do not *harm others*, including the material happiness of society. It could be argued that Mill is not really talking about self-regarding actions here, in that he implicitly claims that as long as actions are not harmfully other-regarding, they are "promotive" of the general happiness. But this is not in contradiction with the notion of self-regarding actions. In Mill's empiricist vision, selfish actions that spring from "love of money, of power, or of fame" can be promotive of the general happiness in a purely arithmetic and indirect manner, by adding up all direct increases of the separate and self-regarding utility of each individual.

The notion of self-regarding actions is thus the fundamental pillar of Mill's system, because, by legitimizing as autonomously productive of utility all selfish and hedonistic actions not yet generating materially and directly harmful externalities, it sanctions their independence relative to virtue/interiority, thus making utility a reality larger than virtue, and thus ultimately independent of it. More generally, this establishes the independence of empirical actions, in their random morality, from the virtuous/noetic essence and principles, which always necessarily sustains them at least to some degree, an emancipation that is the very core of empiricism.

On the other hand, although not directly defining it, the deontological/virtuous dimension is made to stand above the empiricist/selfish one and to limit it from the outside by more poignantly and directly participating in the definition of general utility, that is, of that which selfish and atomistically self-regarding actions cannot injure without denying their legitimacy to exist. This is confirmed by the fact that for Mill such actions, though self-regarding, are not to be protected only from a liberal deontological point of view—that is, as enclosed within the private sphere irrespective of the common good—but also and foremost teleologically and deontically, that is, as arithmetically "promotive" of the general happiness, and thus indirectly of the deontic virtue that of happiness represents the deepest essence. That Mill's ultimate goal is indeed such a growth is revealed by the fact that the most critical purpose of his self-regarding sphere, besides and above the protection of Benthamite actions, is the protection of the higher mental/virtuous element.

"On Liberty" rests on the deep awareness that once unleashed, the selfish, hedonistic, and possessive impulses can easily gain power, as they tend to be spontaneously followed by the masses. Mill believed that only the properly educated few can fully realize inner wholeness and virtue and that only under their guidance will society be enlightened by true utility. This notion of enlightened rather than merely empirical democracy is central to Mill's political philosophy.[21] However social and political enlightenment, and the individual enlightenment that precedes it, requires that the few be protected from what Mill calls the "tyranny of the majority," the totalitarian empowerment of the lower possessive and hedonistic impulses. The self-regarding sphere becomes the main tool to ensure such protection. In fact, Mill's very ideal of individuality has little to do with liberalism, owing much more to the holistic and transpersonal tradition. In describing the nature and value of individuality, Mill quotes from Wilhelm von Humboldt: "The end of man, or that which is prescribed by the *eternal and immutable dictates of reason*, and not suggested by vague and transient desires, is the *highest* and most *harmonious* development of his powers to a *complete* and *consistent whole*."[22] Von Humboldt cannot be considered a liberal, unless liberalism is identified with anything having to do with liberty. He was deeply influenced by both Goethe and Schiller and by their "perennial philosophy" synthesis of romanticism and classicism. Consequently, he profoundly admired the Greek, and more specifically the Socratic, ideal of individuality as a reality that persons must strive to attain by becoming at once inwardly self-sufficient and autonomously capable of acting from the standpoint of universal reason and cosmic responsibility. Inspired by Von Humboldt, Mill's notion of individuality springs from the same roots, although Mill was unable to hold on to them fully and consistently. Even Ten, for whom Mill is more a liberal than a utilitarian, admits that "Mill's notion of individuality . . . paved a middle way between the doctrines of Benthamite utilitarianism and those of later British idealist philosophers."[23] This "middle way," as anticipated in the previous discussion, is merely an *a posteriori dualistic mediation*, whereby the two opposites of deontology and empiricism limit each other externally, though remaining enclosed in their original separate identity. Thus, while deontology is lost in the abstraction of an empirically irrelevant essence, empiricism is reduced to the dullness and precariousness of an empirical reality without foundation, meaning, or end. Their *a posteriori* mediation is then supposed to keep either one from growing each into a unilateral and dangerous absoluteness, while at the same time guaranteeing, through their equally reciprocal limitation, their equal axiological dignity—but in fact it ends by giving priority to empiricism. Deontology rests on the assumption that underneath empirical dualities, with their load of conflicts and relativities, there is a unitary and absolute ethical principle (as represented, for instance, in Kant's categorical imperative) to be understood not as the product of a merely subjective will but as the invisible and concretely indeterminate essence by which the empirical reality, which in a fundamental sense is nothing but the essence itself in its existential articulation and manifestation, is necessarily ruled, if it is not to incur its own self-destruction.

But once deontological principles and virtues are put on the same footing with the accidental empirical reality, deontology is dethroned, and by thus losing that ability to rule—which is its essential hallmark—it cannot but be annihilated. This is precisely what happens when deontological virtue is reduced to a mere part of utility, thus losing its status as utility's essence, and its corollary power to bound selfish utility. This, in turn, makes the latter acquire the dignity of an independent and essential (if not equally worthy) component of utility. In the end, this ennobling of selfish utility brings about a reversal whereby virtue, or the saintly, philosophic and heroic life of Jesus, Socrates, and the Stoic, becomes *supererogatory*—that is, quite irrelevant to the ordinary empirical dimension—and the selfishly utilitarian life is no longer a "noxious" thing, but the ordinary, healthy, and necessary ground of human action.

Here we find the Mill who supports economic competition, and productive and proprietary accumulation, as fundamental components of personal and social development. This Mill identifies progress with economic growth. The standards he has in mind are the capitalistic, growth-economy standards of Europe, while considering "worse than barbarism" the steady-state, sustainable economies of Asian and Native American nations. He even suggests that "to reconcile such people to industry," they must be "compelled to it" through "personal slavery."[24] He uncritically acknowledges that "to grow as rich as possible [is] the universal object of ambition" and admits to the legitimacy of "enormous fortunes . . . earned and accumulated during a single lifetime."

On the other hand, consistent with his inconsistent and dualistic mediation, Mill also wants egoistic and possessive impulses to be limited by considerations of general utility and thus also of the social distribution of wealth. He pleads in favor of "a limitation of the sum which any one person may acquire by gift or inheritance, to the amount sufficient to constitute a moderate independence" and asserts that the best state would be one in which "no one is poor, no one desires to be richer." This is quite close to the perennial philosophy point of view, which Rousseau expresses through the ideal of the individual who is "ni riche, ni pauvre, et peut se suffire a lui-même."[25]

Mill makes indeed significant steps in the direction of a transpersonal political theory, especially when he envisions the workers' cooperative movement progressively displacing the capitalist system of production and when he claims the superiority of a *steady-state economics* on the transpersonal-ecological ground that a stationary economic state "implies no stationary state of human improvement," while the "unlimited accumulation of wealth and population" is inherently destructive. Yet, precisely because they represent the weaker and supererogatory side of Mill, even transpersonal and ecological values are not immune from the influence of his more basic Benthamite utilitarian side. MacPherson correctly notices how, for Mill, "the separate co-operative enterprises were expected to compete in the market, and would be driven by the incentive of desire for individual gain."[26] In the same vein, Mill considers steady-state economics applicable only to the wealthy economies of the West, thinking that "in the backward countries of the world . . . increased production is still an important object."[27] What we see here is a pattern in which selfish and possessive impulses, together with the high-growth, capitalistic economic structures that are supposed to satisfy them, constitute the bedrock of the human life and mind, and the supererogatory transpersonal virtues, together with the corresponding steady-state, cooperative, and ecological socioeconomic system, are superimposed on that bedrock only after its possessive-egoistic requirements have been fully satisfied, and then only as a limit to its probable excesses.

To be sure, Mill sincerely believed that his system fostered a mediation of egoism and virtue, ultimately leading to the triumph of virtue. But his hopes were highly unrealistic. For example, we know today that it is simply impossible for all countries to achieve the overdeveloped standards of production and consumption characteristic of the West, which have been and are made possible by the exploitation of the peoples and resources of the rest of the world. More and more, it has become clear that the possibility of realizing a stationary economic state on a global scale, ecologically sound and distributively just, will depend on the generalized acceptance of lower standards of production, consumption, and waste. Although substantially improved by the development of advanced yet ecologically sound technologies, such a global stationary state will have to adopt the very organizational principles of those self-sufficient economic systems that Mill considered primitive and barbarous.[28] In the same vein, it is highly unlikely that cooperation will be able to survive, let alone thrive, on a psychology whose basic layer consists of possessive egoism.

We have seen that the preeminence of egoistic and possessive utility is the result of reducing virtue into a mere part. By denying virtue the status of the essential core of all truly useful actions, Mill turns it into a particular set of such actions. In so doing, Mill proceeds to a complete *despiritualization of virtue*: He appeals to the virtuous individual and institutional behaviors of Socrates, Jesus, or the Stoics but makes nothing of the inner spiritual states on which those outer patterns are rooted. He writes: "Inactivity, unaspiringness, absence of desire are a more fatal hindrance to improvement than any misdirection of energy . . . [and such absence of desire] generates nothing better than the mystical metaphysics of the Pythagoreans or the Vedas."[29] But detachment from possessions and freedom from the accidental chaos of one's desires are a fundamental moral factor, and in this sense it is wrong to believe that the mystical and contemplative element is intrinsically antisocial and antipolitical. If the Pythagorean mystics built very-well-governed cities in the ancient world, it is because they shared with Socrates, the Stoics, and Jesus a proper understanding of the dialectical relationship existing between contemplative inaction and virtuous action. For those traditions, only the original and thus inactive fullness of one's mind/spirit, a condition that the Stoics called *autarkeia* and Plato *philosophia*, by freeing the person from fears and egoistic desires, makes compassionate action grow strong. Such an inner condition constitutes the heart of the Platonic ideal of the philosopher-king, later brought to life by the Stoic emperor Marcus Aurelius and matched in the East by Prince Arjun of the Hindu Bhagavadgītā, the book dearest to Gandhi.

Mill claims the "reconciling and combining of opposites" as his basic methodological principle, and states that truth is the result of combining "opinions favourable to democracy and to aristocracy, to property and to equality, to cooperation and to competition, to luxury and to abstinence, to sociality and individuality, to liberty and discipline." Yet he does not keep with this principle in relation to the dialectic of contemplation and action, withdrawal into oneself and outer involvement, the former being practically wiped out of the Millian scenario. Mill states that the principle itself applies only to the "antagonisms of the practical life,"[30] and from Mill's overall point of view this implies that the whole picture, virtue included, is crushed within the narrow boundaries of the merely empirical dimension. The reductionist world of empiricism finds in possessive egoism its vital force, its spirit. Having been placed at the roots of the human mind, possessive selfishness becomes unassailable by a virtue that is removed from the psychological depths and reified into a set of traditional rules: "Mankind must by this time have acquired positive beliefs as to the effects of some actions on their happiness; and the beliefs which have thus come down are the rules of morality for the multitude." Mill himself must be aware of the shallowness and inefficacy of such an externalist superimposition of virtue (best represented in Plato's myth of Er, where he who had "become virtuous from habit" chose to reincarnate as a tyrant), as he immediately adds: "and for the philosopher until he has succeeded in finding better."[31] But as opposed to Plato, for whom the philosopher is the one endowed with the fullness of inner wisdom and virtue and is therefore truly capable of managing the moral habituation and education of the people, Mill's philosopher is the intellectual calculator of consequences, who is totally projected into the outer world and therefore weakened relative to those inner egoistic and possessive impulses that in the conquest and consumption of the outer world find their fulfillment. For Mill, the wiser few are professionals and university graduates. That our societies have become corrupt to the point of self-destruction under the very leadership of highly educated entrepreneurs, lawyers, and university professors shows the fatal insufficiency of the Millian project.

Mill's empiricist externalization of the human condition explains why he never was concerned with privacy and "being let alone," a precious condition only for those who believe that truth and virtue are inherent in one's interiority. A Millian commentator has admitted: "The absence of serious discussion of privacy is one of the most remarkable features of the writings of . . . J. S. Mill."[32] The same commentator rightly notices how such a lack of interest in privacy is typical of the whole liberal tradition. But Mill's lack of concern with informational privacy is also the offspring of his utilitarianism. His consequentialism leads him to emphasize the importance of maximizing and centralizing information in order to calculate general utility. As usual, Mill tries to mediate, but the balance between centralization and decentralization that he is here looking for is, once again, rather dualistic and skewed. He pleads for "the greatest possible centralisation of information, and diffusion of it from the centre . . . The central organ should have a right to know all that is done." He identifies liberty with the immunity of the sphere of self-regarding actions and choices, which is not supposed to be seriously hurt by "informational" invasions because these invasions do not appear to stop someone from doing or choosing. Mill was apparently unaware of the "chilling effect," the freezing of one's freedom to choose due to the inner fear of being under scrutiny, as well as of the paralyzing effect that being watched, or the fear thereof, has over one's ability for introspection and privacy. Due to such an underestimation of the inner dimension, Mill's private sphere is quite compatible with the heavy informational requirements of utilitarianism. Once again, however, even in this Mill's intentions are not predominantly utilitarian. In fact, for him the State should expand as much as possible its activity of "informing," and therefore of being informed, and of "advising," or interfering through persuasion:

> A government cannot have too much of the kind of activity which does not impede, but aids and stimulates, individual exertion and development. . . . The worth of the State, in the long run, is the worth of the individuals composing it; and a State which postpones the interests of their mental expansion and elevation . . . will find that with small men no great things can really be accomplished.[33]

This is part of the closing sentence of "On Liberty" and shows that Mill never completely abandoned his transpersonal and deontological side, which was indeed so tenacious that it reappears at the very core of his concrete description of the private self-regarding sphere: "This, then, is the appropriate region of human liberty. It comprises, first, the *inward domain of consciousness*; demanding liberty of conscience in the most comprehensive sense; liberty of thought and feeling; absolute freedom of opinion and sentiment on all subjects." The transpersonal stress on the primacy of the inward domain is explicitly accepted by Mill, who seems also to claim its higher immunity, in practice, relative to actions: "No one pretends that actions should be as free as opinions." Yet Mill justifies such a hierarchy mostly in consequentialist terms: Self-regarding conduct is said not to harm or affect others "directly, and in the first instance," in that it "occasions [no] *perceptible hurt* to any assignable individual except himself." In this sense, thought is considered by Mill to be more self-regarding.

This argument is not very convincing. Thought is the essential stuff of reality, as shown by its being the true source of action. Therefore, although less perceptible, it does in fact harm more deeply and at times more directly than action itself. It is easy to see how the quality of social life depends most of all on the state of mind of its members, and that a bad state of mind is in itself directly harmful, as social apathy, for instance, causes an immediate and deep harm to the communal fabric. Moreover, even when the perceptible harm to others is generated by action, the original source of the harm is the harmful thought, without which there would be no harmful action. The inner noetic and spiritual dimension is, therefore, at once self-regarding and other-regarding; and the fact that it may affect others only indirectly does not diminish but increases its other-regarding character, precisely because of its more subtle and therefore more powerful nature.

To legitimize the special immunity of the noetic and spiritual dimension, we need to change perspective and start thinking in terms of *self-direction*. Although other-regarding in fundamental ways, thought constitutes a privileged dimension because, having itself as its immediate object, it is inherently self-directed: Even when thinking external objects, it thinks them as thoughts, subsisting within itself. Such a noetic selfhood is the deepest layer of the empirical self, and it is in it that existential awareness develops, opening to that essential selfhood whose infinite liberty encompasses universal responsibility. Society has therefore an interest in giving the noetic life special protection, and, more generally, in promoting self-directed and self-sufficient behavior. Contrary to what is suggested by Mill's harm principle, such an interest persists even when society has to bear risks and pay prices, although both the interest of the community and the individual actor require the definition of clear limits to what society can endure.

The "self-direction" approach does indeed save all that is valuable and convincing in Mill's principle of liberty, properly overcoming a notion of self-regarding actions that, besides having been widely criticized,[34] does not even pass Mill's own examination. He writes: "I fully admit that the mischief which a person does to himself may *seriously* affect, both through their sympathies and their interests, those nearly connected with him and, in a minor degree, society at large." Although this seems to invalidate the notion of self-regarding actions, Mill needs it too much not to find reasons for its preservation. He says that the "strongest argument of all" in favor of a self-regarding sphere is that society is likely to interfere "wrongly." This may be a good argument to limit interference, yet there is nothing in it that derives its force from the notion of self-regarding actions itself and in fact can be equally applied in reference to other-regarding actions. But the most revealing passage is found when Mill argues that, although what "a person does to himself" may affect others "seriously," "the *inconvenience* is one which society can afford to bear, for the sake of the greater good of human freedom." Although the action is not and cannot really be self-regarding, society has a duty to leave it alone because of the inherent value of freedom. We have seen how freedom has for Mill a teleological value, related to the ethical development of the individual; and how such a development, without which there remains only the freedom of "noxious" actions, is centered on the virtue that springs from the right noetic-mental growth. The "inconvenience" is thus to be tolerated by society only insofar as liberty promotes such a personal and transpersonal growth. This conclusion, which is logically inevitable if one is to carry the "inconvenience" argument consistently to its end, shows how the implicit essence of Mill's untenable notion of "self-regarding actions" is in fact the transpersonal concept of "self-direction."

Had Mill fully developed this implicit core, he would have had to accept its logical corollaries as well. Given that the immunity of self-directed/other-regarding actions is guaranteed by society because of its critical interest in the development of a freely responsible selfhood, clearly it must be conditioned by such a presupposition and can therefore extend only to the point where: a) the individual still has a significant if minimal measure of ethical self-reliance and potentiality to attain an existential awareness or selfhood; b) the "inconvenience" that society is supposed to bear is still bearable, something that is put into question whenever harmful self-directed actions, that taken by themselves could still be borne, accumulate on such a wide social scale as to endanger the life or the goodness itself of the community and/or nature.

As we are about to see, Mill not only fails to acknowledge but indeed explicitly rejects these conclusions, and the truth is that he uses the "inconvenience" argument to justify a notion of self-regarding actions with which that argument is in complete contradiction. When it comes to the concrete determination of the private self-regarding sphere, Mill shields it with a uniformly absolute immunity, and the hierarchy of thought and action is completely lost. After having stressed the primacy of the "inward domain," as quoted earlier, he writes:

The liberty of expressing and publishing opinions may seem to fall under a different principle, since it belongs to that part of the conduct of an individual which concerns other people; but, being *almost* of as much importance as the liberty of thought itself, and resting in great part on the same reasons, is practically inseparable from it. Secondly, the principle requires liberty of tastes and pursuits; of framing the plan of our life to suit our own character; of *doing as we like*. . . . Thirdly . . . follows the . . . freedom to unite, for any purpose not involving harm to others. . . . No society . . . is completely free in which [these liberties] do not exist *absolute and unqualified*.[35]

The constitution of an "absolute and unqualified" private sphere of immunity creates the typical liberal dualism of private and public that contradicts Mill's philosophical foundations, both transpersonal and utilitarian.[36] Although in opposite ways, dialectical in the former case and liberticide in the latter, both transpersonalism and utilitarianism are monistic philosophies, and it is from them both that Mill derives that awareness of the inextricable unity of public and private that, as we have seen, constantly and surreptitiously surrounds and sustains the contradictory and dualistic device of the self-regarding sphere. Although it is the dualism that ultimately emerges as practically relevant, we have seen how the positively ethical realization of such a unity is the very end of the self-regarding sphere, on the one hand through the transpersonal protection of the heroic, virtuous, and wise individuality and on the other hand through the systematic preservation of the selfish and possessive actions constituting the organically utilitarian society. Mill's dualism was thus born as a function of his double-faced contradictory monism, and in this fundamental respect he can be said to be a liberal only by default.

Mill's essential monism rests most strongly on his transpersonal assertion of the primacy of the "inward domain." Due to such primacy, Mill states that the liberty to express and publish opinions is only "almost" as important as the liberty of thought. Because Mill does not attribute to that distinction any practical relevance, it is clear that his insistence on the higher status of thought and interiority can only be explained as the outcome of his deeply felt adherence to the transpersonal ideal. But because he could not allow the transpersonal side to take over even if only theoretically, Mill is careful to explain once more such a difference in consequentialist terms, by stressing the other-regarding nature of discourse as opposed to the self-regarding activity of thinking. Yet even with that explanation, consistency would have required Mill to still give a higher immunity to thought over its outer expression. But the resulting practical hierarchy of inner and outer, mental and sensuous, with its clear transpersonal undertones, would have denied not only the utilitarian equalization of pleasures but also and more importantly liberal privatism, with its equal shielding of all choices and actions no matter if selfishly hedonistic or virtuous. As we have seen, it is on that very privatism that Mill's project to mediate and thus preserve both utilitarian and transpersonal behavior depended. Thus, in the end he cannot but claim the same absolute protection for the freedom of expression, due to its "resting in great part on the same reasons" that justify the protection of thought and interiority, namely the deep link with selfhood.

Not only opinions are made equal to the inner domain, but so is the realm of "doing as we like," where the very egoistic and possessive actions, that Mill himself considers "noxious," thrive. Mill probably realizes that the practical absolutization of potentially noxious and vicious behavior is untenable and so tries once more a posteriori mediation by acknowledging that the private sphere, though immune from coercion, must be open to moral and educational interferences.[37] This new mediation, which seems to allow for some permeability of the private sphere without questioning the fundamental dualism of private and public, requires a parallel dualism of legal and moral, the former being associated with the public and the latter with the private. Here we meet Mill the legal positivist, for whom the law is defined as an essentially coercive agency molded by the dictates of political majorities and externally limited by a sphere of absolute private rights that only moral persuasion can penetrate.[38] But insofar as he commends ethical interference as a way to foster private virtue, Mill recognizes the possibility and indeed the necessity of morally evaluating and ranking the different types of private action, thus mercilessly exposing the injustice of affording the same absolute immunity to all self-regarding behavior. Whenever such tension emerges, Mill doesn't hesitate to contradict himself by requiring the shielding of the private sphere not only from legal coercion but from ethical interference as well, as shown by the following opposition of liberty on the one hand and morality and law together on the other: "Whenever, in short, there is a definite damage, or a definite *risk of damage*, either to an individual or to the public, the case is taken *out of the province of liberty*, and placed *in that of morality or law*."[39]

Millian liberty, and its private sphere, is said to be normally immune from both morality and law, thus becoming a haven of ethical relativism. In this way Mill, who has never been a liberal in the proper sense, has given to modern liberalism the means to perfect itself into a radical empiricist dualism, whereby the public/private dichotomy is the tool of an ethical relativism that is apparently neutral on the different conceptions of the good but does in fact serve those hedonistic and possessive impulses that for the empiricist tradition essentially characterize human nature.

Mill's liberal and liberal-utilitarian followers have indeed appropriated his empiricist dualism apart from the complexity of his thought and certainly apart from its deep transpersonal inspiration. This explains the gap between Mill and Millianism. Millian influences on jurisprudence follow the same pattern, and it is in this sense that Holmes, at least until his very last years on the bench, can be said to be a Millian.[40] In the end, however, it is Mill himself who legitimized Millianism, as proved by the fact that Holmes's "clear and present danger" test derived directly from Mill's harm principle. It could be objected that Holmes's test is more repressive, both because it substitutes a concrete harm with a hypothetical danger and also because it leaves the determination of what is dangerous to political majorities. But these do not seem substantial differences. Mill himself includes in his notion of harm the case of a "definite risk of damage," which amounts to "clear and present danger." And if it is true that Holmes does not put very demanding constraints on the majority's power, the same can be ultimately said about Mill, although in his case such a result was likely involuntary.

Empirical harm or danger is not something evident in itself, and its assessment depends on the criteria that one adopts. Unless the criteria of goodness and utility, and by contrast of harmfulness, had a self-subsistent character, they are fully dependent on the mutable and accidental market of ideas and thus cannot but be left to the will of majorities. In the end, Mill falls back into a relativism that axiologically equalizes all private behavior, and the price to pay for this abstract absolutization of all "self-regarding" conduct is the relativization of all that is not self-regarding, and thus the attribution to political majorities of the power to decide which of the other-regarding actions are harmful or beneficial.

Moreover, we have seen how unrealistic is the notion of self-regarding actions in face of the complete interdependence of individual, social, and natural life; and how Mill himself recognized its profound limitations. At best, the boundaries of the self-regarding sphere are shaky, and the majority power over the other-regarding sphere, reinforced by Mill's legal positivism, cannot but extend to the determination of what is other-regarding, and thus conversely of what is self-regarding.

In this sense, Holmes' repressive opinion in *Abraham*, though opposite to Mill's transpersonal inspiration, is fully consistent with the pragmatic content of Mill's principle of liberty. We have seen that in his opinion, Holmes admitted to the legitimacy of the government's claim that antiwar propaganda during war times is harmful and must be repressed. Mill could not have said anything different, at least not consistently. He wrote that "even opinions lose their immunity when the circumstances in which they are expressed are such as to constitute their expression a positive instigation to some mischievous act."[41] Certainly anticonscription activity in war time is a direct instigation to an act that, being other-regarding, falls under the State's power to establish it as mischievous. Holmes defended Abraham's right to speech on the sole ground that his leaflet was "silly" and thus unable to produce any serious harm to society. But this Millian line of defense can only protect "silly leaflets," providing fundamental freedoms with very limited, if any, protection. To offer a solid and realistic protection of liberty, as opposed to one that is abstractly absolute and concretely inefficient, we need to go back to that transpersonal and truly deontological vision that penetrated Mill's heart, but, alas, not deeply enough his mind.

BRANDEIS, NON–SELF-DESTRUCTION AND THE PRIMACY OF PRIVACY

Brandeis was one of the major figures of the Progressive movement when, after supporting the failed candidacy of La Follette, he decided to side with Wilson, who became president in 1912. Wilson always considered Brandeis a precious counselor, especially in matters regarding the growth of capitalistic "bigness."

In 1916, despite deep resistance within the Democratic Party, Wilson nominated Brandeis for a position in the Supreme Court. The opposition to the nomination was so strong that the Congressional hearings lasted an exceptional four months before the nomination was confirmed. The opposition came from both conservatives and liberals, from both Democrats and Republicans. This could be explained by the fact that Brandeis was going to be the first Jewish justice of the U.S. Supreme Court. But more likely it was due to the widespread awareness of "how greatly Brandeis differed from his fellow liberals in the Progressive years."[42]

Brandeis belongs to the tradition of transpersonal holism, and although Mill himself was closer to that tradition than his followers, the gap separating Mill from Brandeis was still significant. For instance, the Millian metaphor of the marketplace of ideas, which "suggests the arbitrary character of any given proposed idea ... *was never used by Brandeis.*"[43] He certainly acknowledged the epistemological fallibility of humans, but he thought of it as a merely partial and precarious ability to recognize and re-create eternal and self-subsistent values. This emerges quite clearly, if implicitly, in a crucial passage from *Gilbert v Minnesota*, a case relative to a statute abolishing the "liberty to teach, either in the privacy of the home or publicly, the doctrine of pacifism":

Like the course of the heavenly bodies, harmony in national life is a resultant of the struggle between contending forces. In frank expression of conflicting opinions lies the greatest promise of wisdom in governmental action.... There are times when those charged with the responsibility of Government, faced with *clear and present danger*, may conclude that suppression of divergent opinions is imperative; because the *emergency* does not permit *reliance upon the slower conquest of error by truth*. And in such emergencies the power to suppress exists.[44]

Brandeis's metaphoric use of the cosmic struggle of opposites to justify human and political dialectics is rooted in classical culture (one thinks of Heracleitus, among others), and we shall see in due course that this is not an accident. Brandeis limits the "clear and present danger" to emergencies, on the ground that dialogue is too essential a value to be suppressed because of some ordinary harm or of some falsity that can be conquered by truth through more dialogue. The essence of dialogue is for Brandeis metaphysical, as it represents within the microcosm of human and political life the macrocosmic truth of the harmonic strife of heavenly bodies, ruled by the Logos that posits the essential identity and unity of opposites. For Brandeis, the expression of relative points of view is not an end in itself but a means to promote wholeness, in the same way in which celestial harmony results from the pushes and pulls of heavenly bodies. In the sky and on the earth alike, *wholeness is the truth of partness*. Given that for Brandeis there is no doubt about the existence of truth and error, we can say that for him truth or goodness is perspective wholeness, and error or evil is unilateral and selfish partness, an essentially dualistic and separative state of mind.

In spite of the inner rootedness of outer errors, Brandeis did not think that wrong thoughts and speeches should be repressed only for their wrongness, because he knew that ethical and spiritual development is also and inevitably a process of learning through and from mistakes. Mistaken opinions may of course be harmful, so harmful as to generate situations of emergency. Yet, as opposed to Mill and Holmes, Brandeis believed that speech cannot be legitimately repressed until there is an emergency rather than an ordinary harm or danger. Thus, the harm caused by pacifist propaganda during a war, no doubt a serious harm from the government's point of view, was not for him sufficient to justify repression. In *Gilbert*, Holmes concurred with the majority, leaving Brandeis the only dissenter with the words: "I think you go too far."[45]

R. M. Cover correctly points out that in Brandeis's hands, Holmes' "'clear and present danger test' . . . is turned into an *exception*," acquiring "the status of an emergency exception to political deliberation." But Cover reduces Brandeis's position to a unilateral communitarianism exclusively centered on the political dimension, as if Brandeis were not the father of the modern right to privacy![46] Tribe is right in claiming that Brandeis "did not make the mistake of reducing freedom of speech to its instrumental role in the political system"; but then he unduly forces Brandeis into an opposite reductionism, stating that he considered freedom of speech "an end in itself."[47]

By definition, an end in itself is an absolute. If Brandeis had thought of freedom of speech as an absolute, clearly he would not have allowed its limitation even in emergencies, also because he could not have linked such destructive emergencies to an absolute value to begin with. The reality is that for Brandeis individual freedom becomes a fully immune end in itself only when reaching the deontologically absolute level of essence, thus encompassing universal responsibility and existential self-limitation. In other words, speech is absolutely free only when genuinely directed at the common and cosmic good. Such a dialectical understanding, whereby the end of the private right is the public good (and vice versa), already emerged in *Gilbert*, where Brandeis claimed that the "[f]ull and free exercise of this right [to assemble and speak freely] by the citizen is ordinarily also *his duty*."[48]

This approach is confirmed and further clarified in Brandeis's Concurring Opinion in *Whitney v California*, a 1927 case in which the union activity of a member of the Communist Party was deemed legitimate by the Court. He wrote:

Those who won our independence believed that the final end of the State was to make men free to develop their faculties; and that in its government the *deliberative* forces should prevail over the *arbitrary*. They valued liberty *both* as an end and as a means. They believed liberty to be the secret of happiness and courage to be the secret of liberty. They believed that freedom to think as you will and to speak as you think are *means* indispensable to the *discovery* and spread of political truth; that without free speech and assembly discussion would be futile; that with them, *discussion affords ordinarily adequate protection against the dissemination of noxious doctrines*; that the greatest menace to freedom is an inert people; that public discussion is a public duty."[49]

This passage reveals the implicit presence of the idea of the Whole of Wholes in Brandeis's political philosophy. For Brandeis there can be no freedom, individual or social, if people are inert, if they do not understand public life as a right/duty by learning to take on the larger point of view of the whole. Yet at the same time, the ultimate end of the State is said to be the private wholeness of its citizens, that is, the unhindered development of each individual's faculties. Individuality is not seen as a given, as for the liberal, but as something to be conquered. Like Humboldt, and without the uncertainties and compromises of Mill, Brandeis posits wholeness as the true goal of the individual, knowing however that there can be no private wholeness that excludes and opposes the social and universal other. Indeed, one of his favorite mottos was "Responsibility is the great developer of men."[50]

The prevalence of "deliberative" over "arbitrary" forces in government implies that the egoistic and therefore arbitrary interests composing a merely majoritarian will must surrender to general will and interests and that the public responsibility and compassion inherent in a truly general will cannot come about without being simultaneously present in the private mind of the citizens. This is why Brandeis linked political deliberation, as opposed to arbitrary decision-making, to the development of individual wholeness.

It is this universally responsible wholeness that characterizes liberty as an end, which Brandeis explicitly distinguished from liberty as a mere means. The latter, which is "freedom to think as you will and to speak as you think," is justified only insofar as it supports the "discovery of the political truth," that is, insofar as it is a means to true "deliberation." Because liberty as a means is also and primarily a means to liberty as an end, the latter must be essentially related to political deliberation in a way that shows its deepest core to be the individual's inner identification with political and cosmic universality.

This is implicit in Brandeis's assertion that the secret of happiness is liberty as an end, and the secret of such liberty is courage. We have seen, in Ch. 1, how both in the utilitarian and liberal traditions fear is the central concern, and that courage or any other heroic virtue has no intelligible value. For Brandeis, on the other hand, only the development of fearlessness can make one free: S/he is free who does not depend on the accidental and unpredictable actions of the other and outer, and fear is such dependence. Courage is the secret of liberty as *self-reliance*, and self-reliance is at once private wholeness, the inner completeness that does not depend on the other, and wholistic privacy, the perception that the other is essentially oneself rather than an external obstacle to be feared. We shall see in due course how this notion of self-reliance is central to the overall thought of Brandeis, who already in *Whitney* talked of *"courageous, self-reliant men* with confidence in the power of *free and fearless* reasoning applied through the process of popular government." The explicit identification of courage and self-reliance means that true self-reliance and freedom imply and require the courage of independence, which is also the courage to promote "free and fearless reasoning" in popular government by resisting the egoistic impulses, coming both from one's interiority and from the outside, that dominate the "arbitrary" decision-making of purely majoritarian and interest group politics. The latter is a part, the worst part, of "freedom" as a mere means, that "freedom to think as you will and to speak as you think," which includes the possibility of *falsity* and error. For Brandeis, such a liberty is legitimate only within a context in which the "deliberative forces" of truth and justice prevail, so that error itself—that is, the separative and "arbitrary" element that lives in the human mind—can be channeled toward the formation of a truly general will, without becoming fatally destructive:

To courageous, self-reliant men, with confidence in the power of free and fearless reasoning applied through the processes of popular government, no danger flowing from speech can be deemed clear and present, unless the incidence of the evil apprehended is so imminent that it may befall *before there is opportunity for full discussion*. If there be time to expose through discussion the falsehood and fallacies, to avert the evil by the *processes of education*, the remedy to be applied is more speech, not enforced silence. Only an *emergency* can justify repression. Such must be the rule *if authority is to be reconciled with freedom*.

Authority and freedom are not to be separated, as in liberalism, but dialectically reconciled. But if essential freedom and authority—that is, freedom and authority as ends—are perspectively identical, empirical freedom and authority are not necessarily so. So, whereas unnecessarily repressive authority is to be fought, the free expression of arbitrary and egoistic points of view is to be limited whenever it tends to destroy the legitimate authority of a genuine community. As before in *Gilbert*, Brandeis claims that "only emergency can justify repression," because ordinarily it is through "education" and persuasion, rather than force, that truth can prevail over error. Again, the educational function of the state is something foreign to the liberal tradition and goes back to classical republican and platonist political ideals.

Yet, when does the shift from persuasion to force become inevitable and the danger so "clear and present" as to justify repression? Brandeis's answer is: when "the incidence of the evil apprehended is so imminent that it may befall before there is opportunity for full discussion"; and in a subsequent passage he adds: "There must be the probability of a serious injury to the State." We know that for Brandeis the essence of the State is political deliberation, and therefore genuinely deliberative speech. To qualify as a serious threat, a speech must endanger the "opportunity for full discussion," that is, the possibility itself of open and rational speech. In other words, *to generate a situation of emergency, speech must destroy or threaten to destroy itself.* For Brandeis, speech that results in some harmful act but does not threaten the possibility itself of speech cannot be legitimately coerced. He admits of the need to "punish the first criminal act produced by false reasoning" (a quote from Jefferson) but makes it clear that repression must be directed at the criminal act as such, but at the deliberative level there should be more speech and education: "Among free men, the deterrents ordinarily to be applied to prevent crime are *education* and *punishment for violations of the law*, not abridgment of the rights of free speech and assembly." To be liable to coercion, speech must be *existentially self-destructive*, that is, destructive of either the speaking self or the communal and deliberative environment which that self is essentially one with and existentially part of. In this sense, the underlying *principle of non–self-destruction* was for Brandeis the tool to reconcile freedom and authority. Brandeis conceived of harm as a multilayered reality, so that legal coercion, to be legitimate, must operate within the specific layer in which the harmful action becomes self-destructive: "The fact that speech is likely to result in some violence or in destruction of property is not enough to justify its suppression. There must be the probability of a serious injury to the State."[51] A harm such as the destruction of property, paramount and paradigmatic in both liberal and conservative theories of the time, cannot justify interference into a higher sphere, such as deliberative speech, but ordinarily (apart from more-detailed considerations that we will develop later) only within the same proprietary realm. Supporting this approach is the principle of non–self-destruction. The destruction of property is inherently self-contradictory and thus ultimately self-destructive, because it is always either a *negation* of what one tries to appropriate as a *positive* value for oneself, as when the thief destroys what s/he wants to acquire, namely the secure possession of the goods s/he steals, or it annihilates property at the very moment in which the destroyer, believing to essentially harm the owner, attributes to a merely external good an almost spiritual value.

The same applies to the higher level of personality. With "violence," as opposed to "destruction of property," Brandeis clearly referred to violence against persons. Such a violence constitutes a deeper form of self-destruction, because it springs from a serious lack of respect for persons and thus for oneself as a person. Yet, though involving a higher level of coercion, we shall see that even self-destructive conduct relating to personality cannot justify the coercion of speech and reason.

The principle of non–self-destruction, in its articulation into the three levels of privacy, personality, and property, offers a radical alternative to the liberal conception of liberty. In opposition to the liberal rhetoric of Mill, Brandeis explicitly denies the idea of an absolutely immune sphere of rights: "Although the rights of free speech and assembly are fundamental, they are not in their nature absolute."[52] However, his defense of private liberty is much more efficacious, as he concretely allows for coercive interferences only in self-destructive emergencies and according to a hierarchy of dimensions that makes it the more difficult to interfere with, the more one approaches the higher freedoms of speech and the highest rights of privacy, although not even these can be said to be absolutely immune. Contrary to Mill, Brandeis never abandoned the belief in the reality of an absolute and self-subsistent essence, remaining at the same time always aware that such an essence manifests itself through non-absolute realities, to be ranked according to the relation that each of them has with (their) essence.

He was convinced of the spiritual nature of human beings, in which absolute freedom and universal responsibility merge. Continually, if implicitly, he reasserted the *principle of existential selfhood*, acknowledging it to be the true core of his notion of privacy. That principle commands to leave the self alone, because only by learning to remain deeply within itself, even when acting out in the world, can the self escape the corruptive forces that lure it out of its original nature. The priority of the principle and right of privacy thus rests on a notion of *self-direction* that claims that the more the individual selfhood is at stake, the more individual conduct must be immune from external interferences.

For Brandeis self-directed actions are immediately other-regarding, and we have seen how his defense of free speech, as opposed to that of Holmes, does not require that the speech be harmless and/or socially irrelevant. For Brandeis, the more self-directed the conduct, the more it is other-regarding, as shown by his belief that on the quality of independent thinking and critical speech rest the very possibility of communal life and the survival itself of the State. The heightened immunity of the self-directed conduct is justified by the need to promote the development, both in the individual and in the community, of a morally autonomous self—that is, a self autonomously capable of making ethically responsible choices. Though allowing for a certain degree of interference, the principle of non–self-destruction is fully coherent with the fundamental standard of self-direction, because it makes interference possible only when the existential self, that self-reliant and fearless core of ourselves on which self-direction depends, has lost all actual vitality within the specific layer of which the conduct interfered with is part.

The existential self represents the essentially real and empirically potential capacity for responsible and caring freedom. Conversely, self-destruction is the radicalization of the dualism of self and other, radicalization that is at the root of all evil. In this respect, all conduct that does not fall into such a dualistic error is equally valuable, be it noetic-spiritual, personal, or proprietary. Yet, precisely because all destructive dualism implies the reciprocal externalization of self and other, the more externalized the conduct, the higher the risk of radicalizing dualism into existential self-destruction. This is why Brandeis rejected Mill's equalization of the various dimensions of actions.

From his Supreme Court bench, Brandeis forcefully and repeatedly claimed the independence and priority of the right to privacy relative to the rights of property, thus trying to reverse what was a long established, although not uncontested, jurisprudential axiom.

We have seen how in *Boyd* Justice Bradley, writing for the Court, claimed that property was legally protected as the outer armor of the more essential values of personality and privacy. The decisions following *Boyd* obfuscated that conception. *Boyd* was at times both rejected and reaffirmed, and although in 1927 its decision was officially still in force, its nonpossessive presuppositions were deeply weakened.[53] The private sphere thus protected was conceived more and more in proprietary terms, which was becoming increasingly problematic: "Since this formalist sphere of privacy depended largely on traditional property concepts for its definition, technological change and modern methods of intruding on personal privacy, such as wiretapping, could present problems not readily answered by reference to the old categories."[54]

Such was the central issue emerging in *Olmstead v United States*, a case in which the Washington State police produced evidence collected after months of wiretapping on the telephone of Olmstead, the boss of a powerful band of liquor smugglers during Prohibition.[55] The majority opinion, written by Chief Justice Taft, claimed that because the Fourth Amendment explicitly protects only persons, houses, documents, and personal effects, wiretapping, which neither seizes a person and his properties nor is a search in the sense of "an actual *physical invasion* of his house," cannot be deemed unconstitutional.[56]

This combination of literalism and physicalism is inherently antiprivacy, privacy being the condition of the unmanifest. In spite of its formalist structure, Taft's opinion is not truly formalist, as Formalism was capable of acknowledging immaterial actions and rights, although still within the narrow boundaries of a possessivist and proprietary approach: Justice Butler's dissent, which recognized a right of property on the intangible good of conversation, is representative of such a position. The substance of Taft's opinion, on the other hand, was an absolutization of Legal Formalism's utilitarian side. Taft wanted to grant the police all possible means to fight crime, so as to maximize the social utility of public order, even at the cost of minimizing both individual rights and the ethical and legal duties of the police. In this respect, Taft's opinion is more utilitarian than that of Holmes, whose dissent was more utilitarian in method than in substance.

Holmes abstractly reasserted the primacy of consequentialism. He explained that although he was in agreement with the outcome of Brandeis's dissent, he was not "prepared to say that the *penumbra* of the Fourth and Fifth Amendments covers the defendant." For him, the question was not about principles more or less implicit in the Constitution but about the choice between two desired consequences:

Therefore we must consider the two objects of desire, both of which we cannot have, and make up our mind which to choose. It is desirable that criminals should be detected, and to that end all available evidence should be used. It is also desirable that the Government should not itself foster and pay for other crimes.

Putting things in purely consequentialist terms, the balance could not but bend toward Taft, who explained that the rejection of evidence that "discloses a conspiracy of amazing magnitude . . . would make society suffer and give criminals greater immunity than has been known heretofore." This is not to say that a different consequentialist argument could not be developed. Brandeis developed it by saying that "the tapping of one man's telephone line involves the tapping of the telephone of every other person whom he may call or who may call him." This argument can easily be translated in Millian terms: Although telephone conversations related to activities causing harm to others and society cannot be protected as self-regarding, tapping onto them infringes upon the self-regarding, intimate sphere of all who happen to be accidentally involved in them. But clearly this is a limited argument, which could not withstand the ability of today's computers to tap only on the conversations directly related to the crime. This is why, as we are about to see, Brandeis added a much more practically resilient and deontologically profound argument.

The unilateral consequentialism of the Millian harm principle reinforces positions such as that of Taft. Holmes himself accepted the premises of Taft's argument, siding with the outcome of Brandeis's dissent only because, contrary to what he would have done ten years earlier, he decided to give greater weight to substantively ethical and deontological considerations: "We have to choose, and for my part I think it is a less evil that some criminals should escape than that the Government should play an *ignoble* part."[57] After 1919, Brandeis's influence dug deeply into Holmes's soul. Had Holmes followed his original conception of power and politics, he would have scarcely cared for independent principles concerning nobility. But by incorporating a certain measure of genuine deontology, Holmes moved closer to the muffled core of Millian thought and thus to the resonant and consistent core of Brandeisianism. In this respect, the relation between Holmes and Brandeis exemplifies how Millianism can find its truest realization in a deeper acceptance of its own transpersonal side.

However, the increasingly close relationship between Holmes and Brandeis has often been read in the wrong way. For example, one commentator argues that in *Olmstead* "Holmes and Brandeis joined Chief Justice Taft in reasoning from social consequences." But if this is not fully true of Holmes, as we have seen, it is even less so of Brandeis. The very same commentator has to admit that only "Brandeis' penultimate argument was . . . pragmatic" (that is, in his terminology, consequentialist).[58] In fact, for Brandeis self-subsistent principles of justice are inherently productive of good consequences, but facts are good only insofar as they materially embody such principles. In the transpersonal tradition there is a distinction, not a dualism, between "a priori" and "a posteriori,'' and in fact in *Olmstead* Brandeis rested his consequentialist argument on the spiritually deontological right against forced self-incrimination. Such a right is at once ''a priori'' self-subsistent and ''a posteriori'' beneficial, because its deontological appeal to the intrinsic value of individual interiority is one with the belief that the harmful consequence of letting a criminal escape is nothing compared to the destruction of privacy, the dimension of ''being let alone'' on which the social and political life itself essentially depends.

Brandeis was close to Legal Realism, but only because Legal Realism was a complex movement, whose most sophisticated thinkers restored and enhanced, as against its Formalist ossification, the homeorhetic character of the American natural law tradition.[59] The same realistic and homeorhetic understanding of natural law sustains Brandeis's recognition of privacy as the invisible and concretely dynamic essence of the manifest reality of property and explains his adoption of an interpretive model whereby the written Constitution is perceived as the visible manifestation of unwritten ethical and legal universal principles. Against Taft's literalism, Brandeis quoted Chief Justice Marshall, who in *McCulloch v Maryland* [4 Wheat. 316, 407] wrote: ''We must never forget that it is a Constitution we are expounding''—a sentence that Brandeis interpreted through another quotation from *Weems v United States* [217 U.S. 349, 373]:

Time works changes, brings into existence new conditions and purposes. Therefore a *principle* to be *vital* must be capable of wider application than the mischief which gave it birth. This is peculiarly true of Constitutions. They are not ephemeral enactments, designed to meet passing occasions. They are, to use the words of Chief Justice Marshall, ''*designed to approach immortality* as nearly as human institutions can approach it.''

For Brandeis, thus, constitutions are meant to creatively express, within the space-time horizon, eternal and transcendent values. Writes Grey:

For the generation that framed the Constitution, the concept of a ''higher law,'' protecting ''natural rights,'' and taking precedence over ordinary positive law as a matter of political obligation, was widely shared and deeply felt. An essential element of American constitutionalism was the reduction to written form—and hence to positive law—of some of the principles of natural right. But at the same time, it was generally recognized that written constitutions could not completely codify the higher law. The ninth amendment is the textual expression of this idea in the federal Constitution.[60]

Brandeis operated from within that tradition, and it is quite significant, in this respect, that twice he referred back to Marshall who, like most English and American lawyers, very seldom used the expression ''natural law'' yet adopted a substantively natural law approach.[61] This is also confirmed by Holmes's reference, seen earlier, to Brandeis's appeal to the ''*penumbra*'' of the Fourth and Fifth Amendments. By linking the unwritten Constitution to a penumbral realm, which is never materially self-evident and determined once and for all, Brandeis restores to the natural law tradition its original nonossified character, whereby fundamental principles come alive within and through the concreteness of historical evolution:

> Subtler and more far-reaching means of invading privacy have become available to the Government . . . [and] have made it possible for the Government . . . to obtain disclosure of what is whispered in the closet. Moreover, "in the application of a constitution, our contemplation cannot be only of what has been but of what may be." The progress of science in furnishing the government with means of espionage is not likely to stop with wire-tapping. Ways may some day be developed by which the Government, without removing papers from secret drawers, can reproduce them in court. . . . Advances in the psychic and related sciences may bring means of exploring unexpressed beliefs, thoughts and emotions.

Brandeis's outstanding prophetic power, which earned him the nickname of "Isaiah," was due to his ability to select and evaluate facts not as mere data but as principled seeds of historical growth. His ability to foresee that governmental invasion will reach directly into the inner and psychic life rested on his firm appreciation of the centrality of contemplative and introspective privacy. As a fundamental principle, privacy has always been present in the law, and very appropriately Brandeis defined *Boyd* "a case that will be remembered as long as civil liberty lives in the United States." But Brandeis made fully explicit what *Boyd* had just begun to bring into light, the essential value and significance of privacy in relation to property. In discussing the previous use of the Fourth and Fifth Amendments, Brandeis wrote:

> The protection guaranteed by the two Amendments is much broader. The makers of our Constitution undertook to secure conditions favourable to the *pursuit of happiness*. They recognized the significance of *man's spiritual nature*, of his feelings and of his intellect. They knew that only a part of the pain, pleasure and satisfactions of life are to be found in material things. They sought to protect Americans in their beliefs, their thoughts, their emotions and their sensations. They conferred, as against the Government, *the right to be let alone—the most comprehensive of rights and the right most valued by civilized men.*[62]

This is the passage that more than any other reveals the stature of Brandeis's dissent in *Olmstead*, truly a fundamental contribution to the political philosophy of this century. Any ambiguity is swept away: Property and material goods are only a part of human happiness, and a part that cannot measure up to the spiritual nature of human beings. This is why Brandeis talks of the "pursuit of happiness" as the central goal of the founding fathers, following Jefferson's substitution of "life, liberty and the pursuit of happiness" for the more commercial "life, liberty and property." And this is why the reference to happiness is immediately followed by a reference to "man's spiritual nature": Happiness is essentially a spiritual condition, intrinsic to human nature and independent of external and material goods, useful or pleasant as they may be. Protecting the condition of being let alone promotes the possibility to practice and learn "self-reliance," the courageous independence from the outer that leads to the realization of one's own inner wholeness and that, by shedding away the egoism and the fear generated by "envious comparison" (Rousseau) makes it possible to compassionately identify with others and positively contribute to the happiness of all beings. It is this holographic characterization of the private selfhood in its solitude that sustains Brandeis's paradoxical definition of the right to privacy as the most comprehensive of all rights.

Brandeis could not accept the reduction of privacy to property over intangibles that was advanced by Butler, because, although it would have yielded the same concrete result in the specific case, it obscures the radical difference between a condition presupposing the dualism of owning subject and possessed object and a condition in which the intangible object is recognized as one with the subject's invisible and all-encompassing essence, thus manifesting and promoting non-duality. The different comprehensiveness of privacy and property is not just theoretical. Brandeis reasserted in *Olmstead* the central point of his 1890's article: What is at stake in cases like *Boyd* or *Olmstead* is not the tangible documents or the intangible conversations that are taken away from one's control but the privacy that they embody. This means that the right to privacy, as opposed to a right to property over intangibles, protects also against manipulative invasions of one's interiority, such as the bombardment of minds by TV and other mass-media, which do not take away any possessible good but rather add harmfully, and sometimes even destructively, onto one's essential and morally autonomous nature. This type of corrupting invasion has reached its zenith in our times. But we shall see how for Brandeis the risk of corruption is inherent in civilization as such, which, though full of ennobling potentialities, tends to bury the human spiritual nature under a mass of unnecessary relations and refinements. This is why Brandeis thought of the right to privacy as the right "most valued by civilized men." In the nakedness of privacy, human beings can go back to those free and compassionate roots from which any true civilization grows.

TOWARD A TRANSPERSONAL THEORY OF RIGHTS

In *Olmstead*, Brandeis implicitly applies the tripartite principle of non–self-destruction to legal enforcement by asserting that evidence on criminal economic transactions, such as illegal liquor trade, could not be acquired by violating rights related to higher spheres of human conduct. Although he accepted the power of the police to seize the fruits and instrumentalities of the crime, a power to interfere with objects belonging to the same possessive level of the criminal action, Brandeis rejected wiretapping on two grounds: in that it intruded upon all of Olmstead's conversations, including those of an intimate and personal nature, thus violating the sphere of his personality as protected by the Fourth Amendment; and more importantly, in that it was equivalent to an imposed self-incrimination and thus to a violation of the individual conscience and privacy as protected by the Fifth Amendment. Given that in *Whitney v California*, as we have seen in the previous section, Brandeis applied the principle of non–self-destruction also to the right protected by the First Amendment, it seems clear that he considered it a general, if implicit, constitutional principle.

However, the principle of non–self-destruction represents the emergency standard of a wider principle of existential harm, it itself grounded on the fundamental principle of existential or holographic selfhood, which applies also to ordinary situations, that is, to situations where the person still retains some significant measure of ethical awareness, although diminished by some wrong and harmful conduct. Thus, *existential selfhood*, whose shielding power increases with the increase of *self-direction*, grounds the *principle of existential harm* and becomes the *principle of non–self-destruction* in emergencies.

None of these principles is explicitly claimed by Brandeis, yet I believe that they constitute the very core of his thought. To be sure, they themselves derive from a much older tradition, and it is from this tradition, together with Brandeis's writings and opinions, that my theoretical systematization has taken inspiration.

The principle of existential harm asserts that any harm to others is a harm to self, not just because of the indirect empirical consequences that necessarily befall the agent but more poignantly because of the immediate and direct damage that any harm to others does to that agent's link with his/her holographic essence. On the other hand, any harm to self is a harm to others not just because of the indirect empirical consequences that our self-directed actions always have on others, but more crucially because the very essence of the community, which is a Whole of Wholes and thus a process in which individual parts are helped to become self-reliant wholes, is diminished the more an individual harms himself or herself and the greater the number of individuals who harm themselves.

We talk of existential rather than essential harm because essence lives in nonseparate independence and is thus immune from any direct harm; whereas harm affects that process of transformation whereby the merely empirical self becomes existential, aware of its at once outerly cosmic and innerly spiritual nature.

The empirical duality of self and other retains an important function in the context of self-direction, as this describes and measures the presence in each specific situation of the empirical self, in its physical separation from others, apart from any consideration of its level of existential awareness. But in our approach, the value of empirical self-direction is wholly derived from its relation to the development of existential and ethical awareness. From a mere empirical point of view, we can only descriptively distinguish between "being with others" and "being alone," as well as between the many instances of those conditions, but we cannot say anything about their different meaning and value. "Being alone" is but the principle of privacy, the "withdrawal/forthcoming" discussed in Ch.1, and it is through such a general and pervasive principle that the deeper principle of existential selfhood is brought in to give meaning to each specific instance of those conditions. Only then we can actually say, for instance in relation to "being alone" or "withdrawal/forthcoming," that property-centered solitude is potentially less conducive to such an awareness/selfhood than privacy, or noetic-spiritual solitude. It is thus the principle of existential privacy-selfhood that leads us to establish the hierarchical rights-tripartition of privacy, personality, and property, whereby the merely descriptive "aloneness" is subordinated to normative considerations. It is important to understand, however, that such a normative hierarchy not only does not deny the descriptive dimension, as the duality of self and other still plays an important role in the assessment of self-direction, but in fact refines it, as noetic-spiritual privacy descriptively corresponds to "being alone" more than property-centered solitude, with its externalizing concern for outer goods and matters.

Privacy is placed at the top of the hierarchical tripartition. Yet, precisely because of its existential private/public nature, privacy itself is subdivided into a self-directed privacy and an other-directed or *public privacy*. Brandeis claimed such a twofold priority of privacy when identifying as legally privileged, in relation to both personality and property, both "privacy," the condition of noetic and spiritual aloneness, and "deliberation." Deliberation is the public side of privacy not only because the general will it produces represents the interiority of the community but also because such a communal interiority, though in itself self-subsistent, can only be actualized as an organic convergence of deliberative private interiorities.

On the other hand, we have seen how self-direction is a general principle establishing, within all levels and dimensions, the priority of self-directed over other-directed actions. Within the twofold category of privacy, the principle of self-direction sets the inner life of privacy above the outer realm of political deliberation. This "aboveness" is more gradual than it may appear at first, as there is not only a political deliberation but also a private deliberation whereby the individual will is formed. This is the realm of moral autonomy, where private choices, be they of a proprietary, personal, or political nature, are made from the standpoint of a concrete and perspective universality. Of course choices are also the result of an egoistic or corporatist will, but as such they do not involve real deliberation. As the etymology itself explains, *de-liberation indicates "that which comes from liberation," that is, from the condition that is beyond any inner or outer conditioning, beyond any individual or communal ego.*

Autonomous moral deliberation is different from political deliberation, because, though still involving outer-directed choices, including political ones, it is set within a stage, that of inward and solitary reflection, which is prior to public other-directed expression. This twofold aspect is implicit in the very etymology of "autonomy," which refers both to privacy as self-referentiality (*autos*) and to the law or rule (*nomos*) inherent in every public and relational context. In this sense, the *principle of autonomy*, though an integral part of self-directed privacy, is a bridge between self-directed and other-directed privacy and shows the intimate connection between private and political self-government.

The dimensions of personality and property are also similarly subdivided by the principle of empirical self-direction. We thus obtain an ethical/legal hierarchy articulated on six levels, whereby self-directed privacy is nonseparately independent from the inferior level of other-directed or political privacy, which in turn is nonseparately independent from self-directed personality and so on, down to the last level of other-directed property. Before moving on to a more specific analysis of each of these six levels, we need to further explain the general meaning of the hierarchy itself.

We have seen that the higher the level in such a hierarchy, the higher the level of immunity from coercive interference, and the higher the judicial scrutiny of legal norms and governmental actions that directly or indirectly interfere. But what constitutes a coercive interference? In contemporary liberalism all interferences, including education and persuasion, tend to be delegitimized as implying some axiological hierarchy and thus as at least subtly coercive. Brandeis, on the other hand, proposed widespread education and dialogical persuasion as an alternative to coercion. Indeed, he attributed an eminently educational function to the State, thereby recognizing moral education as the true essence of the law. At the end of his *Olmstead* dissent, he wrote:

The greatest dangers to liberty lurk in insidious encroachment by men of zeal, well-meaning but *without understanding*. . . . In a *government of laws*, existence of the government will be imperiled if its fails to observe the law scrupulously. *Our Government is the potent, the omnipresent teacher*. For good or for ill, it teaches the whole people by its example.[63]

Brandeis's very notion of the good teacher prevented his educational theory of politics from falling into a moralistic paternalism. He considered the most powerful teacher to be the one that teaches "by its example" rather than by imparting notions from the outside. As before in *Whitney*, where he had claimed that "the final end of the State [is] to make men free to develop their faculties," Brandeis recognized law and politics as vehicles of *maieutics* in the Socratic sense, whereby teaching helps the student to give birth to that which is already present in him/her.[64]

From this point of view, apart from the inevitable corruptions of positive laws, the law is essentially freedom, as even its coercive element is but *freedom forced to force the unfree*, those who lack a sufficient measure of selfhood. Of course the empiricist would argue that there cannot be any such loss of self, as s/he identifies the self with the mere body/behavior. But such an empirical self, without the support of that essential and infinite self channeled by the existential and thus ethical awareness, is no self at all, being fully dissolved into sensuous/material interdependence. Given that in all genuine legal systems, coercion is based on the principle of non–self-destruction, thereby intervening when there is no self left to coerce but only a self to restore, we can see that right coercion is but the modality that freedom adopts in emergencies.

As we are talking about the restoration of selfhood, we clearly do not mean to confuse self-destruction with physical self-destruction. Physical self-destruction is the irreversible empirical aspect of the self-destruction of one's capacity for existential selfhood, which does imply bodily self-preservation but at the same time transcends it. The nonseparate independence of the existential from the physical can be seen both when physical self-destruction is the necessary outcome of one's moral and spiritual integrity, as with heroic acts of self-sacrifice; and, conversely, when the preservation of the physical life is accompanied by the loss of one's autonomous selfhood, as with serious addictions or voluntary slavery.

The principle of non–self-destruction, like the principle of existential selfhood that supports it, is articulated into the three dimensions of privacy, personality, and property, and as such it modulates the legitimacy of coercion. Let us start with *other-directed property* and economic action. In the previous section we have explained how such an action, when destructive of the properties of others, is inherently self-destructive. Contrary to common perception, property is a legal relation and is not to be confused with the material goods that bear such relation. Therefore, in order to destroy property, it is enough to destroy the right of property, that is, the control over the possessed object(s). This means that within the category of other-directed property, any harm qualifies immediately as destructive, because even the harm that does not destroy the owner's goods, as in the case of stealing, denies his/her right over it, which is all there is to property. The destruction of other-directed property, in turn, is immediately self-destructive, as we explained in the previous section, because it undermines the very proprietary relationship whose acquisition is the very end of the theft. The distinction between harming and destroying the goods invested by the property relation is of course relevant in assessing the gravity of the crime and thus the required intensity of coercion and punishment. Because at this level any harm constitutes self-destruction, in the realm of other-directed property, preventive coercion is always legitimate (apart from one fundamental exception that we shall see), assuming that it does not infringe upon personality and privacy.

As to punishment, its intensity depends both on the gravity of the harm and on the degree of involvement in the criminal action of the deeper layers of the actor's self. The situation of the occasional street protester who steals or smashes some property is different from that of the regular hooligan or petty thief. In the former case, the other-directed destructive action is the expression of an instinctual self slightly out of balance and possibly even supported by an interiority genuinely concerned with justice. In situations such as these, the punishment cannot but focus on the outer property destroyed, imposing on the protester, according to the circumstances of the case, which may even justify the harmful action altogether, some reparation of the property. In the case of a hooligan or of a recidivous petty thief, on the other hand, the instinctual self has reached or approached self-annihilation, and interference is needed in order to restore such self. Precisely because its goal is restoration, interference must rely on the self's higher layers—for instance, through appropriate psychological counseling, together with participation in the satisfaction of community needs. Finally, both of these cases differ from that of the professional thief or criminal, whose aim is a potentially unlimited accumulation of illegitimate wealth, even through violence against persons. Here, the self's deeper psychological layers, and the freedom and moral autonomy that spring from them, have clearly been overwhelmed by the cancerous overgrowth of the instinctual self. Therefore, coercion is bound to limit the freedom of the individual to act and move. The intensity of coercion, of course, depends on the degree of criminal corruption.

If the difference between petty and greedy stealing is important, that between greedy and needy stealing is paramount. A needy theft cannot be considered other-directed, because its goal is (bodily) self-preservation, and thus its primary and direct object is the self. Without *self-preservation*, there is never a chance to attain full selfhood, and whatever degree of selfhood one has already attained is bound to become irrelevant to the human law, because an honest but dead self is beyond the human reach. Individual self-preservation is therefore an intrinsic requirement of the law, both a natural individual right and a natural communal duty.[65] This is not to deny that needy stealing expresses moral imperfection, as perfect morality would require to value one's honesty more than one's life (the case of s/he who steals *for* the needy is different, showing instead a high level of morality). But morality, although being the very soul of the law, relates to the law in the form of nonseparate independence and therefore is not and cannot be fully encompassed by positive law.

But the individual right and communal duty do not stop at self-preservation, a requirement that could be satisfied even in the case of the slave. In relation to the economic realm of property, the individual right extends to *self-sufficiency*, which implies that enough share, individually and/or cooperatively, in the property of the means of production as to make one economically and thus politically independent. Property for self-sufficiency, then, is the control over the means to ensure self-preservation, which refers to those goods, such as housing, clothes, and food, or the income that buys them, without which it is generally impossible (except in those cases in which deprivation is a conscious spiritual choice) to survive with dignity in the human community; but it is also that which affords the individual the possibility to supplement the mere material survival with a level of prosperity sufficient to cultivate oneself intellectually and spiritually, and to autonomously participate in the life of the community. Property of the means of production, today, refers not only to self-employed workers such as farmers, craftsmen, and professionals but also to tenured public and private workers,[66] although it must be said that the latter, being involved in the mechanical and dehumanizing structure of public and private Bigness, cannot be said to be truly in control of their life or even their self-subsistence. The shift toward a more meaningful and cooperative kind of work is essential to restore the right of property to its original significance.

Of course, the right to self-preservation has priority over the right to self-sufficiency, which means that the latter could be compressed, during emergencies, in order to guarantee the generalized satisfaction of the former. But an important distinction must be made. Of course, in all those cases in which self-sufficiency yields barely enough to survive, there cannot be any compression. This means that the category of self-sufficiency is to be more properly identified with those external goods that produce more than the bare minimum for self-preservation, yet without falling into other-directed property, that is, into a wealth that does not relate any longer to the personal and family needs, be they material, recreational, and/or cultural, of the owner.

The right to self-preservation is essentially linked with privacy and interiority. Therefore, in spite of its definitional inclusion in the general category of property, it verges so intensely on the dimension of self-directed privacy as to be integrated into it for legal purposes, thereby acquiring the strength of a quasi-absolute right. If privacy is essentially interiority, the right to self-preservation, together with the amount of material goods necessary to satisfy it, is such an indispensable presupposition of privacy as to be one with it: With no living body, there is no exteriority in which to find interiority, no privacy relevant to human perception and law, although it can possibly be still relevant beyond the human dimension. As we began to explain in Ch.1, within each level of rights there is a more essential element that represents within that level of rights the general "principle of privacy." Thus, we can say that *physical or bodily privacy*, a privacy whose basic presupposition and most essential layer is the existence of a body, is the representative of the principle of privacy inside the right of property. Such a bodily privacy is to be understood both as self-preservation, as we said, and as that side of the "habeas corpus" that forbids interferences with the body that threaten its physical survival or violate its inner dignity. This means that bodily privacy is usually hidden inside the rights of property, insofar as they guarantee on the one hand the economical survival of the person and on the other hand the immunity of *the body as property of the individual* and as a spatial reality enclosed inside the spatial proprietary sphere. But it also means that in all instances in which property is insufficient to perform its protective function (think only of the many propertyless "free" workers who, lacking control over the ways, means, and time of work, lose control even of their bodies) then bodily privacy emerges in its full autonomy, showing itself to be that *essence of property* that, in emergencies, acquires the very same quasi-absolute strength of the right to privacy. Of course even bodily privacy, which as the property and self-property necessary to *self-preservation* can also be conceptualized as *property-privacy*, or "*private property*" in the strictest sense (self-sufficiency being only partially immune from public interferences), is ultimately subordinated to the interiority that it sustains, and so it can be both voluntarily renounced, as with heroic actions, and legitimately coerced, although only in exceptional circumstances, as when a citizen is forced to take up indispensable yet risky civic duties.

Both self-preservation and self-sufficiency are definitionally related to *self-directed property*, that is, to property in a proper sense. However, the integration of self-preserving property into privacy leaves self-sufficiency to define the category of self-directed property. Therefore, the *right to wealth*, which constitutes the category of *other-directed property*, is defined as the right to accumulate property beyond the level of self-sufficiency. It is the *absolutely relative right*, as it has any force at all against redistributive interferences only after basic self-sufficiency, or the control over the means of production necessary to ensure both the self-preservation and the ethical/noetic development of the individual, is universally guaranteed. This is something that is difficult to achieve in full, and this is why the complete submission of wealth to the redistributive requirements is practicable only in an ideal society. Under a government of wealth, such as in our liberal-utilitarian society, wealth cannot be absolutely subjected to a political power that in fact depends on it. It is important, thus, not only to promote the necessary social redistribution of wealth but also to help wealth transform itself to become a creative rather than destructive factor. Under a government ruled by the principle of wealth maximization the redistribution of private wealth, for the most part, tends to feed into the promotion of governmental and corporate Bigness, often at the expense of small and personal wealth. In such a situation, it is important to have laws that distinguish between the wealth that is a mere end to itself and the wealth that is used for social, ecological, and spiritual goals, finding ways to exempt the latter, at least partially, from taxation, because in such a case the wealth is autonomously performing a genuinely governmental function.

To understand how wealth can also be a factor of growth, it is important to see that one can indeed be wealthy without losing one's healthy self-reliance, including the readiness to renounce wealth if needed. But apart from the dehumanizing temptation inherent in excessive wealth, fully triumphant these days, the very fact that wealth may have to be renounced in order to promote both the autonomous selfhood of others and, in a fundamental sense, even the self that relinquishes wealth, shows how accidental its link with selfhood is.[67]

Although social, economic, and ecological responsibility involves also self-directed property, interference with it must sustain a higher scrutiny. As opposed to other-directed property, *including one's own wealth*, whereby any harm is immediately self-destructive and thus liable to coercion, in the case of self-directed property it is possible to distinguish between self-harm and self-destruction. If I harm or destroy some goods that are legitimately mine through violent behavior, or if I harm my overall patrimony through bad economic management, my proprietary control over the whole of my goods, which may have been reduced but not yet annihilated, is still in force, and my action cannot be configured as self-destructive. Thus, although the economic/ecological education of individuals is to be widely promoted, the shift to coercion in this area is allowed only when a harmful self-directed proprietary action turns existentially self-destructive, that is, either when it reaches the point of destroying one's capacity for self-preservation, or when it directly or indirectly threatens the economic self-sufficiency of the community and/or the survival of the ecological system, on which our own survival depends.

Immunity from coercive interference is further heightened at the level of *other-directed personality*. This is the area of personal relations and extends from relations with strangers to family life, from friendly to sexual intimacy. These relations presuppose a self and an other and so are empirically and legally other-directed, even though their genuine function is the education of the self to perceive the other as self. But the more intimate the relationship, the more immunity increases and becomes progressively closer to that afforded to self-directed personality, because the higher the level of intimacy, the more difficult to separate the selves involved, up to the most-radical intimacy between mother and fetus/baby.

Nevertheless, precisely because the empirical separation of self and other remains a factor even in the most-intimate relations, the falling back from true intimacy into a tendentiously exploitive and abusive dualism of subject and object remains, together with outer interference, always a possibility. But interference becomes increasingly exceptional the more we move from impersonal to personally intimate relations. In the former case, any harm to the other person implies existential self-destruction: By harming a stranger, who is related to us only abstractly, we deny personality as such, and thus even our own personality.

On the other hand, the more personal and intimate the relations, the more difficult it is to identify harms to others as self-destructive. For instance, when parents become moderately violent toward their children or toward each other, the harm may be a serious one, but it is set within a context, chosen or given as it may be, whereby the family members are supposed to learn, even through mistakes, reciprocal love and respect. Such cases allow, and may indeed require, persuasive interferences but do not legitimize any outer coercion until the physical, emotional, or mental integrity of a family member is threatened with destruction, and thus in such a way as to exclude the possibility of an internal resolution and overcoming of the family's conflicts. We cannot deal with the details of such a complex and difficult issue, but it seems possible to establish a general principle for the area of other-directed personality: The more intimate, long, and deep the relation, the more the existential harm needs to approximate existential self-destruction in order to legitimize coercive interferences.

When we move into the area of *self-directed personality*, nothing short of a clear and present danger of thorough self-destruction can authorize coercion. This area is centered on individuality in its material and active self-referentiality, and thus on the immunity of one's body/behavior from external impositions on one's decisional freedom. Here we meet the other side of the ''habeas corpus'': whereas inside the right of property stands a ''passive'' bodily privacy, the shield from all attempts to reduce one's body into someone else's possession, here we find that "active" bodily privacy, relating to one's freedom to use and move and behave within one's body, which is immediately related to and grounded on a more critical "*habeas mentem.*" In fact, although here the body is still involved, it is its activity that is at stake, and the activity and behavior of the body are not a physical reality but the product of a mental energy and impulse. Physical exercise, the freedom to move, and the freedom to care for one's own health, are typical of this category, which also includes all actions expressive of one's personal preferences, both productive, as with the pursuit of certain hobbies, and consumptive, as with listening to a certain music, choosing a certain diet, or consuming certain substances. As before with property, the element of *mental privacy* that lives in and sustains self-directed personality, though ordinarily protected by personality rights, maintains with them a relation of nonseparate independence, and in situations of emergency, when the mind is more directly and nakedly at stake, it emerges as an independent component of the stronger right to privacy. We shall explore this at the end of Ch. 4.

Meanwhile, an important distinction that clarifies the difference between the self-directed personality and the mental privacy that lives in it is that between *taste*, which is an inner reality, and the *behavior* that embodies it. Whereas the latter always implies and requires the former, the reverse is not necessarily true. Taste, though at least partially endowed with the dignity of interiority, cannot claim an absolute right to being actualized, because it could be characterized by wickedness or be incompatible with the material conditions in which its actualization is supposed to take place. Thus, the limiting of the individual freedom of choice is implemented at the level of action, leaving taste itself untouched. Yet, according to the general principle of nonseparate independence, the abridgment of the action depends on the taste from which the action springs, and more precisely on both the intrinsic quality of the taste and on its relation to the outer circumstances. Although the outer context is in this sense important, ultimately it is taste that is more critical, because truly good taste has in itself the ability to minimize harmful impacts on the social and natural environment. As opposed to bad, or merely rich and decadent taste, good taste is attuned to a realm of beauty that does not depend on outer materials and goods but accidentally, and transcends also all merely personal needs and attachments, the true source of the dependence of taste on external goods.

In this respect, the crucial distinction is the one between merely personal taste—which evolves out of external patterns of socialization or *habits*, whose deep but still heteronomous penetration of the human soul leaves ample room for possible corruption—and transpersonal taste, which is at once individual and universal because it is based on an inner spontaneity attuned with the inherent beauty and order of the world. Only in this second sense does taste become a true form of freedom and must be respected also in its outer manifestations. As to personal taste, it is still the element that represents mental privacy within self-directed personality. This means that although its outer manifestations may not be immune from interferences and limitations, no coercive or manipulative interference is possible to forcefully modify one's taste, as it happens for instance with the overwhelming advertising we are subjected to these days. When this happens, it is no longer personality rights that are at stake but again the stronger right to formational and mental privacy.

In relation to productive and expressive activities, the distinction between transpersonal and personal taste means that hobbies, or personally creative habits, are liable to limitations that cannot equally apply to genuinely artistic acts, because they clearly do not contribute as much to the formation of a more insightful social consciousness, and thus to a more genuine political deliberation. I am not belittling creative hobbies, which do perform important individual and social functions. So much so, that in fact the distinction between art and hobbies does not need to be made except in emergencies. We can think of a case, for instance, in which a socially widespread hobby (say woodwork, assuming that it became widely popular) may have to be limited in order to avoid a serious threat to the environment. In such a case, genuine art should lead the way in reducing the use of wood, because beauty can be expressed through all sorts of media. Nevertheless, artists may also want to use wood in order to honor the intrinsic beauty and meaning of the world of trees, or because of some other good aesthetic reason. Thus, the law should exempt genuine artistic endeavors from the limitations imposed on the hobby, on the ground that their cultural, symbolic, and political value is higher than the cost the community may have to pay, and which can never be too high, because genuine art is necessarily less widespread than hobbies. The distinction between art and habit is of course controversial, but when forced by emergencies, we cannot avoid the responsibility of judging, and we can only hope to have the best of judges.

The same principle applies to the second category of self-directed personal action, namely personal consumption, be it food or cultural products. The tension between taste and behavior is equally important in this category, as is the distinction between personal and transpersonal taste and between habit and truly free choice. As opposed to the liberals, we have no delusion about the fact that some choices are ethically superior. For instance, we do not doubt that, from a point of view that is at once deontological and consequentialist, some models of consumption are better than others, both for the person and for the planet. Which are the better choices is not predetermined, but the formal principles that preside over them are, being essentially related to the substantive form of the Whole of Wholes. This means that the determination of such principles into concrete choices requires deep thinking and a wide open principled debate, both in the person and in the community.

Neither liberalism nor the dominant versions of communitarianism can consistently sustain such an approach. For the consistent liberal, there cannot be any debate about what is best, every choice being unquestionable, so long as the legally competent individual desires it. Communitarians, on the other hand, are ready to support both educational and coercive interferences, but mostly when they are representative of the traditional and conventional ethical-legal values of the community, which are generally placed above debate. Dialectical holism, which stresses the value of political deliberation as rooted in the formal/ substantive deontology of the Whole of Wholes, with its implied principle of existential harm, constitutes a radical alternative to both.

For instance, if the "community values" standard had been applied in the recent past, the overconsumption of meat, coffee, tobacco, and alcohol, having become fully entrenched in the way of life of modern capitalistic societies, could never have been questioned. The fact that the liberal structuring of those societies has allowed the criticism of such a way of life, though of course the liberals themselves have remained officially neutral about it, has made it possible to spread a certain awareness of its harmfulness. Yet, on the other hand, the deep-seated sensuous/materialistic and hedonistic foundations of liberal societies have curbed the full development of such a debate and even more the practical implementation of its emerging results. What is intrinsically and deontologically good and beneficial is bound to emerge in the long run as productive of good consequences, and what is intrinsically bad as eventually destructive. Therefore, the maintenance of an open and honest debate about what is good and bad, whereby differences are welcome so long as they do not turn existentially self-destructive, seems to lead quite necessarily toward the eventual emergence and recognition of the good.

But for such a debate to exist, there must be a solid conviction that good and evil are existentially if not ultimately real, and that even though the good can never be concretely predetermined—because what is good here and now may not be good tomorrow—its fundamental and empty form encompasses an infinite number of right answers, and yet only one right solution for each "here and now."

Considering that the excessive consumption of meat on a worldwide scale, in fact on a western scale, is now acknowledged to be one of the main "clear and present dangers" in the destruction of the planet,[68] there doesn't seem to be any rational ground against the legal limitation of the consumption and distribution of meat, unless a sincere but fatally abstract liberalism, or blatantly capitalistic interests, can be said to be rational.

Meat overconsumption is a complex case because, although a self-directed personal action, it allows for a shift from persuasion to coercion mainly on the ground that it compresses property rights of others, thereby involving the category of other-directed property. This shows how proprietary and economic action is inseparable from the emotional and/or aesthetical personality that sustains it, even though the latter, in its nonseparate independence, cannot be reduced to the former. When the risk of self-destruction is more personal than social, though the external good at stake is such that its overconsumption remains within the limits of the self-directed property and also is not economically self-destructive, personality emerges as the independent and primary factor.

For example, the excessive use of alcohol (and the same applies to TV) does not directly involve other-directed property, and apart from those situations in which alcoholism has become an unbearable social plague or in which one becomes unable to take care of one's own self-preservation, it really concerns the management of one's bodily and behavioral personality and through it one's psychological integrity and capacity for rational choices. Like taste, to which it is intimately connected, choice is part of interiority and, when not yet actualized, is still characterized by the freedom inherent in the inner realm. But once reified into personal or proprietary actions, choice acquires the existential quality and limits of such actions, so that the possibility of being freely actualized depends on the measure of its incorporation of the universal responsibility inherent in the realm of essence. This means that true free choice rests on nonchoice, that is, on the freedom from attachment to any of the externals from which one has to choose. Such an attachment, in fact, forces upon the will of the presumed chooser predetermined choices that, although not inherently destructive or self-destructive, may become so due to their inability to change and evolve along with the universe from which the chooser and his/her choices are in fact inseparable. This, in turn, hinders the emergence of the only true free choice, the choice that is right for that individual in that place and time in the universe, and that s/he would spontaneously choose if only s/he could see the larger, infinite picture with which s/he is perspectively and holographically identical.

Whenever a choice becomes so overwhelmingly habitual or obsessive as to threaten the ability itself to choose otherwise, and therefore to choose as such, we talk of personal self-destruction. *Addiction*, widely understood, is the essence of personal self-destruction, though of course not any degree or type of addiction is in that sense self-destructive, because even a good life can involve more or less mild addictions to things and persons. Self-destructive addiction is the process whereby one's whole personality and life are taken over by one or a few obsessive choices. Full-blown alcoholism, drug-dependency (including legal pharmaceutical drugs), pornomania, and so forth, are all forms of self-destructive addiction. The reference to life and personality is important, because an addiction can utterly destroy one's life and personality, though only damaging, no matter how seriously, the deeper realm of interiority and privacy. Even when addiction involves the nonseparate privacy/interiority present within the realm of personality, there always remains a deeper if unconscious layer of inner self-subsistence that transcends all personal preferences and attachments and is therefore open to new and better choices. Thus, although at times all moral autonomy may fully deteriorate, the possibility of its resurgence is never lost, also because often self-degradation brings us closer to that deepest layer, where our power may be reborn like a phoenix rising from its own ashes. Again, in this instance too the level of coercion depends on how much one's capacity for moral autonomy has been involved in the destruction of personality. And here too the interference cannot but be maieutical, working to reestablish the addict's own self-reliance (as in the exemplary experience of Alcoholics Anonymous).

Brandeis applied these ideas to the question of alcohol consumption in a way that was radically different from that of liberalism. For Mill, the consumption of alcohol or drugs belongs to the class of self-regarding actions and can become an object of legal interference only when harmful to others: "The making himself drunk, in a person whom drunkenness excites to do *harm to others*, is a crime against others."[69] Brandeis takes a very different approach. He personally wrote the Court opinions in four different cases establishing the constitutional legitimacy of the Volstead Act, the statute giving rise to the Prohibition Era.[70] Mason comments: "The Prophet stumbles. . . . One sees in these cases evidence of paternalism in the moral sphere. . . . Brandeis took a stand strangely out of key with his customary liberalism."[71] Mason also notices how "conservative" Brandeis's position was relative to the "liberal" position he took many years earlier in 1891. In 1891 he represented the Massachusetts Liquor Dealers Association in front of a legislative committee, thus summarizing the first half of his argument: "Liquor drinking is not a wrong; but excessive drinking is. Liquor will be sold; hence the sale should be licensed. Liquor is dangerous; hence the business should be regulated. No regulation can be enforced which is not reasonable." This passage reveals once again how Brandeis was simply beyond the dichotomy of conservatism/liberalism. Liberals would still consider Brandeis's 1891 position moralistic and paternalistic. Although he distinguished between drinking and excessive drinking, thereby rejecting any bigoted demonization of alcohol, he stated unhesitatingly that excessive drinking is a wrong. There is no need for a harm to others: Excessive drinking is in itself "a wrong," a term that leaves little doubt about the direct legal relevance that Brandeis attributed to such a "moral" mistake. The reason is simple: "Liquor is dangerous," and dangerous existentially, that is, at once for the individual and for the community. Consequently, though representing the liquor business, Brandeis acknowledged the power and duty of the State to license and regulate such business. That the State could use its power of regulation to foster moderate drinking is a concept that Mill himself, let alone the contemporary liberal, considers unacceptable.[72]

At the same time, Brandeis was adamant about the need for reasonable regulations, free from any irrational moralism. This is the very same theoretical position that he took in his Volstead Act pronouncements. In 1919, in *Ruppert v Caffey* (251 U.S. 264, at 282), Brandeis sustained the Volstead Act by explicitly including the regulation of alcohol consumption within the State's general power to promote the health, security, and morality of the community. Yet, at about the same time, in a letter to his wife, he quoted a Biblical passage to praise the wisdom of legalizing the pleasure of drinking.[73] The "reasonable regulation" approach remained unaltered, because Brandeis thought that the Volstead Act was a reasonable regulation. The Act did not prohibit liquors altogether and permitted drinks with an alcoholic gradation varying from 1 percent to 2.5 percent. Though the percentage is low, the fact that low-gradation beers and wines could still be sold, and thus individuals could still enjoy moderate drinking, played an important role in Brandeis's evaluation. Furthermore, in 1920 Brandeis asked P. U. Kellog to survey the social and economic effects that Prohibition was having on the life of American cities: The results confirmed Brandeis's view that the Volstead Act was beneficial and thus a reasonable regulation.[74] Brandeis's pragmatic judgment may be questioned, but that does not extol from the virtue and distinctiveness of his theoretical approach, which ultimately rests on a dialectical and dynamic combination of the necessary amount of regulation with the maieutical promotion of self-regulation, as shown by the second part of Brandeis's 1891 statement: "The better the men who sell liquor, the less the harm done by it. Hence, strive to secure for the business those who are respectable. Self-respect and prosperity are the most effective guardians of morals. Unenforceable or harassing laws tend to make criminals."[75] For Brandeis, the final answer is people's self-government. But only people who strive toward self-reliance and ethical autonomy, thus learning to reconcile freedom and responsibility, can govern themselves. In fact, only people who are in this sense morally autonomous can have "self-respect," and this is why the promotion of self-reliance and self-respect, and of the material prosperity that concretely secures them, are said to be the best guardians of morals.

Brandeis upheld these same ideas in relation to the Volstead Act, the only difference being that circumstances had changed so much as to make him consider alcohol a much more dangerous threat to individual and political self-government. Nevertheless, his goal remained the restoration of an ethically responsible privacy, possibly capable of enjoying moderate drinking. It is very significant, in this respect, that Brandeis's strongest pronouncement in favor of the right to privacy is found in *Olmstead*, which was concerned with the very application of the Volstead Act. Read in relation to his other Volstead Act pronouncements, Brandeis's dissent in *Olmstead* expresses the notion that governmental interference with self-directed personality is legitimate only insofar as it promotes the higher value of privacy.

Coming finally to the level of privacy, we will not repeat how participation in political deliberation and the parallel freedom of expression are manifestations of *other-directed privacy*. Speech and expression, of course, are also present within the levels of property and personality, but only deliberative speech enjoys the heightened protection of other-directed privacy. To be deliberative, speech must be objectively centered on some self-subsistent, general, and universal standard, even when it focuses upon particular facts and actions. This is the case with religious speech, cultural-scientific speech (including philosophical and artistic expression), and political speech, all of which purport to promote the general interest and universal truths (including the universal truths of skepticism and relativism), even when their content and subjective inspiration betray that presupposition. The defining core of deliberative speech, in its higher degree of self-direction and lower degree of particularistic externalization, is the non-separate independence from one's personal and proprietary conditions. Brandeis explicitly adopted this criterion when appealing to the classical jurisprudential distinction of "advocacy" and "incitement" in *Whitney*: "Advocacy of violation, however reprehensible morally, is not a justification for denying free speech where the advocacy falls short of incitement and there is nothing to indicate that the advocacy would be immediately acted upon.'' As long as it remains within the boundaries of thought, which, when it is not yet entangled with harmful and irrational actions, is still open to rational persuasion, speech enjoys a very high immunity. We will return on this in Ch. 4.

To conclude, we need to say a few more things about *self-directed privacy*, the pinnacle of the hierarchical continuum of self-direction. Although it includes bodily privacy (but it is the body as a sacred mask of the human spirit), this category involves primarily mental and spiritual privacy, the realm of thought. It is thus the right of a noetic reflexivity that manifests itself into different aspects: It can be the emotional reflexivity of introspection; the critical reflexivity of intellectual and scientific thought; the symbolic reflexivity of art, myth, or oneiric experiences; the spiritual reflexivity of pure contemplation. Noetic reflexivity has also different degrees of purity, and its purest realization and essence are constituted, whatever the path chosen to reach it, by the mind of enlightenment, that ineffable tautology in which the self has no longer any other as a limit to itself and blossoms into an infinite awareness whose absolute freedom is, immediately and inevitably, universal compassion and responsibility.

But of course reflexivity has also many less enlightened states, down to those corrupt forms of thought that claim the radical and even violent opposition of some self to some other, as with racism, sexism, classism, and selfish individualism. But, as we have already said, as long as it remains within itself, thought and the psychic life constitute the true home of selfhood, the only place that, run down as it may be, the self can go back to its original and enlightened essence. This means that thought cannot be coerced but only helped through to more and better thought, through thoughtful dialogue (according to the Socratic lesson). Coercion can only intervene where bad thinking, which is incapable of self-reliance and is thus inherently bent toward dualistic externalizations, necessarily unfolds into existentially self-destructive speeches and/or actions. Yet even then, what is coerced is the outer manifestation, not the noetic privacy.

This brings us to the question: Is self-directed privacy completely immune from the dangers of self-destruction and therefore from the possibility of coercive interference? On the one hand, it is possible to think of exceptional cases in which even noetic privacy seems to approach self-destruction, as with destructive mental illnesses. The determination of what constitutes a destructive mental illness is too lengthy and complex a subject, and here we can only presume that mental illnesses capable of seriously compromising one's mental capacities do exist and can properly and cautiously be assessed and measured. In such cases, interference becomes inevitable, and in this sense not even noetic privacy can be awarded an empirically absolute right. On the other hand, even in this case interference is legitimate only when directed at the maieutical restoration of the autonomous interiority buried within the illness. This is due to the fact that, as we have seen all along, there is a more fundamental, absolute, and indestructible privacy where essence silently glimmers, ready to emerge into an existential awareness. It is therefore through self-directed privacy that all other dimensions more or less consciously connect with the implicit reality and explicit potentiality of the absolutely free, just, and loving selfhood, the only condition that deserves absolute immunity. This is why the right to privacy is "the most comprehensive of all rights," essentially present within each and every dimension of rights, and approaching, even if without fully attaining, the status of a practically absolute right.

NOTES

1. L. B. Boudin, "Justice Holmes and His World," in *Lawyers Guild Rev.*, III, 4 (1943), p. 37.
2. See Holmes, "The Gas-Stokers Strike," in VII *Amer.L.R.* 582 (1873), pp. 583–84.
3. Holmes, *Collected Legal Papers*, p. 258.
4. J. C. Ford, "The Totalitarian Justice Holmes," in *Catholic World* 159 (1944): 114.
5. See *Patterson v. Colorado*, 205 U.S. 454 (1907), and *Moyer v. Peabody*, 212 U.S. 78 (1909). In both cases Holmes wrote majority opinions that "nullified the freedom of the press guaranteed by the First Amendment." Green, "The Supreme Court, the Bill of Rights and the States," in 97 *Univ. of Penn.L.R.* 608 (1949), 629.
6. *Holmes-Laski Letters*, II, 948.
7. Holmes, "The Gas-Stokers Strike" p. 583.
8. "There are obviously many 'sources' for these views of Holmes. Both the classic liberalism of Mill and the social Darwinism of Spencer converge in their notion that in minorities may reside the seed for future growth of society." R. M. Cover, "The Left, the Right and the First Amendment: 1918–1928" in *Maryland L.R.* 40, 3 (1981); p. 383.
9. 249 U.S. 47, at 52. As noted by Corwin, Holmes was indifferent to the fact that there was no evidence to the concrete effects of the letters, "apart from their content and the fact of their publication." Corwin, "Bowing out 'Clear and Present Danger,' " in XXVII *Notre Dame Lawyer* 325 (1952), p. 329.
10. 250 U.S. 616 (1919), at 630.
11. S. Ingber rightly considers Mill the originator of Holmes's theory of the "marketplace of ideas," though he fails to properly assess their differences. S. Ingber, "The Marketplace of Ideas: A Legitimizing Myth," in *Duke L.J.* (1984): 1.
12. J. S. Mill, "On Liberty" (1859), in *Utilitarianism, On Liberty, Considerations on Representative Government*, London: Everyman's Library, p. 78 and p. 124.
13. Ibid., p. 80, p. 85.
14. Ibid., p. 111.
15. "Whenever liberalism is attacked today, John Stuart Mill's name will almost certainly be mentioned." C. L. Ten, *Mill on Liberty* (Oxford, 1980) p. 1. Ten argues that Mill is a consistent liberal and thus a nonutilitarian.
16. A. and G. Horowitz correctly state that Mill rejected Bentham's thought "in favour of an *almost Platonic* view of happiness, and all in the name of Utility." *Everywhere They Are in Chains* (Canada: Nelson, 1988), p. 172.
17. Mill, *On Liberty*, p. 79.
18. For all the above quotations see Mill, in *Utilitarianism*, pp. 8–18.

19. Mill wrote that "the youth Socrates . . . asserted . . . the theory of utilitarianism against the popular morality of the so-called sophist." *Utilitarianism*, p. 1. Though clearly forcing Socrates' thought, this passage shows how close to the Platonic hero Mill felt. In *On Liberty*, he talks of the "lofty inspiration of Plato and the judicious utilitarianism of Aristotle."

20. For the above quotations and argument see Mill, in *Utilitarianism*, Ch. 4, pp. 36–40.

21. Precisely because the "natural tendency of representative government, as of modern civilisation, is toward collective mediocrity," Mill proposes specific political privileges for the "instructed few," such as: the separate election of representatives of the "instructed minority"; and the attribution of more than one vote to professionals, university graduates, and those with a similar level of education. *On Representative Government*, Chps. 7–8. On the other hand, he believes that political participation in such a culturally enhanced democracy is essential to raise the sentiment of the masses from the narrow horizon of economic and family matters to a universalistic concern with the common good.

22. W. von Humboldt, *The Sphere and Duties of Government*, p. 11, quoted in "On Liberty," p. 125.

23. Ten, p. 72, and generally Ch. 5.

24. *On Representative Government*, p. 213, and Ch. 2.

25. Rousseau, *Du Contrat Social*, II, 10.

26. *The Life and Times of Liberal Democracy* (Oxford, 1977), p. 61, which refers to Mill, *Principles of Political Economy*, IV, vii, 6–7. In sect. 7, Mill claims that only the competitive and ultimately accumulative passions can guarantee the performance of good work and lower prices. The problem is not the fact of outer competition in the market, which may be somewhat inevitable, but the idea that competition is needed as a psychological factor, as if good work could not be the result simply of the love of one's work. Mill was too much steeped into the capitalistic system of production to think that work could actually be enjoyable in itself.

27. For Mill's arguments (and above quotations) on accumulative impulses and steady-state economics, see *Principles of Political Economy*, IV, vi.

28. On steady-state economics, and on Mill's relevance to it, see H. Daly, *Steady-State Economics* (Freeman, 1977). For a discussion of self-sufficient, neither stationary nor growth-oriented economic systems, see F. Schumacher, *Small is Beautiful* (Abacus, 1974).

29. *On Representative Government*, Ch. 3, pp. 228–31.

30. "On Liberty," Ch. 2, p. 115.

31. *Utilitarianism*, Ch. 2, p. 25. For the Myth of Er see *Politeia*, X, 613–20.

32. H. J. McCloskey, "The Political Ideal of Privacy," in *Philosophical Quarterly* 21 (1971): 303, p. 304. The author, who believes that "the case for privacy is basically an ideal utilitarian one" (p. 313), thus adopting a Millian perspective, notices that the lack of discussion of privacy seems to characterize most classical liberal thinkers.

33. Mill "On Liberty" Ch. 5, pp. 183–85.

34. For an anthology of the critical appraisals of Mill's "On Liberty," see P. Radcliffe (ed.), *Limits of Liberties. Studies on Mill's On Liberty* (Wadsworth, 1966).

35. For all quotations, "On Liberty," Ch. 1, pp. 80–81; Ch. 3, p. 123; Ch. 4, pp. 149–52.

36. One of the first to notice the contradiction between Mill's utilitarian premises and

his theory of liberty has been F. Stephens, *Liberty, Equality, Fraternity* (1873), New York, 1882), p. 50.

37. Talking about actions that may be considered by some to be noxious to the actor, Mill writes: "These are good reasons for remonstrating with him, or reasoning with him, or persuading him, or entreating him, but not for compelling him." "On Liberty," Ch. 1, p. 78. In Ch. 4, pp. 150–52, Mill argues in favor of the power, right, and duty of society to educate children so as to "make them capable of rational conduct in life."

38. Mill's legal positivism emerges in his claim that:"*Justum* is a form of *jussum*" and that the "penal sanction . . . is the essence of the law." *Utilitarianism*, Ch. 1, p. 48, p. 50.

39. Mill, "On Liberty," Ch. 4, p. 150.

40. "Clearly his views of reality, ideas and language more closely resembled J. S. Mill's than those of the early utilitarian thinkers. But Mill's idea developed within the utilitarian tradition, and Holmes's methodology ought to be perceived in the same way." H. L. Pohlman, *Justice Holmes and Utilitarian Jurisprudence* (Harvard, 1984), p. 143.

41. Mill, "On Liberty," p. 123.

42. Konefsky, *The Legacy of Holmes and Brandeis* (MacMillan, 1956), p. 75. For a detailed account of the facts described here see A. Mason, *Brandeis: A Free Man's Life* (New York: Viking, 1946), pp. 365–408, pp. 465–508.

43. Cover, p. 373.

44. 245 U.S. 325 (1920), at 343, 338.

45. Holmes's letter to Brandeis, *Brandeis Papers*, 5–13, Harvard Law Library.

46. "Brandeis had not accounted for the many non-political and informal ways that cultures and societies arrive at 'truth.' . . . Brandeis brought philosophy down to earth but may have impoverished it in stressing concrete political processes." See Cover, pp. 381–82.

47. Tribe, p. 788.

48. 254 U.S. 338.

49. 274 U.S. 357 (1927), at 375.

50. See *St. Joseph Stock Yards Co. v United States*, 298 U.S. 38 (1936), at 92.

51. For all quotations, 274 U.S. 357, at 377–78; for Jefferson's quote at 375, note 2.

52. 274 U.S. 357, at 373.

53. In *Johnson v United States*, 228 U.S. 457 (1913), the Court stated that the Fifth Amendment could no longer be invoked against the judicial use of the accused's documents no longer in his possession; in *Adams v New York*, 192 U.S. 585 (1904), *Boyd* was reversed on the ground that the courts needed to inquire neither on the nature of evidence nor on the way it was obtained. But two other cases, *Weeks v United States*, 232 U.S. 383 (1914), and *Gouled v United States*, 255 U.S. 298 (1921), reaffirmed *Boyd*.

54. Note, "Formalism," p. 961.

55. 277 U.S. 438 (1927).

56. 277 U.S. 438, at 466.

57. 277 U.S. 438, at 469–70. For Brandeis's quote, at 476.

58. Note, "Formalism," pp. 963–64.

59. According to J. Shklar, the various American legal realists were united by a common denominator: They "wanted to get away from both natural law and analytical jurisprudence. In the end, however, the radical exponents of the realist doctrine . . . did emerge with only another form of natural law doctrine." Among these "radical realists" was Jerome Frank, whom Shklar calls the "legally most sophisticated among them,"

and who was close both to Brandeis and, on a more personal level, to Justice Douglas. See J. Shklar, *Legalism*, Harvard, 1964, pp. 93–94.

60. T. Grey, "Do We Have an Unwritten Constitution?," in *Stanford L.R.* 27 (1975): 703, 715–16.

61. "Marshall, it is true, refers but rarely to the law of nature. Like the English lawyers, he ordinarily preferred some other term. But it seems clear that his opinions contain many statements indicative of faith in that concept." B. F. Wright, *American Interpretations of Natural Law* (New York, 1962), p. 295. Among other cases, Wright mentions *Johnson and Graham's Lesse v M'Intosh*, 8 Wheat. 543, 572 (1823), where Marshall speaks of "principles of abstract justice, which the Creator of all things has impressed on the mind of his creature man, and which are admitted to regulate, in a great degree, the rights of civilized nations."

62. 277 U.S. 438, at 473–74, 478.

63. 277 U.S. 438, at 485.

64. Maieutics is the art of midwifery and plays a central role in the philosophy of Socrates, for whom the teacher, like the midwife, only helps the student to give birth to what is her own. The classical example of this approach is to be found in the *Meno*, 290–97. Brandeis's sympathy for the notion of education as maieutics is also revealed by his admiration for Whitehead's philosophy of education, directly influenced by Socrates. See L. D. Brandeis, *Letters*, V, p. 378, referring to N. Whitehead, "The Aims of Education," *New Republic* 58 (17/4/1929), pp. 244–46.

65. This has been recognized explicitly by Hegel, who treats needy stealing as a case of "*Notrecht*," or nullification of the positive law. See Hegel, *The Philosophy of Right*, T.M. Knox (ed.), #127. The same has essentially been said by Hobbes, although indirectly and in a way that many seem to have overlooked: For Hobbes, whenever one's life is threatened, either directly or by loss of "the means of so preserving life," one goes back to the state of nature, with no more obligations toward the sovereign and its law. *Leviathan*, Ch. 14, C.B. MacPherson ed., (Penguin), p. 192.

66. For an early formulation of this new idea of property, see C. Reich, "The New Property," *Yale L.J.* 73 (1964): 733

67. The community itself is an individual self in relation to the planetary community and has a right to only enough of the planetary wealth as is compatible with the self-preservation, and possibly self-sufficiency, of all other members of such a community, including animal and vegetable species. The requirement is not that each community has to actively guarantee the self-sufficiency or self-preservation of every other community, because this could sometimes prove impossible. International aid, when it is not a Trojan horse for exploitation, as it is mostly today, is a moral duty. And today, the richer countries have also a duty to compensate the impoverished ones for the ruthless, centuries-old exploitation of their resources. But more in general, the stricter duty should be for each nation not to contribute, directly or indirectly, to the impoverishment of other nations. If only this duty would be enforced, it would go a long way to eliminate both poverty and the loss of sovereignty in our world.

68. Alan Thein Durning, Holly B. Brough, "Reforming the Livestock Economy," in Lester B. Brown et al., *State of the World 1992* (New York, Norton & Company, 1992), pp. 66–82. See also: Jeremy Rifkin, *Beyond Beef* (New York, Dutton, 1992); John Robbins, *Diet for a New America* (Walpole, NH, Stillpoint, 1987); Robbins, *May All Be Fed*. (New York, William Morrow & Co.), 1992.

69. "On Liberty," p. 166ff. Consistent with his inconsistent mediation of liberalism

From Mill to Brandeis 123

and transpersonalism, Mill also allows for a certain number of limitations on the sale of liquors, though the basic principle of the absolute immunity of private choices, at least in the abstract, remains.

70. See *Ruppert v Caffey*, 251 U.S. 264 (1920); *Albrecht v U.S.*, 273 U.S. 1 (1927); *U.S. v One Ford Coupe*, 272 U.S. 321 (1926); *Lambert v Yellowley*, 272 U.S. 581 (1926).

71. Mason, pp. 566–67.

72. Mill rejected the proposal to "tax stimulants for the sole purpose of making them more difficult to be obtained," as well as to impose a "limitation in number, for instance, of beer and spirit houses." "On Liberty," pp. 169–70.

73. Letter of June 14, 1919, to Alice Goldmark Brandeis, quoting Esther 1:8, in *Letters of L. D. Brandeis* (SUNY, 1975), IV, p. 400.

74. See *Letters of L. D. Brandeis*, p. 462, pp. 497–98.

75. For this and for the previous quotation from the same document, see Mason, p. 90.

4
1937–1965: BETWEEN TWO CONSTITUTIONAL REVOLUTIONS

AFTER BRANDEIS

Brandeis was still a member of the Court when, after a tense confrontation with President Roosevelt over some aspects of his reforms, "the Supreme Court dramatically reversed itself and upheld minimum wage legislation in 1937 in *West Coast Hotel v Parrish*,"[1] which explicitly rejected *Lochner*. The 1937 constitutional revolution has been described as a "switch in time that saved nine." According to this view, the Court radically altered its standards out of fear, giving in to President Roosevelt's threat of packing the Court with younger judges, more favorable to his policies. This is a simplistic view, with no factual correspondence. Among the judges opposing Roosevelt's policies were the very same judges who had prepared the 1937 jurisprudential revolution. Brandeis himself was leading such an opposition, clearly not in the name of the Lochnerism he had fought all his life, but because he foresaw the danger of the bureaucratic centralization pursued by the winning wing of the New Deal movement. The fact is, far from being impressed by Roosevelt's threats, the Court autonomously reached the end of a long process of slow but powerful reform of the *Lochner* jurisprudence.[2]

In such a process Brandeis's ideas, which for more than twenty years had been the most organic alternative to Lochnerism, were an obvious source of inspiration. *West Coast Hotel* sanctioned Brandeis's view that property has rights only insofar as it serves the higher values of personality and interiority. The priority of these values was explicitly recognized by the Court in *Palko v Connecticut*, where the extent of the Fourteenth Amendment's incorporation was again the central issue.

In a famous opinion, Justice Cardozo asserted that only the rights that are truly fundamental were to be incorporated at the level of the states. He refused the literal incorporation of the whole Bill of Rights, arguing, mainly in reference to the procedural rights guaranteed by the Sixth and Seventh Amendments, that to "abolish them is not to violate a 'principle of justice so rooted in the traditions and conscience of our people as to be ranked as fundamental.' "[3] This appeal to a principle of justice rooted both in outer history and inner conscience places Cardozo within the homeorhetic tradition of natural law. Cardozo also shared with Brandeis the notion of which rights should be listed as fundamental. Among them, Cardozo placed the rights of speech, press, religion, and assembly, plus the right to legal assistance. Except for the last, they are the rights enumerated in the First Amendment. Like Brandeis, Cardozo deeply believed in the "firstness" of the First Amendment, which for him rested on the primacy of the "liberty of mind" over the "liberty of action": "Freedom of thought and speech ... is the matrix, the indispensable condition, of nearly every other form of freedom." The position of Cardozo and Brandeis has been called "selective incorporation," in opposition to three other positions supposedly present within the Court:

1. Justice Frankfurter's "case-by-case" approach, promoting an ironclad judicial restraint to be overcome only when the case is too shocking to the conscience of the judge and/or contrary to the standards of a civil conduct
2. Justice Black's "total incorporation" of the rights literally enumerated in the Bill of Rights
3. "Total incorporation plus," the position of Douglas, Murphy, and Rutledge who, though accepting the total incorporation of the explicit Bill of Rights, thought that the Bill of Rights implied more than just its literal contents.[4]

But the position of Brandeis and Cardozo is in fact a "selective incorporation plus," because they considered the rights selected in the written Bill of Rights only a part of the wider set of both written and unwritten fundamental rights. The list of fundamental rights presented by Cardozo in *Palko* is only exemplary, and the Bill of Rights itself is considered exemplary of a larger body of fundamental rights *"implicit in the concept of ordered liberty."* For Cardozo, the possibility to apprehend truly fundamental rights, as distinct from less-fundamental ones, rests on the "perception of a *rationalizing principle* which gives to discrete instances a proper order and coherence." This is a perfect example of "realist rationalism" à la Brandeis, whereby specific liberties are concretely defined through a process of substantive and therefore prospective determination of the undetermined and therefore self-subsistent, universal form or principle of liberty. The notion of "ordered liberty," or liberty intrinsically

1937–1965: Between Two Constitutional Revolutions

bound by responsibility, shows how for Cardozo the "rationalizing principle" is the dialectical form itself, the idea of the Whole of Wholes.

The notion that the written Constitution only partially represents the fundamental rights "implicit" in the grounding principle of "ordered liberty" seals the essential homogeneity of the position of Cardozo and Brandeis on the one hand and of the "total incorporation plus" of Murphy, Rutledge, and Douglas on the other. The only concrete difference between the two positions concerns the role of Amendments, such as the Third and the Seventh, that have become practically irrelevant in this century. This shows that for a large majority of the Court, the rejection of *Lochner* did not imply the rejection of "substantive due process" but rather a different understanding of it. The group that was forming in support of this emerging approach was not clearly defined, but by and large the only Justices who maintained radically different approaches were Frankfurter on the one side and Black on the other. The former, although appealing to "immutable principles of justice" and to "natural law," promoted a rigid judicial restraint in relation not only to the economic and proprietary sphere but also to the sphere of personal and political rights. The latter adopted an ultrapositivistic adherence to the letter of the written Constitution, claiming absolute protection only for the literally grounded fundamental rights.[5]

The clash between these different approaches revolved around the central criterion of the 1937 revolution, the so-called *double standard*, which posited the priority of the mental and personal rights and liberties over the economic rights of property. Although the notion of a double standard has been often read from a dualistic viewpoint, Brandeis and Cardozo rejected both sides of such a dualistic reading, the absolute judicial restraint in the field of economic rights on the one hand (Frankfurter) and the absolute immunity of the First Amendment explicit rights (Black) on the other. In reference to the duality of fundamental and nonfundamental rights, Cardozo wrote in his *Palko* opinion that "the dividing line between them, if not unfaltering throughout its course, has been true for the most part to a unifying principle." The unifying principle, as we have seen, is for Cardozo the dialectical principle itself, which in relation to the double standard posits that the rights of mental and personal liberty, although fundamental, are not empirically absolute because they are intrinsically bound by the requirements of order and responsibility; whereas the rights of property, although derivative, are not merely relative, because they are meant to serve the absolute value of ethical and spiritual growth. This is why the dividing line between them, although principled and clear, could not be "unfaltering throughout its course."

The case in which the controversy over the double standard has emerged most forcefully is probably *U.S. v Carolene Products Co.* In his majority opinion, Justice Stone wrote:

The existence of facts supporting the legislative judgment is to be presumed, for regulatory legislation affecting ordinary commercial transactions is not to be pronounced unconstitutional unless in the light of the facts made known or generally assumed it is of such a character as to preclude the assumption that it rests upon some *rational basis* within the knowledge and experience of the legislators.[6]

Here Harlan's position comes finally to the forefront. But without a clear specification of the rational basis test, Stone's criterion was in danger of sanctioning a complete surrender to the will of the legislator. This is why Stone added the famous and highly debated *footnote four*.[7] The footnote hints at three fundamental limits to the presumed power of the legislator to interfere with the economic and proprietary sphere:

1. The rights specifically enumerated in the Bill of Rights
2. The need to defend the political processes vital to democracy
3. The equal right of minorities to participate in those processes

Recently, J. Ely built a whole political and judicial theory upon this footnote. Ely opposes legal positivism and literalism, which, by means of a curious reversal of terms he calls "interpretivism," to all nonpositivistic forms of legal interpretation, which he collects under the label of "non-interpretivism." According to Ely, while the first limiting factor of the footnote four remains within a pure interpretivism, the second and third delineate a limited noninterpretivism immune from the dangers and mistakes of "substantive due process." Ely believes that the two criteria of democratic participation and equality posited by Stone establish the unitary proceduralist principle of "egalitarian participation in the processes of government" as the only standard legitimately able to transcend the letter of the Constitution.[8] There are various reasons why Ely's view is misleading. As H. Garfield correctly points out,

Ely's theory puts more weight on Justice Stone's footnote than it should have to bear. Dictum in a footnote containing such phrases as "there may be" and "it is unnecessary to consider now" could scarcely be considered as drawing a final, definitive line between the polar extremes of rational basis review and strict scrutiny. Viewed in perspective, footnote four is only a cautionary note, designed to prevent the Court's eagerness to repudiate *Lochner* from leading to total abdication of its vital function of safeguarding individual rights.[9]

Garfield stresses how Ely also wrongly attributes to footnote four a general relevance, whereas Stone limited its application to the sole field of economic transactions. Part three of footnote four explicitly asserts that the principle of *Carolene* does not apply to cases such as *Meyer v Nebraska* and *Pierce v Society of Sisters*. This exclusion is important because these cases refer to the right of religious or national minorities to freely and autonomously educate their children, and so, as Garfield rightly reminds us, they represent that uncorrupt side of *Lochner*, that "non economic substantive due process" which is "the most direct precedent for the right of privacy enunciated in Griswold.'' It is true that Stone presented even the "substantive" rights involved in those cases as functional to the equal democratic participation of minorities, but this only apparently justifies Ely's view. In fact, if Stone thought that without substantive rights minorities would scarcely participate in politics, he also conceived of political participation as the basic tool for minorities to protect and foster their substantive and fundamental rights. Thus, in footnote four, he talked of "political processes ordinarily to be relied upon to protect minorities." He too derived, from the very nature of the law, the formal/substantive view of due process. And he too considered fundamental the rights of the mental/spiritual dimension, and political rights but only insofar as they are dialectically related to such a dimension. Three years after *Carolene Products*, Stone wrote that the "Constitution expresses more than the conviction of the people that democratic freedoms must be preserved at all costs. It is also an expression of faith and a command that freedom of mind and spirit must be preserved.''[10]

Furthermore, in *Carolene* Stone hints at the fact that even in the economic and proprietary field there must be some independent standards protecting both the personal and the political rights of individuals and minorities. This shows that he too rejected the dualistic understanding of the double standard in favor of a conception of rights that, though axiologically hierarchical, acknowledges the wholeness of the human experience and the continuity of its material and spiritual aspects.[11]

The problem with the post-1937 jurisprudence is that the Court was unable to maintain such a dialectical holism. The Court began adopting an abstract and dualistic view of rights, whereby the legislator was freed from all judicial control in the economic-proprietary field and subjected to a strict scrutiny only in the field of personal liberties. This dualistic approach was brought to an extreme by Justice Black's advocacy of absolute judicial restraint in all areas not covered by the opposite absolutism of First Amendment rights. In Black's hands, the double standard produced on the one hand *relatively absolute* rights, or rights turned into impossible absolutes within the relative dimension of empirical existence,[12] and, on the other hand, *absolutely relative* rights, or rights fully subjected to the contingent and relative will of political majorities. But Black remained quite isolated, and even Douglas, who was initially influenced by him, after a few years in the Court agreed with Murphy and Rutledge, rejecting Black's absolute judicial restraint in the field of economic and literally unprotected rights, and understanding that the fundamental value of the "preferred rights," even those mental/spiritual of the First Amendment, cannot completely exclude some empirical balancing. With Murphy and Douglas concurring, wrote Rutledge:

The case confronts us again with the duty our system places on this Court to say where the individual's freedom ends and the State's power begins. Choice on that border, now as always delicate, is perhaps more so where the usual presumption supporting legislation is balanced by the preferred place given in our scheme to the great, the indispensable democratic freedoms secured by the First Amendment. . . . Any attempt to restrict those liberties must be justified by clear public interest, threatened not doubtfully or remotely, but by clear and present danger.[13]

Black's literalist absolutism was rejected also by Frankfurter, but in his case the alternative was a tendency to expand judicial restraint into the very area of First Amendment liberties. The Court never abandoned the substantive scrutiny of social and economic legislation, that is

never wholly abandoned the position that legislatures, at least in their regulatory capacity, must always act in furtherance of public goals transcending the shifting summation of private interests through political processes. The pluralist thesis that there exists no public interest beyond that summation never became judicial dogma in economic life any more than in other sectors of human concern.[14]

But Frankfurter held this idea only abstractly, reducing the transcendent public interest to the majoritarian and/or institutional will. The same reduction was operated by Black, whose strong judicial restraint was at least tempered by the absolutist defense of the explicitly enumerated rights.

Thus, a compromise was forged whereby the Court avoided for the most part scrutinizing economic legislation and focused instead on the protection of the preferred rights of individual privacy and political liberty, an area in which important decisions were indeed made. Although the language of substantive due process was abandoned for fear of a return of Lochnerism, the Court applied an implicit substantive due process that created remarkable difficulties in logic and argument. *Skinner v Oklahoma* was a direct antecedent of that "right to reproductive autonomy" that pioneered the constitutionalization of the right to privacy in the 1960s. The right of a petty delinquent against an Oklahoma statute forcing sterilization on recidivous criminals was affirmed by the Court on the ground of the "equal protection" clause of the Fourteenth Amendment. H. Garfield points out that the "equal protection" rationale was a "subterfuge" allowing the Court "to protect the substantive due process rights surrounding marriage and procreation without unduly disturbing the ghost of *Lochner,* so recently laid to rest."[15] That the hidden rationale of the decision was not "equality" but "substantive due process" is shown by Douglas's opinion for the Court, which defined Skinner's right "one of the basic civil rights of man . . . a basic liberty."[16]

Two more cases of this period, both relating to the so-called right to silence, can be considered forerunners of the constitutional right to privacy. Though in *West Virginia Board of Education v Barnette* [319 U.S. 624 (1943)], dealing with the "right to remain silent," the Court "considered the individual conscience a private sphere constitutionally guaranteed,"[17] in *Kovacs v Cooper* [336 U.S. 77 (1949)] the Court began to acknowledge the growing social concern with the technological invasions of personal tranquility and peace of mind.[18] In *Kovacs*, Black, Douglas, and Rutledge dissented in the name of free speech, invoking the precedent of *Saia v New York* [334 U.S. 558 (1948)]. But *Saia* dealt with the generalized and preventive power of the police to silence public loudspeakers, whereas in *Kovacs* the police could only interfere with obnoxious loudspeakers already in action. Of course the question of how to determine the limit between obnoxious disruption and valuable communication is debatable, but the three dissenters did not even bother debating, claiming that any limitation of the public use of loudspeakers would represent a constitutional violation. This could be an example of Black's influence on young Justice Douglas. Yet, the participation of Rutledge makes it plausible to think of the dissent as an understandable if extreme reaction to the growing phenomenon of McCarthyism, which was well under way in 1949. Nevertheless, the abstract rights-absolutism that inspired it laid itself open to Frankfurter's criticism of the "preferred freedoms" doctrine:

"The preferred position of freedom of speech" . . . I deem it a mischievous phrase, if it carries the thought, which it may subtly imply, that any law touching communication is infected with presumptive invalidity. . . . The phrase . . . expresses a complicated process of constitutional adjudication by a deceptive formula. . . . Such a formula makes for mechanical jurisprudence.

Frankfurter developed also a more substantive argument:

It is not for us to supervise the limits the legislature may impose in safeguarding the steadily narrowing opportunities for serenity and reflection. Without such opportunities, freedom of thought becomes a mocking phrase, and without freedom of thought there can be no free society.[19]

This is a strong argument, more faithful to the spirit of the "preferred freedoms" doctrine than Frankfurter himself would have admitted. But he adopted it only because it allowed him to practically reaffirm a judicial restraint that, at that point, he had almost come to idolize. If serenity and reflection, and thus privacy, are so essential to the free society, judges should not just restrain from interfering when legislation protects them but should also stop legislation from allowing or promoting violations of them. This second side of the equation was never acknowledged by Frankfurter, and his judicial restraint became so extreme as to stop only in the face of violations that would "shock the conscience." When the propulsive thrust of the 1937 revolution came to an end, first with the death of Chief Justice Stone in 1946 and then with those of Rutledge and Murphy in 1949, Frankfurter's position became dominant, giving rise to the McCarthyism of the Vinson Court.

THROUGH THE TUNNEL OF McCARTHYISM

Although McCarthyism, one of the most evident forms of totalitarian democracy, represented in some ways a break from Roosevelt's New Deal, particularly in relation to the restriction of union activities, there is a significant continuity between the two periods, shown for example by the fact that President Truman, who promulgated the Loyalty and Security Program, had been Roosevelt's Vice President. It is true that the New Deal tried to build a "pluralistic mass State" in which to integrate "those who had been forgotten by [classical] liberalism."[20] But Justice Douglas, who himself was an important figure of the New Deal movement, has reminded us that it was integration into a system based on the unquestioned centrality of oligopolistic capitalism, a system whose reorganization produced, together with an economic centralization whose costs had to be borne by the community through the development of the welfare state, a huge central bureaucracy growing in symbiosis with the powerful interest groups and economic interests that it was supposed to regulate.[21]

This centralization of powers and functions under the banner of the capitalistic principle generated an unprecedented attack on both the economic/political autonomy of local communities and the individual privacy, through both integration and repression. If McCarthyism was the time for full-blown repression, the New Deal was integration that also did not refrain from using repression, as the first acts of a McCarthyist nature were promulgated during the New Deal.[22] When repression became predominant, the issue of political and individual privacy emerged as more crucial than ever, but alas not for the "Frankfurterian" Vinson Court. The inner dynamic of a Court is too complex to be fully captured by schematic generalizations, and certainly Frankfurter himself did sometimes, if rarely, embrace the defense of privacy. But the new line of the Court was essentially based on Frankfurter's rejection of the "preferred freedoms" doctrine, which produced a specific blend of judicial restraint and the balancing test. For Frankfurter, judicial restraint meant full subordination to the arbitrary majoritarian determination not only of policies but also of political ends. Such a view rested on an arithmetical conception of public interest and will, which also led to the distortion of another classical legal tool, the *balancing test*. When public and private are understood as mere empirical realities, their balancing cannot but result in the preeminence of the quantitatively massive public sphere over the quantitatively insubstantial private sphere, as with most communitarians. The balancing of public and private was thus reduced to a mere fiction, so that the balancing test ended up being concretely applied only to conflicts between different private interests.

However, this had never been the position of the Court. We have seen how even Legal Formalism theoretically accepted to balance public and private interests, and how the homeorhetic and dialectical holism of Harlan, Brandeis, and Cardozo, and again of Rutledge, Murphy, and Douglas, acknowledged that not only in the economic field but even in the area of fundamental or preferred freedoms, the empirical balancing of private rights and public powers, although in different degrees for different types of liberty, was inevitable. The only one who thoroughly rejected any balancing whatsoever, opposing the two unequal spheres of arbitrary public will and positivistic rights, each abstractly absolute in its own realm, was Black, behind whom stands Justice Holmes and the whole empiricist tradition.

But Harlan, Brandeis, and those who followed in their footsteps were not empirical absolutists. Theirs was, if we can say so, a *dialiminal absolutism*, that is, an absolutism of the essence concretely unfolding in and through existential limits and modulations. According to this position, behind the private/public duality there stands a "unifying principle," a common essence under the rule of which the empirical and thus more or less accidental manifestations of the public and of the private need to be reciprocally balanced. Because such a common ground, the very real idea of the Whole of Wholes, posits the priority of mental/spiritual rights as the necessary tools to foster that ethical and cultural growth of individuals that is indispensable to any well-organized community, it is clear that the proper "balancing" of public and private requires attributing a "preferred" status to those rights, thus showing how "balancing test" and "preferred freedoms" do indeed support each other harmoniously.

Frankfurter's position is a perverse mediation of the opposite approaches of Brandeis and Black. Like Brandeis, Frankfurter acknowledged the need to pervasively balance the public and private. But unlike Brandeis, and like Black, he adopted empiricist and quantitative premises, leading to an almost unlimited subordination to the majoritarian will. Thus, his undue appropriation of Brandeis's critique of empirical absolutism becomes the Trojan horse to subject even the preferred personal and spiritual freedoms to a quantitatively superior, rather than deliberative, political will. The only and very thin limit to the omnipotence of governmental agencies was, for Frankfurter, the requirement not to act in such an "uncivilized" way as to "shock the conscience" of an ordinary person.[23]

In 1953, when Vinson died and was replaced by Earl Warren, a new attitude began to emerge in the Court, particularly in relation to the rescue of the "clear and present danger" test. But change was slow, and the McCarthyist standards of national security were for the most part maintained throughout the 1950s.[24] There emerged, however, the first limited recognition of a "right to associational privacy";[25] and in *Mapp v Ohio* [367 U.S. 643 (1961)], the right not to have one's private sphere penetrated without a "probable cause" was incorporated at the state level. In *Mapp* the only dissenters were Frankfurter, Whittaker, and Harlan (old Justice Harlan's nephew).

Harlan Jr.'s early position was quite influenced by Frankfurter, whose "shock the conscience/no-preferred-freedoms" standard he seemed generally to accept. But in *Poe v Ulmann* [367 U.S. 497 (1961)], concerned with a Connecticut statute prohibiting contraception, Harlan moved to a partial constitutional recognition of the right to privacy, dissenting with Frankfurter's majority opinion that left the case undecided. For the dissenting Douglas, the statute constituted "an invasion of the privacy that is *implicit* in a free society" and also hindered the serene and proper medical counseling of couples in need of contraceptive assistance.[26] In *Poe*, Harlan abandoned Frankfurter's extreme restraint in favor of a more active defense of certain fundamental liberties, while Douglas distanced himself radically from Black by embracing substantive due process. The stage was ready for "the most important substantive due process decision of the modern period, *Griswold v Connecticut*."[27]

GRISWOLD v *CONNECTICUT*

In *Griswold v Connecticut* [381 U.S. 479 (1965)], the Court declared unconstitutional the same Connecticut statute already discussed in *Poe*. The opinion of Douglas for the Court stated that reproductive autonomy and free family planning are protected by a *constitutional right of privacy* implicit in the *penumbras* and *emanations* of various articles of the Bill of Rights.

Douglas's opinion has been considered by many a bad compromise between natural law and legal positivism or literalism,[28] and similar thoughts must have also been entertained by the rest of the *Griswold* Justices if, apart from the dissenters Black and Stewart, only Clark subscribed to Douglas's opinion with no further remarks.

Both Harlan and White criticized Douglas, for they thought that his notion of "penumbra" did not really overcome Black's literalism. This seemed to be confirmed by Black himself who, while accusing Harlan and White of holding a "natural law due process theory," tried to minimize the distance between Douglas and himself by calling their disagreement "a narrow one."[29] Was Black correct?

To answer this question, we need to understand Douglas's overall theoretical posture. Douglas was a complex and controversial figure, whose opposition to the Establishment (as he liked to call it) reminds one of Brandeis, to whom Douglas felt very close. Like Brandeis, Douglas was a man of the New Deal who soon became disillusioned with it. Like Brandeis, he was a profound naturalist and environmentalist when the concern for the environment was still uncommon,[30] and he always fought against both oligopolistic capitalism and bureaucratic centralization in the name of a federalism of decentralized and ecologically sound communities. During the time in which he was Chairman of the Securities and Exchange Commission, he wrote:

The growth of bigness has resulted in ruthless sacrifices of human values. The disappearance of free enterprise has submerged the individual in the impersonal corporation. . . . He is denied a chance to stand on his own before man and God. He is subservient to others and his thinking is done for him from afar. . . . His opportunities to become a leader, to grow in stature, to be independent in mind and spirit, are greatly reduced.

Widespread submergence of the individual in a corporation has an insidious effect on democracy as has his submergence in the state in other lands.[31]

It is because of the feared totalitarian character of capitalistic corporations that Douglas initially supported the expansion of governmental intervention, though remaining a staunch supporter of individual rights.

He was a great admirer of the Native American civilization and had a deep sympathy for heretics and minorities, beginning with the hoboes, who were often also Wobblies, that is, members of the socialist union IWW. His sympathy for anti-Establishment dissenters reemerged intact during the 1960s when, already quite old and subjected to ferocious attacks from the right, he sided with the anti–Vietnam War youths against the oppressive power of the "military-industrial complex" and the huge governmental bureaucracies.[32]

In an address dedicated to his beloved Brandeis, he wrote: "The democratic way when it places the worth and dignity of the individual first recognizes the essential unity of mankind.... The strength of the democratic way is its respect for the minority.... Foremost is the smallest minority of all—the individual conscience."[33] Although Douglas's conception of minorities is partially influenced by Mill, as we shall see, his reference to the inherent link between individual conscience and mankind as a whole points to the more essential nature of his thought, which will develop into a full-blown acceptance of the transpersonal and Brandeisian understanding of individuality and privacy. The philosophical affinity between Douglas and Brandeis grew with their friendship, although at the beginning they were divided by some jurisprudential differences.[34] Douglas was of a different generation and remained always somewhat entangled in the ambiguity of Legal Realism, which brought together natural law realists such as J. Frank (for whom Douglas felt deep friendship and admiration) and legal positivists such as Holmes and Black.[35]

Douglas always thought of Black as a good friend and teacher, and even when he embraced more fully the Brandeisian natural law approach, he tried not to break up completely with Black, making constant if vain efforts to reconcile the different views of Brandeis and Black: "I was ideologically closer to Brandeis and to Black than to any others [on the Court].... For some reasons I do not understand, Black and Brandeis were never close.... They were indeed brothers under the skin."[36] Brandeis and Black found themselves on the same side in the post-1937 rejection of Lochnerism, but we have seen how their motivations for such a rejection were radically different. In *Olsen v Nebraska* [313 U.S. 236 (1941)] Douglas, who in the meanwhile had replaced Brandeis in the Court, expressed his firm opposition to Lochnerism. But *Olsen* was concerned with socioeconomic legislation and so did not address the noneconomic side of substantive due process, that dimension of "preferred freedoms" that divided Brandeis and Black. In *Adamson v California* [332 U.S. 42 (1947)], which concerned the Fourteenth Amendment's incorporation of the Fifth Amendment, Douglas sided with Black's literalist "total incorporation" and against Murphy's "total incorporation plus." But during the 1950s Douglas extended his political and economic Brandeisianism to the legal field,[37] and in *Poe* he reversed his position by explicitly supporting Murphy's dissent in *Adamson*: "Though I believe that 'due process' as used in the Fourteenth Amendment includes all of the first eight Amendments, I do not think it is restricted and confined to them."[38]

The shift looks even more radical if we consider that Douglas, having rejected the literalist view of the "preferred freedoms," opened to substantive due process even in the area of socioeconomic legislation, where Black consistently claimed an almost absolute judicial restraint. He wrote: "The error of the old Court, as I see it, was not in entertaining inquiries concerning the constitutionality of social legislation but in applying the standards that it did."

Moreover, Douglas connected this new substantive due process to natural law, implicitly in *Poe*, where he extensively quoted from a natural law article, and explicitly in a volume he had written only three years earlier:

Natural rights were often invoked by the laissez-faire theorists of the late nineteenth and twentieth century.... Conspicuous is the case of *Lochner v New York*.... The natural rights of which I speak are different. They have a broad base in morality and religion to protect man, his individuality, and his conscience.... Some are written explicitly into the Constitution. Others are to be implied.[39]

Against the natural law background of his dissent in *Poe*, it has been said that Douglas's opinion in *Griswold* represented an anticlimax, "a retreat from ... earlier flirtation with natural rights" that "captured the majority of the Court and relied exclusively on the penumbral theory rather than a natural rights approach."[40] Undoubtedly, in *Griswold* Douglas avoided as much as he could relying explicitly on natural law. However, this does not necessarily mean that he intended to abandon his natural law–substantive due process approach, and could very well be explained both by a strategical shift in the mode in which the natural law discourse was to be applied and by the need to differentiate the substantive due process thus generated from Harlan's own version. After all, we should not forget that in *Griswold* itself, Douglas alluded quite directly to the legitimacy of a non-Lochnerian and noneconomic substantive due process.[41]

This is not to deny that Douglas approached substantive due process with great caution, so that Emerson can rightly claim that he missed a great opportunity to entrench his alternative version of substantive due process into the official constitutional doctrine.[42] But the natural law foundations still implicitly existed, and Douglas's opinion, if cleaned of its conceptual ambiguities and read together with Goldberg's concurring opinion, offers important indications for the development of a genuine substantive due process.

Although Douglas read quite peculiarly *Pierce* and *Meyer*, the two crucial antecedents of noneconomic substantive due process, his reading is not as arbitrary as some have claimed.[43] He wrote that the two cases, decided by the

Court under the due process clause of the Fourteenth Amendment and involving the right of families to privately educate their children, are more essentially related to the right to knowledge implicit in the First Amendment. The shift away from the Fourteenth Amendment's due process is not a rejection of the substantive and natural law understanding of judicial review. That understanding is now developed through the alternative notion of substantive rights implicit in the written Constitution. He introduced that notion by talking of "peripheral rights" without which "the specific rights would be less secure." These peripheral rights supplement the written specific rights and taken individually are indeed only supplementary. Yet, their existence as a whole points toward a deeper and wider realm that transcends and encompasses the visibility of the text, thus playing not a peripheral but a foundational role. For instance, Douglas states that the specific rights of free speech and press include a whole series of peripheral rights, such as the right to think, read, study, distribute printed material, teach, and freely educate one's children. Those peripheral rights, in turn, embody that "spirit of the First Amendment" wherefore "the State may not . . . contract the spectrum of available knowledge." In other words, the peripheral rights manifest the reality of an implicit yet comprehensive right to knowledge that represents the true foundation of the written freedom of speech and press. It is my conviction that this is the true meaning of Douglas's theory of *penumbras*, which he so introduces:

In other words, the First Amendment has a penumbra where privacy is protected from governmental intrusion. . . . The foregoing cases suggest that specific guarantees in the Bill of Rights have penumbras formed by emanations from those guarantees that help give them life and substance.

The reference to a *substance* that the rights enveloped in the nontextual half-darkness give to the explicit rights, shows that the substantive and natural law approach of *Poe* is not abandoned. But of the two sides of Douglas's theory of penumbras, the peripheral and the foundational, only the first has been perceived by most commentators, who have thus made it possible for themselves to emphasize the contradiction between the supposedly quasi-literalist theoretical ground and the de facto natural law result of the opinion. This is a typical comment: "*Griswold* is probably better understood as a calculated compromise. Douglas sacrificed the *Poe* dissent, which was closer to his own true philosophy, in an effort to attract a majority of the Court to an opinion that would constitutionally legitimate the right of privacy."[44] This only partially hits the mark. Douglas had no need to compromise in order to attract the majority of the Court. Besides Harlan and White, a natural law-substantive due process approach was explicitly accepted by Goldberg, with whose opinion both Warren and Brennan concurred. Possibly, the "compromise" won Clark over to the majority. But this doesn't seem a sufficient reason, given that even without Clark, Douglas could have constitutionally entrenched his *Poe* position with the support of five more judges.

I think a better explanation can be found in Douglas's will both to maintain his friendly relations with Black and to distance his own from Harlan's conception of substantive due process. Moved by this twofold concern, Douglas developed a theory of penumbras, rescuing it from within the homeorhetic natural law tradition (remember how the concept of penumbras emerged in Brandeis's *Olmstead* dissent), whereby *the constitutional text was transcended not by being made irrelevant but by being considered in its visible organic wholeness*. Douglas's understanding of penumbras as both peripheral and foundational emerges clearly in his treatment of the right to privacy.

He claimed that zones of privacy are present as penumbras not only in the First Amendment but also in the Third, in the Fourth and Fifth, and in the Ninth. The shadowy right to privacy is thus spread through various Amendments and in each of them may have a peripheral function to play toward the rights there explicitly asserted. But in its penumbral wholeness, the right to privacy appears to be more comprehensive than any of the specified rights it supports. In fact, Douglas clearly moves from the empirical apprehension of the peripheral *rights of privacy* to the recognition of a *principle of privacy*, which is a general "right" in its legal quality, as a fundamental if penumbral foundation of the Bill of Rights as a whole: "We deal with a right of privacy older than the Bill of Rights—older than our political parties, older than our school system."

In *The Right of the People* Douglas wrote: "The penumbra of the Bill of Rights reflects human rights which, though not explicit, are implied from the very nature of man as a child of God."[45] Here, as opposed to *Griswold*, it is the Bill of Rights that is a penumbra projected by the whole of fundamental natural rights. But even in *Griswold*, although placed in the penumbral realm, the fundamental right of privacy is said to be older than any political and civil institution, a natural right preceding and thus grounding the Bill of Rights itself. This means that what we see in *Griswold* is not an abjuration but a change in perspective. From the point of view of natural rights, *the written Constitution is, like the cave in the Platonic myth, a shadowy reflection of the essential light of the ontological law*. But from within the Cave itself, from the existential point of view of historically determined rights and laws, the natural law and fundamental rights remain in the dark, too powerful to be directly gazed at by ordinary human eyes. In *Griswold*, Douglas adopted this latter point of view, which fully confirmed his most intimate natural law convictions, yet had the parallel advantage of not clashing too evidently and harshly with Black's legal empiricism.

The presence of two levels in Douglas's opinion, an essential-esoteric and an existential-exoteric, was so widely perceived that Douglas had to keep protesting against the allegation that *Griswold* resuscitated substantive due process. He did so without too much conviction, as in *Doe v Bolton*, where he wrote that there are "those who have believed that the reach of due process in the Fourteenth

Amendment included all of the Bill of Rights but went further. Such was the view of Mr. Justice Murphy and Mr. Justice Rutledge. Perhaps they were right; but it is a bridge that neither I nor those who joined the Court's opinion in *Griswold* crossed."[46] Because that bridge had already been crossed by Douglas in *Poe*, his protest in *Bolton* is clearly meant for the protection of those who, like Clark, adhered to the *Griswold* opinion with no intention of subscribing to substantive due process. In fact, the reference to the fact that "perhaps" Murphy and Rutledge were right anticipates Douglas's statement, contained in the second and posthumous volume of his autobiography, that Murphy's and Rutledge's was a position "with which, in the years to come, I was inclined to agree."[47]

As we said, Douglas's attempt in *Griswold* to develop a substantive due process position without relying on the Fourteenth Amendment was also motivated by the need to distance himself from Harlan. Harlan rejected Black's literalism by realistically pointing out that creative interpretation is inevitable even when the judge tries to stay as closely as possible to the written formulas of the law. This does not mean that Harlan was indifferent to the constitutional text,[48] which becomes relevant for him as a *rational continuum*, as he explained in *Poe*:

The full scope of the liberty guaranteed by the Due process Clause [of the Fourteen Am.] cannot be found in or limited by the precise terms of the specific guarantees elsewhere provided in the Constitution. This "liberty" is not a series of isolated points.... It is a rational continuum which, broadly speaking, includes a freedom from all substantial arbitrary impositions and purposeless restraints.

For Harlan, the constitutional rational continuum of liberty "spells out the reach of the Fourteenth Amendment due process . . . [and thus] those rights 'which are . . . fundamental.'" Because due process, by implying the "rational continuum of liberty," autonomously defines fundamental rights, Harlan claims its self-subsistence: "The Due Process Clause of the Fourteenth Amendment stands, in my opinion, on its own bottom."[49] Harlan's "rational continuum" does in some ways embody a principled holism that connects back to Brandeis, and such connection is reinforced by Harlan's simultaneous appeal to historical realism and thus implicitly to the homeorhetic character of Brandeis's legal rationalism: "Each new claim to Constitutional protection must be considered against a background of Constitutional purposes, as they have been *rationally* perceived and *historically* developed."[50] The seeming affinity between Brandeis and Harlan has fooled many, including such an astute commentator as H. Garfield, who posits the existence of a "Brandeis-Harlan approach" in opposition to Douglas's position.[51] But the affinity between Brandeis and Harlan is an optical illusion. Harlan's rationality, as opposed to Brandeis's formal/substantive and transcendent/immanent "logic of facts," is only the logical consistency of values that are inherently and completely historical and traditionalist. Harlan belongs to the *communitarian legal tradition*, although in the "liberal" way that characterizes many current communitarians and that is rather different from that of Frankfurter, to whom Harlan remained nevertheless always related. We cannot forget Harlan's reliance on Frankfurter's methodological combination of judicial restraint and empiricist balancing he never discarded, although he did modify it in part. For Harlan, judicial restraint meant rejecting the appeal to a self-subsistent and universal reason inherent in the human conscience of the judge and bowing instead, if not to the mere majoritarian will as with Frankfurter, to the fully historical reason of the American juridical tradition. In a passage from *Griswold* in which, not accidentally, he referred back to Frankfurter's *Adamson* opinion, Harlan wrote: "Judicial self-restraint . . . will be achieved, in this area as in other constitutional areas, only by continual insistence upon respect for the teachings of history [and] solid recognition of the basic values that underlie our society."[52]

The significance of this passage can be fully appreciated only in relation to Harlan's reading of the balancing test in *Poe*:

Due process has not been reduced to any formula; its content cannot be determined by reference to any code. The best that can be said is that through the course of this Court's decisions it has represented the balance which our Nation, built upon postulates of respect for the liberty of the individual, has struck between that liberty and the demands of organized society. If the supplying of content to this Constitutional concept has of necessity been a rational process, it certainly has not been one where judges have felt free to roam where unguided speculation might take them. The balance of which I speak is the balance struck by this country, having regard to what history teaches are the traditions from which it developed as well as the traditions from which it broke. That tradition is a living thing.[53]

This passage is extremely revealing of Harlan's ambiguity. The appeal to self-subsistent rational principles seems important, as when Harlan talks of "postulates" of liberty. One would expect these postulates to be also the essence of "due process" and thus the proper guide of the rational speculation by which the judge reaches a decision. Instead, Harlan tells us that due process is "the balance struck by this country," the traditional way of dealing with the opposition of individual autonomy and social interdependence and responsibility. There remains, at the theoretical level, an unresolved tension between tradition and reason. Although tradition takes priority, Harlan cannot avoid acknowledging that tradition itself is grounded upon rational postulates: His reference to the fact that tradition is constituted also by breaks away from tradition implies that tradition itself must rest upon something that transcends tradition, some unchangeables that keep defining every new historical turn in reference to the essential character and identity of the tradition. There are two possibilities: Either such "rational postulates" are transcendent ontological principles, or else they are simply the historically established principles chosen by "our society." The latter is clearly the most evident presence in Harlan's doctrine, as it is revealed, for instance, by his polemic against "unguided speculation."

To be sure, judges cannot roam freely wherever speculation takes them. But the guide of judicial thinking could very well be the spiritual privacy of the judge, his/her ability to attain the self-subsistent natural or ontological principles that live both in the world and within ourselves. In fact, whenever radical innovations are required, speculation cannot but rely upon itself alone! Though abstractly acknowledging the need for breaking at times with tradition, Harlan still chastises as "unguided" the speculation that doesn't take tradition as the only legitimate source of right answers. Like his opponent Black, Harlan wants judicial reason subordinated to purely external standards of justice, even though the standard is for him tradition rather than majoritarian/governmental will.

But Harlan's thought is more complex than that. If "rational postulates" were purely historical, they would still be part of the tradition they are supposed to found, which means that they too would need to be overcome when the need for breaks from tradition arise. If the evolution of tradition is not inherently controlled by truly independent and metahistorical, although nonseparate, principles of justice, then any shifts in the tradition, including arbitrary majoritarian interpretations and/or modifications of it, are legitimately part of the tradition itself. Not only could they not be legitimately subjected to judicial scrutiny and criticism, but in fact, if anything, they should require the subjugation of the judges in virtue of their quantitatively higher "democratic" value. This is why Harlan talks of his "rational postulates" always maintaining a certain ambiguity about their historical or metahistorical status. Indeed, his concept of tradition can act as a self-subsistent foundation only by surreptitiously and silently incorporating the idea of a metahistorical character into rational postulates that ultimately remain merely historical and thus essentially relativistic.

In *Poe*, for example, Harlan made it clear that his opposition to the Connecticut statute had nothing to do with its substantive command, because "Connecticut's judgment is no more demonstrably correct or incorrect than are the varieties of judgment, expressed in law." For Harlan, substantive judgments are moral judgments in "forum internum," whereas the realm of the law is primarily concerned with the "forum externum":

We are not presented simply with this moral judgment to be passed on an abstract proposition. The secular state is not an examiner of consciences: it must operate in the realm of behaviour, of overt actions, and where it does so operate, not only the underlying moral purpose of its operation, but also the choice of means becomes relevant to any Constitutional judgment on what is done.[54]

Here we find another of Harlan's ambiguities. He does not conceptually erase moral purposes from the picture, because they supposedly remain the "underlying" factor of legislative actions. Yet not only does he focus on the external side of those actions but, by declaring the impossibility of axiological choice among different moral judgments, he makes those "underlying moral purposes" de facto irrelevant to legal decisions. The reality is that Harlan fully buys into liberal dualism, which radically splits between the inner and outer, ethical and legal, private and public. As with modern liberals, the reference to deontology (rational postulates) and self-subsistent ethical principles is purely rhetorical, it is only the ennobling mask of historicism and relativism. Thus, in *Poe* he argued uniquely against the "choice of means" and procedures that break down the barrier between private and public, that is, against the "intrusion of the whole machinery of the criminal law into the very heart of marital privacy." In other words, though all policies and ends are substantively legitimate, there is a *barrier of rights* that should simply be immune from public policies and "experimentation," a liberal private sphere separated and immune from the public sphere precisely because they are both equally arbitrary.[55]

The true contours of Harlan's doctrine begin to emerge, presenting us with a picture whereby liberal dualism, together with its legalistic formalism, is both legitimized and mediated by a traditionalist understanding of substantive values. The postulates or fundamental principles of which Harlan talks are the formalistic and dualistic principles of classical liberalism. They are indeed metaphysical principles, resting on a certain view of reality that, as we saw in Ch. 1, comes from a certain part of the human soul. Although Harlan does not discard their metahistorical character, he prefers to present them as the principles of "our society," because the relativism that they propose could not tolerate to be grounded upon deontological or metaphysical absolutes of any kind. This is the essential contradiction of liberalism as the deontology that asserts the impossibility of any deontology, that is, of any a priori and thus superior ethical value. This makes for that merely abstract deontology that is totally useless when concrete and practical judgments are needed. We have seen how the fact that liberalism simply establishes a private sphere of immunity, leaving judgments and choices to the relativistic battle of wills of majorities, in the end endangers the existence itself of the private sphere, whose practical boundaries are too shifting not to fall under the decision-making power of political majorities. This is why Harlan supplemented the formalistic and abstract principles of liberalism with the substantive ways of balancing provided by tradition. Tradition represents the solid platform that, though inevitably imposing some limits to the abstractly absolutist rights-deontology of liberalism, gives it the realistic ground that it needs.

Harlan developed a specific type of the a posteriori dualistic mediation that we encountered in Mill, one that involves on the one hand a *substantive historicism or traditionalism* constituted by the arbitrary ways of balancing dualisms that "our community" has traditionally chosen and on the other hand a metahistorical (although still vested in a historical dress) *formalism of rights* supposedly protecting the private sphere and individuals from the arbitrary and thus potentially totalitarian will of relativistic majorities and/or traditions. Harlan's position is in this respect a forerunner, although only methodologically, of Dworkin's current attempt to give liberalism a more communitarian flavor.[56] On the other hand, it shows how in the end liberalism and communitarianism, in-

1937–1965: Between Two Constitutional Revolutions 143

sofar as they both rest on a merely empirical and historicist conception of community and tradition, are not so far apart from each other (and we shall see shortly how the communitarian Michael Sandel claims Harlan's theory of privacy to his camp).

In *Poe* we have a concrete example of Harlan's liberal traditionalism. After criticizing the Connecticut statute for breaking down the barriers between private and public, Harlan delimited the immunity of the private sphere in the traditionalist terms of "marital privacy" and more generally of family privacy:

Certainly the safeguarding of the home does not follow from the sanctity of property rights. The home derives its pre-eminence as the seat of family life. And the integrity of that life is something so fundamental that it has been found to draw to its protection the principle of more than one explicitly granted Constitutional right.

Although he followed Brandeis in rejecting the all-encompassing nature of property rights, Harlan fails to identify privacy as a right to be let alone and as the most comprehensive of rights. Harlan repeats with insistence that privacy is the "privacy of the home," the "private realm of family life," explaining that "it is difficult to imagine what is more private or more intimate than a husband and wife's marital relation."[57]

Although Harlan's theory of rights stops at the dimension of personality rights, which is a typically liberal trait, his identification of personality and intimacy with family life is a manifestation of his traditionalism. Of course family life is central to personality and intimacy but does not exhaust it, and only in a traditionalist framework such as Harlan's does it become so encompassing as to exclude other, "irregular" forms of intimacy. Wrote Harlan:

The right of privacy most manifestly is not an absolute. Thus, I would not suggest that adultery, homosexuality, fornication and incest are immune from criminal inquiry, however privately practiced. . . . Adultery, homosexuality and the like are intimacies which the State forbids altogether.[58]

This is a clear example of how liberalism and traditionalism are mediated within Harlan's system, the extension of the former, abstractly axiomatic, being concretely determined by traditional practices.

The nonabsolute nature of the sphere of personality and intimacy is another element that seems to unite Harlan and Brandeis. But again this is mere appearance. For Brandeis, the criteria that legitimize the compression of private behavior are not borrowed from tradition but are intrinsic to privacy itself and to its essential unity with the public. So, from a Brandeisian point of view, incest and family violence are to be interfered with because they are the farthest from what is most genuinely private or intimate. But when considering homosexuality and fornication, by which Harlan seems to indicate all sorts of irregular family arrangements (including polygamy and the like), the Brandeisian approach takes a very different route.

To be sure, homosexuality and the like are complex issues, to be analyzed in "the light of reason" (Brandeis). But Harlan takes the simpler and much more dangerous shortcut of entrusting the whole thing to tradition. Although his appeal to tradition may be sustained by his desire to preserve and reinforce a certain measure of traditional liberal rights and private autonomy, it ultimately leads to a situation whereby privacy and the derived rights of the private personality that are at stake in cases such as *Poe* are given over to the dominant ways of the various historical and geographical contexts, to a tradition that, insofar as it is only historical, can easily and arbitrarily reverse itself.

Resting his theory of substantive due process on the sole Fourteenth Amendment would have meant, for Douglas, running the risk of confusing his own position with Harlan's, thus creating a Douglas-Harlan block in radical opposition to Black, Stewart, and possibly even Clark. Douglas avoided this by more or less consciously articulating one exoteric and another esoteric level. But it is possible to reconstruct the true core of Douglas's opinion, especially with the help of Goldberg's concurring opinion, which draws directly from Douglas's *Poe* dissent. Read together, the esoteric level of Douglas's opinion for the Court, and Goldberg's concurring opinion, gives us a good sense of what the official *Griswold* position would have been had not it been for the oppositions and mediations between the different ideological blocks in the Court, of which Douglas himself was the crucial catalyst.

There is a twofold theoretical element linking Goldberg's opinion to that of Douglas: the appeal to the Ninth Amendment as a way of opening up toward the unwritten Constitution, and therefore a conception of the Constitution as a whole inclusive of its invisible foundations. It is important to understand how Goldberg wrote in a truly concurring spirit stressing the deeper elements of Douglas's opinion. Goldberg accepted Douglas's penumbras, and, instead of focusing on their "quasi-positivistic" pretensions, emphasizes their being a source of fundamental although implicit rights. It is precisely in order to assert the priority of penumbral fundamental rights over penumbral peripheral rights in Douglas's opinion that Goldberg insisted upon the direct link between penumbras and the Ninth Amendment:

Reaching the conclusion that the right of marital privacy is protected, as being within the protected penumbra of specific guarantees of the Bill of Rights, the Court refers to the Ninth Amendment. I add these words to emphasize the relevance of that Amendment to the Court's holding.[59]

Goldberg's "Fourteenth-Amendment-substantive-due-process-incorporation-via-Ninth-Amendment" strategy gives the right to privacy a different meta-positivistic foundation than Harlan's direct and exclusive appeal to the Fourteenth Amendment. Goldberg rejects the idea that some article can in itself be an independent source of fundamental implicit rights, and this applies also to the Ninth Amendment, which only

> shows a belief of the Constitution's authors that fundamental rights exist that are not expressly enumerated in the first eight amendments. . . . In sum, the Ninth Amendment simply lends strong support to the view that the "liberty" protected by the Fifth and Fourteenth Amendments from infringement by the Federal Government or the States is not restricted to rights specifically mentioned in the first eight amendments.[60]

This means that, rather than standing "on its own bottom," analogous yet unrelated to the Bill of Rights (as believed by Harlan), the Fourteenth Amendment incorporates and represents that integral Constitution that lives in the link that the Ninth Amendment establishes between the whole written Constitution and its unwritten foundations and peripheries. This is a very different holism than that of Harlan's traditionalist "rational continuum." On the other hand, the notion of the integral Constitution, the true if undeveloped core of the Goldberg/Douglas approach, focuses on the whole Constitutional text as a "limited Whole" mirroring, through the door of the Ninth Amendment, the universal and ontological Constitutional form, that which we have defined as the principle of the Whole of Wholes.

The overall form of the Bill of Rights, which is the very soul of the Constitution, with its hierarchy of amendments and rights, is more essential than the specific content of the various amendments themselves, because that very content can be properly assessed only in relation to the overall frame. Such a constitutional form/structure has itself a penumbral character, given that nowhere are its architectural principles explicitly or textually posited. And yet, it is a potent form, as the fundamental principle of liberty of the Fifth and Fourteenth Amendment's due process, for instance, cannot be understood apart from the overall constitutional form, from that "firstness" of the First Amendment that gives a higher degree of protection to the inner liberty of the noetic and deliberative mind over the outer and more accidental liberty of personality or proprietary conduct.

Such an implicit constitutional form/structure, which presents us with *the image of a well-differentiated totality*, is nonseparately independent not only from the historical accidents of the constituted community but also from the text that manifests it. Indeed, it is indestructible and always available for those who have eyes creative enough to see its constantly renewed appearances. When the determinate substance of the text is reunited with its implicit form, and through it to the universal form of the Whole of Wholes, the written Constitution comes alive, absorbing the "logic of facts" (onto-logic) and moving from the dry abstraction of a self-enclosed language to an apprehension and regulation of experience whereby the authority of the historical community and the liberty of its mortal members are reconciled in their reciprocally encompassing wholeness. Wrote Goldberg: "I agree fully with [the] Court that . . . the right of privacy is a fundamental personal right, emanating 'from the totality of the constitutional scheme under which we live.' "

The right to privacy itself, which is fundamental to any genuinely free society, is not written in the constitutional text, yet it "emanates" from the living architecture that such a text represents.

Like Douglas, Goldberg considered the right to privacy a general constitutional right, of which family privacy is, although important, only one of its aspects.[61] He extensively quoted from Brandeis's *Olmstead* dissent in order to reassert that the right of privacy is the "most comprehensive of rights and the right most valued by civilized men," and to show how the hierarchical architecture of the constitutional totality has noetic-spiritual privacy as its essence and ground.[62] The idea that the right to privacy is rooted in the penumbral living constitutional scheme beyond the written Constitution is attributed by Goldberg to Douglas's majority opinion in *Griswold*, in accordance with a correct understanding of its esoteric core. The very sentence just quoted by Goldberg ("from the totality of the constitutional scheme under which we live") was taken from Douglas's dissent in *Poe*.[63] A similar conception was affirmed a year after *Poe*, in 1962, by Redlich:

When the question of standards is posed within the context of the Ninth and Tenth Amendments, rather than in terms of due process, a definite pattern starts to emerge. To comply with the purposes of these Amendments, the textual standard should be *the entire Constitution*. The original Constitution and its amendments project through the ages *the image of a free and open society*. The Ninth and Tenth Amendments recognized—at the very outset of our national experience—that it was impossible to fill in every detail of this image.[64]

The constitutional image is the *founding juridical myth*, the constantly retold story from which the significance of the principle of dialectical wholeness can be learned. It is this mythical intelligence, the will to represent the paradoxical and ineffable Idea/Form of the holistic-dialectic constitution of reality, that stands at the core of the Ninth Amendment understanding of due process. Redlich presented this view as an alternative to due process. But given that the formula "due process" by definition expresses only the legal commandment to interpret and regulate concrete experiences in accordance with the fundamental juridical ideal (or constitutional myth), Redlich's posture seems to make sense only insofar as it intends to overcome Harlan's Fourteenth Amendment and traditionalist substantivism. Goldberg, who by Redlich was partially influenced, rightly perceived the same general approach as a different form of substantive due process. Contrary to Harlan, he thought of the Fourteenth Amendment as a smaller "limited whole" incorporating at the local level the larger "limited whole" of Bill of Rights, which in turn reproduces in its structure the unwritten ontological constitution of the world, or macrocosmic whole (in a way similar to the macro-microcosmic conception that is found, for instance, in the contemporary theory of fractals). Goldberg went directly back to Brandeis's and Cardozo's "selective incorporation," which, like Douglas's "total incorporation plus," was meant to open itself up toward the unwritten constitution.[65]

By finding in the concrete wholeness of the constitutional text the transcendent form that becomes the living substance of a well-ordered liberty, the Douglas/Goldberg position represented, in the context of *Griswold*, the only genuine form of due process, formal/substantive due process. The regret is that Douglas, for reasons that we have tried to explain, did not explicitly develop such an approach. This uncertainty throws a shadow on an otherwise great judge. Nevertheless, Douglas's understanding of fundamentals has always been unfaltering, and fundamental were for him the very same values that Brandeis considered fundamental, with privacy at the very top of the list. To him, privacy was the cornerstone of the Constitution and the most essential First Amendment, and it was so as a right that protects not the freedom to act and choose arbitrarily, but the liberty to be alone and to return inside:

Liberty in the constitutional sense must mean more than freedom from unlawful governmental restraint; it must include privacy as well, if it is to be a repository of freedom. The *right to be let alone* is indeed the beginning of all freedom.[66]

NOTES

1. 300 U.S. 379 (1937). L. Tribe, *American Constitutional Law* (Foundation Press, 1988), 581.

2. See also A. Mason, *Brandeis: A Free Man's Life* (New York: Viking, 1946), 624–27.

3. 302 U.S. 319 (1937), at 325, quoting *Snyder v Massachusetts*, 291 U.S. 97, at 105.

4. H. J. Abraham, *Freedom and the Court* (Oxford, 1988), pp. 107–17.

5. See Frankfurter, "Concurring Opinion," in *Adamson v California*, 332 U.S. 46 (1946). In the same case Black wrote a dissenting opinion in which he accused the majority of the Court of practicing "natural law."

6. 304 U.S. 144 (1938), at 152.

7. See, among recent interventions, B. Ackerman, "Beyond 'Carolene Products,' " in *Harvard L.R.* 98 (1985): 713; and Powell, "Carolene Products Revisited," in *Columbia L.R.* (1982): 1087.

8. J. Ely, *Democracy and Distrust* (Harvard, 1980), p. 77.

9. H. Garfield, "Privacy, Abortion and Judicial Review: Haunted by the Ghost of *Lochner*" in *Washington L.R.* 61 (1986): 287, 300–2. That Stone did not assign to footnote four the general relevance presumed by Ely is confirmed by Lusky himself, who materially wrote the note. According to Lusky, who was at the time Stones's legal assistant, the note was offered "not as a settled theorem of government or Court-approved standard of judicial review, but as a starting point for debate." Lusky, "Footnote Redux: A *Carolene Products* Reminiscence," in *Columbia L.R.* 32 (1982): 1093, note 52, p. 1098.

10. *Minersville School District v Gobitis*, 310 U.S. 586 (1940), at 606–7.

11. "Thus the attempt to distinguish the rights protected during the Lochner era from the preferred rights [of the 1937 revolution] in terms of a supposed dichotomy between economic and personal rights must fail, and a wider conception of what human beings require becomes unavoidable." Tribe, p. 779.

12. For a theoretical statement of Black's rights-absolutism, see H. Black, "The Bill of Rights," in *New York Univ. L.R.* 35 (1960): 866.

13. *Thomas v Collins*, 323 U.S. 516 (1944), at 529–30.

14. Tribe, p. 582.

15. Garfield, p. 303. The Supreme Court itself had previously defined the "equal protection clause" the last resort of constitutional argument. *Buck v Bell*, 274 U.S. 208 (1927).

16. 316 U.S. 535 (1942), at 541.

17. A. Baldassarre, *Privacy e Costituzione* (Roma, 1974), p. 137. The case involved the right of a Jehovah witness not to salute the American flag.

18. The case established the legitimacy of a municipal regulation prohibiting the use of noisy loudspeakers on vehicles circulating in public streets, on the ground that in "his home or on the street [the unwilling listener] is practically helpless to escape this interference with his privacy by loud speakers except through the protection of the municipality." *Kovacs v. Cooper*, 336 U.S. 77, at 87.

19. *Kovacs v Cooper*, 336 U.S. 77.

20. Baldassarre, p. 163.

21. W. O. Douglas, *Go East, Young Man: The Autobiography of W. O. Douglas* (New York, 1974), 343–76.

22. "These investigations of subversives neither started in the New Deal nor ended with it. The first Un-American Activities Committee in the House during the days of the New Deal was created in 1934." Douglas, *Go East, Young Man,* p. 385, in a chapter entitled "The Witch Hunt in the New Deal," pp. 377–92. Of the same period is another repressive law, the *Smith Act* (1940), 18 *U.S. Code* 2385 (1958).

23. Frankfurter himself seemed to be shocked only by physically disgusting behavior, as when, in *Rochin v California* [342 U.S. 165 (1952)], the police had made Rochin vomit capsules containing narcotic drugs by force-feeding him with an emetic. Other cases showing the liberticide posture of the Vinson Court are: *Dennis v United States*, 341 U.S. 494 (1951), where the "clear and present danger" test was abandoned in favor of a much more relaxed "grave and probable danger" test; *American Communication Association C.I.O. v Douds*, 339 U.S. 382, at 397; the cases involving the so-called "sensitive positions," or jobs considered relevant for the national security, which for the Court included even teaching in public schools. See *Garner v Los Angeles Board of Public Works*, 341 U.S. 716 (1951); *Adler v Board of Education*, 342 U.S. 485 (1952).

24. See the upholding of *Dennis* in *Yates v United States*, 354 U.S. 299 (1957); as to "sensitive positions" see *Konisberg v State Bar of California*, 366 U.S. 36 (1961); and for the "right to silence" see *Uphaus v Wyman*, 360 U.S. 72 (1959) and *Barenblatt v United States*, 360 U.S. 109 (1959).

25. In the famous case, *N.A.A.C.P. v Alabama* [357 U.S. 449 (1958)], where the N.A.A.C.P. claimed the right to disregard an Alabama law imposing on associations the disclosure of their membership to the government. The Court recognized such a right, but only on the ground that the N.A.A.C.P. could not be considered subversive or communist-infiltrated. The McCarthyist point of view remained, yet the sentence is important, as it gives the right to privacy a first if limited constitutional recognition.

26. 367 U.S. 497, at 521.
27. Tribe, p. 775.
28. Goldberg wrote a separate concurring opinion, adhered to by Warren and Brennan, but Harlan concurred in the judgment but not in its reasoning, proposing as an alternative rationale a substantive due process independently sustained by the Fourteenth Amendment. Finally White, in a separate opinion of his own, supported Harlan's general position yet remained skeptical about the constitutional character of the right to privacy. See, for example, P. G. Kauper, "Penumbras, Peripheries, Emanations, Things Fundamental and Things Forgotten: The *Griswold* Case," *Michigan L.R.* 64 (1965): 197, where Douglas is criticized for not having developed an explicit natural law solution; and Note, "On Privacy: Constitutional Protection for Personal Liberty," in *New York Univ. L.R.* 48 (1973): 670.
29. Black, "Dissenting Opinion," 381 U.S. 479, at 511 (including note 3).
30. On Douglas's love of nature and naturalistic experiences see his autobiography, *Go East, Young Man,* especially Ch. 14, "Conservation." Exceptional for a Supreme Court Justice, Douglas has been a very prolific writer. Among his thirty-two books we find various environmental works, two of which are true green manifestos ahead of their time: *A Wilderness Bill of Rights* (Boston, 1965); *The Three Hundred Years War: A Chronicle of Ecological Disaster* (New York, 1972).
31. In J. Allen (ed.), *Democracy and Finance: Addresses and Public Statements of W. O. Douglas* (Yale, 1940), p. 16.
32. W. O. Douglas, *Points of Rebellion* (New York, 1969). For his relations with Native Americans and hoboes, *Go East, Young Man*, pp. 69ff and 75ff.
33. Douglas, "The Lasting Influence of Mr. Justice Brandeis," in *Temp. L.Q.* 19 (1946): 361, 362.
34. Interested in Douglas's work at the SEC, Brandeis invited him over for a discussion in 1934. Since then, the two met regularly almost every week. In his autobiography, Douglas claims that Brandeis himself chose him as his Supreme Court successor. He writes: "When I learned, after the event, that Brandeis had gone to FDR and asked that I be named to take his place on the Court when he retired on February 13, 1939 I was the proudest human alive." *Go East, Young Man,* pp. 449, and more generally pp. 441–53.
35. Douglas, *Go East, Young Man,* pp. 374–76, 423–25, 462 (on Douglas's relation with Frank).
36. Ibid. pp. 449–53.
37. "As the decade progressed, Justice Douglas was increasingly influenced by the legal theories of Brandeis, Chafee and Meiklejohn." Note, "Toward a Constitutional Theory of Individuality: The Privacy Opinions of Justice Douglas," *Yale L.J.*, 87, 8 (1978): pp. 1597–1600, p. 1584. However, Chafee is closer to Holmes than to Brandeis and Meiklejohn, which shows how Douglas was still entangled by some ideological confusion.
38. 367 U.S. 497 (1961), p. 516 and p. 521, note 13, for his quotation of Murphy's *Adamson* dissent.
39. W. O. Douglas, *The Right of the People* (New York, 1952), 1972 ed., p. 58.
40. Note, *Toward a Constitutional Theory*, pp. 1585–86.
41. "Overtones of some arguments suggest that *Lochner v New York* should be our guide. But we decline that invitation. . . . We do not sit as a super-legislature to determine the wisdom, need, and propriety of laws that touch economic problems, business affairs

or social conditions. This law, *however*, operates directly on an intimate relation of husband and wife and their physician's role in one aspect of that relation." 381 U.S. 479 at 482.

42. T. I. Emerson, "Nine Justices in Search of a Doctrine," in *Mich. L.R.* 64 (1965): 219, p. 223.

43. According to Kauper, p. 253, Douglas's interpretation of *Pierce* and *Meyer* would have surprised Justice Reynolds, who wrote the Court opinion in both cases.

44. Note, *Toward a Constitutional Theory of Individuality*, p. 1586, note 44.

45. Douglas, *The Right of the People*, p. 58.

46. 410 U.S. 179 (1973), at 212, note 4.

47. W. O. Douglas, *The Court Years* (New York, 1980), p. 55.

48. "The basis of judgment as to the Constitutionality of state action must be a rational one, approaching the text, which is the only commission for our power not in a literalistic way, as if we had a tax statute before us, but as the basic charter of our society, setting out in spare but meaningful terms the principles of government." *Poe v Ullman*, 367 U.S. 497 (1961), at 540.

49. See *Poe v Ullman*, 367 U.S. 497, at 543, 541, and *Griswold v Connecticut*, 381 U.S. 479, at 500.

50. *Poe v Ullman*, 367 U.S. 497, at 544.

51. Garfield, p. 311, note 108.

52. 381 U.S. 479, at 501.

53. *Poe v Ullman*, 367 U.S. 497, at 542.

54. 367 U.S. 497, at 547.

55. "[Although] the States are and should be left free to reflect a wide variety of policies, and should be allowed broad scope in experimenting with various means of promoting those policies, I must agree with Mr. Jackson that 'There are limits to the extent to which a legislatively represented majority may conduct . . . experiments at the expense of the dignity and personality' of the individual." 367 U.S. 497, at 555.

56. Dworkin, too, claims that liberalism is indeed communitarian insofar as it is the basic content of "our tradition" and "our community." See R. Dworkin, "Liberal Community," in *Calif. L.R.*, 77, 479 (1989), p. 483; and *Law's Empire* (Harvard, 1986). For my criticism of Dworkin's position, whose substantive contents are indeed quite different from Harlan's, see *Privacy, Rights and Natural Law*, Ph.D. thesis, University of Toronto, 1993, Ch. 4 (6).

57. 367 U.S. 497, at 548–52.

58. 367 U.S. 497, at 552–53.

59. 381 U.S. 479, at 486–87.

60. 381 U.S. 479, at 492–93.

61. "The Connecticut statutes here involved deal with a particularly important and sensitive area of privacy—that of the marital relation and the marital home." Goldberg, Concurring Opinion, at 495.

62. 381 U.S. 479, at 494. It must be said that sometimes Goldberg seems to partially fall under the traditionalist spell, as when he sides with Harlan in supporting the State's power to repress homosexuality and fornication (at 499).

63. 367 U.S. 497, at 517, 521.

64. N. Redlich, "Are There 'Certain Rights . . . Retained by the People'?" in *New York Univ. L.R.* 37, 787 (1962): 810–11. In support of Redlich's position as applied to

Griswold see R. B. McKay, "The Right of Privacy: Emanations and Intimations," *Univ. of Mich. L.R.* 64, 259.

65. "Although I have not accepted the view that 'due process' as used in the Fourteenth Amendment incorporates all of the first eight Amendments . . . I do agree that the concept of liberty protects those personal rights that are fundamental, and is not confined to the specific terms of the Bill of Rights." 381 U.S. 479, at 486.

66. W. Douglas, Dissenting Opinion, *Public Utilities v Pollak*, 343 U.S. 451 (1952), 467.

5
ABORTION AND THE NEW PRIVACY PARADIGM

PRIVACY AND ABORTION

The prevalence of the Douglas/Goldberg approach gave rise to an extensive development of the right to privacy, although the mediatory character of Douglas's official exoteric opinion "acquiesced in a conception of privacy that was susceptible to constriction by the more conservative Burger Court."[1] But before that constriction could be felt, the right to privacy was able to grow, if somewhat distortedly, in three main areas:

a) The privacy of conscience and thought, generally associated with the First Amendment[2]
b) The privacy of body and home, associated with the Fourth Amendment
c) The privacy of the accused, protected by the Fifth Amendment[3]

This was a time of growing popular concern over the technological invasions of privacy, and in various dissenting opinions both Douglas and Brennan had forcefully voiced such concerns.[4] In this area, the proprietary rule of physical trespass established in *Olmstead* was still in force. But after a slow erosion,[5] *Olmstead* was finally reversed in *Katz v United States*, which stated that "the Fourth Amendment protects people, not places." The Court added that the right to privacy cannot be limited to the Fourth Amendment, being instead a general constitutional principle.[6] Things began slowing down with the advent of the

Burger Court, which nevertheless has not been as reactionary as one might have expected. Besides the partial reversal of the liberal *Miranda* criteria in the field of criminal law and procedures,[7] in the field of freedom of expression, the Burger years have brought about a "net diminution in the boundary of the free speech clause for those without money to pay as against the enlarged prerogatives of those with the means to advertise."[8]

Undoubtedly, the Burger Court has gradually been able to partially reestablish the priority of economic and proprietary rights, including some of the old *Lochner* standards.[9] But we must be careful not to confuse property rights *tout court* with the "bigness" rights of public and private oligopolies defended by the Burger majority. This is a common mistake, often linked to that dualistic interpretation of the "double standard" that opposes proprietary rights as a whole to personal and privacy rights abstracted from their material base. Van Alstyne, for instance, claims that due to the reemergence of property rights during the Burger era, the "nascent revolution of Millian autonomy has been altogether checked," and liberty has been understood "more in the mode of John Locke and of Adam Smith and somewhat less in the mode of John Mill (or of John Rawls)."[10]

Apart from the fact that there are more affinities between Locke and Rawls than Van Alstyne may think, the reality is that the privacy revolution of the 1960s, with its foundations in the 1937 revolution of "preferred freedoms," had very little to do with Millianism, at least until *Roe v Wade*. The Warren Court as a whole never justified its decisions in terms of the public/private opposition nor accepted the liberal-Millian dualism of deontological rights and economic goods/policies, with its parallel dualistic reading of the "double standard." This is shown clearly by the very case that Van Alstyne considers the best example of the reemergence of the property paradigm during the Burger years, and whose majority was formed, contrary to what Van Alstyne's interpretive framework would make one think, by the very Justices who directly promoted the supposedly "Millian revolution."

In *Lynch v Household Finance Corp.* [405 U.S. 538 (1972)], Stewart, Douglas, Brennan and Marshall were the majority; Burger, White, and Blackmun dissented. Mrs. Lynch was a worker whose employer was depositing a percentage of her salary into a savings account, and who had been sued by Household Finance Corp. for the insolvency of a promissory note. Before trial the corporation, under the provisions of a Connecticut statute, garnished her savings account. The District Court rejected Mrs. Lynch's appeal on the ground of a dualistic interpretation of the double standard giving the legislator full control over economic matters. Stewart's opinion rejected any judicial abdication in matters of distributive justice, as well as any abstract conception of individual rights:

This Court has never adopted the distinction of personal liberties and proprietary rights. ... The dichotomy between personal liberties and property rights is a false one. Property does not have rights. People have rights. The right to enjoy property without unlawful deprivation, no less than the right to speak or the right to travel, is in truth a "personal" right, whether the "property" in question be a welfare check, a home or a savings account. In fact, a fundamental interdependence exists between the personal right to liberty and the personal right to property. Neither could have meaning without the other.[11]

Stewart may be exaggerating the equal footing of property and liberty. But he understood the value of property from a personalistic point of view, as proven by the fact that his decision protected the personal right to property of Mrs. Lynch against the impersonal proprietary interests of a capitalistic corporation; and, as confirmed by the unconditional concurrence in Stewart's opinion by Douglas, a most consistent opponent of "bigness." The allegation of Lochnerism should thus be limited only to a minority of the Burger Court, and only in relation to the economic sphere. Instead, it has often been extended to the majority of the Court, especially in reference to the line of privacy cases following *Griswold*.

The most controversial case in that respect has certainly been *Roe v Wade*, where the woman's right to decide about abortion has been established as rooted in the constitutional right of privacy:

This right to privacy, whether it be founded in the Fourteenth Amendment's concept of personal liberty and restrictions upon state action, as we feel it is, or, as the District Court determined, in the Ninth Amendment's reservation of rights to the people, is broad enough to encompass a woman's decision whether or not to terminate her pregnancy.

Blackmun managed to reconcile Harlan's approach with the Douglas/Goldberg position by correctly recognizing them as different versions of substantive due process. He connected them with the formal/substantive due process of Brandeis and Cardozo by stating that because the "Constitution does not explicitly mention any right of privacy," both approaches cannot but refer to those "personal rights that can be deemed 'fundamental' or 'implicit in the concept of ordered liberty' " (a famous quote from Cardozo's opinion in *Palko*). Thus, a unitary thread of substantive due process emerges, running from *Meyer* and *Pierce*, to Brandeis's dissent in *Olmstead*, to *Griswold*. Given the nondualistic conception of the "double standard" that unites Brandeis, Cardozo, and the post-*Griswold* Justices of the *Lynch* case, such a notion of due process should not be called "noneconomic," but "formal/substantive."

Though purportedly siding with Harlan on the question of the Fourteenth Amendment's grounding of substantive due process, Blackmun converges even technically toward the Douglas/Goldberg doctrine of due process by acknowledging the existence of a wide textual-logical basis for the constitutional right to privacy, and therefore opening to the notion of constitutional totality. At the same time, by treating abortion as a simultaneously individual and social problem, he seems to refuse not only Harlan's traditionalism but also liberal atomism.

Blackmun grounded the right to privacy on various constitutional amendments (First, Fourth, Fifth, Ninth, Fourteenth), and more generally on that form of "ordered liberty" that is the true essence of the Constitution. With this methodological move, Blackmun substantively dropped Harlan's privacy-familism, upholding instead the notion of a general and comprehensive right to privacy that also "has some extension to activities relating to marriage, procreation, contraception, family relationship, child rearing and education."[12] Furthermore, by resting the Fourteenth Amendment itself on the whole of the constitution, written and unwritten, Blackmun made the esoteric content of *Griswold* explicit. In this, he was supported by Stewart who, in a concurring opinion, wrote that "*Griswold* stands as one in a long line of ... cases decided under the doctrine of substantive due process, and I now accept it as such."[13] The uncertain and indulgent rebuttal of Douglas in *Doe v Bolton* implicitly acknowledged the possible emergence of a unitary conception of substantive due process involving the majority of the Court.

Although Blackmun's unitary version of formal/substantive due process is still afflicted by important limits, it represents a positive methodological step in the right direction. Yet, apart from a few sympathetic if not uncritical articles,[14] most commentators have simply refused *Roe* as a whole. John Ely has led the attack by accusing *Roe* of resurrecting Lochnerism and of developing a "noninterpretive" and thus constitutionally unfounded substantive due process.[15] But allegations of judicial arbitrariness have been advanced by thinkers that Ely himself would consider "noninterpretivists."[16] The criticism generally advanced against *Roe* has been that it has produced "judicial legislation" through a decision that, rather than merely invalidate the Texas statute under scrutiny, has specified the basic criteria of legitimacy for all state and federal legislation. The criteria themselves have also been criticized for breaking the proper judicial boundaries and falling into a "medical approach" structured on hospital-like rules and regulations.[17]

Indeed, the second and more substantive element of Blackmun's opinion is the medical criterion of the fetus's viability, which set the limit of the woman's right to privacy in the abortion situation. This criterion is questionable, but for different reasons than for its "medical" character or "legislative" nature. In fact, one of the main merits of Blackmun has been his attempt to overcome, through the notion of viability, the unilateral and polarized attitudes of abdicating to the majoritarian or traditionalist will on the one hand and requiring an absolute noninterference with the private choice of the woman on the other. Though acknowledging the fundamental character of the woman's right to privacy in reproductive matters, Blackmun made it clear that her right cannot be an absolute, because there are important public interests with which it must balance. He thus asserted that such a right can be compressed by a vital and therefore compelling interest of the State.[18]

For Blackmun, the compelling public interest in the abortion situation comprises two complementary elements: the protection of the mother's health and

Abortion and the New Privacy Paradigm

the protection of the potential human life of the fetus. This twofold interest becomes stronger the more advanced the pregnancy: "With respect to the State's important and legitimate interest in the health of the mother, the 'compelling' point, in the light of present medical knowledge, is at approximately the end of the first trimester. . . . With respect to the State's important and legitimate interest in potential life, the 'compelling' interest is at viability." As to viability, Blackmun wrote that it "is usually placed at about seven months (28 weeks), but may occur earlier, even at 24 weeks" and described it as the moment when the fetus "presumably has the capability of meaningful life outside the mother's womb" if sustained by appropriate technologies. The Court concluded that during the first three months of pregnancy, the State can only prescribe that abortion be practiced by a regularly registered medical doctor; during the second trimester, the public interest in the mother's health authorizes appropriate governmental regulations of the ways in which the abortion is practiced; and only after viability, around the beginning of the third trimester, the State "may go so far as to proscribe abortion . . . except when it is necessary to preserve the life or health of the mother."[19]

Having decided to determine the limits of legislation on abortion, the Court had to tackle the substance of the problem, and the problem being eminently scientific precisely where it is ethical, it could not avoid considering the medical and physiological factors involved. Therefore, the allegations of medicalization are misleading. As to the allegation of *Roe* being "judicial legislation," the argument that the Court should not have interfered with the States' power to decide on abortion has been advanced not only by antichoice writers but also by those who thought that the States would have recognized the woman's right to choose anyway, thus giving such right a fuller political legitimacy.[20] Had this argument been followed by the Court, a great disparity among the different States would have resulted in a field involving fundamental values and rights. Tribe has rightly pointed out that the "fatal flaw of the 'legislative solution' argument is that it presumes that fundamental rights can properly be reduced to political interests . . . [and] it ignores the choice of a fundamentally different form of government that was made for our nation two centuries ago: 'The very purpose of a Bill of Rights was to withdraw certain subjects from the vicissitudes of political controversy.' "[21]

But some have simply denied that the right at stake in *Roe* was truly fundamental. J. Ely, for example, claims that no right to privacy was really involved in *Roe*, because the Court merely established a constitutionally unsupported right to abortion.[22] Helen Garfield has rightly written that when

> the right to privacy is fragmented in this way, it becomes possible to attack any segment of the right as judicial legislation. . . . The distinction between the right to abortion and the right to make the abortion decision is crucial to the definition and scope of the right. A right to abortion would protect the pregnant woman only if she decided to have an abortion. Protecting the decision protects also her right not to have an abortion.[23]

This means that the right at stake in *Roe* does not protect abortion as a value but rather the woman's freedom from constraints and necessities, including the freedom not to be forced to have an abortion by the circumstances. In this sense, the ultimate goal of the right to privacy in the abortion context is to reduce the painful and harmful necessity of abortions, thus allowing the woman to take into full account the interest of her critical others: the fetus, the family, the community. This brings us back to Blackmun's nonatomistic premises. He wrote that the "pregnant woman cannot be isolated in her privacy," the abortion situation being "inherently different" from other forms of familial privacy in that it involves the collective interest to the life of the fetus and to the health of the mother. Because of this, and in spite of the fact that he mediates these elements of substantive and communitarian ethics with stronger elements of liberal relativism and atomism, as we shall see, Blackmun has been subjected to harsh allegations of conservatism by various liberal and/or radical thinkers. According to Grey, the contraception and abortion cases are "dedicated to the cause of social stability through the reinforcement of traditional institutions and have nothing to do with the sexual liberation of the individual."[24] We should indeed be thankful that the contraception and abortion cases have nothing to do with the sexual liberation ideology, which, at least in its dominant versions, is a by-product of capitalism and its generalized consumeristic attitude toward both things and persons.[25] Grey argues for a normalization of sexual instincts and practices whereby they would be perceived as something no more special than eating a sandwich.[26] The powerful force of instincts, both healing and dangerous, is completely erased, together with their intrinsic and precious potential for self-transcendence. The spiritual and transpersonal significance of instincts and desires, and of pleasure as their ruling principle, is especially revealed in erotic relations and orgasm, sensuous forms of self-transcendence that, due to their intense materiality, require strong ethical limits, first of all the commandment of not using the other.

Grey places both Douglas and Blackmun among the conservatives, opposing them to "a modern, rationalist, individualist outlook reflecting the perspective of J. S. Mill, Professor Hart" and others.[27]

Although he flirted with Millianism in his attempt to forge a compromise between Brandeis and Black, in the end Douglas remained true to Brandeis's transpersonal natural law. Blackmun, instead, belongs to a new generation of judges, including Brennan and Marshall, who have drawn from Millianism like never before, although they too have had to balance liberal dualism with the dialectical holism inherent in the very nature of the law. Interestingly enough, the resulting mediation has been more faithful to Mill than Millianism has ever been. We have seen that Mill ended up with a two-layered type of mediation whereby the transpersonal and ecological values were superimposed on a more fundamental bedrock of utilitarian possessivism and liberal dualism. This is what the new breed of judges has generally done, and only with them, and after *Roe*, has it become possible to confuse the discourse of privacy with the discourse

Abortion and the New Privacy Paradigm

of Millian liberty, as one Millian commentator of *Roe* has done: "Mill found impermissible laws predicated on either the state interest in the enforcement of morality or in paternalism. Mill's principle of liberty would, therefore, overlap many claims that might otherwise be couched in terms of privacy." Yet, the same writer admits that the new position emerging in the Court is not reducible to Millianism. In commenting on *Paris Adult Theatre v Slaton* [413 U.S. 49 (1973)], involving the public consumption of pornography, he writes:

The Court acknowledged the state interest in the prevention of physical harm to others and the prevention of non-physical offense, but was apparently eager to demonstrate that the state's interest does not end there ... [and] gave explicit recognition to the state's interest in protecting "the social interest in order and morality."[28]

Paris, a decision of the Burger-Rehnquist majority in which Blackmun concurred, is quite representative of that mediatory and dualistic superimposition of holistic values over a base of liberal dualism (Mill's harm to others), an approach that can be also found in the *Roe* majority opinion.

That the "compelling state interest" does not emerge until the "viability of the fetus" means that the state cannot interfere until the fetus, being able to live outside and independently of the mother, has become *other* than the mother and thus capable of being protected by the "harm to other" principle. From this point of view, whatever happens before viability is the private business of the woman, the only legally relevant subject, a separate self that the Millian principle makes immune from any responsibility toward individual or communal others. But this is truly untenable, because from around the end of the third month, when the fetus's quickening or animation occurs, it becomes impossible to talk of a separate self for either the mother or the fetus. Starting from that moment, there are two empirical selves in one, and pregnancy becomes materially symbolic of the delusory character of any empirically separate selfhood. The corporeal unity of mother and fetus, unique as it is, manifests, in the most physical and evident way, the universal condition of existential interdependence: We all, like the child in the womb, breathe the air filtered by mother earth's green lungs, are nourished by her various digestive and transformative organs, and develop our sensibility through the stimuli coming from the environment she provides.

The principle of interdependence has always been at the core of the legal tradition, and this is why Blackmun cannot simply uphold Mill's principle of liberty. Aware of the special interdependence between mother and fetus, which in turn mirrors the general interdependence of all members of the community, including those who are to be born, Blackmun recognized that the "pregnant woman cannot be isolated in her privacy." It is just a statement of principle, but it is enough to stir up accusations of "paternalism" and "glaring departure from Mill's principle."[29]

In fact, the crucial limit to Blackmun's opinion is that such a recognition of interdependence remains quite undeveloped in practice, which leads to an excessive acceptance of Millian liberalism. Blackmun put together in a purely mediatory and contradictory way on the one hand the principle of harm to others and on the other hand a nonrelativistic principle of harm to self, implicit in his legitimization of the public power to limit the harm that the pregnant woman may inflict to herself through the abortive practices. The two sides of his discourse only limit each other externally, each enclosed in itself and untouched by the constitutive influence of the other. Thus, the only relevant harm before viability is the possible self-harm to the separate self of the mother, with no concern whatsoever for the fetal side of the physically existential and unitary self that emerges in pregnancy. This is the most serious limit of Blackmun's solution, condemning to irrelevance the supposedly yet-non-other fetus, and therefore also the delicate and sometimes tragic intimacy and inseparability of mother and fetus, both before and after viability.

Had Blackmun taken a truly holistic and dialectical approach, he would have had to adopt something like the principle of existential harm, which the pregnancy situation, whereby the harm to the fetus is an immediate mental and physical harm for the mother herself, exemplifies in the most intense way. The adoption of such a principle would have also revealed the insufficiency of the viability standard and of its physicalism, because the recognition of the material unity of self and other would have brought to the surface the essentially holographic nature of each self. Consistent with his mediatory approach, Blackmun has added to his physicalism a limited awareness of life as a spiritual, rather than merely physiological, reality. When he wrote that abortion can be a lesser evil relative to the bad life that an unwanted pregnancy may cause to both mother and child,[30] he recognized the superior value of a *life worth living* over the still important value of *life as such*, thus going back to the classical teleology of the good life, or life leading toward the most profound ethical and spiritual self-realization.[31]

For Ruth Colker, who explicitly adopts such a spiritual perspective, "the more appropriate route, which would have been more respectful of the value of life, would have been to recognize that the state has a compelling interest in ensuring *the valuation of fetal life*, but that criminalizing abortion is not a necessary means to achieving that end." This route is not in opposition to women's interests and feelings, because a "woman who chooses an abortion may still value fetal life. . . . Women may value fetal life but also hold other values [i.e., good life and a true caring relationship for both her and the child to be born] which lead them to choose an abortion."[32]

Colker's position is thus an alternative both to the pro-lifers' attempt to criminalize abortion and to the liberal-relativistic attempt to shield the woman's freedom of choice from any ethical and spiritual valuation. She develops here, to a fuller extent, a premise somewhat abstractly stated by Blackmun himself in the muffled holistic side of *Roe*. She writes:

My defense of women's ability to choose an abortion is not absolute. It is contingent upon existing social circumstances.... From the perspective of love and compassion, I accept the argument that women have the responsibility in this world to nurture love and life. Since we are connected selves, we have no claim to act in ways to protect our bodily integrity in isolation from society.

Colker underlines how pro-lifers are often blinded toward the circumstances that make an abortion necessary. Though recognizing that they give voice to deeply felt needs and feelings, including those of women who have gone through traumatic abortion experiences,[33] she rightly states that their criminalization of all abortions under all circumstances sheds a malignant light on women, which multiplies the suffering already generated by the abortion experience. Pro-lifers discount the importance of the social and economic conditions surrounding pregnancy and abortions; pretend not to see the tragedy of back-alley abortions, which mostly affects poor and uneducated women, and which is a direct product of the criminalization of abortion; and too often supplement their fight against the right to the abortion decision with a fight against contraception, which only increases the cycle of more unwanted pregnancies and more abortions.[34] Due to these factors, writes Colker,

Society must allocate the responsibilities of its members compassionately and respectfully. A woman, in my view, has the right to seek an abortion to protect the value of her life in a society that disproportionately imposes the burdens of pregnancy and child care on women and does not sufficiently sponsor the development and use of safe, effective contraceptives.

Expanding on this approach, we are able to say that abortion may at times also protect the fetus itself, from a society that imposes miserable living conditions on too many people, that promotes the breakdown of families and communities, and that pollutes the planet to the point of making life itself more unlikely and newborns' malformations much more likely. A true and radical solution can only come from a deep transformation of the social, economic, and cultural conditions of the world in which we live, overcoming the wide gap between poor and rich, educated and uneducated, women and men, and making joyful sexuality, reproductive responsibility, and loving childrearing ordinary realities. As long as unjust conditions endure, abortions are bound to be present, even, if necessary, in the most painful and dangerous illegal forms. Thus, the right to the abortion choice needs to be maintained, not only to guarantee safe conditions to those who would otherwise abort in danger but also and foremost as a crucial means toward the minimization of abortions.

For this, the pregnancy/abortion decision must come through a proper decisional process, where women, and possibly men, can develop a deep valuation of the fetal life in relation to their material and emotional-spiritual condition, and from the point of view of that essential unity of self and other on which all true caring, including parental caring, rests. Were such a decisional process widely promoted, unnecessary abortions would be substantially reduced, and sexual partnership, reproductive choices, and parenthood would be highly improved.

Unfortunately, in *Akron v Akron Center for Reproductive Health*, the Supreme Court stated that informing the woman about the life of the fetus and the abortion procedure is unconstitutional. The decision itself was reasonable, given that in the specific case, as the Court wrote, "much of the information required is designed not to inform the woman's consent but rather to persuade her to withhold it altogether."[35] But the Court turned the criticism of the instrumental use of "informed consent" into a general and absolute principle, thus shutting off any possible discussion of how to promote a genuinely informed consent.

From the transpersonal point of view, "informed consent" is only the basis for a deeper involvement of the woman's conscience and interiority in the process of choosing about abortion. Colker, for instance, proposes that the law recognize "the need for women to be confronted with conflicting opinions about the abortion decision and to have a safe space in which to consider them." She would "support legislation requiring hospitals and clinics that perform abortions to make available group counselling sessions," both in the form of consciousness-raising meetings where women could talk to each other in an open and nonjudgmental way; and in the form of counseling sessions for all women (irrespective of whether they are considering an abortion or not, lest women considering abortion be singled out), where "pregnant women and their partners [can] discuss the quality of their own lives, the implications of raising a child or having an abortion, and the meaning or value of the fetus' life. These counseling sessions should be run by trained ethicists, not physicians, and should be voluntary." This should be complemented by giving women *a chance to be left alone* after having taught them how to go inside themselves through *meditation*, so as to internally reelaborate all the dialogue absorbed from consciousness and counseling sessions from the point of view of that essential privacy where liberty and responsibility, selfhood and otherness, are intimately fused. If that essential place is sufficiently approached, then the decision, whatever it may be, will necessarily yield the best possible solution available to the woman, the fetus, and the world.[36]

Given the stress she puts on meditation and on " 'inner peace' as the result of self-examination," it seems contradictory that Colker criticizes both the substantive due process methodology of *Griswold* and *Roe*, which deeply involves the ethical-spiritual privacy of the judge, and the formulation of the abortion issue in terms of privacy.[37] This is probably due to the fact that she identifies privacy with liberal privatism, therefore reactively falling into the political majoritarianism and judicial positivism of people like Ely. Given a genuine and spiritual understanding of privacy, corresponding to the original Brandeisian meaning, I am sure that Colker herself would agree that privacy is deeply implicated in the right to the abortion choice. In the abortion conundrum, the *mystery of life and death* comes to the surface, together with the mystery of birth as a primordial form of self-individuation over the background of the essential unity of self and other. As we have seen in Ch. 1, this places abortion in that general category of life and death issues that, pertaining to the most-intimate essence of being human, cannot but belong to the area of privacy and of its right. Although family and reproductive matters belong more specifically to the area of personality rights, abortion must in this sense be placed within the higher right of privacy as interiority (an idea that is even physically represented by the fact that the fetus is indeed "inner" to the mother). This makes the abortion choice immune from any outer interference and imposition, as spirit cannot be coerced but inherently subjected to the ethical and spiritual requirements characterizing the right of privacy and interiority.

There is at least one abortion law, the Italian "Legge 22 Maggio 1978, n. 194," which has opted, at least theoretically, for a similar approach. The "194," still deeply cherished by the Italian feminist movement, opens with the following statement: "The State guarantees the right to a conscious and responsible procreation, recognizes the social value of motherhood, and protects human life from its beginning." Starting from such a proper valuation of fetal life, the law asserts that the "voluntary interruption of pregnancy," although legally authorized in forms that we will discuss, "is not a means to birth control" (Art. 1). The "Consultori Familiari" (family counseling centers), instituted in 1975 and present in most Italian towns, are invested by the law with the task to minimize the use of abortion as a birth control device. They have the duty to inform the woman on her rights and on all forms of assistance available to her and to "contribute to remove the causes that could induce the woman to interrupt the pregnancy" (Art. 2, a–d). Furthermore, the "Regioni" are required to collaborate with the "Consultori" in promoting courses and seminars, both for the counseling and medical personnel, and for the public as a whole, concerning "sexual education, the course of pregnancy, birth, contraceptive methods, and abortion techniques" (Art. 15). Finally, in the development of all such activities, the "Consultori" are asked to collaborate with "the appropriate grassroots social groups and voluntary service associations" (Art. 2). Unfortunately, this aspect of the law has not been fully or properly developed, mostly due to a paralyzing confrontation between pro-choice and pro-life groups, which has made the pro-choice movement quite suspicious of any attempt at a spiritual and ethical treatment of the abortion issue, even though lately something seems to be changing.

The "194" is remarkable also in that it allows the performing of abortions only "within the first 90 days" of pregnancy (Art. 4–5). During the second trimester, abortion "can be practiced . . . when pregnancy or childbirth involve a grave danger for the life of the woman"; and in case of "pathological processes, including those relative to relevant anomalies or malformations of the fetus, which may determine a serious danger for the physical and psychological health of the woman" (Art. 6). After viability, abortion can be practiced only when there is a serious danger for the woman's life, but "the physician who performs the intervention must adopt any necessary measure to save the life of the fetus" (Art. 7). The "194," thus, still adopts a trimestral approach, but the point at which the State's interest in the fetal life becomes compelling is moved back to the beginning of the second trimester. This seems a much more sensible solution, both from a spiritual and a secular point of view.

Most spiritual and ethical traditions make a distinction between conception and animation. They see life as a function of the soul, thus placing the beginning of sentient life at animation (anima = soul). Aristotle and most ancient Greeks thought that the fetus does not become animated until at least forty days after conception for a male and eighty-ninety days for a female. This view was accepted into Christianity, and remained the official position of the Catholic Church until nearly a century ago. Of course, it is difficult to establish with precision the timing of such a subtle event as animation. But the distinction between conception and animation is important, because it acknowledges the shift from a merely material to a sentient and psychological life, while establishing the starting point of the progressive humanity of the fetus. This is confirmed by the concrete experience of pregnant women, who "feel" the fetus more like a person the more the pregnancy progresses.

Generally, in legal contexts deeply influenced by religion, as with the classical common law, animation has been identified with the quickening. This was the position taken by the great common law jurist Bracton, and "it is undisputed that at common law, abortion performed before 'quickening' ... was not an indictable offense."[38] This is very reasonable: Articulate and sensory reactive movement, as opposed to mere organic growth, is what distinguishes animals from the vegetable kingdom, thus marking the perceivable shift from a living but inanimate being to a sentient animated being. Quickening, whose date cannot be uniformly established, although certainly does not occur before the end of the first trimester, represents thus a significant practical notion both from a spiritual and a secular point of view. This is very important, given that, as Justice Stevens reminded us in *Webster v Reproductive Health Services* [109 S. Ct. 3040] "our jurisprudence ... has consistently required a secular basis for valid legislation." Manifesting in an empirically undeniable way the presence of a sentient though unviable life inside the womb, quickening has all the characteristics to constitute a secular criterion for determining that the interest of the State has become existentially compelling, that is, compelling because of the simultaneous harm to the fetus as a (physically) inseparate other, and to the mother in her deep existential, and thus inherently loving and responsible, selfhood.

The need for a shift from viability to quickening seems to have been implicitly acknowledged in *Webster* by Justice Stevens, who rightly insisted on the importance of differentiating between the various stages of fetal development, against the unjust equalization of a fully developed fetus and an embryo. Stevens has pointed out that even from a religious point of view it is possible, and indeed necessary, to recognize the difference between an embryo and a sentient/animated fetus. In so doing, he also implicitly admitted that a sentient fetus, having moved beyond the stage of a vegetable-like embryo, qualifies as a self, and thus as an other inside the physiological self of the mother. Although he did not say it, Stevens seems to have suggested the possibility of an alliance between the religious and secular around the notion of quickening, as he wrote: "Focusing our attention on the first several weeks of pregnancy is especially appropriate because that is the period when the vast majority of abortions are actually performed."[39] Making an effort to take the abortion decision within the first trimester is a due act of loving responsibility. This of course doesn't mean that before quickening the fetus is to be perceived as disposable matter, because even vegetable life is life, and in the case of the fetus it may be vegetable life already linked to a human soul, if only in a latent form.[40]

This is why it is always important that the decision on abortion be as introspectively aware and as globally responsible as possible, and this is why privacy is essential to the pregnancy/abortion decision. Such a link is reinforced at the symbolic level by the fact that pregnancy constitutes the most powerful embodiment of true privacy by revealing with full material clarity the essential inseparability and identity of self and other, of all private selves with each other, and of each with the cosmic mother/father, the universally public Self.

THE GROWING ATTACK ON THE RIGHT TO PRIVACY

The post–*Roe v Wade* antiprivacy trend has had a global impact. In the area of financial privacy the Burger Court, in *California Bankers Ass. v Schultz* [416 U.S. 21 (1974)], validated the Bank Secrecy Act of 1970, imposing on the banks a duty to maintain microfilm copies of all checks and account documents, and to make them available to the inspection of certain governmental agencies. This would seem to contradict the Burger Court's return toward a new economic Lochnerism,[41] but it is not so, because the result of *California Bankers* was in support of fiscal policies directed at subordinating personal liberty to the processes of capitalistic Bigness.

The growing fusion of governmental agencies and powerful economic groups under the leading principle of profit maximization has made fiscal activities more and more central for the reproduction of the capitalistic economic polity. The centralization of resources in the hands of big government has become essential to sustain the welfare state, the positive side of the modern capitalist state. But the welfare state is merely an instrument to guarantee social stability and is subordinated to the most essential function of the contemporary state—the participation in, and the administrative and military sustenance of, the overall mechanism of unlimited economic growth. Against such primary function, the welfare state gives in and shrinks whenever an economic crisis requires that resources be directed at pushing back up a sinking level of profits. In order to preserve the public/private oligopolistic structure, which may include different measures of welfare assistance, it is indispensable to have a properly working fiscal machine, capable of transferring resources to the main actors of the centralized, unlimited growth economy.[42] Indeed, what characterizes the Bank Secrecy Act discussed in *California Bankers* is its focus on very personal forms of property, such as individual checks and bank accounts, in a context whereby the privileged internal channels of tax evasion by both banks and multinational enterprises remain generally untouched. Douglas, in dissent, wrote:

In a sense a person is defined by the checks he writes. By examining them the agents get to know his doctors, lawyers, creditors, political allies, social connections, religious affiliation, educational interests, the papers and magazines he reads and so on ad infinitum. These are all tied to one's social security number; and now that we have the data banks, these other items will enrich that storehouse and make it possible for a bureaucrat—by pushing one button—to get in an instant the names of 190 million Americans who are subversive or potential and likely candidates.

For Douglas, the wide control advocated by the government over individual accounts has nothing to do with fighting crime and tax evasion, "unless we are to assume that every citizen is a crook, an assumption I cannot make." To fight crime and tax evasion, we do not need a "sledge-hammer approach" but a "delicate scalpel": The penetration of one's financial privacy is authorized by the Constitution when there is a "probable cause" of crime. The approach chosen by the government, and sustained by the Court, is right only "if Big Brother is to have his way."[43]

The aversion of the Burger Court to personal financial and fiscal privacy is part of a more general antiprivacy posture that Tribe calls the "retreat from Katz," or from the principle stating that the Fourth Amendment protects persons, not places. In this context, the theme of data banks has been underlined strongly by the late Douglas,[44] but when the Court took up the issue directly in 1977, he was no longer among its members. In *Whalen v Roe*, the Court validated a New York statute establishing that doctors, when prescribing certain heavy drugs for therapeutic purposes, must inform health authorities, who in turn must keep a computerized record of such prescriptions for a period of five years. The decision reversed the District Court, which claimed, in strong Douglasian terms, that the statute violated the right to privacy of patients, and especially the privacy of the doctor-patient relationship.[45]

In spite of the positive fact that Stevens's unanimous opinion made clear that the Court would have been much less tolerant toward data banks that do not fully guarantee against the risk of embarassing or harmful disclosures, the Court took the idea that bureaucratic and informational centralization serves administrative efficiency for granted. But we have seen in Ch. 1 that such an idea is a delusion, and no less delusory is the hope that procedural and technical guarantees may be sufficient to prevent abuses against privacy and the democratic process. Only Brennan, in his concurring opinion, forcefully stressed the need to prevent the governmental power to accumulate information from growing beyond clearly defined limits, in order to secure privacy and liberty.[46]

The antiprivacy trend of the Burger period is also quite visible in the area of associational privacy. As Tribe points out, associational privacy has a "dual character," because "the right of one person or group to exclude others is inevitably a limitation upon the freedom—including the associational freedom—of those others."[47] In two related cases, the Court established some basic criteria in order to solve the "dual character" conundrum, the most important being "intimacy," which makes exclusion legitimate only when the association promotes "the formation and preservation of certain kinds of highly personal relationships ... [from which] individuals draw much of their emotional enrichment ... [and develop an] ability to define [their] identity that is central to any concept of liberty."[48]

We must not exaggerate the special nature of the dual character of associational rights. All rights possess such a character, each implying a limitation upon other people's power to access its related sphere of liberty. The only difference is that the right to exclude others is in one case individual and in the other collective. At the same time, both individual and associational rights and privacy can exclude others only insofar as they, in a deeper sense, encompass and respect their fundamental rights/interests. Thus, the holder of the right to a certain property has full control over other people's access to that property, but only as long as his/her enactment of such control does not clash with the general requirements of material justice and social and ecological integrity. Similarly, the right to associational privacy, which implies the power to discretionally define the boundaries of the association, is valid only insofar as it does not transform *legitimate diversity* into illegitimate discrimination. Within this more general standard, the criterion of intimacy offered by the Court is certainly important, intimate and personal relations being the most basic forms of legitimate diversity. But there are others as well, as we have seen earlier with the *Belle Terre* case (see note 48), where the right to exclude was attributed to such a nonintimate association as a town because its communal and anticonsumeristic lifestyle could have been spoiled by an unlimited inclusion, which would have dissolved its legitimate diversity into the dominant socioeconomic and cultural models. In this sense, the general standard of legitimate diversity is constituted both by the criterion of personal intimacy and by that of a cultural, sexual, and ethnic homogeneity that is legitimate as long as it represents the core object of the association and does not become the element to unduly prevent culturally, sexually, or ethnically different people from participating into wider activities that do not intrinsically require such homogeneity. In other words, a feminist or a male-identity group, in which gender and its problems are the object of the association, have all the right to exclude people of the opposite sex, as do groups of black consciousness, or groups of white males coming to terms to their story and role in society. In all such cases, of course, there is a necessary requirement that such groups focus on the characters and problems of their homogeneous and distinctive identity and not on the attempt to demean, hate, or threaten the opposite group/identity. On the other hand, when for instance the object of the association is the organization of generally cultural or recreational events, charity, and beneficence, and so on, the exclusion of any group or person, based on gender, race or ideology, becomes clearly an act of unjustified discrimination.[49]

Generally speaking, the Burger Court has maintained an ambiguous position in relation to privacy, although toward the end its antiprivacy posture has become more radical (as we shall see). But the attack on privacy has undergone a great acceleration with the advent of the Rehnquist Court, which, in *Webster v Reproductive Health Services* [109 S.Ct. 3040 (1989)], has imposed the first serious revision of *Roe*. In the sixteen years between the two cases, the Court had essentially maintained the principle that reproductive decisions are protected by the right to privacy, confirming on the whole both *Griswold* and *Roe*.[50] On the other hand, some important limitations were imposed on the right to the abortion decision. A majority of the Court, including the anti-*Roe* and some of the pro-*Roe* judges, has continually asserted that the State may refuse to pay for abortion. It was established, in a series of cases, that the state can decide to pay all expenses relative to childbirth though contributing nothing to abortions, and can even forbid the practice of abortion in public hospitals.[51] In *Harris v McRae* [448 U.S. 297 (1980)], the same view was reaffirmed, with the further specification that the State can refuse to pay for abortion even when abortion is necessary to save the life or to protect the health of the mother.

McRae and other related cases, decided against the constant dissent of Brennan, Marshall, and Blackmun, and with the less constant dissent of Stevens, have become the target of a heavy feminist criticism, which has stressed how their outcome deprived indigent and economically dependent women—that is, the majority of women—of a right that is formally theirs. Such criticism has also focused on the limits of the privacy semantics, with the argument that treating the freedom to decide on abortion as a privacy right reduces abortion to a private business, logically justifying the argument that public powers cannot be responsible for it. C. MacKinnon, commenting on *McRae*, writes:

The private world of [children's] abuse and poor women's unfunded abortions, is the "free world." For those who use and abuse women and children, it is. . . . The doctrinal choice of privacy in the abortion context . . . reinforces what the feminist critique of sexuality criticizes the public/private split.[52]

MacKinnon, too, reduces privacy to its liberal and corrupted version, separative privatism. She overlooks the fact that Blackmun's *Roe* opinion is only in part grounded on the liberal conception of the private and that it also contains the claim that privacy is not atomistic isolation and it intrinsically implies social and public interests. It is this latter side that sustained the opposition of Blackmun, Brennan, and Marshall to the private/public dualism of *McRae*.

In *Webster v Reproductive Health Services*,[53] Rehnquist acknowledged, as the lower court had done [851 F.2d. 1071 (1988)], that the Missouri statute contrasts with *Roe* in that it "creates what is essentially a presumption of viability at 20 weeks, which the physician, prior to performing an abortion, must rebut with tests indicating that the fetus is not viable." But according to Rehnquist the statute does not substantially contravene *Roe* because the tests, contrary to the opinion of the lower court, are not mandatory, and there can be, as the lower court itself had admitted, "a 4-week error in estimating gestational age, which supports testing at 20 weeks."[54]

Stevens stressed, against Rehnquist's reversal of the Missouri District Court's reading of the statute, that the Missouri statute, which for Rehnquist leaves the tests to the discretion of the physician, "twice uses the mandatory term 'shall' and contains no qualifying language." In the same vein, Stevens rejects Rehnquist's depiction of the claim that life begins at conception, advanced in the statute's preamble, as a mere value judgment without relevant practical consequences, by reminding the Court that both *Roe* and *Akron* had prohibited the States to adopt any specific theory of when life begins, especially in the case of a theory that is "non-secular" and represents an "unequivocal endorsement of a religious tenet of some but by no means all Christian faiths."[55]

Although recognizing that the performance of tests at twenty weeks will make second-trimester abortions more expensive and more difficult, the Court considered it a legitimate burden in that it "permissibly furthers the State's interest in protecting potential human life." But because the "permissibly furthers" standard is based on the recognition of "the State's 'compelling interest' in protecting potential human life throughout pregnancy," clearly the decision is in evident opposition with *Roe*'s assumption that the State's compelling interest starts only at viability. And indeed Rehnquist, though formally reassuring us that the decision does not involve the validity of *Roe*, does not hesitate to say that the "trimesters and viability" approach of *Roe* is "unsound in principle and unworkable in practice."[56]

The ugliness of Rehnquist's opinion derives not from its intention to revise *Roe* (we too think it should be revised) but to radically yet surreptitiously undermine it through a falsely "proceduralist" position, which claims that all substantive decisions on abortion should be left to the various states, yet rests such claim on the very substantive presupposition that the compelling interest of the State is present "throughout pregnancy." If the compelling interest is equally present at all stages of pregnancy, the life of a nine-month-old fetus is equally valuable as the life of a fertilized egg. But, as Justice Stevens acutely pointed out, if there is no difference between a fertilized egg and a fully mature fetus on the eve of birth, their destiny could "scarcely be left to the will of state legislatures."[57]

Such logical contradictions do not overly worry Rehnquist, to whom logic seems to be an unnecessary option. With the same logical licentiousness, if we can say so, Rehnquist states that nowhere does the Constitution mention a right to abortion or a trimestral scheme, in a most obtuse literalist manner, which, says Blackmun, if adopted would practically erase most constitutional jurisprudence; and that *Roe* resembles more a code of regulations than a constitutional doctrine, even though he himself had shortly before asserted that "[m]any branches of the law abound in nice distinctions that may be troublesome but have been thought nonetheless necessary."[58]

Rehnquist's last argument, that there is no reason why the State's interest in potential human life should become irresistible only in the last trimester, seems to carry more weight, not because of its own logical strength but because of a parallel weakness in *Roe*. Blackmun rightly dismissed Rehnquist's "permissibly furthers" standard as "circular and totally meaningless," in that it takes the question (Where does the State's power to interfere extend?) for the answer (Wherever the State's power to interfere extends!). This tautological reasoning, says Blackmun, shows the arbitrary and brutal nature of Rehnquist's jurisprudence.[59] Nevertheless, Rehnquist's focus on the State's interest during the first two trimesters hits indirectly on Blackmun's thin treatment of the same period in *Roe*. We have seen that for Blackmun the woman can never be isolated in her privacy, not even during the first two trimesters. This would seem to justify the more or less active role that the community and its political organs may want to play. But we have seen that such a line of argument is never seriously developed by Blackmun, because it would question the whole viability approach, with its dualistic and atomistic roots. The vacuum thus left is filled by Rehnquist's criticism, which is itself very weak but which can take advantage of the ambiguities of the pro-privacy judges. This is unfortunate, because Blackmun and friends have themselves the resources to fill that vacuum, thereby revealing the irreparable thinness of Rehnquist's arguments. Although the liberal formalism of rights is ultimately prevalent in Blackmun's overall position, it is balanced by genuinely holistic considerations of individual/social happiness and goodness, which could easily unmask Rehnquist's "communitarian" appeal to state powers and traditional morality. Thus in *Webster*, Blackmun, focusing on the ideal of the good life previously appealed to in *Roe*, convincingly attacked the "lack of compassion" of the Rehnquist Court, accusing it of throwing women back to the "unclean and unsympathetic hands of back-alley abortionists" and forcing them into such desperate conditions as to make them "defy the law" by performing "abortions upon themselves, with disastrous results."[60]

In spite of the menacing premises developed in *Webster*, the next episode in the infinite battle over abortion has offered an interesting reversal of perspectives and alliances, which seems to move at least in part in the right direction. In *Planned Parenthood of Southeastern Pennsylvania v Casey* [112 S.Ct. 2791 (1992)], three of the judges who had previously opposed *Roe*—Sandra O'Connor, A. Kennedy, and D. Souter (who appears to be more autonomous from Rehnquist than one originally expected)—have written a joint Majority Opinion, asserting that *Roe* has become too much of a legally established and socially accepted precedent to be completely reversed, as demanded by Rehnquist and the three judges supporting him—Scalia, White, and Thomas. The

Majority Opinion claims the need to preserve the "central" or "essential holding" of *Roe*, namely the right of the woman to choose if to abort or not within the period previous to viability. Yet, it does not take *Roe*'s trimester approach for granted, and it tries to rescue from oblivion the side of *Roe* that stresses the need to balance the individual right to free choice with more holistic and communal considerations:

> It must be remembered that *Roe v. Wade* speaks with clarity in establishing not only the woman's liberty but also the state's "important and legitimate interest in potential life." This portion of the decision has been given too little acknowledgment and implementation by the courts in its subsequent cases. . . . What is at stake is the woman's right to make the ultimate decision, not a right to be insulated from all others in doing so.

Implicitly moving toward a revision of the viability standard, the three judges continue:

> We reject the rigid trimester framework of *Roe v. Wade*. To promote the state's profound interest in potential life, throughout pregnancy the state may take measures to ensure that the woman's choice is informed, and measures designed to advance this interest will not be invalidated as long as their purpose is to persuade the woman to choose childbirth over abortion. These measures must not be an undue burden on the right.

The "undue burden" standard has, in the analysis of the Court, two main aspects, both relating to the necessity that there be no "substantial obstacle to a woman seeking an abortion": On the one hand, the states cannot impede the woman's freedom of choice *materially*, for instance through "unnecessary health regulations" clearly directed at making it difficult for a woman to have an abortion; on the other hand, the states, though having a legitimate power to inform the woman about the pregnancy/abortion dilemma she faces, cannot obstruct the woman's choice *spiritually*, by using such a power only in order to psychologically force her not to abort.

Both Blackmun and Stevens, in their Concurring Opinion, have rejected this part of the Court's position, fearing that its approach, based on the idea of "informed consent," including the provision that the woman undergoes a waiting period between the request and the actual performance of the abortion, could be used by the states characterized by an antichoice position to limit the woman's right through psychological terrorism. The concern is to be taken seriously, and there is no doubt that there will be those who will try to misuse the position taken by the Court in order to impose "undue burdens" on the woman. But this risk cannot be attributed to some intrinsic limit of the Court's opinion, which in fact is precisely geared toward preventing the states from imposing any "undue burden." If the "undue burden" standard is to have any logical coherence, it cannot but impose on the states the duty to inform the woman objectively and without any psychological terrorism, be it by showing her horror images of actual abortions or by attaching to the abortion choice an intrinsic sense of wrongness and guilt.

As to the waiting period between request and performance, it is not clear why it should be an "undue burden" on the woman's choice, unless reflection itself, and the ability to adequately ponder a choice that is certainly dramatic and very important, is to be deemed as useless. On the whole, the fears of the pro-choice judges and movement seem quite unfounded: In Italy, again, the law establishes a waiting period of one week rather than just twenty-four hours, yet women have not felt unduly burdened in their choice to abort when it is truly necessary, and I am sure they are grateful to have such a possibility to reflect in those cases in which abortion would be a hastened and not truly necessary choice. This has probably been a major factor in the success that the Italian law has achieved in greatly reducing the number of abortions without violating women's liberty.

There is one further controversial point to discuss. The Court asserts that, within the limits of not imposing an "undue burden," the states have the power not only to inform but to "persuade the woman to choose childbirth over abortion." It has been thought that this could be a possible weapon in the hands of the antichoice forces, but again this seems to me a mistaken fear. The pro-choice and feminist movement itself should claim this preference of childbirth over abortion as its own, and indeed generally it does, by acknowledging that the women themselves experience abortion as a painful, tragic, and undesirable alternative to the impossibility of choosing for the best, that is, for childbirth. Of course, persuasion cannot become the Trojan horse for psychological terrorism, but the Court's opinion, if properly applied, is there precisely to avoid this. The Italian law explicitly imposes on the officials of the "Consultori Famigliari" (who are often women) the duty to invite the woman not to abort, providing her with the best possible alternatives. This is an important norm, because it forces or at least it stimulates the public powers to "care" for women in need. At the same time, it has not prevented women from choosing abortions whenever necessary, also because the provision has on the whole been applied with equanimity and understanding, and with respect for the woman's situation and ability to choose.

Though Blackmun's strong attachment to *Roe* is somehow understandable, Stevens's mistrust for the Majority Opinion seems to contradict his previous implicit acceptance of the possibility to shift the fulcrum of the right to the abortion choice from viability to quickening, giving in, if only in this circumstance, to Blackmun's theoretical posture, which ambiguously mediates between such a holistic-spiritual understanding and the liberal ideology of rights.

The tension between dialectical holism and liberal dualism, and its solution through a contradictory "liberalism plus," does indeed characterize the overall position of the pro-privacy judges after Douglas's retirement, with the partial exception of Stevens. *Bowers v Hardwick* [106 S.Ct. 2841 (1986)] perfectly exemplifies the ongoing opposition between the new and contradictory pro-privacy approach and the brutal antiprivacy posture of the Rehnquist majority. Hardwick was charged with sodomy under a Georgia statute after an officer accidentally caught him having consensual sexual intercourse with another man.[61]

Following Rehnquist's methodology, White said that the case could not be construed in terms of privacy, because the constitutional right to privacy deals with "family, marriage [and] procreation," and there is "no connection between [these] on the one hand and homosexual activity on the other." The question, thus, was not to determine if homosexual relations "are wise or desirable" but only "whether the Federal Constitution confers a fundamental right upon homosexuals to engage in sodomy."[62]

The reduction of privacy to the level of personality rights, concerned with sexual and reproductive freedoms, is a conscious way of weakening the right to privacy. White performs such a reduction even though only three weeks before *Hardwick* he had said the very opposite, that the right to privacy does not cover only family, marriage, and procreation but also individual autonomy.[63] Even White's treatment of the question in terms of homosexuality was deceitful, as the Georgia statute prohibits sodomy in general, and the "sex or status of the persons who engage in the act is irrelevant as a matter of state law." But clearly the question of homosexual rights was for White and Rehnquist more easily disposable than that of the police power to enter "the sacred precincts of marital bedroom."[64]

White appealed to Cardozo's test of fundamental liberties (Is the right at stake "implicit in the concept of ordered liberty"?), but he did so only instrumentally, as he showed no sign whatsoever of understanding the appeal to implicit fundamental rights that is at the core of Cardozo's test. In reality, the only test at work in White's opinion was the *history and tradition test*. White listed a long series of historical antecedents to show that homosexuality has always been considered a crime in American law. Blackmun rebutted such an argument by calling upon Justice Holmes, who once wrote that "[i]t is revolting to have no better reason for a rule of law than that so it was laid down in the time of Henry IV . . . and the rule simply persists from blind imitation of the past."[65] Drawing from Brandeis's dissent in *Olmstead*, Blackmun questioned the intellectual integrity of the majority, and most particularly their attempt to break up the right to privacy into many fragmented and thus less-defensible rights:

This case is no more about a "fundamental right to engage in homosexual sodomy," as the Court purports to declare, than *Stanley v. Georgia* was about a fundamental right to watch obscene movies, or *Katz v. United States* was about a fundamental right to place interstate bets from a telephone booth. Rather, this case is about "the most comprehensive of rights and the right most valued by civilized men," namely "the right to be let alone."[66]

Blackmun is absolutely right. Yet his own conception of privacy is also not immune from reductionism, although of a different type.

Michael Sandel has defined the new post-*Roe* privacy paradigm as "voluntarist," that is, based on an "ideal of a neutral state" and "of a self freely choosing its aims and attachments." In opposition to this, he posits the old "substantive" privacy paradigm of Brandeis, Douglas, and Harlan, which referred only to "keeping intimate affairs from public view" and which was "unabashedly teleological.... The privacy the Court [of *Griswold*] vindicated was not for the sake of letting people lead their sexual life as they choose, but rather for the sake of affirming and protecting the social institution of marriage."[67] Sandel is right that there is a difference between the old Brandeisian and the new post-*Roe* privacy paradigm, but his analysis of that difference is misleading. First of all, the "old" privacy paradigm was not limited to the informational dimension. We have seen that (a) for Brandeis privacy was, as the "right to be let alone," the "most comprehensive of all rights"; (b) Douglas had the same wide and comprehensive view, as finally confirmed in his Concurring Opinion in *Doe v Bolton* (we discuss this Opinion, together with [a] and [b] as a whole, in Ch. 6). What is more important, however, is that Sandel confuses Harlan's "substantive" approach with the formal/substantive approach of both Brandeis and Douglas. Harlan's notion of privacy can certainly be described as centered upon social institutions and traditional morality. But we have seen how Brandeis's and Douglas's theory of privacy, as well as of family and morality, was fundamentally different. As Sandel upholds that very type of communitarianism characterizing the traditionalist side of Harlan, individuality is for him a product of communal and traditional structures, and that view he misleadingly projects onto Douglas and his *Griswold* opinion. But Douglas concurred also in *Roe*, and it is not clear why Sandel does not place him within the "new" privacy paradigm, which was started by Blackmun's *Roe* decision. The reality is that neither can Brandeis and Douglas be reduced to communitarianism, nor can the post-*Roe* judges be reduced to the liberal and atomistic individualism with which Sandel completely identifies the "new" privacy paradigm.

There is no question that the "new" privacy paradigm has moved away from Brandeis and toward a more liberal and dualistic conception of privacy and rights. Yet, we have seen that it too acknowledges, to an important degree, the dialectical and holistic requirements inherent in the law. The result is an *a posteriori dualistic mediation* of formalistic liberal privatism and substantive communitarianism, which emerges in *Hardwick*'s dissent with utter clarity. Commenting on *Bowers v Hardwick*, Sandel upholds his communitarian and "substantive" solution, although he shows to be at least in part beyond Harlan's ethical traditionalism:

The voluntarist answer holds that people should be free to choose their intimate associations for themselves, regardless of the virtue or popularity of the practices they choose so long as they do not harm others.... By contrast, the substantive answer claims that much that is valuable in conventional marriage is also present in homosexual unions....

Abortion and the New Privacy Paradigm

It defends homosexual privacy the way *Griswold* defended marital privacy, by arguing that, like marriage, homosexual union may also be "intimate to the degree of being sacred . . . a harmony in living . . . a bilateral loyalty."[68]

In fact, however, both conceptions are present in Blackmun's dissent in *Hardwick*. The liberal-atomistic side emerges when he writes that what is at stake in the case, and thus in the right to privacy, is "the freedom of an individual to choose the form and nature of . . . intensely personal bonds." There is nothing wrong with freedom of choice if it is understood as a condition that one attains, through a process in which mistakes are tolerated to the point of existential self-destruction, by becoming capable of making the right choices. But here freedom of choice tends to be perceived as a given, as a deontological right due to everyone and at all times, no matter what the choice. This absolutization of the freedom to choose is paired with a dualistic view of privacy and public life: "We protect those rights not because they contribute . . . to the general public welfare, but because they form so central a part of an individual's life. The concept of privacy embodies the 'moral fact that a person belongs to himself and not to others or to society as a whole.'" Blackmun was here quoting Stevens in *Thornburg*, who in turn was quoting from Charles Fried's radically atomistic and ultimately possessive theory of privacy. This strong liberal element in Blackmun's opinion is reinforced by his adoption of Mill's harm principle, as when he argued that homosexual behavior should not be encroached upon because, like any other intimate choice, it "involves no real interference with the rights of others."[69]

Yet, Blackmun wrote also that the "sexual intimacy"/"intimate association" of homosexuals is constitutionally protected for the same reasons that heterosexual intimacy/marriage is protected, namely because it "is an association that promotes a way of life . . . a harmony in living . . . a bilateral loyalty." This is the very same sentence from *Griswold* that Sandel presents as the best example of the "old" and "substantive" conception of privacy. Blackmun could not center his opinion on the question of homosexuality, because of his refusal to treat the Georgia statute as involving only homosexuals. However, he wrote in a footnote that homosexuality, although not a disease as once was thought, is neither "simply a matter of deliberate personal election" and "may well form part of the very fiber of an individual's personality." He concluded that to deprive homosexuals of the right to associate intimately among themselves would leave them with "no real choice but a life without any physical intimacy." This is the Blackmun who wants to protect the privacy of homosexual relations not in the name of free choice, as the other Blackmun does, but from the much more "substantive" point of view of the loving self-realization of individuals naturally characterized by a different type of sexuality, based on the communitarian presupposition that "we all depend on the 'emotional enrichment from close ties with others.'"[70] The fact is, this opinion, like the overall approach of the post-*Roe* pro-privacy judges, is a bit schizophrenic and never quite manages to coherently synthesize its two conflicting sides. On the other hand, the dualistic coexistence of the formal-liberal and substantive-communitarian sides indirectly rescues at times the formal/substantive transpersonalism of Brandeis, which includes them both into a higher synthesis.

In spite of the ambiguity that plagues the "new" privacy paradigm, there is still hope, mostly because the increasing attack on privacy, which is now reaching into the most subtle and deep layers of interiority, is forcing the judges to acknowledge the absolute value of subjectivity as a spiritual dimension independent of a more or less arbitrary freedom to act and choose. This is what is happening on the newest frontier of the right to privacy, the dilemma of euthanasia, with which the lower courts have been wrestling for the last twenty years. In *In re Quinlan*, [70 N.J. 355 A.2d 647 (1976)], the New Jersey Supreme Court allowed Karen Ann Quinlan to die—that is, she was to be no longer kept alive by an artificial life support system—basing their decision on her constitutional right to privacy. As anticipated in Ch.1, there exists a deep link between death, the ultimate withdrawal from our body, and spiritual privacy, the temporary withdrawal from our social and relational personality. The right to die with dignity and in peace may very well restore the constitutional right of privacy to its original spiritual meaning.

In the lower courts, the tension between the "free choice" and the "formal/substantive" notion of privacy has surfaced in the form of a conflict between the *substituted judgment* standard—whereby the right to choose of an incompetent patient, technologically kept in a vegetative state, is transferred to someone else who is supposed to choose as the patient would have done if able—and the *best interest* standard—whereby the substituted judgment by the family is subjected to judicial control, so as to guarantee that the decision be taken in accordance with, so to speak, the "objectively subjective" interest of the patient.[71]

There is a further standard, the clear and convincing proof standard, which authorizes the suspension of the technological furtherance of life only when explicitly required by an expressed will of the incompetent patient. This is the standard adopted by the State of Missouri, whose normative has been the object of the first Supreme Court's decision in the field, *Cruzan v Director, Missouri Dept. of Health*.[72] The Missouri law had imposed on Nancy Cruzan a purely vegetative life for many years, during which she was force-fed through tubes implanted in her stomach and left with no awareness other than great pain caused by the treatment. Once again, the Rehnquist majority managed to sustain that law through an absurd level of judicial restraint and a parallel pretense of substantive neutrality.

The dissent of Brennan, Marshall, and Blackmun, on the other hand, is a further example of their liberal/holistic ambiguity. On the one hand, Brennan referred to the value of a "proud death" and to the abhorrence of an "ignoble end." Here, the motivation is human dignity and a substantive vision of what is to be human beyond the mere freedom to choose, which in itself includes also the possibility of choosing an ignoble death. On the other hand, however, Brennan ended up basing his opinion on free choice, stating that the "determination needed in this context is whether the incompetent person would choose to live in a persistent vegetative state." The conclusion was for the substituted judgment of the family, which is supposed to know best what the patient would have chosen. Undoubtedly, the value of empirical self-determination and free choice is important, but cases like *Cruzan* show its inherent limits, its inability to be an end in itself: Nancy Cruzan could simply not choose her destiny, and other criteria, related to what's intrinsically valuable in the person besides and beyond her freedom to choose, are needed.

In order to avoid acknowledging this logical conclusion, which would have radically questioned the "free choice" horizon of his opinion, Brennan had to distort the notion of "substituted judgment" by reducing it into a mere "substituted choice." Substituted judgment is the judgment, as Brennan himself recalled, that parents or tutors have to make for children or mentally incapacitated subjects. Brennan identifies "substituted judgment" with choosing-as-the-incompetent-would-choose, possibly in the sense that the family or the tutor are supposed to choose what the child would choose as a grown-up, the mentally handicapped as a mentally competent person, and Nancy Cruzan as a physiologically whole person. But this reading of "substituted judgment" erases a very important difference between the case of children and the mentally handicapped on the one hand and the case of Nancy Cruzan on the other. As opposed to Nancy Cruzan, children and the mentally handicapped can choose, only they are generally unable to independently choose in their own best interest. This fact cannot be covered up by bringing in the adult that the child will be, and the mentally sound person that mentally handicapped would be. No one could ever know what such an adult would concretely choose, and in fact s/he could very well choose something that no family or tutor, moved by the desire to help the child or the mentally handicapped flourish, would ever choose. If the "substituted judgment" standard needs any reference at all to the competent adult that the child or the mentally handicapped would be, that adult is clearly an ideal, an image of the reason that dwells in each individual soul, and in which judgment, as opposed to arbitrary choice, is rooted.

The important difference outlined earlier—the fact that Nancy Cruzan cannot choose at all, not even badly—brings the problem of choice more to the forefront, making the reduction of "substituted judgment" to "substituted choice" apparently more plausible. But in spite of the greater urgency to find a substitute chooser, the requirement that the substituted choice be a sound judgment in the patient's best interest maintains its primacy. When Brennan says that the Cruzan family is "more likely to make the choice that the patient would have made," he clearly puts an ideological blanket on reality. The family cannot know what their incapacitated relative would actually choose any more than anyone else. The family is only more likely to decide in the best interest of the person they care for, although not even this is sure, given that sometimes there may be little closeness between the relatives and the patients, and given also the wide dysfunctional nature of families in today's world. This is why in the *In re Conroy* case, the Court rightly subjected the family itself to judicial supervision, not in order to take the decision away from the family but to make sure that the family's decision would take into account all relevant factors in a complete and honest way.

This is in line with the traditional requirements of the "substituted judgment" standard, if properly understood as implying the "best interest" standard. It is true that families are free from judicial supervision, but only as long as they do not fall into serious violations that threaten the integrity and proper development of the child, that is, in a fundamental sense, as long as they do not approach or cross the line of "existential self-destruction." The higher frequency with which tutors of the mentally handicapped are generally subjected to judicial supervision is justified by the very fact that the mentally handicapped are inherently more prone to (self-) destructive behavior. As to incompetent patients who stand at the brink of life and death, their situation is even more special, because the decision to be taken is ultimate and irrevocable, thus plunging into *the very last layer of existential self-destruction*, and simultaneously involving the patient, family, and society. Existential self-destruction, which is ethical and spiritual before being physical (the latter being, in the case of terminally ill patients, possibly unavoidable), is the worst answer to the interest of the person. This means that it can be avoided only by appealing to her "best interest," which is indeed the interest not to betray and harm one's ethical and spiritual nature. Because such best interest transcends the level of family or for that matter political relations, the judicial supervision in the sense described earlier is a must.

In solitary dissent, Justice Stevens appealed to the "best and most essential interests of Beth Nancy Cruzan," making it clear that such interests are ultimately identifiable with the protection of that essential selfhood and autonomy that grounds, yet is not reducible to, one's capacity for choice and action. That transcendent interiority, which in conditions such as those suffered by Nancy Cruzan may still nourish the unconscious mind of dreams and visions or live in the mute nakedness of a soul withdrawn into itself, is the absolutely valuable essence beyond our spatial and behavioral being. Stevens has acknowledged the importance of self-determination and free choice, stating that "if there was any evidence that Nancy Cruzan herself defined life to encompass every form of biological persistence by a human being, so that the continuation of treatment would serve Nancy's own liberty," then her choice should be respected.

In fact, it is not clear that the patient's choice, if known, should be respected in all cases—for example, as when it runs deeply afoul of his or her own "best interests" through a blind attachment to a hopelessly vegetative body, while the collectivity has to bear the very high costs of treatment, thus increasing the enormous profits of the medico-pharmaceutical industry while taking resources away from its existential and planetary duty to support human lives still rich in potentialities. Stevens did not explicitly discuss these problems, and even though the sense remains that he has given freedom of choice more than its due, he clearly set "free choice" below more-essential values, such as the "quality of life," "human dignity," and the "sanctity and individual privacy of the human body," that no human being should ever be deprived of, not even with his/her consent. With this, Stevens moves beyond a merely "spatial" and/or "decisional" understanding of privacy:

Just as the constitutional protection for the 'physical curtilage of the home . . . is surely . . . a result of solicitude to protect the privacies of the life within,' so too the constitutional protection for the human body is surely inseparable from concern for the mind and spirit that dwell therein.

The fact that Stevens recognizes the relevance of mind and spirit in Cruzan's condition, a condition that he believes cannot be considered "life" in a proper sense ("there is a serious question as to whether the mere persistence of . . . bodies is 'life' as that word is commonly understood"), shows his belief in our transcendent yet nonseparate spiritual nature. Rescuing a basic transpersonal idea, Stevens gets at the very core of the link between privacy and death, both forms of withdrawal from life, yet both indispensable if life is to have any meaning at all:

Death is not life's simple opposite, or its necessary termination, but rather its completion. . . . Many philosophies and religions have . . . long venerated the idea that there is a "life after death," and that the human soul endures even after the human body has perished. . . . It may, in fact, be impossible to live for anything without being prepared to die for something.

Life itself, and thus actions and choices, make sense only if related to that essential silence/inaction that death brings forth, and whose absolute value grounds the empirically quasi-absolute and thus natural rights of mental/spiritual privacy. It is to such a spiritual ground of natural rights that Stevens appeals when he connects privacy to the "inalienable rights to life and liberty endowed to us by our Creator." Privacy is thus returned to its original meaning, and its fundamental right is given back its foundational role relative to all other rights. This is why, like Brandeis before, Stevens reclaims the privileged link between privacy and the First Amendment in its "firstness." It is not an accident, thus, that in referring to the line of privacy cases that he deems relevant to *Cruzan*, Stevens sealed his opinion by quoting, from Brandeis's dissent in *Olmstead*, the very passage that states that "the makers of our Constitution . . . recognized the significance of man's spiritual nature."[73] The right to privacy has been made to journey through ambiguous victories, corrupting defenses, and crashing defeats, but its original flame lives on.

NOTES

1. Note, "Toward a Constitutional Theory of Individuality: The Privacy Opinions of Justice Douglas," in *Yale L.J.* 87 (1978), p. 1600.

2. In *Stanley v Georgia* [394 U.S. 557 (1969)] the Supreme Court established that the private use of pornographic material is protected by the constitutional right to privacy. See also: *Paris Adult Theatre v Slaton*, 413 U.S. 49 (1973), dealing with public consumption of pornography, *United States v Thirty-Seven Photographs*, 402 U.S. 363 (1971) and *United States v Twelve Reels*, 413 U.S. 123 (1971), both dealing with public distribution of pornographic material. In 1965 a new approach to free speech was developed, with important implications for the right to privacy, an approach drawing at least in part from Meiklejohn's doctrines. We discuss this briefly in Ch. 4.

3. As to the Fourth and Fifth Amendments, we know how they "run into each other." In *Shapiro v Thomson* [394 U.S. 618 (1969)], through a substantive due process approach, the Court acknowledged the fundamental constitutional character of the right to travel, a right inherent in the active side of the individual bodily sphere. In a crucial Fifth Amendment decision, *Griffin v California* [380 U.S. 609 (1965)], the Court reasserted in almost absolute terms the privilege against self-incrimination. Then, in the historic case *Miranda v Arizona*, the Court gave an unprecedented boost to the protection of the accused and his/her dignity, by elaborating in great detail a set of rules for all inquisitorial activities that widened and strengthened the right against self-incrimination, the right to counsel, and the right to silence. 384 U.S. 436 (1966). The Court also asserted that confessions obtained through methods that violate the accused's dignity cannot be presented in judgment. *Miranda* had been prepared by *Escobedo v Illinois*, 378 U.S. 478 (1964). The near absolutist standards of *Miranda* were partially tempered in *Schmerber v California* [384 U.S. 757 (1966)], which nevertheless maintained the main features of *Miranda*, adding the provision that the use of a lie-detector violates the right against self-incrimination.

4. See Douglas, Dissenting Opinion, *Osborne v United States*, 385 U.S. 323 (1966), and Brennan, Dissenting Opinion, *Lopez v United States*, 373 U.S. 468.

5. See *Silverman v United States*, 365 U.S. 505 (1961), and *Wong Sun v United States*, 371 U.S. 471 (1963).

6. 389 U.S. 347 (1967), at 351ff. The expansion of privacy rights in these areas was partially balanced by a parallel expansion of the police's powers in the field of ordinary (nonelectronic) searches. See, for instance, in *Terry v Ohio* [392 U.S. 1 (1968)].

7. The reversal of *Miranda* is concerned particularly with the exclusionary rule. See also *Harris v New York*, 4091 U.S. 222 (1971); *Oregon v Hass*, 429 U.S. 714 (1975); *Rakas v Illinois*, 99 S.Ct. 421 (1978). The criteria for the formation of criminal juries were relaxed in *Williams v Florida*, 399 U.S. 78 (1970) and *Apodaca v Oregon*, 406 U.S. 404 (1972). In *Kirby v Illinois*, 406 U.S. 682 (1972), the Court eased the procedure for the identification of suspect and alleged criminals; in *United States v Martinez-Fuerte*, 428 U.S. 543 (1976), it narrowed the extent to which searches need judicial authorization as a prerequisite.

8. W. W. Van Alstyne, *The Recrudescence of Property Rights*, p. 68. See, for instance, *Greer v Spock*, 424 U.S. 828 (1976) (handbilling on government property limited); *Hudgens v NLRB*, 424 U.S. 507 (1976) (picketing on private property limited); and on the other hand, *First National Bank v Bellotti*, 435 U.S. 765 (1978) (corporate

funds to campaign against ballot issues protected); *Buckley v Valeo*, 424 U.S. 1 (1976) (restrictions on personal electioneering expenditures invalidated).

9. The economic rights of big private and public corporations, although on the whole reinforced, have been sometimes partially compressed by the Burger Court. In *Prunyard Shopping Center v Robins*, 447 U.S. 74 (1980), the Court decided that a shopping mall cannot be considered property in a traditional sense and so could not forbid the collection of signatures for a petition promoted by a group of students. In spite of the result, the general idea that ownership of productive and commercial properties gives the right to exclude public speech remained. But in *Bates v State Bar*, 433 U.S. 350 (1977), and *Virginia State Board of Pharmacy v Virginia Citizens Consumer Council*, 425 U.S. 748 (1976), the Court included commercial advertising among the types of discourse protected by the First Amendment, thus considering it equivalent to political speech.

10. Van Alstyne, pp. 68–70.

11. 405 U.S. 538 (1972), at 542, 552.

12. For the above discussion see 410 U.S. 113 (1973), at 152–53.

13. 410 U.S. 113, at 168.

14. See, for instance, Heyman and Barzelay, "The Forest and the Trees: *Roe v Wade* and Its Critics," in *B.U.L.R.* 53 (1973): 765, and Wellington, "Common Law Rules and Constitutional Double Standard: Some Notes on Adjudication," in *Yale L.J.*, 83 (1973): 221.

15. J. Ely, *Democracy and Distrust* (Harvard University Press, 1980), pp. 2–3; and specifically on *Roe*, "The Wages of Crying Wolf," in *Yale L.J.* 82 (1973): 920.

16. A. Bickel, *The Morality of Consent* (1975), p. 27; Perry, "Substantive Due Process Revisited: Reflections on (and beyond) Recent Cases" in *Nw.U.L.R.* 71 (1976): 417, p. 420; I. Lupu, "Untangling the Strands," *Mich.L.R.* 77 (1979): 981, pp. 998–99.

17. See A. Cox, *The Role of the Supreme Court in American Government* (1976): 113; and P. Freund, "Storm over the Supreme Court," in *A.B.A.J.* 69 (1983): 1474, p. 1480.

18. In case of a conflict between a governmental interest and a nonfundamental private interest, the less exacting "rational relation test" is applied.

19. 410 U.S. 113, at 157–67, and especially 163–64.

20. For the former position see the U.S. Solicitor General's *amicus curiae* brief, similar in content to Rehnquist's and White's dissent. For the latter, see Ruth Ginsburg, "Some Thoughts on Autonomy and Equality in Relation to *Roe v. Wade*," in *North Carol.L.R.* 63 (1985): 375.

21. L. Tribe, *American Constitutional Law* (New York: Foundation, 1988), 1352, quoting *West Virginia Board of Education v Barnette*, 319 U.S. 624, 638 (1943).

22. Ely, "The Wages of Crying Wolf," esp. pp. 931–39. The same position is taken by Rehnquist in his *Roe* Dissenting Opinion. Behind this reductionistic antiprivacy approach stands the utilitarian tradition. Ely explicitly claims his link with utilitarianism and Bentham in "Constitutional Interpretivism: Its Allure and Impossibility," in *Indiana L.J.* 53 (1978): 399, 405–8.

23. H. Garfield, "Privacy, Abortion and Judicial Review: Haunted by the Ghost of *Lochner*," in *Washington L.R.* 61 (1986), 316–18.

24. T. Grey, "Eros, Civilization and the Burger Court," in *Law and Contemporary Problems* 43, (3) (1980): 88, p. 88.

25. See C. Lasch, *Haven in a Heartless World* (New York: Basic Books, 1977).

26. Grey, *Eros*, p. 97. Grey mentions Bertrand Russell as a source for this position.

27. Grey, *Eros*, pp. 85–87. As to Douglas's conservatism, Grey indicates as another example his decision in *Village of Belle Terre v Boraas*, which upheld a regulation of the town of Belle Terre, Long Island, authorizing residence only to stable family groups, and thus excluding from within the municipality the students of a nearby university, who brought suit against the town. But Grey does not see that the town's normative included in its definition of "family" common law couples and even singles, and that therefore Douglas's opinion did not have anything to with a traditionalist protection of ordinary families. The focus of Douglas's decision was the protection of smallness, of the autonomy of local communities respectful of fundamental individual rights. The town's regulation was an attempt to escape from the circuit of oligopolistic and consumeristic bigness and in fact excluded from within the town's borders shops, supermarkets, and even door-to-door distribution of mail. Grey's allegations of traditionalism refer also to the Court's decision in *Moore v City of East Cleveland*, 431 U.S. 494 (1977), which reversed a municipal regulation establishing a legal definition of "family" whereby it was illegal for a grandmother to live in the same house with two nephews who were cousins rather than brothers. Does Grey's modernity imply the governmental power to mold and dissolve interpersonal bonds at will?

28. Note, "*Roe* and *Paris*: Does Privacy Have a Principle?" in *Stanford L.R.*, 26 (1974):201161, 1168–70.

29. Ibid., p. 1170, note 50.

30. "Specific and direct harm medically diagnosable even in early pregnancy may be involved. Maternity, or additional offspring, may force upon the woman a distressful life and future. Psychological harm may be imminent. Mental and physical health may be taxed by child care. There is also the distress, for all concerned, associated with the unwanted child, and there is also the problem of bringing a child into a family already unable, psychologically or otherwise, to care for it. In other cases, as in this one, the addictional difficulties and continuing stigma of unwed motherhood may be involved." 410 U.S. 113, at 153. The reference to "all concerned" includes the child too.

31. On abortion in those cases in which the life of the newborn cannot be expected to be a "good life," in the sense of leading toward the realization of such superior values, see Plato, *The Republic*, V, 461; Aristotle, *The Politics*, 1335b.

32. She continues: "For instance, it is apparently not uncommon for women who have had abortions to note mentally when the baby would have been born and to experience special sadness on the anniversary of that date. . . . Even a woman who has an abortion to destroy the life of a particular fetus may still value fetal life. Many women, for example, choose abortion to defer child-birth. They do not bear a child now in order to bear a child later. It is because of their love and concern for the value of potential fetal life that they choose to defer child-birth. . . . Such women want to have a child when they can best love and care for it." "Feminism, Theology and Abortion: Toward Love, Compassion and Wisdom," in *Calif L.R.* 77 (1989), p. 1058.

33. Colker notices how one of the main groups within the "pro-life" movement is Women Exploited by Abortion (WEBA), formed by women who have undergone deep emotional and spiritual crises after having had an abortion. *Feminism, Theology and Abortion*, p. 1065, note 192.

34. I should like to add, on my part, that one important contribution is being made by those nonfundamentalist pro-lifers who do not oppose contraception as such, and that is the attempt to promote and refine the methods of natural contraception. Considering that the methods of chemical contraception are known to be harmful to the health of

women, the development of nonharmful, natural contraception systems corresponds to the general interest of both women and society.

35. 462 U.S. 416 (1983), at 444. The Court held the same position in *Thornburg v American College of Obstetricians & Gynecologists*, 106 S.Ct. 2169 (1986).

36. As Colker points out, it would be a mistake to think that from the point of view of "inner peace" only childbirth can be chosen. She reports this exemplary story: "Having an abortion seemed to be the most thoughtful and loving decision we could make, in fact, it seemed to be the only decision we could make which would still maintain our life goals and plans in helping serve others as we had hoped. I was a Christian then, as I am now, and constant prayer asking for guidance through peace is how I was able to feel that God had guided me toward that decision, also. Since the abortion in 1977 I have helped hundreds of emotionally disturbed children, counseled twice as many parents about the loving ways of parenting. . . . In 1979 I married a Pediatrician who has been a wonderful husband and father to our four year old boy and our seven months old boy in utero. . . . God has given me blessings and much peace since 1977." Colker, *Feminism, Theology and Abortion*, p. 1067, note 193, quoting Paltrow, "Amicus Brief: Thornburg," *Women Rts.L.Rep.* 9 (1986): 3, 21.

37. Colker, *Feminism, Theology and Abortion*, p. 1052, note 148.

38. *Roe v Wade*, 410 U.S. 113, at 132; more generally, see 129ff.

39. See Stevens, Dissenting Opinion, *Webster v Reproductive Health Services*, 109 S.Ct. 3040, 3079–85, at 3082, 3084.

40. The Hindus, as probably did the Pythagoreans, think that although ensoulment occurs later in the pregnancy, the specific individual soul is already associated at conception with the body it will enter.

41. In *United States Trust Co. v New Jersey*, 431 U.S. 1 (1977), and *Allied Structural Steel Co. v Spannaus*, 438 U.S. 234 (1978), the Court invalidated statutes limiting the freedom of contract for the first time after the abandonment of *Lochner*. In *Kaiser Aetna v United States*, 100 S.Ct. 383 (1979), the Court forbade the government from imposing an unpaid-for public servitude upon a valuable commercial development on the ground of the "takings" clause of the Fifth Amendment. Writes Van Alstyne: "None of these is a 'revolution' in constitutional law . . . [but] they tend to show that some of the 'old' liberties have not yet wholly yielded to the social impulse to regulate or to redistribute" (p. 72).

42. Although questionable for some of its immediate ideological aspects, J. O'Connor, *The Fiscal Crisis of the State* (New York, 1973), remains very instructive.

43. *California Bankers Ass. v Schultz*, 416 U.S. 21, at 85 (1974).

44. Besides his dissent in *California Bankers*, Douglas repeated his attack on the bureaucratic abuse of technology and data banks in his Dissenting Opinion in *Laird v Tatum*, 408 U.S. 1 (9172), where the Court upheld the military power of electronic and data banks surveillance over civilians.

45. *Roe v Ingraham*, 403 F.Suppl. 931 (SONY 1975).

46. "The central storage and easy accessibility of computerized data vastly increases the potential for abuse of that information, and I am not prepared to say that future developments will not demonstrate the necessity of some curb on such technology." 429 U.S. 589, at 606–7.

47. Tribe, p. 1400–1.

48. *Roberts v United States Jaycees*, 468 U.S. 609 (1984), at 615. The case referred to the right of women, who already participated in most activities of the "Jaycees" club,

to acquire full membership, including the right to vote, from which they were previously excluded. Brennan, writing for the Court in favor of the women, explained that the concerned association did not have the necessary requisites of intimacy and exclusivity, and denied that such attributes could be possessed by associations having influence on the economic life. Likewise, in *Rotary International v Rotary Club of Duarte*, 107 S.Ct. 1940 (1987), Justice Powell asserted that the club could not exclude women because "the relationship among Rotary Club members is not the kind of intimate or private relation that warrants constitutional protection." 107 S.Ct. 1940 (1987), at 1946. On the topic in general, see K. L. Karst, "The Freedom of Intimate Association," in *Yale L.J.* 89 (1980): 624.

49. In the more specific area of the privacy of political associations, the Burger Court "[s]ometimes ... has appeared to adhere to the earlier strict scrutiny standard" (established in the *N.A.C.C.P.* case), but other times "has discarded strict scrutiny in favor of a more deferential rational basis standard" (also called rational relation test). K. A. Young and P. B. Herbert, "Political Association under the Burger Court: Fading Protection," in *U.C.D.L.Rev.* 15 (1981): 53, p. 54.

50. In *Carey v Population Services Intern.*, 431 U.S. 678 (1977), the Court reaffirmed the principle that the use and distribution of contraceptives can be limited by the State only due to a compelling interest. As to abortion, besides *Akron* and *Thornburg*, discussed in sect. 3 earlier, *Planned Parenthood v Danforth*, 428 U.S. 52 (1976), invalidated a Missouri statute imposing the adoption of a specific abortion technique not widely available in that state. Again, in *Colautti v Franklin*, 439 U.S. 379 (1979), a statute was struck down because it did not clearly specify that the life and health of the mother always have priority over the life and health of the fetus.

51. See *Beal v Doe*, 432 U.S. 438 (1977); *Maher v Roe*, 432 U.S. 464 (1977); and for the prohibition of abortion in public hospitals, *Poelker v Doe*, 432 U.S. 519 (1977).

52. C. MacKinnon, "Abortion: On Public and Private," in *Toward a Feminist Theory of the State* (Harvard, 1989), 184–94.

53. 109 S.Ct. 3040 (1989). There have been numerous doctrinal reactions to the decision, and various monographic issues of legal journals have been devoted to it. See *Penn.L.R.* 138, 1 (1989), for both pro-life and pro-choice critical comments; *Amer.J.of Law and Med.* 15, 2–3 (1989), 153, reporting the numerous briefs of the various amici curiae of the two sides; and C. Crain, "Judicial Restraint and the Non-Decision in *Webster*," *Harvard J. of Law and Pub.Pol.* 13 (1990): 263, for a pro-life point of view.

54. 109 S.Ct. 3040, 3054–56.

55. 109 S.Ct. 3040, 3079–80, 3082, and 3083, note 12.

56. 109 S.Ct. 3040, 3056–58. The tricky ambiguity of the decision is also revealed by the opinions of O'Connor and Scalia, who both concurred only in the result. For O'Connor, the Court should not have reexamined *Roe* at all, and this shows how she did not believe Rehnquist's claim that *Roe* remains undisturbed. Scalia, on the other hand, criticizes the Court for not having gone further to an explicit reversal of *Roe*.

57. Stevens, Dissenting Opinion, 109 S.Ct. 3040, 3075, quoting his own dissent in *Thornburg v American College of Obstetricians and Gynecologists*, 476 U.S. 747 (1986), at 778–79.

58. 109 S.Ct. 3040, at 3072–73, which quotes Rehnquist in *Daniel v Williams*, 106 S.Ct. 662 (1986), at 667.

59. "The opinion contains not one word of rationale for its view of State's interest. This 'it-is-so-because-we-say-so' jurisprudence constitutes nothing other than an at-

Abortion and the New Privacy Paradigm

tempted exercise of brute force; reason, much less persuasion, has no place.'' 109 S.Ct. 3040, 3075–76.

60. 109 S.Ct. 3040, 3077–78.

61. See D. J. Richards, "Constitutional Privacy and Homosexual Love," in *N.Y.Rev.of Law and Soc.Change 14* (1986): 895; R. D. Mohr, "Mr. Justice Douglas at Sodom," in *Columbia Human Rights L.R. 18* (1986): 43–110.

62. 106 S.Ct. 2841, at 2843–44.

63. White, Dissenting Opinion, *Thornburg v Am. College of Obstetricians & Gynecologists*, 106 S.Ct. 2169 (1986), at 2194. The same inconsistency characterizes Rehnquist. In 1976 Rehnquist claimed, in *Paul v Davis*, 424 U.S. 693, 713, that the right to privacy cannot be applied to questions of Fourth Amendment searches and seizures because it is limited to questions of family and procreation. This is the exact opposite of what he had said in opposition to *Roe*, where he stated that by extending the right to privacy to questions of procreation the Court had deviated from the traditional core of privacy, namely Fourth Amendment searches and seizures.

64. 106 S.Ct. 2841, at 2849, 2856, and 2858 (which quotes *Griswold*, 381 U.S., at 485).

65. 106 S.Ct. 2841, at 2844–45 (White's argument), at 2848 (Blackmun's answer).

66. 106 S.Ct. 2841, at 2848.

67. M. J. Sandel, "Moral Argument and Liberal Toleration: Abortion and Homosexuality," in *Calif.L.R., 77* (1989): 521, pp. 524–27.

68. Ibid., p. 534, quoting from *Griswold*, 381 U.S. 479 (1965), at 486.

69. 106 S.Ct. 2841, at 2851–52 [quoting Stevens in *Thornburg*, 476 U.S. at 777, which quotes Fried, *Correspondence, Phil. & Pub. Affairs 6* (1977), pp. 288–89]; and at 2856.

70. Quoting *Roberts v United States Jaycees*, 468 U.S. 609, at 619. For all quotations from Blackmun's dissent, see *Bowers v Hardwick*, 106 S.Ct. 2841, at 2850–52.

71. For the "substituted judgment" standard, see *Superintendent of Belchertown State School v Saikewicz*, 373 Mass. 728.370 N.E.2d 417 (1977); for the "best interest" standard, see *In re Conroy*, 98 N.J. 321, 486 A.2d 1209 (1985).

72. 110 S.Ct. 2841 (1990). A previous case, *In re Westchester County Medical Center on behalf of O'Connor*, 72 N.Y.2d 517, 531 N.E.2d 607 (1988), had established a similar standard, but in that case, as opposed to the *Cruzan* case, the patient was not in a coma but was partially conscious and could answer simple questions.

73. Stevens, Dissenting Opinion, *Cruzan*, 110 S.Ct. 2841 (1989), at 2878–92, especially at 2884–85.

6

BRANDEIS, DOUGLAS, AND THE TRANSPERSONAL THEORY OF RIGHTS

THE TRANSPERSONAL ROOTS OF POLITICAL AND LEGAL BRANDEISIANISM

The transpersonal political ideal has been criticized in R. Bellah's survey of American society and culture with the same arguments that communitarians, mainly of an Aristotelian ascendant, generally adopt to charge the Platonic-Stoic tradition of antipolitics. Bellah and his cowriters thus liquidate the political significance of transpersonalism:

> Another way out of the dead end of radical individualism, a way inherited from Wordsworth, Emerson and other romantics, and presently found among some humanistic and transpersonal psychologists, is to assume that at the core of every person is a fundamental spiritual harmony that links him or her not only to every other person but to the cosmos as a whole. Here, too, external authority, cultural tradition, and social institutions are all eschewed. The self in its pristine purity is affirmed. But somehow that self, once discovered, turns out to be at one with the universe. Romantic and psychologistic pantheism is, indeed, linked to one strand of our religious heritage.... But such romantic individualism is remarkably thin when it comes to any but the vaguest prescriptions about how to live in an actual society.[1]

However, contrary to what Bellah et al. believe, the "self" is not discovered in an all-or-nothing like fashion. Full self-realization involves generally a difficult and long process. Yet, we all may catch a glimpse of it at times in the most natural ways, and we have at all times the possibility of accessing some degree of transpersonal awareness. We can all raise our eyes to the skies above and sense our cosmic interdependence. And we can look inside ourselves to rescue that natural feeling of compassion upon which Rousseau, a most political philosopher, believed any society needs to be built. Genuine transpersonalism does not reject authority, tradition, and institutions. It only refuses to pay a blind homage to them, knowing that they can survive and flourish only when they embody creatively and dynamically the *a priori* and self-subsistent idea/reality of the Whole of Wholes, which is implicit at least to some degree in every community that can still be called so. Bellah and his colleagues accuse the transpersonal tradition of a lack of realism and of having an excessively thin political theory. In fact, unrealistic is to think that there can be true community without communion.

The thickest and most-realistic indications on how to regenerate American society have come from those, such as Brandeis and Douglas, who have followed in the steps of Emerson and other "romantic individualists." Their legal and political activity may have been historically marginalized by the triumph of the oligopolitical "bigness," but it has provided the most articulate, intelligent, and practical solutions to the crisis of the contemporary world, as some are beginning to realize.[2]

We have already discussed Brandeis's legal thought, showing its implicit yet very clear transpersonal inspiration. That such a philosophical inspiration has not been easily perceived by everyone may be due to the fact that Brandeis has never written any systematic work, but only journal articles, letters, and legal sentences. One major obstacle to the understanding of Brandeis as a transpersonalist is the widespread opinion of him as an empiricist scientist of the law. Such a view mistakes for empiricism what was instead his natural law conviction that justice and morality are inherent in the facts.[3]

Brandeis said once that he "had no time for metaphysics," and D. Riesman notices how that was one of his "severe self-limitations." Another author has written that "Brandeis's morality was not based on metaphysics. He was indeed a worldly philosopher."[4] But this is true only if Brandeis's rejection of metaphysics is understood as a rejection of dry intellectualism and if by "worldly philosopher" we mean someone capable of recognizing unchanging fundamental truths within a constantly changing world. Dean Acheson reports the following anecdote:

I remember one evening during the twenties listening to professor Manley Hudson of Harvard (later Judge Hudson of the World Court) hold forth on Brandeis, the Scientist of the Law, who had brought the methods of the laboratory into the courthouse, who put facts through test-tube treatment, and so on. While this was going on, I found out that the Justice was free and would receive my friend and me. It was easy to guide the conversation to the growing political issue of prohibition and, in the course of it, to provoke Mr. Hudson into asserting that moral principles were no more than generalizations from the mores or accepted notions of a particular time and place. The eruption was even more spectacular than I had anticipated. The Justice wrapped the mantle of Isaiah around himself, dropped his voice a full octave, jutted his eyebrows forward in a most menacing way, and began to prophesy. Morality was truth; and truth had been revealed to man in an unbroken, continuous and consistent flow by the great prophets and poets of all time. He quoted Goethe in German and from Euripides via Gilbert Murray. On it went—an impressive, almost frightening, glimpse of an elemental force.[5]

This episode alone is enough to clear all misunderstandings about Brandeis's liberalism or empiricism and gives us a better understanding of Brandeis's relation to philosophy and metaphysics. Philippa Strum has argued that Brandeis rejected philosophy because he considered it "the 'cyclone cellar for finer souls' as the monasteries had been during the Dark Ages; that is, philosophy was a hiding place."[6] But given Brandeis's personal and political predilection for privacy, hiding places should not have been such a bad thing for him, especially if they protected "finer souls," among whom he certainly ranked "the great prophets and poets of all times" he so often quoted. The fact that Brandeis did not pretend to be a philosopher may only testify to his honesty in recognizing that higher philosophical insight, which always transcends language and linear reason, was beyond his direct grasp. Yet, he also thought that the degree of one's true philosophical understanding is to be seen in one's living. P. Freund, who was Brandeis's assistant, has rightly said: "He was not a philosopher in his leisure moments. . . . His philosophy is found in his living."[7] But his living philosophy always drew its force from the spiritual and ethical insights of the great prophets and poets of all times. His letters are filled with innumerable quotations of Goethe, the Greeks, and the Bible, and this shows how for him genuine thinking had to be of a spiritual and thus deeply felt nature.

Nevertheless, in spite of his constant reference to "man's spiritual nature," Brandeis's spirituality has rarely been taken seriously. One author has written that he "was not at all religious. In fact, he was puzzled by people who relied on God and religious institutions."[8] To be sure, Brandeis's notion of spiritual self-reliance excluded any dependence on institutional and sectarian dogmatism and on any type of radically separate God. But he had a deep sense of religion in the etymological meaning of *re-ligo*, the universal interconnection of all beings as intrinsic to each of them. Even when he made use of the concept of God, he did so in reference to the moral self-regeneration of human beings. Dawson reports how he asserted the need for a "righteous leader to preach 'the fear of God' . . . and turn his powers towards arousing the nation to repentance and cleansing." Therefore, Urofsky's opinion that Brandeis "had a curious gap in his knowledge of things religious" seems quite unjustified. Writes Dawson:

Brandeis's letters, particularly in early years, show familiarity with the Old Testament. Indeed, his moral system, with its strong emphasis on social justice, has a strong affinity with the prophetic tradition. . . . Not without reason did Roosevelt call Brandeis "Isaiah," partly in jest and partly, one suspects, in awe.[9]

Brandeis's understanding of the unity of philosophy, poetry, and religion was at once strongly humanist and deeply spiritual, contrary to Strum's definition of him as a "secular humanist." He certainly was a humanist, but his understanding of humanity was spiritual rather than secular. Strum herself reports the following sentence by Brandeis: "Man's work is, at best, so insignificant compared to that of the Creator—it is all so Lilliputian one cannot bow before it." This sentence is extremely revealing. Man as a doer is a little thing, just one among the infinitely many creatures of the universe. Yet Brandeis had a strong sense of the distinction between "doing" and "being," and if human doing was for him limited and fallible, he attributed to human nature or being the same spiritual quality that is the essence of any creativity and thus of the Creator itself. It is precisely for its essential unity with all beings, that "the Creator that Brandeis envisioned was tied to no specific religion."[10]

It is *spiritual humanism* (another way to say transpersonalism) that connected Brandeis to Ralph Waldo Emerson, as understood by Dorothy Glancy:

Warren's and Brandeis' insistence on self-determination as an exercise of and means to attain and protect individual freedom reflected the traditional American emphasis on spiritual independence and self-reliance associated with Emerson, Thoreau, Dickinson. . . . Theirs was a social and psychological tradition concerned with introspection and solitude, as well as interpersonal relationships. Viewed by its inventors as an important safeguard for the individual control over his or her spiritual development and intimate relationships with others, the right to privacy fits within this tradition and perhaps only makes sense within that context.[11]

In his youth, Brandeis used to collect in an *Index Rerum* relevant quotations from various works, from the Bible to Shakespeare, but "Emerson was . . . Louis' favourite author, and quotations from his work ranged from short excerpts to full pages."[12] In a letter of 1876, Brandeis wrote: "I have been indulging in Emerson also—and can conscientiously say, that my admiration for him is on the increase. I have read a few sentences of his which are alone enough to make a man immortal."[13] This admiration grew over the years to encompass the philosophical sources that inspired Emerson himself. As we said, prominent among Brandeis's references are not only the Biblical prophets but above all Goethe, of whom Emerson wrote that he, "the most modern of the moderns, has shown us, as none ever did, the genius of the ancients." Emerson's work abounds with references to Greek tragedy, Socrates, Plato, and the Stoics, and it is again not accidental that over the years Brandeis felt increasingly closer to the "Greek genius," as he called it.[14] Glancy notices how the "Emersonian tradition of individualism relied heavily on 'solitude' as essential for cultivation of individuality," and then adds:

The Transpersonal Theory of Rights

Warren and Brandeis deliberately turned inward to focus on each individual's need to protect his or her internal, spiritual existence, his or her feelings, thoughts, sentiments. ... [In this] Warren and Brandeis were consciously the disciples of Emerson, not of Adam Smith. ... [Furthermore] In arguing for the right to privacy of all persons, whatsoever their position or station, Warren and Brandeis were also emphatically not the apostles of ... social Darwinism. ... It was, they felt, particularly fitting and necessary for the law to recognize and encourage respect for each individual's right to privacy. After all, encouraging such respect for privacy reinforced the mutual respect essential to bind together a community of free and self-determined individuals. ... Warren's and Brandeis' right to privacy was a practical embodiment of that Emersonian ideal.[15]

As Glancy remarks, "solitude" is a term more frequently used by Emerson than is "privacy," but it is clear that Emerson understood the two terms as equivalent. He constantly refers to "private" and "private life" not as opposite but as dialectically complementary to the universal and public:

There is one mind common to all individual men. ... Of the universal mind each individual man is one more incarnation. ... Each new fact in his private experience flashes a light on what great bodies of men have done. ... We are always coming up with the emphatic facts of history in our private experience and verifying them here. All history becomes subjective; in other words, there is properly no history, only biography. ... The priestcraft of the East and West, of the Magian, Brahmin, Druid, and Inca, is expounded in the individual's private life.[16]

Elsewhere, he categorically asserts: "The private life of one man shall be the most illustrious monarchy. ... For a man, rightly viewed, comprehendeth the particular natures of all men. Each philosopher, each bard, each actor has only done for me, as by a delegate, what one day I can do for myself."[17] This unity of private and public has for Emerson two dialectical sides, what we have named Interdependence and Independence:

Man is a stream whose source is hidden ... [and is] that Unity, that Over-Soul within which every man's particular being is contained and made one with all other. ... We live in succession, in division, in parts, in particles. Meantime within man is the soul of the whole; the wise silence, the universal beauty, to which every part and particle is equally related, the eternal ONE. ... Of this pure nature every man is at some time sensible. ... We know that all spiritual being is in man. ... We lie open on one side to the deeps of *spiritual nature*.[18]

This notion of "spiritual nature" appears frequently in Emerson, and it cannot be an accident that Brandeis used the very same expression in his most important writings on privacy. For Emerson, it is because of his spiritual nature that "the deeper [man] dives into his privatest, secretest presentiment, to his wonder he finds this is the most acceptable, most public, and universally true."[19] This passage rests on the same paradoxical dialectics that one finds in Brandeis, for whom "the most important office, and the one which all of us can and should fill, is that of a private citizen.... There is a wide field of usefulness for a public private citizen."[20] Again, the same unity of opposites characterizes Emerson's notion of *self-reliance*, defined as the power to be alone with others:

The virtue in most request is conformity. Self-reliance is its aversion ... It is easy in the world to live after the world's opinion; it is easy in solitude to live after our own; but the great man is he who in the midst of the crowd keeps with perfect sweetness the independence of solitude.

In the same essay on self-reliance, one of those that Brandeis admired most, Emerson writes that the great problem of man is that his genius does not "put itself in communication with the internal ocean, but it goes abroad to beg a cup of water of the urns of other men. We must go alone.... So let always sit."

Self-reliance at its best requires meditation and prayer, which Emerson defines as "the soliloquy of a beholding and jubilant soul." But this contemplative nature of self-reliance does not exclude action and life, because "prayer is the contemplation of the facts of life from the highest point of view."[21] This conception of self-reliance, with its insistence on facts as carriers of fundamental principles, resonates deeply with Brandeis's legal theory and more generally with his way of life and personal ethics. F. Frankfurter wrote that he "had the utmost attainable intellectual and moral autonomy," and a student of Brandeis has said that "Brandeis's primary standard of action was his own conscience. If he believed he was right, that settled the matter for him, no matter what others might think."[22] Needless to say, his autonomy was not capriciousness, but independence from the prejudices that blind human beings toward the rational truth spoken by facts. Mason, the friend and biographer of Brandeis, says that "Brandeis learned from Emerson the self-reliance he practiced all his life."[23]

It could be argued that Brandeis did not develop the contemplative aspect of Emerson's self-reliance. This may be true in reference to the lack of a specific meditative practice on the part of Brandeis, though these are things difficult to establish, given the extreme privacy of such practices. But Brandeis did undoubtedly absorb from Emerson the notion of a human essence transcending action, to which human beings need to return in all possible ways, including through those forms of action, such as play, in which the active intention is subordinated to the contemplative attitude of watching things happen disinterestedly. In 1890, his fiancée Alice Goldmark sent him the following poem by Longfellow:

O gift of God / A perfect day; / Whereon shall no man work but play;

/ Whereon it is enough for me, / Not to be doing but to be.

Brandeis answered: "Of course you are right, Alice ... for it has been a pet opinion of mine, formed early and often recurred to."[24]

To maintain a proper relation between "being" and "doing" was crucial to

Brandeis's way of life. He used to regularly take time away from work daily for relaxation and reflection, and periodically for vacations, because he was convinced that "there must be time also for the unconscious thinking which comes to the busy man in his play."[25] To get in touch with the unconscious is indispensable to the "busy man," because action must nourish itself at the sources of unconscious thinking, which in its purposeless mental watching has a somewhat contemplative quality. Brandeis's implicit acceptance of the unity of contemplative and active is confirmed by his acceptance of another fundamental distinction, that between Reason and Understanding, the former transcending the linear and intellectually conscious thinking of the latter. Writes Emerson: "The understanding adds, divides, combines, measures, and finds nutriment and room for its activity in this worthy scene. Meantime, Reason transfers all these lessons into its own world of thought. . . . [The] universal soul [we] call Reason."[26] In a letter to Frankfurter, Brandeis implicitly makes a similar distinction:

But I guess that only a very small part of the causes are technical or professional; and that one will have constantly to bear in mind "Sie sprechen eine Sprache, die ist so lieb, so schon / Dock keine der Philologen kann diese Sprache verstehen" (They [the stars] speak a language that is so majestic, so beautiful, and yet no philologist can understand this speech).[27]

The language of the stars is clearly the Logos or universal Reason, and such Logos cannot be captured by the analytical language of the philologist, which parallels the measuring language of technical and professional causes.

For Emerson, universal Reason is at once independent of and intrinsic to the Cosmos: "We are its property," so that It cannot depend on us; yet at the same time the universal Reason, "considered in relation to nature, we call Spirit," and Spirit is fully "within or behind . . . individual life."[28] The link with Emerson explains why Brandeis did not use the term "spiritual" with the vagueness with which it is too often used. In many of his writings, his *Olmstead* opinion foremost, he explicitly distinguishes between "spiritual," "intellectual," and "moral," and between "man's spiritual nature," "his sentiments," and "his intellect." Human spirit transcends, while encompassing, both intellect and sentiments, and this is the reason why it can only be found by moving beyond relatedness, and thus beyond both analytical understanding and emotional feeling. In a letter to his wife, Brandeis wrote: "I have practiced solitude, save a call on Holmes J. this afternoon." Solitude becomes a "practice," an exercise in self-discipline to delve more deeply into one's "unconscious thinking" and into one's "spiritual nature." Resisting excessive social contacts, something on which Emerson insists throughout his writings, is the presupposition to plunge more deeply into one's nature, both within and without. The world of outer nature is indeed the "symbol of spirit," the realm of presocial and preconventional authenticity, at least when still uncorrupted by human destructive manipulations. Writes Emerson: "To go into solitude, a man needs to retire as much from his chamber as from society. I am not solitary whilst I read and write, though nobody is with me. But if a man would be alone, let him look at the stars."[29] In the infinity without, the starry cosmos to which Brandeis so often refers in his writings, every single event acquires meaning in light of its unlimited interdependence and is thus the complementary side of the infinity within: "And, in fine, the ancient precept, 'Know thyself,' and the modern precept, 'Study nature,' become at last one maxim."[30] In this, Emerson is a disciple of his friend and disciple Thoreau, the master of contemplation in and through nature. Emerson's and Thoreau's thought can be characterized as *ecological transpersonalism*, and they are both to be considered the philosophical and spiritual fathers of American environmentalism. It is as a disciple of such forefathers that Brandeis proposed, among the reforms he envisioned for the New Deal, important environmental actions:

He advocated permanent investments for projects of lasting social value. Although he did not describe the projects in detail, he mentioned such things as afforestation, flood control, soil erosion control, irrigation efforts, navigation improvements, and the creation of lakes and ponds.[31]

Of course he also had other important proposals, especially directed at fighting the power of oligopolistic capital, and at remedying the dramatic social and economic problems that "bigness" and "big business" had created. But his fight against "bigness" cannot be properly understood apart from his Thoreauian sensitivity. His own habits testify to his Thoreauianism, and it was no accident that his places of vacations were very Thoreauian places such as Dedham, Maine, the Canadian woods, or Cape Cod.

Brandeis wanted to give back to agriculture the central role that it had in the Jeffersonian model of decentralized democracy, not only because of the economic self-sufficiency that the land guarantees to individuals but also because of the daily personal contact with the beauty and order of nature that was for Brandeis a way to moral autonomy and spiritual self-reliance. This is why "he disapproved of farm machinery," and "linked agricultural recovery with the recovery of society as a whole."[32] He was also suspicious of much of modern technology: "He avoided telephones whenever he possibly could. He hated the automobile and much preferred to walk. . . . Modern advertising was, to him, a pernicious vice, and he complained about it for all of his mature life. The modern obsession with fashion repulsed him."[33] His was not another kind of prejudicial conservatism, because Brandeis was very open to truly useful, principled, and ecologically sound technology. He was one of the first to talk of the scientific management of industry, although he understood it only as a means whereby to reduce the waste created by oligopolistic capitalism and to decentralize power in the hands of industrial workers.[34] At the same time, he knew that most modern technology screens human beings from spiritually experiencing nature within and without. For instance, he perceived with his usual premonition the dangers of an automobile-centered society. In a letter dated 1/3/1935, he asked Frankfurter to find someone who could research and write the history of the harm that the automobile had caused in the United States. Dawson comments: "In the light of recent developments (e.g. air pollution and the energy crisis), one wonders if Brandeis was being prophetic rather than anachronistic."[35] However, he was not contrary to technology as much as to the artificialization of human sentiments and relations that most modern technology embodies and promotes. Like Rousseau, he stigmatized artificialization as deeply rooted in the "envious comparison" generated by *"amour propre"*:

We are living in [an] artificial age, and artificiality is ruining many of those just starting out in life.... Seeing others far better off in this world's goods, enjoying the luxuries and good things of life, they deem it necessary to do likewise, for fear, I suppose, that they might be ridiculed for their thrift or sufficient strength of character to say no.[36]

Brandeis was a radical critic of consumerism and mass society, yet not from an elitist point of view, as he thought that everyone's capacity for spiritual and ethical self-reliance would be reinforced if luxurious standards of living were drastically reduced: "Pompei & Alexandria are being emulated. I guess a heavy batch of adversity wouldn't hurt American morals."[37] He also put an "almost obsessive emphasis on the virtues of the past,"[38] but this, far from being a symptom of traditionalism, was precisely connected to that individual withdrawal from material greed and attachment without which there cannot be any spiritual self-realization. Thus, "many who commented upon him ... remarked upon the simplicity of his life-style, his austerity, his hatred of luxury, his spare diet.... His personal habits and preferences seemed like a righteous rebuke to the stupidities, the complexities, the frills of the twentieth century."[39] In his final will, he wrote: "I have made for my wife and daughters, provision larger than will be required for that *simple living* which we have *practiced* from conviction and which I assume each will continue."[40] "Simple living," which Brandeis seems to describe as an ethical and spiritual practice, is a direct heir to the Stoic *homolegoumenos te physei zen*, the way of living and acting according to the inactive and fundamental nature of being, cosmic and individual. Like the Stoics, Brandeis was adamant, if discreet, about the reality of the natural law, and in this too he was a direct disciple of Emerson. Recognizing the identity of supreme Reason and Logos, Emerson talks of the Over-Soul of the cosmos as the "Highest Law," and declares:

All things are moral, and in their boundless changes have an unceasing reference to spiritual nature.... This ethical character so penetrates the bone and marrow of nature, as to seem the end for which it was made.... The moral law lies at the centre of nature and radiates to the circumference.[41]

In his article on the "living law," Brandeis refers to the time "when Euripides burst out in flaming words against 'the trammelings of the law which are not of the right' "; and reports a whole poem of Goethe, whom he defines a "poet-sage . . . imbued with the modern scientific spirit," which ends with the words: "As for the law, born with us, unexpressed / That law, alas, none careth to discern."[42] Brandeis, like Goethe, thought that true modernity and science do not grow by abandoning the eternal moral principles, but by constantly renewing the understanding of their silent yet most eloquent language. For such an understanding, privacy/interiority is essential, both as privacy of the person who judges (and thus of all of us when judging) and as the inherent truth of things that mirrors the interiority of the judging person. Brandeis always insisted on the privacy of the judge, stressing at the same time the importance of anchoring his or her interiority to the reality of facts. For him, judicial reason and the reason inherent in things constituted a hermeneutical circle, whereby the spiritual reason of the judge enlightens the facts, while the logic itself of facts confirms and fleshes out such inner reason. In *Schafer v U.S.* (251 U.S. 466, 482–3), Brandeis explained how judicial reason needs a sort of contemplative withdrawal from the turmoil of facts:

This is a rule of reason. . . . Like many other rules of human conduct, it can be applied only by the exercise of good judgment; and to the exercise of good judgment, calmness is, in times of deep feeling and on subjects which excite passion, as essential as fearlessness and honesty.

It is through this inner calmness that the judge, for Brandeis, can access the fundamental reason that mirrors, from within the human soul, the rational truth that lives in things. This essential correspondence of inner and outer reason was expressed by Brandeis on the one hand through the motto he applied to judicial review, "*If we would guide by the light of reason*," and on the other hand through another crucial motto, borrowed from the Roman-Stoic natural lawyers, "*ex facto oritur jus*," "the right emerges from the fact." The dialectical unity of such two mottos gives us a complete picture of Brandeis's homeorhetic natural law.

At this point, we need to dispel some misunderstandings regarding Brandeis's attitude toward judicial restraint and substantive due process. Brandeis has always been an advocate of judicial restraint, and was originally against substantive due process. His opposition to substantive due process, however, was directed against legal formalism, with its conservative imposition of arbitrarily "substantive" standards meant to stall legal and political change. At the same time, his support for judicial restraint was due to his appreciation of democratic deliberation, especially if decentralized, and to his conviction that such deliberation, when genuinely developed, could promote justice. In neither case was Brandeis's position proceduralist, because he was confident that judges have not just the legitimate power but also the duty to make sure that the democratic decision-making is truly deliberative. In *New York State Ice Co. v Liebmann*, [285 U.S. 262 (1932), at 311], he wrote:

To stay experimentation in things social and economic is a grave responsibility. . . . This Court has the power to prevent an experiment. We may strike down the statute which embodies it on the ground that, in our opinion, the measure is arbitrary, capricious or unreasonable. We have the power to do this, because the due process clause has been held by the Court applicable to matters of substantive law as well as to matters of procedure. But in the exercise of this high power, we must be ever on the guard, lest we erect our prejudices into legal principles. If we would guide by the light of reason, we must let our minds be bold.

Brandeis finally accepted substantive due process, although he was still cautious about its possible misuse by judicial arbitrariness. What worried Brandeis was the abuse of substantive due process "to stay experimentation in things social and economic," which concerns the relation between ends and means and is thus within the competence of democratic powers. But this does not mean that he wanted to abandon the judicial control of the ends pursued and of the reasonable connection between the ends declared and the means adopted. This is why Brandeis concludes his opinion with the same motto he used to support Harlan's test of reasonableness, "If we would guide by the light of reason, we must let our minds be bold." Precisely because the opposite of deliberative decision-making is for Brandeis arbitrariness, including procedurally democratic and majoritarian arbitrariness, the criterion with which to distinguish deliberative from arbitrary politics is the reason that comes from the facts, the holistic reason living in that substantive form of the Whole of Wholes that sustains the "general will" and that leads the genuine search for the common good.

Indeed, Brandeis's opposition to substantive due process relaxed in the course of the 1920s, and turned into acceptance and support when the threat was no longer represented by a *Lochner* jurisprudence trying to arbitrarily stop deliberative political majorities but by those same majorities having become arbitrary decision-makers. In spite of his personal closeness to Roosevelt and to the New Deal movement, Brandeis did not hesitate to strike down, through an essentially substantive due process, the New Deal's legislative measures that he perceived as promoting "bigness" and the growth of oligopolistic capitalism.[43] R. A. Burt has attributed to Brandeis a proceduralist approach even in this case, on the ground that he did not develop an analysis of the "substantive provisions" of the legislation but objected to the fact that it "was not enacted by a publicly visible or accessible process of reasoning."[44] But clearly the procedural aspect is only one aspect of Brandeis's fight against economic and political centralization. Centralization is "bigness," and bigness is bad not only because it centralizes, but also because it strips human beings of their freedom and dignity. Clearly he would have objected to "bigness" and centralization even if it had been approved through a publicly visible and participative decision-making, because a decentralized establishment of centralization would have been inherently contradictory and thus self-destructive. In a 1912 speech, he said: "The real fight today is against the inhuman, relentless exercise of capitalistic power . . . for social and industrial justice. . . . We must have right living conditions [and political rights] . . . but they are only means to the real end, which is the declaration of the rights of man."[45] The relentless capitalistic drive makes it impossible to have "right living conditions" for everybody, because it centralizes the management of the economy and resources in fewer and fewer hands. Even more important, it destroys the possibility of true citizenship, which, as Rousseau pointed out, requires that "no citizen be so rich as to be able to buy another, nor anyone so poor as to be forced to sell himself."[46] But the true goal of a just distribution of property is the establishment of the "rights of man," and thus of a more complete type of freedom.

This reference to the "rights of man" is one of the few explicit natural law expressions used by Brandeis and has nothing to do with the liberal "natural rights" approach. In *New York Central v Winfield* [244 U.S. 147 (1917), at 165], he rejected "our individualistic conception of rights" as the protective shield of possessive egoism and ethical arbitrariness. Not only is the classical Lockean approach involved in his rejection but also the post-Millian liberalism of the "enlightened selfishness," as Brandeis claimed that "We ought to develop enlightened unselfishness, as a substitute for the old, so-called enlightened selfishness."[47] "Enlightened unselfishness" meant for him, on a larger scale, abandoning the utilitarian wealth-maximizing and centralizing drive. Brandeis was convinced that a New Deal would not have been possible unless the "extreme mal-distribution of wealth" had been straightened out by forcing great wealth "out of existence through income and inheritance taxes." The revenues of such a taxation should have been used by the government to curb unemployment through "projects of lasting social value," such as the environmental programs mentioned earlier. But Brandeis was also convinced that the government, rather than building a parallel bureaucratic bigness, should redistribute wealth so as to promote a general economical and political self-sufficiency of individuals and communities. It is in this sense that he proposed that the Federal and State governments appropriate land and other productive means in order to lease them at a low cost to agricultural and workers' cooperatives.[48]

We have seen how the subordination of property to privacy was a central tenet of Brandeis's thought. Precisely due to the spiritual quality of his concept of privacy, his criticism of property absolutism cannot be limited to the idea of a more equal distribution of wealth, as even equality of distribution could not offset his rejection of excessive wealth and widespread consumerism. Brandeis knew that the core of the problem is the tension between inner self-reliance and the externalized life of accumulation and consumption, and that outer problems, such as wealth inequalities, socioeconomic injustices, and ecological destruction, are but the necessary results of the inner dominance of property over privacy. This is why the opposition between "bigness" and "smallness," so central to

The Transpersonal Theory of Rights

Brandeis's thought, is not to be read only in relation to the conflict between oligopolistic powers and the small property of workers and farmers but also, and more fundamentally, in relation to the indispensable value of smallness for spiritual and ethical self-development. In *Liggett v Lee*, decided a few years after the Great Depression, a dissenting Brandeis explained how the "maldistribution of wealth" is primarily a problem of political and cultural domination, and how the growth of oligopolistic "bigness" leads toward a "rule of plutocracy," which in turn leads to a social and spiritual corruption of the country and of its citizens:

There is a widespread belief that the existing unemployment is the result, in large part, of the gross inequality in the distribution of wealth and income which giant corporations have fostered; that by the control which the few have exerted through giant corporations individual initiative and effort are being paralysed, creative power impaired and human happiness lessened; that the true prosperity of our past came not from *big business*, but through the courage, the energy, and the resourcefulness of *small men*; that only by releasing from corporate control the faculties of the unknown many, only by reopening to them the opportunities for leadership, can confidence in our future be restored and the existing misery be overcome; and that only through participation by the many in the responsibilities and determinations of business can Americans secure the *moral and intellectual development* which is essential to the maintenance of liberty.[49]

The socioeconomic battle between "big business" and "small men" is the spiritual battle between the dominance of things over men and the spiritual-ethical privacy (courage, resourcefulness, creativity) that all can attain in their small individuality. "True prosperity" depends on "moral and intellectual development," which in turn depends in fundamental ways on "smallness." Writes Strum:

For Brandeis, the infinite fallibility of human beings was balanced by their infinite educability. That ability to learn is one of the keys to Brandeis's philosophy and his perception of human nature. Because human beings are fallible, their endeavour, whether economic or political, must be kept small.[50]

As Rousseau with his notion of "*perfectibilité*," Brandeis complemented the existential fallibility of human beings with their potential perfectibility. Like Rousseau, Brandeis appreciated the infinite existential perfectibility of human beings as springing from a fundamental spiritual nature that is already essentially perfect and that lives in the smallness of one's privacy. That privacy, in turn, tends to flourish in decentralized and participative politics, where endeavors can "be kept small." D. Acheson reports that Brandeis continually insisted on

the curse of these metropolitan maws which, having first corrupted with promise of money and power, sucked in and devoured the youth and promise of the country. He spoke of the impotence of an individual really to affect the course of any big community or organization. They ran themselves by a mechanics ungovernable by man. To govern and shape a community no larger than New Jersey would stretch the capacities of a Pericles. It could be done; but better still in smaller communities.[51]

Apart from a few heroic individuals, such as Emerson and Thoreau, people generally tend to depend heavily upon their context. Therefore, the possibility for them to attain true freedom depends on their living in small and participatory communities, because only by taking direct charge of the common good can the ordinary individual move beyond the limitations of his/her empirical individuality, achieving that responsible and thus truly moral autonomy without which there can be no real freedom. In various occasions, when talking of the development of individual autonomy and liberty, Brandeis repeated that *"the great developer is responsibility"*:

Always and everywhere the intellectual, moral and spiritual development of those concerned will remain an essential—and the main factor—in real betterment. This development of the individual is, thus, both a necessary means and the end sought. . . . The great developer is responsibility. . . . Democracy in any sphere is a serious undertaking. It substitutes self-restraint for external restraint. . . . It demands continuous sacrifice by the individual and more exigent obedience to the moral law than any other form of government. Success in any democratic undertaking must proceed from the individual. It is possible only where the process of perfecting the individual is pursued. His development is attained *mainly* in the process of common living.[52]

The inner "intellectual, moral and spiritual" growth of the individual is both the prerequisite and the end of public democratic life. Such development "is attained *mainly* in the process of common living" (where "mainly" indicates the parallel importance of self-sufficiency and privacy even for people who are *mostly interdependent*) and thus in small and decentralized political societies where true common living is possible. However, Brandeis's "common living" is not the merely empirical community of empiricist democrats or communitarians. "Common living," as the "living" explains, is not a descriptive given, but a process whereby individuals learn and practice the "moral law," growing toward the inner apprehension and outer embodiment of the transcendental form of the Whole of Wholes. Like the classics and Montesquieu before him, Brandeis believed that democracy is the most difficult regime to sustain, because it requires that everyone realize the moral law both within oneself and with others. There is no doubt, therefore, that for Brandeis democracy could only be a spiritual democracy.

The spiritual character of democracy has a twofold manifestation. From an inner or essential point of view, each citizen is endowed with an essential and practically potential independence, and thus with the duty to realize it in its intrinsic unity with responsible interdependence. From an outer or existential point of view, where independence and interdependence tend to move apart, there are individuals who are mostly interdependent and need to absorb from the context the elements necessary in order to perfect their potential wholeness, and there are others who are mostly independent and can more easily find within themselves their essential wholeness. It is these independent individuals who are to concretely embody the guiding power of the moral law.

Acheson reports that Brandeis used to talk of a "rounded and full understanding of life, the only wisdom that can be trusted with leadership," and this seems to confirm that for Brandeis only individuals who have developed their spiritual, intellectual, and moral wholeness can and must be leaders.[53] His admiration for Pericles' democracy was also admiration for the maieutical leadership of Pericles, because he knew that no "rule of law" can guarantee justice without being creatively perceived and dynamically embodied by just individuals ("rule of men"). His call for the advent of a "righteous leader" was based on the conviction that enlightened minorities are the key to spiritual democracy, because the "quality and spiritual value" of communities "can only come about through the concentrated, intensified strivings of smaller groups."[54] Writes D. Acheson:

New "functional" governments, "social discipline" and all that sort of things leaves him cold. But he can believe that all through this mass of blubber, society, there are individual minds which are working and which may be able to guide a handful of followers out of the wilderness, if they are let alone. But that "if" is a very big one. No one is ever let alone.[55]

Such a link between privacy and enlightened minorities has nothing to do with elitism. As we have seen before, Brandeis had a maieutical conception of leadership, grounded on the Socratic and Emersonian notion that essentially each individual has the power to become enlightened, and that the existential need for guides is justified only insofar as it helps people become more self-reliant and thus more worthy of self-government.[56]

It was the lack of spiritual/ethical integrity and capacity for self-government that brought about for Brandeis the democracy of "bigness," with its general equalization at the lowest common denominator of hedonistic and possessive egoism and its unlimited growth economy that such an egoism pretends to satisfy. Brandeis lucidly foresaw the totalitarian dangers inherent in the fusion and centralization of great political and capitalistic powers under the "technically" democratic banner of "bigness." In a 1905 speech he talked of "inconsistency . . . of political democracy and industrial absolutism," a concept that he later repeated by claiming that there is a "necessary conflict . . . between our political liberty and our industrial absolutism," as financial and capitalistic oligarchies resemble the despotisms of the past.[57] With this, he set himself in clear contrast with both liberals and conservatives, who, in spite of their differences, share the axioms of the "bigness" ideology: "Neither liberal nor conservative found him altogether acceptable: the former distrusted his compromising conservatism, the latter damned his anarchist-radicalism."[58] This comment by Mason, confusing his organic and coherent position for a combination of anarchism and conservatism, reveals that even those who were personally close to Brandeis found it difficult to grasp his paradoxically complex approach. Most commentators have had problems in classifying Brandeis within the liberal-conservative spectrum and have often solved the difficulty by placing him in the middle.[59] But Brandeis was heir to the uncompromising transpersonal tradition, whose "centeredness" or middle-path is altogether outside and beyond that spectrum. He acted as the guide of an enlightened minority defeated and scorned by the triumph of capitalistic bigness in its either liberal or conservative versions. Liberal-minded economists believed that "to dwell on the 'curse of bigness' on the contemporary scene is to be guilty of a purely 'emotional antagonism.' "[60] Even H. Laski, one of the main representatives of post-Millian liberalism, wrote that Brandeis's *The Curse of Bigness* was "like the pronouncement of a believer in the Ptolemaic astronomy that the new Copernican world will not do." The reality is that Brandeis was much closer to Copernicus and Galileo (who were in fact heirs to the Platonic tradition) than liberals such as Laski, who accepted the "bigness" dogma with the same blind faith of Ptolemaic believers (who were, interestingly enough, Aristotelians). It has been said: "He fought the 'curse of bigness' in business, and the industrial collapse seems to have justified him. . . . He finds now that it has been transferred to government. And he is still fighting it, which may make him, in the eyes of many, another Don Quixote."[61] Copernicus and Galileo were too treated like Don Quixote, and yet they literally changed the world. A few decades after his death, as the spiritual, ecological, and socioeconomic destructiveness of capitalistic bigness has reached unprecedented proportions, we may soon be forced to call upon Don Quixote Brandeis and the great chain of thought of which he has been a link. Only, this time, to save the world.

PRIVACY, RIGHTS, AND THE BRANDEIS-DOUGLAS CONSTITUTIONAL TRADITION

In *Olmstead,* Brandeis defined the right to privacy, or "right to be let alone," as "the most comprehensive of rights and the right most valued by civilized men." To Brandeis, civilization is both liberating and corrupting, and it is precisely privacy, as the withdrawal/forthcoming to/from the interiority in which lives our originally spiritual and universally compassionate nature, that shifts the balance from corruption to liberation, from self-destruction to happiness. The right to privacy is thus absolutely primary, and Brandeis considered it the apex of the hierarchy of rights, as well as the implicit ground upon which the rights of personality and property rest.

At the end of Ch. 2 we presented a theory of rights centered on the hierarchical tripartition of privacy, personality, and property, with each level innerly subdivided into a more private or self-regarding dimension and a more public or other-regarding dimension. Although that tripartition, and the parallel concepts of existential harm and non–self-destruction, are implicit in his position,

Brandeis's concrete legal elaboration of such an approach was adapted to the specific American constitutional framework and history. In the American constitutional tradition, the dimension of personality rights has generally been unified with that of human interiority and spiritual privacy. A clear example of this is constituted by Justice Bradley's unification of the Fourth Amendment right against searches and seizures, referring specifically to the physical immunity of the active personality, and the Fifth Amendment right against self-incrimination in *Boyd*, which rests directly on the notion of the inherent freedom of the human conscience. But such a unification did not signify the mutual collapse of the two levels, because Bradley clearly insisted on the fact that the outer layer of bodily and proprietary immunity from searches and seizures finds its essential ground in the protection of the individual conscience and interiority.

The same happens with Brandeis. He focused on the great divide between the then dominant rights of property on the one hand and those of privacy and personality on the other. He was right in doing so, because that was indeed the main field of confrontation in 1890 and during his whole career on the bench. In the 1890 article, Brandeis treated the "right to be let alone" and the "right to an inviolate personality" as coextensive, and in *Olmstead* he widened that coextension to include the "right to privacy." The fusion of privacy and personality rights is confirmed by the fact that in *Olmstead* Brandeis, like Bradley before, unifies the Fourth Amendment's rights of physical/personal immunity and the Fifth Amendment's right against self-incrimination. Yet, we have seen how that unification retained a critical distinction: Brandeis's argument from the Fourth Amendment established a relative right, but his argument from the Fifth Amendment was meant to assert the absoluteness of the right of the human conscience. Such a distinction of spiritual-noetic privacy and private personality is confirmed by Brandeis's insistence on their different degree of immunity from interference, as when he attributed the private consumption of alcohol, which properly belongs to the sphere of self-directed personality, a lesser right than the privacy of the individual interiority, which was for him an absolute, indeed the only absolute, right. Brandeis's understanding of "absolute rights," however, was implicitly based on the distinction between essential and existential. In *Duplex Printing Press Co. v Deering* [254 U.S. 443 (1921), at 479], he wrote: "All rights are derived from the purposes of the society in which they exist; above all rights rises duty to the community." Brandeis is here referring to the need for essentially absolute rights to be existentially implemented through the limits imposed by the context of responsibility toward others and toward the common good. Brandeis was aware of the fact that limits are not only inevitable but indeed necessary for true liberty, and he expressed this idea in a letter to N. Hapgood, dated 27/11/1927, by quoting his beloved Goethe: "Everything which frees our spirit without giving us control over ourselves is fatal." This is why he always thought that even those rights that he deemed essentially absolute, such as the rights concerned with the life of the mind and with deliberative politics, had to be subjected to the test of "clear and present danger," where the danger is, as we saw in Ch. 2, that of an existential, at once private and cosmically public, self-destruction.

Brandeis distinguished also between the spiritual and noetic life from the life of political deliberation. The latter he considered essentially related to privacy, both because it is a teacher in the development and expression of that responsible liberty that is essential to true privacy, and because without true privacy genuine "deliberation" is bound to turn into "arbitrariness," a distinction that he constantly stressed. Hence, the paramount and "most comprehensive" category of privacy rights included for him the rights related to freedom of expression and participation in deliberative politics. Yet, he distinguished between a stronger right to "being let alone" in self-contemplation, thinking and autonomous moral reflection/deliberation—a right *almost* immune even from the strict "clear and present danger" exception—and a somewhat weaker right of political deliberation and participation that is instead to be more ordinarily subjected to the "clear and present danger" analysis. On the other hand, this right of political deliberation, given its inherent link with *thought*, was by Brandeis attributed a higher degree of immunity than the rights of the self-directed personality, which are more deeply infused by the general principle of privacy, but are also bound to the existentially lower realm of *action*.

The existential priority and nonseparate independence of thought in relation to action, grounded on the classical distinction of the contemplative and active life, is expressed in the American Constitution through the "firstness of the First Amendment." Such a notion inspired Brandeis's and Cardozo's understanding of the "preferred freedoms" doctrine with its "double standard" of judgment. Frankfurter reports that in his 1923 conversations with him, Brandeis included among the fundamental rights to be protected through substantive due process, the rights to appeal, to education, to choice of profession, and to locomotion. Together with the right to education, with its implicit link to the freedom of thought, Brandeis considered fundamental certain rights, such as those concerning the choice of one's profession and to locomotion, that refer to the active personality and are therefore inherently more liable to public regulations and limitations. This would appear as a possible contradiction in Brandeis's thought, and it is difficult to make sense of what look like contradictions in Brandeis's thought because he never wrote any systematic theoretical work. However, if we look more deeply into Frankfurter's report, we begin to see a consistent pattern. Brandeis's placement of both personality and privacy rights under the same general category is in line with his somewhat tactical unification of all rights transcending the proprietary dimension. Yet, in the end, the inner differentiation of privacy and personality, within such a unitary category, nevertheless emerges. Brandeis completed his argument, according to Frankfurter's report, by explictly defining the above unitary category of fundamental rights in opposition to property rights as conceived within the Lochner framework, concluding that though these are ordinarily liable to limitations, the "right to your education and to utter speech is fundamental except in clear and present

The Transpersonal Theory of Rights

danger."[62] In the end, thus, the only fundamental rights that are said to enjoy the stronger protection of the "clear and present danger" test are those relating to the formation and deliberative expression of thought rather than those relating to the active personality.

This gives a different character, gradual rather than dichotomous, to Brandeis's conception of the hierarchy of rights and thus to his understanding of the "preferred freedoms" and "double standard" doctrines. It has been claimed that "double standard" meant for Brandeis that only privacy and personality rights were to be protected by a substantive due process, leaving property and contract rights under the protection of a merely procedural due process. Writes H. Garfield: "Although he opposed special due process protection for liberty of contract, Brandeis was willing to use substantive due process to protect personal rights he deemed fundamental."[63] This expresses one important truth, namely that Brandeis did believe in "substantive due process," although in its formal/substantive version. But it is a wrong statement if it intends to present a dichotomous view of Brandeis's theory of rights. Brandeis's "double standard" dualized between privacy/personality and property rights on the ground of a hierarchical continuum that neither collapsed privacy and personality into one another nor completely excluded property rights from a fundamental protection. Mental/spiritual rights of privacy and material rights of property were for him the two faces of a unique problem, because there is a relation of inverse proportionality between the two: The more property becomes dominant, fostering wealth maximization and capitalistic "bigness," the less the room for spiritual privacy and moral autonomy. Emerson expresses such inverse proportionality:

The reliance on Property, including the reliance on governments which protect it, is the want of self-reliance . . . that which a man is, does always by necessity acquire; and what the man acquires is *living property*, which does not wait the beck of rulers, or mobs, or revolutions, or fire, or storm, or bankruptcies, but perpetually renews itself wherever the man breathes.[64]

If there is a property that stands in opposition to privacy and self-reliance, there is also a "living property" that serves such fundamental values. Though constantly fighting against the attempt "to endow property with active, militant power which would make it dominant over men,"[65] Brandeis also worked to make the true meaning of "private property" as *privacy-grounded property* emerge. This view, besides being consistent with the whole of Brandeis's approach, is confirmed by Frankfurter's (somewhat obscure) summary of their conversations: "Property, it is absurd as Holmes says, to deem fundamental in the sense that you can't curtail its use or its accumulation or power. There may be some aspects of property that are fundamental—but not regard[ed] as fundamental specific limitations upon it."[66] Property has two sides. One is not fundamental and can therefore be limited in the name of more fundamental rights and interests: It involves the "use" of property, which has necessarily social and ethical implications, and even more the "accumulation" of wealth and the power associated with it. But there is also a fundamental side that, as it is easy to understand by contrast, refers to property before accumulation, to the property that gives no power over others but preserves one's material independence from external powers, and, of course, even more fundamentally to the property indispensable to one's self-preservation. This view has been consistently maintained by Brandeis, who in the 1890 article had already written: "The right of property, in its widest sense, including all possession, including all rights and privileges, and hence embracing the right to an inviolate personality, affords alone that broad basis upon which the protection which the individual demands can be rested."[67]

Here, Brandeis talks of property "embracing" privacy, and this would seem to contradict his repeated description of privacy as the most comprehensive of all rights. Yet again there is no contradiction, because the two claims are made again from *two different points of view*, the *essential* and the *existential*. From an existential point of view, privacy is the foundation of property and thus encompasses it. But from an essential point of view, that is, when property grows toward its own essence, property is privacy in that it embraces within itself the ethical and spiritual meanings associated with privacy. Property's essential embracing of personality and privacy implies, therefore, its existential subordination to those larger and deeper layers of human existence. In this sense, Brandeis had an implicitly *holographic* conception of language, whereby each word/concept, like any self, inherently contains all the others. Behind this vision there is, once again, the theoretical work of Emerson: "Every universal truth which we express in words, implies or supposes every other truth. *Omne verum vero consonat*. It is like a great circle on a sphere, comprising all possible circles, which, however, may be drawn and comprise it in like manner."[68] This metaphor perfectly expresses the equality and reciprocal encompassing of all selves and concepts at the level of essence. Brandeis implemented such a holographic approach to the question of rights by developing a hierarchy of dimensions and rights that never overlooked the essential value of each of those dimensions and rights.

As we know, this model of rights and privacy only partially survives in the "new" paradigm that emerged in the 1970s and that is torn between liberalism and transpersonalism. *Bowers v Hardwick* [106 S.Ct. 2841 (1986)], is very revealing in this respect. The dissent by Blackmun, Brennan, Marshall, and Stevens (although we have seen that Stevens often goes beyond the model presented by Blackmun in *Bowers*) presents a theory of the right to privacy that, though in the context of a contradictory/mediatory approach, in the end remains within the liberal horizon:

In construing the right to privacy, the Court has proceeded along two somewhat distinct, albeit complementary lines. First, it has recognized a privacy interest with reference to certain *decisions* that are properly for the individual to make.... Second, it has recognized a privacy interest with reference to particular *places* without regard for the particular activity in which the individuals who occupy them are engaged. . . . The case before us implicates both the decisional and the spatial aspect.[69]

Blackmun upholds the liberal spatialization of privacy by returning to that subordination of privacy to "places" that Brandeis had criticized in *Olmstead* and the Court had finally overcome in *Katz* by asserting that privacy protects persons, not places. This subordination to physical space tends to externalize privacy into the lower dominion of property, and Blackmun's understanding of privacy's "decisional" aspect further reinforces such a tendency.

Blackmun identifies decisional privacy with the individual freedom of choice, although he does not specify what he means by freedom of choice. As we have seen in Ch. 2, choice too is articulated into different levels: the inner freedom to form and behold one's tastes and preferences; the freedom to act out or impersonate such preferences; and the freedom of economic and proprietary choice. Thus, one can develop an inner preference that may be either too unjust or too impractical to be implemented in the outer world, and yet, in spite of its complete or partial limitation by ethical and material factors, autonomy in choosing is a valuable component of interiority, and must be respected as such. The liberal, on the other hand, collapses freedom of choice into the freedom to act as one chooses.

It is the last understanding of decisional privacy that ultimately prevails in Blackmun's mediatory scheme. For Blackmun, spatial and decisional privacy are clearly entitled to immunity from interferences "without regard for the particular activities in which the individuals who occupy [it] are engaged." This is of course very liberal. Furthermore, in Blackmun's conception privacy is reduced both to personality, the "decisional" sphere, and to property, the "spatial" sphere, and its essence is thus lost into that mix of utilitarianism and liberalism, into that utilitarian liberalism, which is so prevalent today. Blackmun's further justification of privacy as a force promoting a "good life" ("a harmony of living," "the happiness of the individual") only tempers *a posteriori* the arbitrariness of liberal "privacy," into a model that we called "liberalism plus." We have seen in Ch. 3 that such a dualistic/mediatory conception of privacy was already implicitly present in *Roe v Wade*, and this explains why Douglas preferred to concur in Blackmun's *Roe* decision with a separate opinion, in order to present an alternative conception of privacy explicitly centered on the Brandeisian primacy of interiority and the human "spiritual nature."

In *Doe v Bolton* [410 U.S. 179 (1972)], the companion case to *Roe v Wade*, Douglas asserted that the questions at stake "involve the right of privacy" and then claims that the general right of privacy encompasses different rights and privileges, all of which "come within the meaning of the term 'liberty' as used in the Fourteenth Amendment." The intimate connection of privacy and liberty has always been forcefully asserted by Douglas, and one author has rightly claimed that "for Douglas, the conventionally separate concepts of privacy and liberty coalesced."[70] The sense of this coalescence is explained by Douglas's repeated claim that "the right to be let alone is indeed the beginning of all freedom": Privacy is the essence of the continuum of liberty-rights and is thus essentially involved in each and every right and liberty. This is the very picture offered by Douglas in *Bolton*. After having identified privacy and liberty as overlapping, he sets the following hierarchy of rights:

First is the autonomous control over the development and expression of one's intellect, interests, tastes, and personality. These are rights protected by the First Amendment and, in my view, they are absolute. . . . *Second is the freedom of choice in the basic decisions of one's life respecting marriage, divorce, procreation, contraception, and the education and upbringing of children.* These rights, unlike those protected by the First Amendment, are subject to some control by the police power . . . [but] a "compelling state interest" must be shown in support of the limitation. . . . *Third is the freedom to care for one's health and person, freedom from bodily restraint or compulsion, freedom to walk, stroll, or loaf.* These rights, though fundamental, are likewise subject to regulation on a showing of "compelling state interest."

This is Douglas's most organic presentation of his theory of privacy. Its brevity and sketchiness should not surprise, because Douglas "was a pragmatist; he left theory-building to others."[71] Although there remain some contradictions in his theory, it is immediately clear that Douglas adds, above the spatial ("freedom to walk, stroll, or loaf") and the decisional ("freedom of choice in the basic decisions of one's life"), the more fundamental level of privacy as the autonomous interiority and its expression. With his identification of liberty and privacy, Douglas establishes a general *principle of privacy*, that which is holographically present in all rights as "private" rights. With his hierarchical structuring of the three levels, he sets the more specific *right to privacy*, entitled to the dignity of an absolute immunity, above the rights of self-directed (third level) and other directed (second level) personality, both of which are subjected to the possibility of a "compelling state interest."

The encompassing quality of the principle of privacy includes property rights as well, although in *Bolton* Douglas limits his analysis to the privacy and personality complex, in line with the previous American tradition. Coherent with his political and economic Brandeisianism, Douglas posited a deep link between property and self-direction, explicitly claiming that property is important both as a "project of one's own personality" and as a "guarantee of privacy."[72] In Ch. 3 we have seen how he, though forcefully fighting "bigness" and its instrumental attempt to give priority to property rights, was ready to defend the right to private property when supportive of individuality, as in the *Lynch* case. He thus accepted the distinction between self-directed and other-directed property or wealth.

The case of personality rights is more complex. In *Bolton*, Douglas inserted in the first level of absolute rights the term "personality," and this would seem to contradict the fundamental distinction between privacy and personality rights. But Douglas uses here the word "personality" in the psychoanalytical meaning of the "inner persona," referring to interiority, as shown also by the fact that he puts it together with "intellect," "tastes," and "interests." Personality as referring to our active and socially related being is clearly confined within the second and third levels of the hierarchy. The second level of rights, referring to self-reproduction, family, and sexuality, corresponds to what we have defined as other-directed personality or intimacy. The third level, referring to self-care and more generally to personal freedom of movement and action, coincides with what we have called self-directed personality. The fact that Douglas distinguished this last level is important. The freedom to care for one's health and person clearly includes the externalization of one's tastes, because taking care of one's health necessarily implies choosing one's diet and way of life. This confirms what we said earlier, namely that "taste," as used by Douglas in relation to the first level of absolute rights, does not in itself involve the actions that embody it and is thus referred to interiority. Douglas's concrete hierarchy of inner and outer shows how far from Millianism he had come by the end of his life. D. Glancy, in her otherwise commendable defense of Douglas's theory of privacy, claims that the tripartition presented in *Bolton* is directly derived from Mill.[73] But I think she is wrong. We have seen in Ch. 2 how Mill's tripartite sphere of private liberty, while putting first the "inward domain of consciousness" in accordance with his transpersonal side, claims for both such a domain and for the second domain of free private choice and action the same absolute protection, as opposed to Douglas's explicit confinement of the liberal "freedom of choice," or freedom to act as one chooses, to a conditioned form of protection.

By looking more carefully, it becomes quite evident that Douglas's scheme of rights is directly, if somewhat confusingly, inspired by classical natural law, and not surprisingly so, given that he explicitly appealed to natural law and rights throughout his life. The level of economic and property rights corresponds to the general natural law category of *self-preservation*. The second level of intimacy, family, and reproductive rights, with its general reference to the interpersonal life, is immediately connected to the natural law fundamental category of *self-reproduction*, which also includes the third level of bodily self-care, habits, hobbies, and more generally self-directed decisions, both because care of oneself as a person is the presupposition of intimate and family relations and because we reproduce ourselves, in a moral rather than biological sense, through our habits and socially learned behaviors. Finally, the first level, referring to the development and the outer expression of interiority, is but the twofold natural law precept sanctioning the natural human impulse toward spiritual self-realization and sociopolitical life, which are truly, for Douglas too, *complementary opposites*.[74]

However, it is at this point that Douglas's theory of privacy and rights shows itself to be irresolvably, if only partially, entangled with Millian liberalism.

Douglas adopts, in relation to the first level of rights, a position of rights-absolutism, which he extends equally both to interiority and to its expression. These elements are more Millian than Brandeisian. We have seen how Douglas has been torn all his life between those two ways of thinking, possibly confused by their important similarities. His *Bolton* opinion manifests some remnants of that tension and yet shows how Douglas did, in the end, radically depart from Millianism. In fact, both his rights-absolutism and his equalization of interiority and expression have a pragmatic and instrumental value, rather than a substantively theoretical one. It is true that in some cases he actually upheld the absolute immunity of speech from interference, the most famous instance being his dissent in *Paris* involving pornography. But it is also true that he was aware of the fact that expression cannot receive the same absolute protection enjoyed by interiority. In questions of free speech, he upheld the "speech brigaded with action" test: "The only time suppression is constitutionally justified is where speech is so closely brigaded with action that it is in essence a part of an overt act . . . as when fire is shouted in a crowded theatre." This test is clearly an offspring of Brandeis's "clear and present danger" test. The main difference between Brandeis's and Douglas's approaches is that the former recognizes that speech can by itself constitute a clear and present danger, something that Douglas was reluctant to fully and concretely accept. In many concrete instances Douglas did sever speech and action so radically as to make speech as absolutely immune as thought. But if he did so in practice, he did not do so in theory. His very shouting-fire example of a "speech brigaded with action" refers to a speech that is in itself the whole of the action. This shows Douglas's openness to the possibility of subjecting speech itself to the "clear and present danger" exception, a possibility that he thus acknowledged in the very same work in which he presented the definition of his test: "It is clear that the First Amendment does not give complete free rein to utterances. The Bill of Rights does not underwrite all irresponsible talk."[75] He also concretely envisioned such a possibility. In *Beauharnais v Illinois* [343 U.S. 250 (1952)], he accepted the idea that the government can regulate racist and discriminatory speech, even though he dissented against the actual regulation implemented because it was not based on a sufficient showing of a clear and present danger. The fact that Douglas resisted concretely applying his own theoretical standard of free speech is likely due to what he considered a very threatening expansion of governmental interferences in all walks of life. But he knew that speech and expression, the beginning and most-essential forms of one's active membership in the community, cannot enjoy the same absolute immunity of the spiritual interiority they represent.

There is no doubt that "spiritual nature" was for Douglas the essence of privacy, and through it of all rights. Like Brandeis, he was a transpersonalist in the tradition of Emerson and Thoreau, whom he repeatedly presented as the champions of true liberty. He did not hesitate to confess his transpersonalist beliefs in his autobiography:

I came to believe that Jesus was, like other men, the son of God, that, as Alan Watts wrote, he had "intense experiences of cosmic consciousness—of the vivid realization that one's self is a manifestation of the eternal energy of the universe, the basic 'I am.' " The powerful lesson of the New Testament is that if Jesus could identify with God, every person can do the same. The Hindus and Buddhists believe that. Each of them can say "I am God" without being guilty of subversion or blasphemy. For that represents the striving for a goal of which all people are capable of seeing, and fulfilling in part.

In line with the ecological transpersonalism of his predecessors, he insisted that spiritual self-realization implies ecological responsibility and integrity, and he admired both Eastern philosophies and Native-American spirituality for their having "respect for all forms of life, animal as well as human" and for their knowing that "Man is not on earth to dominate, destroy, and kill" but to become "one with the life of his area of earth."[76] His relentless environmentalism, both through action and writings, testifies to the ecological depth of his spirituality.[77] Precisely because of his faith in the spiritual nature of human beings, his protection of human interiority against the conforming pressures of both society and organized religion was inflexible. The fact that in *Bolton* freedom of religion and the right to be silent are, as "aspects of the right of privacy," the first two examples of the first level of rights, cannot be accidental. N. Strossen, building upon Professor Powe's work, has claimed that Douglas's approach to the religion clauses and the freedom of conscience of the First Amendment has been characterized by a stern "evolution to absolutism." And yet, even in this area Douglas always maintained a distinction between inner belief and outer conduct. For him, although "freedom to practice a religion is as much a part of religious freedom as freedom to believe," religious conduct constituting a "clear and present danger" can be limited. Strossen concludes that "Douglas's mature view of the Free Exercise Clause still drew some distinction between beliefs and conduct, holding only the former to be absolutely protected," although she also notices how Douglas often failed to concretely apply such a standard.[78] Beyond his philosophical contradictions and practical inflexibility in face of very threatening governmental powers, Douglas was aware of the fact that there can be no practical rights-absolutism, because even the most essential and spiritual reality is necessarily embodied to some degree in conduct, so that not even the most absolute privacy escapes the possibility of limitations, as extremely exceptional and unlikely as they may be.

In the end, Douglas's conception of privacy and rights reaffirms the approach that lives within Brandeis's theory of law and rights. In such an approach, the right of privacy/to be let alone is at once "the beginning of all freedom," or the highest layer in the hierarchy of rights, and the "most comprehensive of rights," the encompassing essence or principle of each and every right, including personal and proprietary rights. The existential primacy of privacy manifests itself through a hierarchical tripartition that is structured vertically along the polarity interiority/thought versus exteriority/action and horizontally through the distinction of self-direction and other-direction. In *The Right of the People*, Douglas generalizes such a subdivision by distinguishing all individual rights into two general categories, the rights "to be let alone" and the rights of "expression." There are thus three different senses and levels of intensity in which privacy is implicated with rights: There is an existential *principle of privacy*, which participates in all rights insofar as they are rights of a private individual, and more importantly as they are supposed to serve the ethical and spiritual growth (the growth of an existential awareness) of the person; there is a further *principle of selfhood*, which is the empirical and dualizing aspect of the general principle of privacy and which regulates the horizontal distinction between self-direction and other-direction, allowing us to give priority to the actions that have self and interiority as their primary object; and finally there is the *right to privacy* proper, which is the general name for the liberty and immunity of thought, interiority, education, and so forth, plus the rights to self-preservation and of life/death that are inherently part of our deepest being. Such a transpersonal and Brandeisian theory of privacy and rights can be visually summarized as in Figure 6.1. The first thing to notice about the scheme is that it resembles quite closely the natural law tripartition of self-preservation, self-reproduction, and sociopolitical/spiritual life (which in turn follows the Platonic tripartition of money/body/soul). Though maintaining the overall approach, we have developed the three general categories into a six-layered model by adding dimensions that in the classical natural law model were only implicit, and by shifting a few elements.

For instance, we have maintained the general definitional link between property and self-preservation, the latter being the true essence of property. Yet we moved such core of property, "material self-preservation," to the level of self-directed privacy, because there could not be any legally and politically relevant interiority to begin with without the preservation of a human bodily exteriority. In the same way, because the essence of material self-preservation is the question of life and therefore of death, we have included in such a category the life and death issues. All the rights included in the category of self-directed privacy, or privacy *tout court*, are ordinarily immune from coercive interferences (apart from the case of mental illnesses). Yet, they are inherently at one with the ethical and spiritual self-duties that ground the right to privacy to begin with. This means that cultural and educational stimuli, as long as they are maieutically bent toward the promotion of the inner and autonomous self-development and self-introspection, do not violate but rather promote the absoluteness of right to privacy, as with the promotion of the autonomous self-reflection on the part of the pregnant woman in the abortion situation. Of course, as soon as the interiority manifests itself into an action, which is inherently enmeshed in interdependence so as to become immediately potentially relevant for the law,[79] interference becomes possible, as when spiritual and religious practices, precisely because they are practices, may become violent or dangerous; or when, in the abortion case, it becomes plausible to think that the fetus has reached the

Figure 6.1
Scheme of Liberty and Rights

Private / inner / thought

PRIVACY

Private interiority individual conscience spiritual privacy sensations, emotions **Private Autonomy** inner taste/choice inner will/deliberation **Material Self-preservation** privacy-property life and death issues	**Public interiority** General Will (Common Good, Whole of Wholes) **Public Autonomy** political deliberation associational privacy freedom of deliberative speech/participation

PERSONALITY

Private Personality private self-directed action outer taste/choice habits, hobbies, self-care	**Interpersonal Intimacy** intimate relations marriage, sexual and reproductive freedom

PROPERTY

Private Property private economic freedom for self-sufficiency	**Wealth** private use of common, socially responsive wealth

public / outer / action

(Left axis: **Self-Direction   Right to be let alone**)
(Right axis: **Other-Direction   Expression   Participation**)

condition of *spiritual otherness* as opposed to that of empirical and separative otherness that characterizes the Millian approach of *Roe*.

At this point, we need to explain why property for self-sufficiency, being a prerequisite for a full political participation, is not raised within the category of political deliberation/expression, or other-directed privacy. The reason is that, although it is a very important support for political participation, self-sufficiency is not indispensable to it in the absolute way in which bodily survival is indispensable to the existence of human interiority and privacy. Even in situations in which self-sufficiency cannot be fully and generally guaranteed, the rights of political participation and expression are still active, indeed more active than ever. For example, in crises in which the government would need to redistribute even the property necessary for self-sufficiency, in order to guarantee the universal right to self-preservation, not only would the rights of political participation and self-expression have to be maintained, but in fact they would have to be extended to the utmost, so as to increase control over the government and its expanded powers.

Within the category of other-directed privacy, or political participation and expression, speech plays a critical role. We have seen how Brandeis (and Douglas too, even if with some ambiguity) acknowledged the fact that speech, though enjoying a high degree of immunity, is liable to certain limitations. In the case of speech "brigaded with action," or speech that is the action itself (as when shouting "fire" in a crowded theater), this is easy to see. More difficult is to establish the limits to be applied to speech as such. Even in the area of speech, Brandeis implicitly applied the principle of non–self-destruction, whereby wrong speech should be tackled only with more and better speech, as long as it does not threaten the life of the community and of itself as the "communicative" esence of community, thus creating a situation of "emergency." This concept was developed into a consistent theory by Alexander Meiklejohn, which, when corrected of some contradictions that plague it, furnishes us with a *test of relevance* that can actually constitute a proper guide in all "free speech" issues.[80]

Following the formal/substantive methodology, Meiklejohn refuses to limit speech because of its content (falsity versus truthfulness), establishing instead the discrimination line at the level of the form of the speech, of its wholistic-universal versus particularistic character, and thus of its *relevance* to the common good. The question, for Meiklejohn, is not one of letting everyone say what they want to say, but rather of letting everything that needs to be heard for proper political "deliberation," and thus for the proper search for the Whole of Wholes, be heard. Of course, this holistic form of the speech is immediately substantive, because it excludes from the absolute protection guaranteed to "relevant" speech, all speeches that express inherently particularistic or discriminatory interests, such as the corporate lobbying, the manipulatory speeches moved by a politician's or a party's selfish interest, the racist and sexist speeches, and the speech whose only reason is gossip. This is not to say that these speeches enjoy no protection, but as opposed to the "relevant" speeches protected by the absolute force of the First Amendment, they are entitled to the more limited protection of the Fifth.[81]

The problem with Meiklejohn's theory (and unfortunately here we have to greatly simplify Meiklejohn's rich and complex thought) is that he ends up crystallizing his test of relevance into a formalistic dualism of public versus private, on the ground that what is public is relevant for the common good, and what is private is not. But as there are public institutions that work against the common good, so are there private citizens (Brandeis called them "public private citizens") who deeply promote it. This is why Meiklejohn's concept of "relevance for the common good," which is too vague because any action, including speech, necessarily impinges on the communal life, should become "relevance for the promotion of the common good." For instance, any speech made by a corrupt president, or by some representative of a House committee controlled by some corporate lobby, is nevertheless relevant for deliberation, given the public quality of the speakers. But if we look at such speeches under the light of their relevance for the promotion of the common good, looking for the *wholistic or particularistic origin and direction of their intention*, then even such speeches could end up being limited. This is in line with that basic constitutional doctrine of the "implied limitations of government," whereby the courts, although they cannot interfere with the choice of means and policies, can control the ends concretely pursued by the public powers, and so can also control the political speeches that are moved by illegitimate selfish or corrupt ends.

The shift from the nominalistic to the formal/substantive notion of relevance rescues Meiklejohn's theory from its own limitations. When it adopted Meiklejohn's nominalistic test of relevance in the field of the freedom of the press, the Supreme Court repeatedly bumped into the practical impossibility of establishing what or who is public or private, falling into a series of deep contradictions.[82] There the problem was that of deciding, in reference to the higher degree of legitimacy attributed to the publication of personal information on publicly relevant people, who is a "public figure," and the problem was made difficult by the fact that we all may become public figures by "voluntarily injecting ourselves into a public controversy" (as stated by the *Gertz* Court), or by participating more actively in politics. By adopting the standard of "relevance for the promotion of the common good," we overcome the nominalistic dualism of public versus private. Instead of establishing a priori definite rules that would inevitably fall into a nominalistic and static acquiescence to what is thought of as relevant according to the dominant public opinion, we would favor an a posteriori analysis of how a certain action or speech has tried, or not tried, to promote the common good. On the one hand, this would make for a less mechanical jurisprudence, more intelligently bent toward searching for the fundamental ends of the political life. On the other hand, the lack of fixed but dull rules would stimulate people to autonomously search for what is best for the Whole of Wholes, giving a more creative contribution to the common good.

Given the minimization of fixed rules, it is clear that the Courts would have to give more weight to the *intention* of the speaker, writer, publisher, and so on.

This is not to say that there would not be guidelines, or a set of relatively standardized rules. In fact, it would be easier to have both. For instance, from the point of view of the nominalistic distinction of public and private, gossip seems to have become the more and more "relevant" for the majority of the public. But in reference to the promotion of the common good, gossip would have a very little immunity from interference, and there would certainly be a pretty final rule against, for instance, the publication of the names of rape victims. Furthermore, if we consider the issue of the publication of personal information on more or less public figures, we can see that, in reference to the promotion of the public good, the a priori determination of who is a "public figure" is not really necessary: We could simply adopt a general guideline stating that the smaller the geographical and political area in which one becomes public, the lower the level of the information that can be published. So, for instance, on a small town politician nothing personal should be published, not even relating to his or her economic situation (unless of course the information concerns something illegal), both because in a small town everybody can know his or her character and quality on a more personal level and because the level of responsibility is anyway quite low. But the more we move up the political ladder, the more the politician must accept to release information on his or her economic, personal, and political life, as long as it is information that is useful to understand who the person is as a political leader, rather than being mere gossip. Anyone who candidates himself or herself to be a President of the United States (or of any other country) should not only be squeaky clean (a standard that has nothing to do with the pathetic notion of excluding someone because s/he smoked a joint when s/he was twenty!), but, given that government is indeed the great teacher, should embody the highest moral standards.

There is only one last criterion that needs to be sketched out. When deciding the quality of speech, we need to make distinctions. On one hand, there is *existentially false speech*—the racist or sexist speech that denies the universal inclusiveness of discourse, thereby denying itself as a discourse while entering the opposite dimension of violence. This type of speech can be tolerated only insofar as its racist or sexist content has not yet taken over the intention to maintain an open and inclusive communication, so that a contradiction remains between the exclusionary content and the inclusionary method. This may be the case of the person who is convinced that blacks are inferior and thus not worthy of participating in political deliberation, and yet remains open to reasoning with them, thus remaining somewhat open to change through better speech. On the other hand, there is *empirically false speech*—which does not claim to exclude anyone from speech and deliberation as racially, sexually, or morally lower, and is always protected as long as its empirical falsity does not reach the level of existential self-destruction, thereby threatening fundamental aspects of the community and thus the possibility itself of discourse. For instance, often economic

The Transpersonal Theory of Rights

lobbying starts on the conviction that the good of a certain economic sector (say, forestry) coincides with the common good; and even if it were an empirically false claim, it could not be interfered with until there emerges a situation of emergency. When the maintenance of that economic sector may become existentially self-destructive (as it has happened with the lumber industry, which, while destroying nature, is unable even to produce profits for itself, apart from the growing governmental funds it receives), its political propaganda, which still claims to be "relevant" for the promotion of the common good, reaches such a degree of empirical falsity as to promote existential self-destruction. Then, the possibility of interference, even if only in the form of a partial limitation, becomes legitimate.

Coming back to our general scheme, we can acknowledge that the classical natural law tripartition organizes the highest dimension of rights in the same way we have done, by distinguishing between a spiritual dimension (which the medieval natural lawyers identified with the natural impulse toward God) and a sociopolitical dimension (which the classical and medieval thinkers identified with the human impulse to live in society as a "zoon politikon" or political animal). The transpersonal understanding of the spiritual impulse is of course quite different from the impulse toward a personal God as conceived by mainstream Christianity and points rather to that inner search for our inner divinity associated with the Platonic and Stoic precept "know thyself." A genuinely homeorhetic and transpersonal conception of natural law should radically transcend the models, old and new, that have been produced from within the Aristotelian-Thomistic tradition, which has partially moved toward a dismantling of the proper order of the three precepts/dimensions (sometimes to the point of claiming the full-fledged priority of the proprietary dimension of self-preservation over the spiritual and sociopolitical dimension[83]) and has generally ossified natural law into a code of predetermined and traditionalist rules.

Our six-partition, while being specifically a scheme of liberty and rights, implicitly contains a scheme of responsibility and duties. As privacy is stronger the more it integrates responsibility, so the right to privacy enjoys the highest immunity precisely because it incorporates the best potential for fulfilling the moral duty to oneself and others. Essentially, the higher the right, the higher the duty. On the other hand, rights and duties are empirically and thus legally opposed. If the highest right of privacy is to be fully realized, the coercive or manipulative enforcement of the duty of privacy, of going inside one's interiority in order to grow spiritually and ethically, would clearly contradict the freedom that is inherent in spiritual and moral life, being thus a violation of the right's guarantee against interference. A legal scheme of responsibility and duties would thus be the complete reversal of the scheme of rights. The right to wealth, the weakest of all rights, corresponds to the strongest and most enforceable duty, the duty to ensure that wealth be as common as possible. In this sense, the scheme of liberty and rights represents the private side of a whole whose public side is the scheme of responsibility and duties.

The dialectical nature of our approach emerges also with our notion of *public privacy*, identifiable with that "general will" that is intrinsic to the community as a Whole of Wholes. The notion of public privacy is the one side of a whole whose other side is "private publicity," or the privacy that grows toward an inner identification with community. Our concept of privacy is thus at once distinct from and coherent with the concept of publicness, thereby fulfilling the requirement of distinctiveness/coherence presented in Ch. 1. The right to privacy, though being distinctively defined by the process of withdrawal/forthcoming and by the reality of an invisible universal communion, implies, like a hologram, all other rights. In spite of the allegations of "vagueness" against such an essential and therefore "most comprehensive" conception of privacy, rights would be meaningless without it.

Without the the *existential principle of privacy*, whereby every right is penetrated, as a private right, by its teleological essence—that is, by the fundamental end of the ethical and spiritual development of the individual—it would be impossible to understand what are the limits intrinsic to each specific right, and to determine, within each layer of rights, that most essential core that requires to be raised to the privacy level of quasi-absolute rights (as with the right to the abortion choice in the category of personality rights, or the right to self-preservation within the category of property rights).

Furthermore, without the *principle of selfhood, or empirical principle of privacy* (which in our Scheme of Rights corresponds to the general "right to be let alone," covering its left side together with its tripartition), it would be impossible to distinguish, at all levels, between self-directed and other-directed spheres of actions and rights. What distinguishes the sphere of personal liberty from that of intimate and family relation is indeed the degree of "withdrawal," that is, of empirical privacy or aloneness. If we could not make such a distinction, we would not be able to modulate the degrees of immunity and interference to which the two different categories of rights are to be entitled. This again shows how a "most comprehensive" concept of privacy, rather than being "vague" (as with the vagueness that characterizes the all-encompassing concept of property upheld by reductionistic thinkers), is indeed the perfect tool to refine and detail our understanding of rights.

The simultaneous interplay of the vertical distinction of private and public (inner/outer, thought/action) and of the horizontal distinction of self-directedness/being alone and other-directedness/being with others, gives the hierarchical continuum of rights the form of an *ascending spiral*, progressively and circularly rising from level 6 to level 1. The form of the spiral symbolically represents the holographic nature of our scheme: Existentially, the spiral of rights is a hierarchical ladder; essentially, it can be flattened into a series of concentric and continuous circles having the same center or inherent nature (notice the similarity with Emerson's image of the reciprocally encompassing circles). The center is the top of the spiral, the subtle line where existential privacy turns into the essential privacy of universal communion, wholeness, and responsibility. This means that all conditions and rights, wealth itself included, have spiritual privacy as their ultimate and true self and existentially must be modulated accordingly.

We have seen how the dominant philosophical approaches tend to pull down privacy and its right within their ontological and legal horizon, reducing it to a manifestation of the basic right that expresses such a horizon. Thus, the utilitarian reduces privacy to an aspect of property; the liberal to a basic right of personality, identifying it with the private sphere that shields free choices and autonomous personal decisions; the communitarian, when s/he does not reject it altogether, to mere associational privacy, or to a space defined by traditional and majoritarian morality. The result of all such reductions is the loss of that center of the spiral of rights that constitutes the true ground not only of rights but also of the very values that are essential to those philosophical approaches, namely happiness, freedom, and community.

NOTES

1. R. Bellah et al., *Habits of the Heart* (New York: Harper & Row, 1985), p. 81.

2. "[Brandeis's] views on American society and government represent such a fundamental and creative attack on the central problem of the twentieth century as to make him a truly significant political thinker." S. J. Konefsky, *The Legacy of Holmes and Brandeis* (1956) (New York, 1961), p. 15. This is why "Brandeis has always attracted considerable academic attention and . . . we are in a particularly productive phase of Brandeis scholarship." N. L. Dawson, (ed.), "Introduction," *Brandeis and America* (University Press of Kentucky, 1989), p. 1.

3. "Brandeis not only read the 'signs of the times' aright, but with an insight which was focused on 'fundamental conceptions.' " S.J. Konefsky, p. 71, quoting L. D. Brandeis, *The Curse of Bigness* (New York, 1934), 72.

4. N.L. Dawson, *Louis D. Brandeis, Felix Frankfuter and the New Deal* (Archon, 1980), p. 11; which also reports D. Riesman, "Letter to Justice Frankfurter," May 22, 1936, *Frankfurter Papers*, Library of Congress, box 127.

5. D. Acheson, *Morning and Noon* (Houghton Mifflin, 1965), 95–96.

6. P. Strum, *Louis D. Brandeis: Justice for the People*, 1984, p. 310, which quotes L. D. Brandeis to F. Frankfurter, January 27, 1927, *Letters*, V, 260.

7. Quoted in Konefsky, *The Legacy*, pp. 71.

8. L. J. Paper, *Brandeis* (Prentice-Hall, 1983), p. 4

9. Dawson, *Louis Brandeis*, 12–3, and p. 186, note 3; M. Urofsky, *A Mind of One Piece: Brandeis and American Reform* (New York, 1971), p. 98.

10. P. Strum, p. 230, p. 44.

11. D. Glancy, "The Invention of the Right to Privacy," in *Arizona L.R.* 21, 1 (1979): 1, p. 25. Another author stresses the crucial connection of privacy with the figure of the poet. See E. J. Jensen, "Privacy and the Power of Art," in *Univ. of Toledo L. J.* 15, 2 (1984): 437–47, (spec. ed. on the right of privacy).

12. A. Mason, *Brandeis: A Free Man's Life* (New York: Viking, 1946), p. 39.

13. M. Urofsky and D. Levy (eds.), *L. D. Brandeis' Letters* (SUNY, 1971–78), Vol. 1, p. 12.

14. See Acheson, p. 50; and for Emerson on Goethe, "The American Scholar," in *Selected Essays* (Penguin, 1982), pp. 83–106.
15. Glancy, pp. 32, 39, 26.
16. R. W. Emerson, "History," in *Selected Essays*, 149–173.
17. Emerson, "The American Scholar," in *Selected Essays*, 99–100.
18. Emerson, "The Over-Soul," in *Selected Essays*, 206–8.
19. Emerson, "The American Scholar," in *Selected Essays*, p. 97.
20. Interview in the *Boston Herald*, April 14, 1903; and letter to C. Snyder, 11/3/1913, quoted in Mason, p. 122 and 395.
21. Emerson, "Self-Reliance," in *Selected Essays*, 1, 191–92, 195.
22. F. Frankfurter, *Of Law and Men* (New York, 1956), p. 188; J. Danelski, "The Propriety of Brandeis Extrajudicial Conduct," in Dawson (ed.), *Brandeis and America* (University Press of Kentucky, 1989), p. 28.
23. Mason, *Brandeis*, p. 39.
24. Ibid., p. 75.
25. L. D. B. to W. Dunbar, 2/2/1893, *Letters*, Vol. I, p. 109.
26. Emerson, "Nature," in *Selected Essays*, p. 49, 55.
27. *Letters*, Vol. V, p. 204. The quotation is from H. Heine, *Buch der Lieder*, 1851 (misquoted by substituting "lieb" for "reich").
28. Emerson, "Nature," in *Selected Essays*, p. 49.
29. Ibid., pp. 48, 37.
30. Emerson, "The American Scholar," in *Selected Essays*, p. 87. This theme of nature as the realm of withdrawal from the world to meet one's deepest self is also Rousseauian. See, for example, *L'Émile*. It is also a theme of the Perennial Philosophy, whereby the search for the Absolute takes both the path of the God within and of the God without. A. Huxley, *The Perennial Philosophy* (1946) (London, 1985), p. 20.
31. Dawson, *Louis D. Brandeis*, p. 30.
32. Ibid., p. 193, note 2, 122; p. 72.
33. D. W. Levy, in Dawson (ed.), *Brandeis and America*, p. 103.
34. For an exhaustive account of Brandeis's thought in relation to industrial democracy, see Philippa Strum, *Brandeis: Beyond Progressivism* (University of Kansas Press, 1993), Ch. 2.
35. Dawson, *Louis D. Brandeis*, p. 193, note 122.
36. L.D.B., *New York Herald*, 3/3/1912, in Mason, pp. 423–24.
37. Letter to Alfred Brandeis, 18/10/1914, *Letters*, Vol. III, p. 331.
38. Konefsky, p. 74.
39. Levy, p. 104.
40. Mason, p. 639.
41. "The Over-Soul" and "Nature," in Emerson's *Selected Essays*, pp. 206–7 and pp. 58–59, respectively.
42. Brandeis, "The Living Law," in *The Curse of Bigness* (New York: Viking, 1934), p. 317.
43. See *Panama Refining Co. v Ryan* 293 U.S. 430 (1935); *Humphreys Executor v United States*, 295 U.S. 602 (1935); *Louisville Bank v Radford*, 295 U.S. 555 (1935); *Schecter Poultry Co. v United States*, 295 U.S. 528 (1935).
44. A. Burt, *Two Jewish Justices* (University of California, 1988), p. 25. Burt reports that Brandeis told T. Corcoran, after the *Schecter Poultry* decision: "This is the end of

this business of centralization, and I want you to go back and tell the President that we're not going to let this government centralize everything."

45. *Chicago Record-Herald*, 3/1/1912, cited in Mason, p. 372. For Brandeis's attack to the "sacredness of private property," see "The Living Law," in *The Curse of Bigness*, pp. 316ff, p. 318–19.

46. Rousseau, *The Social Contract*, II, xi.

47. Brandeis, *The Curse of Bigness*, p. 87.

48. See Dawson, *Louis D. Brandeis*, pp. 28–35, 70ff, quoting from various Brandeis writings. Dawson (p. 20) comments: "[Brandeis] was willing to use the power of the State, sometimes in surprising ways, to secure and guard the traditional values of Jeffersonian democracy."

49. 288 U.S. 517, at 541, 580.

50. P. Strum, "Brandeis and the Living Constitution," in N. Dawson (ed.), *Brandeis and America*, 1989.

51. Acheson, *Morning and Noon*, pp. 50–51.

52. Letter to Mr. Bruère, 25/2/1922, in which Brandeis summarizes a speech given to the federal Council of Churches, quoted in Mason, p. 585.

53. Acheson, p. 51.

54. Letter to the *Survey*, 7/11/1920, quoted by Mason, p. 603.

55. Acheson, p. 53.

56. Brandeis, who certainly appreciated the role of important leaders such as La Follette, and then Wilson, in 1912 accused Theodore Roosevelt, Wilson's opponent, of "purposing only to take a certain *paternal* care of the American workingman, who, if given a fair field, could, in the main, take care of himself." In Mason, p. 382. This reference to paternalism acquires a special meaning if we remember how Brandeis explicitly subscribed to Whitehead's maieutical conception of education and how politics was for him essentially based on education.

57. Brandeis, "The Opportunity in the Law," to the Harvard Ethical Soc., in *Business: A Profession* (Boston, 1914) (2a e 3a ed., 1925, 1933); *The Curse of Bigness*, p. 72; and *Other People's Money and How the Bankers Use It* (New York, 1914) (2d ed., 1932).

58. Mason, p. 640.

59. "It is difficult to analyze Brandeis" philosophy using the traditional categories of liberal and conservative. . . . Brandeis took the middle road between the liberals' excessive reliance on governmental power and the conservatives' distrust of political activism. . . . One could say that he advocated the use of liberal means to obtain conservative ends." Dawson, *Louis D. Brandeis*, p. 20.

60. "This phrase was used by Mr. Lilienthal to describe a dissent by W. O. Douglas, in which the Justice may be said to have spoken as a disciple of the man he succeeded on the bench." Konefsky, pp. 161–62, quoting D. Lilienthal, *Big Business: A New Era* (Harper, 1952).

61. M. Lerner, *Herald Tribune*, 3/31/1935, quoted in Dawson, *Louis D. Brandeis*, p. 33, together with the quote from Laski's letter to Holmes, 3/1/1935. See, more generally, pp. 28–35.

62. Brandeis-Frankfurter Conversations, *Brandeis Papers*, Harvard Law Library, quoted in R. M. Cover, "The Left, the Right and the First Amendment: 1918–1928," in *Maryland L. R.*, 40, (3) (1981): 349, note 101, pp. 377–78.

63. H. Garfield, "Privacy, Abortion and Judicial Review: Haunted by the Ghost of Lochner," in *Washington L.R.*, 61 (1986): 287, p. 299.

64. Emerson, "Self-Reliance," in *Selected Essays*, pp. 201–2.
65. *Truax v Corrigan*, 257 U.S. 312, at 368.
66. *Brandeis Papers*, Harvard Law Library, in Cover, p. 378, note 102.
67. "The Right to Privacy," in Schoeman, *Philosophical Dimensions of Privacy* (Cambridge University Press, 1984), p. 85.
68. Emerson, "Nature," in *Selected Essays*, p. 60.
69. 106 S. Ct. 2841 (1986), at 2850–51.
70. N. Strossen, "The Religion Clause Writings of Justice W. O. Douglas," in S. L. Wasby (ed.), *He Shall Not Pass This Way Again. The Legacy of W. O. Douglas* (University of Pittsburg Press, 1990), 91–107, p. 95.
71. L. A. Powe, "Justice Douglas, the First Amendment, and the Protection of Rights," in S. L. Wasby, 69–90, p. 75.
72. Douglas, *A Living Bill of Rights* (New York, 1961), p. 56.
73. D. Glancy, "Douglas's Right of Privacy: A Response to His Critics," in S. L. Wasby (ed.), 155–177, p. 167.
74. For Elizabeth Schneider, Douglas's theory of privacy shows "affirmative dimensions" that integrate communal values, thus moving toward the overcoming of the liberal dualism of public and private. She argues that in so doing Douglas accepts the feminist rejection of privacy as a fundamental right. But for Douglas true privacy, far from being in opposition to communal life, is the basic presupposition and goal of community. E. Schneider, "The Affirmative Dimensions of Douglas's Privacy," in S. L. Wasby, pp. 179–85.
75. Douglas, *The Right of the People* (1952) (New York: Arena, 1972), p. 34, 22.
76. Douglas, *Go East, Young Man: The Autobiography of W. O. Douglas* (New York: Random House, 1974), pp. 113–4.
77. For a critical discussion of Douglas's environmentalism see S. L. Wasby (ed.), Part Four, pp. 189–253.
78. See N. Strossen, "The Religion Clause Writings of Justice W. O. Douglas," in S. L. Wasby (ed.), 91–107, p. 98, which quotes from W. O. Douglas, *The Anatomy of Liberty* (New York, 1963), pp. 26–27. See also L. A. Powe, "Evolution to Absolutism: Justice Douglas and the First Amendment," in *Columbia L.R.*, 74 (1974): 371.
79. There is a sense in which thought too is immediately an action, is immediately responsive to interdependence and to goodness or evilness. But its relevance is of an ethical or religious type, whereas the law can only make the sphere of thought immune from outer interferences, being ready to interfere itself as soon as evil thought turns into an outer action.
80. I have discussed Meiklejohn's theory of free speech in my Ph.D. thesis, *Privacy, Rights and Natural Law* (University of Toronto, 1993), Ch. 4. The section is now contained in Ch. 4 of my *Privacy* (Roma: Editori Riuniti, 1994). The essay is also a more detailed analysis of the position on "free speech" sketched out here.
81. For Meiklejohn, there is "a 'freedom of speech' which the First Amendment declares to be non abridgable. But there is also a 'liberty of speech' which the Fifth Amendment declares to be abridgable." A. Meiklejohn, *Political Freedom* (Oxford, 1965) (orig. ed. Harper, 1960), pp. 36–37.
82. See the sequence of decisions in: *New York Times v Sullivan*, [376 U.S. 254 (1964)]; *Time, Inc. v Hill*, [385 U.S. 374 (1967)]; *Rosenbloom v Retromedia*, [403 U.S.

29 (1971)]; *Gertz v R. Welch, Inc.* [418 U.S. 323 (1974)]; *Dun & Bradstreet, Inc. v Greenmoss Builders, Inc.* [472 U.S. 749 (1985)].

83. J. Finnis, for example, advances the strong (and partially questionable) claim that "the 'first-order' good of life may not, in [Thomas's] view, be deliberately attacked even in order to preserve the 'third-order' good of friendship with God." J. Finnis, *Natural Law and Natural Rights* (Oxford, 1980), pp. 94–95, which refers to *Summa Theologiae*, Iia, Iiae, 64(5), ad 2; IIIa, 68(11), ad 3. This is in line with the contemporary Catholic attribution of an absolute value, which in the past was linked to the notion of an ethically and spiritually "good life," to biological life as such.

7
WHAT TO DO ABOUT PRIVACY?

To conclude this historical and philosophical journey, let us address the crucial and urgent problem of what to do in practice about privacy. Although we will briefly discuss the vast array of technologies and legal measures that can be used to slow down the increasing invasion of our informational privacy, the battle for informational privacy cannot be won by simply establishing technical and legal barriers, barriers that repeatedly grow obsolete and insufficient, but by radically altering our way of thinking about rights, about their hierarchy and limits, and ultimately about the importance of the inner and spiritual over the outer and material.

It would be silly to think, however, that technical and legal measures cannot indeed contribute to transformation, in the same way in which it is delusory to think that they alone, without a deep cultural and philosophical change, can do all the work. One measure that would seem to be capable to promote a paradigmatic shift in our relationship to constitutional privacy is the idea of a "Privacy Amendment" to the Bill of Rights. As noted by one author, the "states that have adopted explicit privacy amendments have emerged, in many areas, as the leaders of privacy discourse in the United States."[1] However, the amendments seem to have focused mostly on a specific privacy area, in some cases that of decisional privacy, in others that of physical privacy (searches and seizures).[2] The risk, thus, is that the amendment may become a tool that, though securing the protection of privacy, ends up restricting the impact and scope of the right of privacy, thus having it fall back under the tutelage of other and lesser principles, such as those of personality (freedom of choice) or utilitarian property (wealth maximization).

But the risks should not make us forget the important potentiality present in the idea of a privacy amendment, namely the official recognition of privacy as a fundamental right-principle. If a privacy amendment were to be adopted, it should not be restricted by too specific definitions, so as to encompass all the layers of privacy that the law has already, in different measures, recognized, and remain open to those that law and experience still have not met. Specifications would have to be added not as limiting factors but as clarifications and exemplifications of the general principle that, given the direction our history is taking, would have to refer to the highest and most-threatened layers of privacy, the informational and the formational. Although this open-texture may displease positivists, Courts have understood the importance of using privacy amendments not as restrictive but rather as expanding and enlightening interpretive tools. The Alaska Supreme Court, for instance, has for the most part used the privacy amendment "as a justification for a broad reading of other constitutional provisions," something that after all is both inevitable, given that the principle/right of privacy is deeply intertwined with other constitutional provisions (First, Third, Fourth, Fifth, Ninth, Fourteenth Amendments), and proper, because constitutional provisions must indeed be general principles shedding light on more-specific rights and legal situations.

The appeal to a "sliding scale test," which emerged in some of the privacy cases discussed by the Alaska Supreme Court, is also important, because it helps to define the different layers of the right to privacy and their hierarchically varying degree of immunity. Although the first priority of a nonreductionistic privacy amendment would be the maintainance of a general and open texture, the further step in a transformational and transpersonal direction would be the establishment of a "sliding scale" whereby the inner and mental take precedence over the outer and material, thus making explicit something that has always been deeply implicit in the constitutional text, architecture, and jurisprudence. Privacy would thus emerge as a general principle governing the structure itself of rights and immunities and giving meaning to the other layers of constitutional rights, those referring to personality and to property.[3] There could then be more-specific references to informational and formational privacy.

In the field of informational privacy there has been quite a lot of legislative and judicial work done around the world, which has generated both a general set of principles regarding the legitimacy of data banks and their activities and different institutional settings to supervise and sanction the application of such principles. David Flaherty, in his book on the international experience of privacy protection, reports a complete set of principles of data protection from government personal information systems, which include: *publicity and transparency* (no secret data banks); *necessity and relevance* in regard to the collection and storage of information; *minimization* of collection and storage to the maximum extent possible; *finality* (purpose of collection established in advance); *respon-*

sibility of the information keepers; limitation and control of the networking between different data banks (that we could call the principle of *separation*); *informed consent* on the part of those who relinquish control of their personal information; *accuracy and completeness* of the stored and circulating information; the principle of *data trespass*, making the abuse of personal information subject to both civil and criminal sanctions; special rules for protecting *sensitive personal information*; the *right to access and correction* of the stored personal data; the *right to be forgotten*, including the ultimate anonymization or destruction of almost all personal information.[4]

These principles have been applied only partially in different countries and very sparingly in the United States, which, though at the forefront of the promotion of the general constitutional value of privacy, has been quite in the rear regarding the protection of informational privacy, also due to a widespread and extremist ideology stating the absolute freedom of the press. Though generally these principles are complementary, some seem to be redundant, and others are quite incompatible. In particular, there emerges a strong tension between the principles of necessity/relevance, minimization, finality, sensitive data, limitation of data banks linkages on the one hand, and the principle of informed consent on the other. If indeed personal data were collected only when and to the minimum extent necessary for a legitimate and recognized purpose, keeping out unnecessary sensitive personal data and most of all making it impossible to freely transfer personal information into data banks or even personal computers that have nothing to do with such original purpose, then the requirement of informed consent would be utterly superfluous. The reality is that the ideology of informed consent, together with its parallel elements of access and correction on the part of the individual, is generally used as a smoke screen to avoid applying the other and stricter measures of privacy protection. It is reknown that, at the level of speed and complexity reached by the current collection and management of information, the notion of the individual knowing, consenting, accessing, and then correcting data on himself, is at best only an empty hope. Furthermore, consent should not be sufficient to allow others to use our persona, which is truly a sacred icon, in any way they want, in the same way that it is not possible to consent to slavery. The power of consenting to someone else using information on ourselves, apart from legitimate governmental purposes attained through the means and within the conditions defined earlier, should be limited to specific instances: interpersonal and intimate relations; legitimate commercial and properly remunerated uses of one's image and personal information (excluding, for instance, the situation of criminals making money by selling the story of their crimes; or of people selling their or their children's image to pornographers); and, in the case of advertising, firms should explicitly ask for the individual's consent to sell his or her address to other firms, specifying which type of firms they would sell it too, so as to allow each individual to choose the type of commercial information s/he desires to receive. Giving the individual more protection than the one bestowed by consent means that the individual is not left to herself against the free hand of giant governmental and corporate forces. Furthermore, only when the volume of personal information stored and circulated is minimized according to the stricter informational criteria defined earlier, and ultimately in accordance with the common good rather than with profit, would the individual right to consent, access, and correct become a plausible and enforceable reality.

In Ch. 1, we saw that the disastrous state of privacy in contemporary society is due precisely to the constant violation, in fact total disregard, for the principles sketched earlier: information is freely collected and circulated by potentially everyone, regardless of status and purpose; it is freely circulated and exchanged between different public and private data banks having no common legitimate purpose; its main purpose is on the one hand profit-making, as information has become, in the Information Age, the hottest commodity, and on the other hand bureaucratic self-reinforcement, according to that tautology of centralizing Bigness that is the truth behind the rhetoric of governmental and corporate efficiency. Accordingly, its collection is maximized on the ground of the delusory and surreptitious argument that more information makes better decisions, whereas in fact it is the quality and not the quantity of information that determines the wisdom of political decisions. Finally, it is precisely sensitive data that are most sought after, because they are the most profitable commodities to be sold.

If we want to do something serious about informational privacy, beyond the empty rhetoric of individual consent, access, and correction, we must intervene at the source of the problem. The first thing to be established very clearly is that all personal information is potentially sensitive, because all such information can today be used against the individual. There is no doubt, as Flaherty reports about the Scandinavian position, that "racial, religious, political, criminal, and sexual matters, health information, and the use of intoxicants" are "particularly sensitive information." But then what about financial information, which can be extremely sensitive if put in the wrong hands, or information about one's life-style, shopping habits, family and interpersonal behavior, and so forth, all of which can be used against the individual by people with dubious intentions and which also can reveal something very intimate about the person?

In the end, there should be a basic presupposition whereby no personal information can be collected but in the minimum amount strictly necessary to the attainment of a legitimate and recognized governmental purpose; by the sole institution competent for that purpose; and with the limitation that the transfer of information between different branches of the government has to be done only when there is an overlap in which certain legitimately collected information is legitimately indispensable to another branch, in transparency and accordance with the law and, if the purpose of the branch is of an investigative nature (police, fiscal, etc.), under the supervision of the courts. This should constitute the main bulk of the principle regulating informational privacy, be it contained or not in a privacy amendment.

What to Do about Privacy?

Given that such a principle ultimately depends on what are established as the governmental purposes legitimizing the collection of information, the protection of privacy rests on what idea of political and administrative knowledge will prevail. As long as the idea that more information produces better government prevails, forgetting that intelligent political decisions require wisdom rather than a mass of overwhelming details obscuring central issues at stake and that the interests involved in the development of the computer state and the information economy have little to do with efficiency and productivity, any effort to protect privacy will have only scarce success and will be repeatedly made obsolete by new and more powerful informational technologies.

Even the issue of how to concretely enforce the principles of privacy protection ultimately depends on the maximization versus minimization of data collection, because any system of enforcement is doomed to fall short of its task in the face of the massive informational circulation that pervades every pore of our society, although of course some systems of enforcement work better than others. On the ground of the international experience, H. Jeff Smith has proposed the following institutional model:

A Data Protection Board, based on the Data Commissioner model, should be created with advisory powers. Such a board ... would be expected to assist corporations in developing codes of acceptable practices, as the British Registrar has, and to field citizen complaints. This board should serve in an educational role.... However, should corporations refuse to cooperate with the board voluntarily, the legislatures should stand ready to ... [grant] some measure of regulatory power.

Although this model refers specifically to corporations, it can also easily be applied to governmental agencies, who are neither too different nor really separate from the corporate world. What I would add to Jeff Smith's model is the following.

When facing the question of the composition of the Data Board, the main issue is its independence from both government and corporations and its ability to forcefully lead a battle for privacy protection culturally, politically, and legally. The question of independence is a difficult one, and Flaherty has warned us of how over time governments have tried to name more-obsequious Commissioners.[5] Although imperfect, the only body with a long history of institutional and experiential independence from government is the judiciary. The Data Board should be nominated by the Supreme Court and should be composed of judges with privacy experience. The only exception should be the Data Commissioner, who should be chosen among nonjudicial leaders of the pro-privacy movement.

As to the system of control, whereas the licensing system seems to be too burdensome and oppressive, the lack of any form of registration would leave untouched the current situation of total informational anarchy. Given the fact that the principles of finality, necessity, minimization, and separation involve not just the activity of the data bank, but its very constitution, the registration system would allow the Board to check the legitimacy of data banks at the very moment of their formation. The strength itself of those principles would reduce the volume of circulating information, thus making the work of the Data Board more manageable. This in turn would avoid furthering the development of another giant bureaucracy.

Although Flaherty is right in warning that in a time when "enthusiasm for deregulation currently exists in most countries, data protection is not an appropriate area for the exercise of such sentiments," it is also true that a genuine downsizing of Big Government and more generally Bigness (including corporate Bigness), deriving from a strong political and economic decentralization, is the only true guarantee against the constant invasion of privacy and violation of individual autonomy and also against the need of a bigger and bigger *pro-privacy bureaucracy* (a contradictory concept, as any big bureaucracy, even when working for privacy, has inherent antiprivacy tendencies).

In fact, Flaherty himself, though supporting strong legal and institutional means to protect privacy, such as the ones discussed here, constantly expresses the feeling that all such means may be at best very weak tools and at worst a way to further justify, through the delusion that something is being done, the pervasive and totalizing dismantling of privacy. It is not only that privacy protection cannot but cave in within a social and economic system that values informational maximization above all, but it is also: a) that there are "no technical limits to electronic surveillance and social control at the present time"[6]; b) that technological change is so rapid that any legal and institutional remedy risks becoming obsolete very quickly, unless it rests on strong privacy principles pointing toward a different set of fundamental social values; c) that the management of the protection of privacy is entrusted to the very same body, the government, which is today, in its profound interpenetration with the corporate and financial world and its growing information economy, a major agent of the dismantling of privacy; d) that preying on personal information has become an activity that can be done from any personal computer, which has created a totally uncontrollable situation, one that no registration system or data board could even come close to surveying.

The reality is that in the Information Age and Information Economy, where personal information has become the major source of both power and profit, informational privacy can only become the sacrificial lamb in the altar of Bigness, with its twofold drive toward unlimited wealth maximization and self-reinforcing bureaucratic centralization.[7] In this respect, although strong policies of informational privacy protection are very important, the reality is that privacy as a *"postmaterialistic issue* ... will inevitably be overshadowed as long as predominantly materialistic values and interests elect our democratic governments and sustain the policies they administer."[8] What is required for the protection and promotion of genuine privacy is then a paradigmatic cultural and political shift, a concept strongly asserted by James Rule: "The alternative to endless erosion of privacy through increased surveillance is for organizations to relax the discriminations which they seek to make in their treatment of people. ... We propose a reallocation of resources toward less discriminatory, less 'informational-intensive' ways of dealing with people."[9] At the core of informational centralization is the drive toward a centralizing and thus discriminatory allocation of resources (of which information itself is part). This means that discriminatory and intensive informational practices can be overcome only by abandoning the drive toward wealth, information and power maximization/centralization. More fundamentally, this is possible only by redirecting the empiricist metaphysical drive, which misplaces our innate absolute-impulse into the folly and delusion of an absolute sensuous/material fullness into its proper spiritual dimension. The movement, then, must be twofold, on the one hand transforming the productive, distributive, and power model, on the other creating the inner change toward postmaterialistic values that is indispensable to any outer progress. We have thus a *circle of privacy protection*, whereby privacy can be ultimately guaranteed only through an overall political and economic change; yet such a change will be possible only as long as privacy, the shield of the individual critical autonomy indispensable to change, will resist the current devastating attack on it.

But in order to close the circle and make it strong, it is necessary to bring back in that which is most protective of our mental freedom and spiritual nature and on which every other dimension of privacy depends, namely *formational privacy*. Although it is the informational aspect of privacy that is at the center of public attention today, in fact the informational invasion of privacies is but a preparation for the more strategic attack on formational privacy, that is, on the interiority of our thoughts and emotions. *Most of today's accumulation of personal information is done in order to be more efficient in addressing advertising, sales, political propaganda, and TV shows to the right persons at the right time.*[10] Even TV, the great formational invader, feeds on the constant flow of personal and private information, from gossip on public figures and on ordinary citizens who unwillingly fall under the spotlight, to the solicitation of the public disclosure of both known and unknown people's private lives, to serials and movies that are essentially but a fictional reproduction of gossip. To be sure, gossip, as stated by the hypercapitalistic Richard Posner, is a powerful "educational" force as it educates people to release their most prurient selves, while involving their mind deeply in the lives of the rich and famous as the best possible life pursuit.[11]

In the end, the question of privacy is a question of mental colonization. The defense of privacy has been very weak, so far, precisely because this link has been radically missed. If one looks at privacy only in informational terms, the gravity of its disastrous situation seems much less important than if we were to realize that *the demise of privacy is the demise of the independent mind*, a fact that cannot be balanced by any utilitarian or communitarian gain. From a strict utilitarian point of view, information is indeed such a valuable economic as well as political commodity that privacy carries almost no weight against it. Even many pro-privacy activists have conducted their battles from within the dominant paradigm without any deeper desire to promote the ethical and spiritual trans-formation of the capitalistic drive and forces. And there has been a general inability to grasp the ethical and spiritual significance of privacy, due either to the atomistic and ultimately utilitarian understanding of human personality and rights that characterizes liberalism, and/or to a certain communitarian insensitivity to the fact that true *part*icipation requires the inner wholeness of individual *parts* to begin with.

Unless the transpersonal understanding of privacy will prevail, together with the awareness of the priority of formational privacy, even the genuine attempts at a strong defense of informational privacy, such as Rule's notion of a less discriminatory, less centralized, and less information-intensive society, would ultimately fail. One can easily imagine a world in which informational accumulation and surveillance on the part of centralizing bureaucracies and corporations are replaced by a decentralized system in which every individual becomes a "free" active promoter in both the dissemination of personal information, mostly of the gossiping type, and in the formational colonization of both his and other people's minds. With the current demise of the welfare state, and with the growing substitution of human workers with intelligent machines, the need for external surveillance will begin to fade together with controlling welfare bureaucracies on the one hand and entrepreneurs selecting and evaluating workers through data banks on the other. The fading of the distinction between those who control and those who are controlled, through everyone's involvement in reciprocal and self surveillance and mental penetration, will not eliminate, but only modify, the fundamental dualism characterizing our societies.

The situation that appears to be emerging is one in which an increasingly richer and more powerful tier of society would leave the rest of the community to fend for itself, creating a schism in which a larger and peripheral community of the poor, unemployed, and culturally nonintegrated would develop their own social and economic system, possibly with some financial help from the richer center. This is not so far off as it may sound. There are already examples of it, and even Rifkin's proposals to overcome what he aptly, if hyperbolically, terms "the end of work" appear to go in the direction of simply guaranteeing some kind of reduced income to a peripheral world of outcasts participating in various volunteering and nonprofit activities.[12] Being in the care of themselves, such a peripheral people would be subjected to much less information-intensive individual discrimination, and in such a state it could even begin to develop solidaristic forms of production and distribution, as hoped by Rifkin. In the possible schism of a peripheral socialism for the outcasts and a more central absolutist and globally integrated capitalism, surveillance through the acquisition of personal information would probably be limited to the upper people, in order to make sure that they individually do share the values and the behavior of the capitalistic center. For the rest of the people, who would be cut off from relevant interactions with the higher world, a general form of statistical and social surveillance would be more than enough. What I am describing here is only a very dangerous possibility, which makes the battle to strongly protect informational privacy, in order to block the selecting mechanism that would let into the social and economic center only "values integrated" people, more urgent than ever.

Once again, however, the battle for formational privacy is even more pressing, because it is in the formational field that the predominance of values is established. The powerless many are already, for the most part, involved in an active and satisfying participation in the decentralized mechanisms of mind alteration, promoting the inner rise to power of our lower (consumeristic, wealth-maximizing) selves, and today, when the money to consume and accumulate is becoming scarce for most, of the *fantasizing self*[13] that lives in TV and media dreamland.

It is very likely that giant governmental and corporate bureaucracies will be replaced by more agile, decentralized, and networking economic and political actors,[14] and that therefore the central accumulation of information will become obsolete. The new economy is very information-intensive, but in an unexpected way. We have seen how the wealth of personal information that today's technology puts at the disposal of pollsters, salesmen, advertisers, and so on, allows for a much more individualized penetration of the human mind. This will continue mainly to control more thoroughly the upper world of participants in the central capitalistic economy. On the whole, however, surveillance will remain as a backup to the more formational goal of providing gossip and entertainment for the fantasizing minds of the lower classes on the one hand and participation in the worldwide informational web to the integrated classes on the other.

The growth of a nonintegrated social and economic dimension, especially if connected to the alternative and green dimension of production, consumption, and services, could be an excellent opportunity to develop a more compassionate, less profit-seeking, and consumption-driven world, which in the long run could reunify society on a different set of ethical and spiritual principles. But this depends in large part on how much formational privacy will be preserved, and although informational privacy protection is very important in halting the corrupted side of the information economy, a direct intervention is urgently required to shield the realm of interiority from the forces pulling it out of itself, out of introspection and silence and into consumeristic and/or fantasizing noises. Something needs to be done very soon about the totalitarianism of TV mass culture, which is now invading, in an even worse form, the Internet.

There is no doubt that the Internet, which lets us play a much more active role than TV, has interesting interactive educational potentialities and gives people the concrete feeling of being a planetary individual. But again, the Internet is the site of a battlefield between the transformational forces that want to use it for educational and ethical purposes and the lower capitalistic forces that use the Internet as a Trojan horse, one that is much more powerful than TV precisely because it does not simply penetrate a passive mind, but it solicits our lower selves to actively participate in and further spread the capitalistic and fantasizing way of life. This active involvement becomes more powerful the more it gives us the possibility to construct our own "virtual" reality, in the same way in which an artist could do, with the difference that an artist undergoes a training in order to express his inner visions, involving both self-knowledge and a penetration into the deeper reality of the world; whereas "virtual reality" can be easily constructed by anyone, with no need for training or discipline, and thus with the danger of very easily falling into the materialization of our lowest and most-shallow desires.

People will be able to fully and "happily" enter an unreal world of cheap but pain-assuaging fantasies, or one of unlimited if imaginary satisfaction of desires (but what are desires if not the children of our fantasy?), the latter being most likely reserved to the fewer "well integrated." By falling asleep into the dreamland of absolute capitalism, people will not even realize that the Dispenser of Great Powers is indeed the soul-stealing Mephistopheles, that absolute capitalism is indeed the worst totalitarianism that humanity has ever experienced, a *totalitarianism of souls*.

Of course, the question of formational privacy implies many more factors, such as education, social habituation, the loss of places of silence and quiet, tourism that destroys all natural retreats, and so forth. But the worst threat of all today is the generalized fall from inner visualization (creative imagination, dreams, archetypal myths) to outer and outerly controlled screens. If the Net is left to itself, with no regulations and most of all without any educational soul, absolute capitalism will take it over, with an unprecedented defeat of privacy and autonomy, also because decades of TV watching have already weakened minds, thus thoroughly preparing the field.

Many now warn us about the dangers of TV, especially for children, asking for antiviolence chips and other protective measures. Even Popper, who did a lot to promote relativism, although he would deny that, at the end of his life pointed out what transpersonal and transformational circles have said for a long time, namely that TV, beyond the problem of what it broadcasts, contains in itself the risk of corruption. As with the Internet, the battle for better programming content and a better use of the TV is essential, but it is not enough. The outer-spection of TV is the exact opposite of inner-spective privacy as the experience of that aloneness that transcends the I/other dualism of the egoic personality and the subject/object dualism of possessive property. To be sure, watching a piece of art or a scenery is also an outer-spection, but you do not watch a painting for hours every day, and the meditative quality of watching a painting or a scenery is something that in fact puts one in better touch with oneself. TV is, in this respect, utterly different. Its ability of transporting us into fantasy worlds (with TV even the foreign geographical worlds we watch on the news are reduced to a fantastic spectacle) eradicates us from our own deep roots, turning us into easy and even cooperating preys. *To spend one's life in front of the TV makes us go through the utmost externalization whereby otherness, the lives of the fictional characters, penetrates our own identity, creating a harder, crystallized selfhood, one that is more impermeable to ethical growth precisely because it is not fully ours, so that we can neither modify it nor, even more importantly, personally feel the ethical dilemmas implied in the human condition.* The fact that people are less and less sensitive to behaving unethically, or that "criminal" children seem to be possessed by criminal characters on TV and in movies, has to do precisely with such a dehumanizing mechanism.

Transformational forces should forcefully promote the educational potentialities of both TV and the Internet, which may imply, given the emergency situation and the "clear and present danger," having laws that will force TV networks to broadcast a certain amount of culturally nutritious programs, avoiding certain levels of trash culture, and forbid certain uses of the Net, beginning with pornography (which is much more dangerous and mind-capturing, especially for the young, when coupled with "virtual sex"). We will also need laws that will limit the merely commercial use of those powerful tools, first of all by imposing limits to the amount and nature of advertising and by prohibiting the subliminal advertising currently present in most programs. But most of all we will need a cultural revolution to take people off the hook of a purely "mediatic" (and artificially mediated) life, something that may require even the possibility of limiting the time people may spend in front of a screen.

Although the latter could be done by intervening on the supply side, by limiting the amount of broadcasting time, this is also a difficult and risky avenue to pursue. In the end, the question we must ask is: Why do people spend so much time in front of their screens? Because they do not want to think about their painful lives, they want to escape out of their limited selves. The TV and the Internet are ultimately *ecstatic* instruments, although theirs is a false ecstasy that gives us only the delusion of transcendence, while in fact closing upon us the cage of a smaller and smaller self. The magic of TV and the Internet is the magic of feeling unlimited, of watching and knowing universally like a God. The only way of getting people off the hook of TV and media addiction is by promoting our ability to experience the beauty of our inner visions, which help us expand ourselves through the sense of our cosmic and planetary communion, and of the outer visions of nature as a wonderful metaphor and carrier of spiritual meaning. To give spiritual and natural privacy its primary status not only in the law but also in our life, we need a New Deal for the age of information, a National Meaningful Plan helping people relearn to be with themselves, with real others, and with the real magic in nature and in our mind. We need to offer to as many people as we can alternative opportunities to meet, study, dialogue, all of which could not be truly accomplished without learning to be happily alone and to meditate. With the coming "end of work" there will be even more educated people unemployed. They could be taught to help the people get off the screens into themselves, and thus with real others, thereby promoting a "revolution of privacy" which, as Brandeis knew very well, is the most valuable to "civilized men."

NOTES

1. K. Gormley and R. G. Hartman, "Privacy and the States," in *Temple L.R.*, 65 (1992), 1279–1323, p. 1283.
2. Five states (California, Alaska, Montana, Hawaii, Florida) added strong decisional privacy amendments to their constitutions between 1972 and 1980. Others (Hawaii, Illinois, South Carolina, Louisiana) amended their constitutions with reference to a stronger search and seizure privacy.
3. On the approach of the Alaskan Supreme Court to privacy, including the quotation, see John F. Grossbauer, "Alaska's Right to Privacy Ten Years after *Ravin v State*: Developing a Jurisprudence of Privacy," in *Alaska L.R.* 2 (1985), pp. 159–183.
4. D. Flaherty, *Protecting Privacy in Surveillance Societies* (Chapel Hill: University of North Carolina Press, 1989), p. 380.
5. Ibid., "Controlling Surveillance," pp. 371ff.
6. Ibid., p. 402.
7. On the informational stage of absolute capitalism, see S. Scoglio, "Privacy, Inequality and Transformational Politics. The Right to Privacy in the "Airy" Age of Absolute Capitalism," presented at the 1996 APSA Meeting, San Francisco, August 29–September 1.
8. Colin J. Bennet, *Regulating Privacy. Data Protection and Public Policy in Europe and the U.S.* (Cornell University Press, 1992), p. 254.
9. J. Rule et al., *The Politics of Privacy* (New York, 1980), p. 154. In the same vein, D. Burnham asks: "How can a society devoted to the notion that the free flow of information is essential to the development of sound public policy make a deliberate decision not to collect certain kinds of information?" *The Rise of the Computer State* (New York, 1983), p. 187.
10. See Jeffrey Rothfeder, *Privacy for Sale* (New York: Simon and Schuster, 1992).
11. R. Posner, "*A Sibley Lecture: The Right to Privacy*," in *Georgia L.R.*, 12–3 (1978), p. 396.
12. Jeremy Rifkin, *The End of Work* (Putnam's Sons, 1995).
13. Of course the faculty of imagination is an essential human resource, and there is a whole world of myth, literature, and art that promotes human intelligence. But when they are true to themselves, myth and art reinforce the human ability to see reality unveiled, in its deeper truth, the opposite of the current formational forces that promote the blindness and denial of the fantasizing self, also a very powerful yet destructive human force.
14. J. Naisbitt, *The Global Paradox* (New York: William Morrow and Co., 1994).

SELECTED BIBLIOGRAPHY

Abraham, H. *Freedom and the Court*. New York: Oxford, 1988.
Acheson, D. *Morning and Noon*. Boston: Houghton Mifflin, 1965.
Ackerman, B. *"Beyond 'Carolene Products.' "* In *Harvard L.R.* 98 (1985).
Amer. J. of Law and Med. 15 (1989) (monographic issue on abortion).
Arendt, H. *The Human Condition*. University of Chicago Press, 1958.
———. "Public Rights and Private Interests." In *Small Comforts for Hard Times*. F. Stuber and M. Mooney (eds.), Columbia University Press, 1977.
Bailyn, B. *The Ideological Origins of the American Revolution*. Harvard University Press, 1967.
Baldassarre, A. *Privacy e Costituzione*. Roma: Bulzoni, 1974.
Becker, Ted. (ed.). *Quantum Politics*. Praeger, 1991.
Bellah, R. et al. *Habits of the Heart*. New York: Harper & Row, 1985.
Benn, S. *Privacy, Freedom and Respect for Persons. Privacy. Nomos XIII*. J. Chapman and R. Pennock (eds.) New York: Atherton, 1971.
Bennet, C. J. *Regulating Privacy. Data Protection and Public Policy in Europe and the U.S.* Cornell University Press, 1992.
Bentham, J. *The Works of Jeremy Bentham*. J. Bowring (ed.) (Edinburgh, 1843), 11 vols., reproduction ed. New York: Russell and Russell, 1962.
Berman, H. *Law and Revolution*. Harvard University Press, 1984.
Blackstone, W. S. *The Sovereignty of the Law. Selections from Blackstone's Commentaries*. Toronto: University of Toronto Press, 1973.
Bloustein, E. *Privacy As an Aspect of Human Dignity: An Answer to Dean Prosser*. In *N.Y. Univ. L.R.*, 39 (1964).
Brandeis, L. D. *The Curse of Bigness*. New York: Viking, 1934.

———. *Business: A Profession* (1914). New York: A. M. Kelley, 1971.
———. *The Letters of L. D. Brandeis* (5 v.). Eds. D. M. Levy and M. I. Urofsky. Albany: SUNY, 1971.
———. *Other People's Money and How the Bankers Use It* (1933). New York: Harper and Row, 1967.
Brandeis, L. D., and S. Warren. "The Right to Privacy." In *Harvard L.R.*, 4 (1890).
Burnham, D. *The Rise of the Computer State*. New York: Random House, 1983.
Burt, A. *Two Jewish Justices*. Berkeley: University of California, 1988.
Capuyoa, E. "On Privacy and Community." In *Small Comforts for Hard Times*. F. Stuber and M. Mooney (eds.). Columbia University Press, 1977.
Colker, R. "Feminism, Theology and Abortion: Toward Love, Compassion and Wisdom." In *Calif. L.R.* 77 (1989).
Corwin, E. S. The 'Higher Law' Background of American Constitutional Law." In *Harvard L.R.* 42 (1928).
Cover, R. M. "The Left, the Right and the First Amendment: 1918–1928." In *Maryland L.R.* 40, no. 3 (1981).
Daly, H. *Steady-State Economics*. San Francisco: Freeman, 1977.
Dawson, N. L. *Louis D. Brandeis, Felix Frankfurter and the New Deal*. Hamden, Conn.: Archon, 1980.
———. (ed.) *Brandeis and America*. University Press of Kentucky, 1989.
Douglas, W. O. *The Anatomy of Liberty*. New York: Trident, 1963.
———. *The Court Years: The Autobiography of W. O. Douglas*. New York: Random House, 1980.
———. *Go East, Young Man: The Autobiography of W. O. Douglas*. New York: Random House, 1974.
———. *A Living Bill of Rights*. New York: Doubleday, 1961.
———. *The Right of the People* (1952). New York: Arena, 1972.
Dworkin, R. "Do We Have a Right to Pornography?" In *Oxford J. of Leg. Stud.* 1 (1981).
———. *Taking Rights Seriously*. Harvard University Press, 1978.
Ely, J. "Constitutional Interpretivism: Its Allure and Impossibility." In *Indiana L.J.* 53 (1978).
———. *Democracy and Distrust*. Harvard University Press, 1980.
———. "The Wages of Crying Wolf." In *Yale L.J.* 82 (1973).
Emerson, R. W. *The Collected Works of R. W. Emerson* (4 v.), A. R. Ferguson and R. E. Spiller, (eds.). Harvard University Press, 1971.
———. *Selected Essays*. Penguin Classics, 1982.
Emerson, T. I. "Nine Justices in Search of a Doctrine." In *Michigan L.R.* 64 (1965).
Finnis, J. *Natural Law and Natural Rights*. Oxford University Press, 1980.
Flaherty, D. *Protecting Privacy in Surveillance Societies*. Chapel Hill: University of North Carolina Press, 1989.
Frankfurter, F., Justice. *Of Law and Men*. New York: Harcourt, Brace, 1956.
Garfield, H. "Privacy, Abortion and Judicial Review: Haunted by the Ghost of *Lochner*." In *Washington L.R.* 61 (1986).
Gavison, R. "Privacy and the Limits of Law." In *Yale L.J.* 89 (1980): 421–71.
Georgia Law Review 12, 3 (1978) (monographic issue on privacy).
Glancy, D. "The Invention of the Right to Privacy." In *Arizona L.R.* 21, 1 (1979).
Gormley, K., and R. G. Hartman. "Privacy and the States." In *Temple L. R.* 65 (1992).

Selected Bibliography

Grey, T. "Do We Have an Unwritten Constitution?" In *Stanford L.R.* 27 (1975).
———. "Eros, Civilization and the Burger Court." In *Law and Contemporary Problems* 43, 3 (1980).
Grossbauer, J. F. "Alaska's Right to Privacy Ten Years after *Ravin v State*: Developing a Jurisprudence of Privacy." In *Alaska L.R.* 2, 1985.
Hegel, G. W. F. *The Philosophy of Right*. T. M. Knox (ed.). Oxford University Press, 1952.
Horwitz, M. *The Transformation of American Law*. Harvard University Press, 1977.
Huxley, A. *The Perennial Philosophy*. London: Grafton, 1985.
Journal of Legal Studies 9, 4 (1980) (monographic issue on privacy).
Kauper, P. G. "Penumbras, Peripheries, Emanations, Things Fundamental and Things Forgotten: The *Griswold* Case." In *Michigan L.R.* 64 (1965).
Kennedy, D. "Toward a Historical Understanding of Legal Consciousness: The Case of Classical Legal Thought." In *Research in Law and Sociology* 3 (1980).
Konefsky, S. J. *The Legacy of Holmes and Brandeis*. New York: Macmillan, 1956.
Lasch, C. *The Minimal Self*. New York: Norton and Co., 1984.
Law and Contemporary Problems 31, 2 (1966) (monographic issue on privacy).
Linowes, D. *Privacy in America*. Urbana: University of Illinois Press, 1989.
Locke, J. *A Letter Concerning Toleration*. J. Tully (ed.). New York: Hackett, 1983.
———. *Two Treatises of Government* (1689). Cambridge University Press, 1988.
Lowi, T. *The End of Liberalism*. New York: Norton and Co., 1969.
Lusky, L. "Footnote Redux: A *Carolene Products* Reminiscence." In *Columbia L.R.* 82 (1982).
MacIntyre, A. *After Virtue*. Indiana: University of Notre Dame, 1984.
MacKinnon, C. *Toward a Feminist Theory of the State*. Harvard University Press, 1989.
MacPherson, C. B. *The Political Theory of Possessive Individualism*. Oxford University Press, 1962.
Mason, A. *Brandeis: A Free Man's Life*. New York: Viking, 1946.
———. *The Supreme Court from Taft to Burger*. Baton Rouge: Louisiana State University Press, 1979.
McCloskey, H. J. "The Political Ideal of Privacy." In *Philosophical Quarterly*, 21 (1971).
McLaughlin, C., and G. Davidson. *Spiritual Politics*. New York: Ballantine Books, 1994.
Meiklejohn, A. *Political Freedom* (1960). New York: Oxford University Press, 1965.
Mill, J. S. *The Collected Works of J. S. Mill*. University of Toronto Press, 1963.
———. "On Liberty" (1859), in *Utilitarianism, On Liberty, Considerations on Representative Government*. H. B. Acton (ed.). London: Everyman, 1972.
Miller, A. *Assault on Privacy*. Ann Arbor: University of Michigan, 1971.
Milsom, S. F. C. *Historical Foundations of the Common Law*. London: Butterworths, 1981.
Moore, B., Jr. *Privacy: Studies in Social and Cultural History*. New Jersey: M. E. Sharpe, 1984.
Nedelsky, J. "Reconceiving Autonomy." In *Yale Journal of Law and Feminism* I, 1 (1989).
Note, "Formalism, Legal Realism and Constitutionally Protected Privacy under the Fourth and Fifth Amendments." In *Harvard L.R.* 90 (1977).
Note, "On Privacy: Constitutional Protection for Personal Liberty." *New York Univ. L.R.* 48 (1973).

Note, "*Roe* and *Paris*: Does Privacy Have a Principle?" In *Stanford L.R.* 26 (1974).
Note, "Toward a Constitutional Theory of Individuality: The Privacy Opinions of Justice Douglas." In *Yale L.J.* 87 (1978).
O'Connor, T. "The Right to Privacy in Historical Perspective." In *Mass. L.Q.* 53 (1968).
Packard, V. *The Naked Society*. New York: McKay Co., 1964.
Paper, L. J. *Brandeis*. New York: Prentice-Hall, 1983.
Parent, W. A. *Recent Work on the Concept of Privacy*. In *Amer. Philos. Q.* 20 (1983).
Pennock, R., and J. Chapman. (eds.). *Nomos XIII Privacy*. New York: Atherton, 1971.
Plato. *The Collected Dialogues*. H. Cairns and E. Hamilton. (eds.). Bollingen Series. Princeton University Press, 1961.
———. *The Republic*. F. M. Cornford (ed.). Oxford University Press, 1941.
Posner, R. *A Sibley Lecture: The Right to Privacy*. In *Georgia L.R.* 12, 3 (1978).
Postema, G. J. *Bentham and the Common Law Tradition*. Oxford University Press, 1986.
Powe, L. "Justice Douglas, the First Amendment and the Protection of Rights," in *He Shall Not Pass This Way Again. The Legacy of W. O. Douglas*. L. S. Wasby (ed.). University of Pittsburgh, 1990.
Prosser, W. L. *Privacy: A Legal Analysis. In Calif. L.R.* 48 (1960).
Raines, J. C. *Attack on Privacy*. Valley Forge, PA: Judsons, 1974.
Redlich, N. "Are There 'Certain Rights . . . Retained by the People'?" In *New York Univ. L.R.* 37 (1962).
Rothfeder, J. *Privacy for Sale*. New York: Simon and Schuster, 1992.
Rousseau, J. J. *Discourse sur l'origine et le fondement de l'inégalité parmi les hommes* (1755). Paris: Nathan, 1981.
———. *Du Contrat Social* (1762). Paris: Seuil, 1977.
Rule, J., et al. *The Politics of Privacy*. New York: Elsevier, 1980.
Sandel, M. "Moral Argument and Liberal Toleration: Abortion and Homosexuality." In *Calif. L.R.* 77 (1989).
Schoeman, F. (ed.). *Philosophical Dimensions of Privacy*. Cambridge University Press, 1984.
———. *Privacy and Social Freedom*. Cambridge University Press, 1992.
Spurlin, P. M. *Montesquieu in America: 1760–1801*. Octagon, 1969.
Strum, P. *Louis D. Brandeis: Justice for the People*. Harvard University Press, 1984.
———. (ed.), *Brandeis on Democracy*. University Press of Kansas, 1995.
Thoreau, H. D. *Cape Cod* (1865). New York: Penguin, 1987.
———. *Walden Pond* (1854) and *Civil Disobedience* (1849). New York: Norton, 1966.
Tribe, L. *American Constitutional Law*. New York: Foundation, 1988.
Unger, R. "The Critical Legal Studies Movement." In *Harvard L.R.* 96 (1983).
Urofsky, M. *A Mind of One Piece: Brandeis and American Reform*. New York: Scribner, 1971.
Wasby, S. L. (ed.). *He Shall Not Pass This Way Again. The Legacy of W. O. Douglas*. University of Pittsburgh, 1990.
Weinstein, W. L. "The Private and the Free: A Conceptual Inquiry. In *Privacy. Nomos XIII*, R. Pennock and J. Chapman (eds.). New York: Atherton, 1971.
Westin, A. *Privacy and Freedom*. New York: Athenaeum, 1967.
Wilber, K. (ed.). *The Holographic Paradigm*. Boston: Shambhala, 1985.

Selected Bibliography

Wolin, S. "Democracy and the Welfare State." In *Political Theory* 15, 4 (November 1987).

Wright, B. F. *American Interpretations of Natural Law*. New York: Russell and Russell, 1962.

INDEX

Abe, Masao, 50 n.32
Abortion, 153–65; *Akron v. Akron Center for Reproductive Health*, 162; animation and conception, 159–65; and medicalization, 156–57; fetus's viability, 156–57; *Harris v. MacRae*, 168; informed consent, 162, 171; Italian law on, 163–65, 172; *Planned Parenthood of Southeastern Pennsylvania v. Casey*, 170–72; pro-life vs. pro-choice, 160–65; *Roe v. Wade*, 155–65; reflection and meditation, 160–65, 172; transpersonal view of, 162–65, 168–72; *Webster v. Reproductive Health Services*, 168–70
Abraham, H. J., 147
Abraham v. United States, 78, 92
Absence: as the metaphysical ground, 40; One-Absence, 44
Absolute impulse, 3, 28, 42, 231; as misdirected into the search for bad infinity, 3–4, 231; capitalism as its materialistic channeling, 3

Acheson, Dean, 188–89, 199–200, 201
Action, 79; and choice, 115; and taste, 112–14; and thought, 204, 211–12; liberty of, 126, 176
Adamson v. California, 135, 140
Addictions, 107, 115
Advertising. *See* Television
Agriculture: Brandeis on, 194; Jeffersonian agrarian democracy, 62; oligopolies and yeoman farmers, 53
Akron v. Akron Center for Reproductive Health, 162, 169
Alaska Supreme Court, 226
Alcohol, 114–18; Alcoholics Anonymous, 115
Archetypal forms. *See* Platonic forms
Arendt, Hannah, 32, 48 n.1; and privacy as privation, 33–34
Aristotle, 2, 32–33, 164; and abortion, 182 n.31
Aristotelian-Thomistic tradition, 25, 27, 32–34; and the concept of "synolon," 32

Aristotelianism, 34–35, 187; and the dualism of theoretical vs. practical, 34
Art, 118; and hobbies, 113
AT&T, 9
Atomism: in the abortion situation, 155–65, 170; legalistic and personalistic, 23; liberal, 67
Autonomy, 21, 178; definition of, 105; Millian, 154; principle of, 105; reproductive, 130
Awareness: existential, 88; self-awareness, 42; transpersonal, 188

Bahagavad Gita, 86
Bailyn, Bernard, 50 n.33, 64
Beauharnais v. Illinois, 210
Beauty, 25, 112
Becker, Theodore, 48 n.3
Bellah, R., 187
Benn, Stanley, 48 n.1
Bentham, Jeremy: and Panopticon, 7; and reductionism, 25–26, 80; and relativism, 81; and wealth, 26, 49 n.12; Benthamite tradition, 25
Berlin, Isahia, 49 n.20
Berman, Harold, 39, 60
Bible, 116, 189, 211
Big Brother, 13–14
Bigness, 108, 165, 188, 194, 197, 230; and externalization, 4; as the spiritual power of capitalism, 3–4; Big Government, 15, 165, 230; corporate, 110; rights of, 154
Bill of Rights, 13, 128, 134, 137, 138, 144, 157, 210, 225; unity of its form and substance, 39, 145
Birth, 34, 47, 156–65. *See also* Life/death
Black, Justice Hugo, 133, 134; and Fourteenth Amendment's incorporation, 126–27; dualistic interpretation of double standard, 127–30; his theory of rights, 129 vs. Harlan, Jr., 141
Blackmun, Justice, 32, 154, 168, 176; and abortion, 155–65; and the new generation of post-*Roe* judges, 158–59, 206–7; new privacy paradigm as the dualistic mediation of liberalism and holism, 158–59; 170–72, 174–75, 206–7; his version of substantive due process, 155–56
Blackstone, William, 64–65
Blade Runner, 5
Bloustein, Edward, 48 n.5; his personalist and spiritual concept of privacy, 22
Body: as a mode of self-consciousness, 24–25; as property of the individual, 109; as mask of spirit, 118
Bohm, David, 51 n.38
Bowers v. Hardwick, 172–76, 206–7
Boyd v. United States, 58–59, 98, 203
Bradley, Justice, 58–59, 98, 203
Brandeis, Justice Louis D., 25, 37–38, 47, 48, 71, 174, 187; advocacy vs. incitement, 117–18; and agriculture, 194; and alcohol consumption, 115–18; and automobiles, 194–95; and Cardozo, 125–31, 147; and Emerson, 188, 190–95; and individual wholeness, 95; and fearlessness, 95–96, 196; and Greek thought, 189–90, 196; and Legal Realism, 101; and natural law/rights (homeorhetic), 101, 135, 188–89, 195–96, 198; and self-direction, 98; and self-reliance, 96; and technology, 194–95; as a transpersonalist, 63, 93, 100, 187–202; as Isaiah, 102, 189, 190; as People's Lawyer, 61; and logic of facts, 61–62, 139, 196; and metaphysics, 93, 188–89, 193; beyond liberal conception of rights, 198; Big Government, 15; Bigness, 3, 4, 93, 134–35, 188, 194, 197, 201–2; Brandeis briefs, 61–62, 69; Brandeisianism, political, economic and legal, 187–202; civilization, concept of, 103, 202; common living, 200; contemplation and action, 192–93; democracy, theory of, 194, 196, 200; dialectical identity of opposites, 94, 191–92; dissent in *Olmstead*, 98–103, 173, 179, 202; double standard, preferred freedoms, balancing test, 126–34, 204–5; deliberation, 94, 117, 196, 203–4; deliberative vs. arbitrary forces, 95–96, 197; environmentalist, 134, 194–95; formal/substantive due process, 139, 155, 174, 196–98,

204; fusion of rights of privacy and personality as against property, 203; Goethe, 189–90, 196, 203; government as teacher, 106; government, concept of, 95–96, 198; harm, concept of, 97; holographic conception of language, 206; leadership, concept of, 189, 199–202; liberty, notion of, 95–96, 199; living law, 62, 196; living philosophy, 189; maieutics, 106, 122 n.64; "man's spiritual nature," 43, 54, 98, 102, 179, 189; mistaken either as a communitarian or as a liberal, 94, 116, 139, 174–75, 201–2; morality essential, 189, 195–200; nomination to the Supreme Court, 93; on property/wealth, 53–58, 107–11, 143, 198–99, 205–6; persuasion as alternative to coercion, 106; political and economic theory, 135, 194–95, 198; principle of non–self-destruction, 97, 202–6; privacy, conception of, 103–19, 135, 189, 191, 196, 202–6; privacy as the most comprehensive of rights, and most valued by civilized men, 102–3, 146, 198, 202; Progressive movement, 93; prophets and poets, 189–90, 196; Reason and Logos, 144, 193, 195; responsibility, notion of, 95, 200; right to privacy, 54–58, 94, 174, 189, 202; selective incorporation of Fourteenth Amendment, 126–31, 147; simple living, 195; smallness, value of, 198–99; social justice, 189, 198; speech, freedom of, 95–97; spiritual, notion of, 193–94; spirituality, 189–90, 192; theory of rights, 93–119, 202–6; theory of penumbras, 99–101, 138; *The Right to Privacy* (1890), 54–58; Thoreauianism, 194; workers's cooperatives, 198
Brennan, Justice, 32, 137, 153, 154, 158, 168, 206; in *Whalen v. Roe*, 166–67; on euthanasia, 176–79
Buddha, 38
Buddhism, 27, 40, 48–49 n.8, 50 n.32, 211; and the Gods, 34
Bureaucracy: private and public, 2–3, 15; governmental, 10, 132, 166–67, 228; pro-privacy, 230

Burger, Chief Justice, 154
Burger Court, 153–54, 166, 167; dualistic interpretation of double standard, 154–55; on rights of corporations, 181 n.9
Burnham, David, 6, 8, 9, 11, 236
Butler, Justice, 99, 103

California Bankers Ass. v. Schultz, 166
Campbell, Joseph, 50 n.34
Capitalism: absolute capitalism, 1ff.; absolutistic impulse of, 3–4; and market economy, 3–4; and the dialectic of liberalism and utilitarianism, 16, 67; as a dreamland, 234; as the materialistic channeling of the absolute-impulse, 3–4; as Bigness, 3–4, 165; as corrupt spiritual power, 14–15; as totalitarian, 3, 16–17, 135; global capitalistic economy, 3–4, 232; its contradictory balance of centralization and decentralization, 14–16; military-industrial complex, 135; oligopolistic, 53, 59, 132, 194, 197
Capra, Fritjof, 48 n.3, 50 n.30
Capuoya, E., 43
Cardozo, Justice: selective incorporation, 126–27, 147; non-dualistic theory of double standard, 127, 155, 204; test of fundamental liberties, 127, 173
Categorical imperative, 36, 84
Central Intelligence Agency (CIA), 10
Centralization: as a tautological phenomenon, 15, 228, 230; bureaucratic, 1–17, 166–67, 228, 230; economic, 132; irrationality of, 14, 166; of information, 8, 87, 166–67; through decentralization, 232; transcendental centralizing mechanism and centralizing agents, 14; transpersonal/ecological approach, 16, 197
Choice: between interiority and action, 115, 207; right and wrong, 113–15. *See also* Freedom, of choice
Christianity, 33, 164; and abortion, 164, 169. *See also* Aristotelian-Thomistic tradition
Church, 33; Catholic, 164

Citizen: civic duties, 110; good man and good citizen, 37; wholeness of, 95
Civil disobedience, 78
Civilization, 54, 103
Clark, Justice, 134, 137
Clear and present danger. *See* Legal tests
Coercion, 97, 111; on taste, 112–13
Colker, Ruth, 160–63
Common good, 69, 82, 94, 197; utilitarian, 68; arithmetical conception of, 132
Common Law: and abortion, 164; and right of privacy, 53–58; English tradition, 71, 164; its precommercial values, 59
Communitarianism, 24, 25, 94, 132, 174; and community values, 113–14; and family's privacy, 34; and feeling, 35–36; and liberalism, 142–43; and Justice Rehnquist, 170; and spirited-emotional soul, 35; criticism of the Platonic-Stoic tradition, 187; defined, 32–38; in Justice Blackmun, 158, 170–72, 174–75; in Justice Harlan, Jr., 139–40; privacy as privation, 33; religious, 32–34; secular, 34–35; political-associational privacy as its highest horizon, 35, 232
Community: and abortion, 158–65, 170; and communion, 188; and dialogue, 38, 113; as collective person, 47; associational privacy, 35; its interiority, 37, 105; its moral sense, 59; its planetary duties, 122 n.67; local, 132; small, 63, 199–200; utilitarian conception of, 17; values, 114
Compassion, 44, 95, 118, 161, 188, 233
Computer: computer crimes, 8–9; computer industry and centralization, 16; computer information flawed, 6; computer matching, 14; computer state, 6–11, 228; computer control, 6, 230; computerization and loss of responsibility in the workplace, 7; educational and cultural potentialities, 10
Conscience: and history, 126; liberty of, 88, 203; privacy of, 78, 104, 153; right of, 130; of the woman in the abortion situation, 162–65

Consciousness: cosmic, 211; inward, 88, 209; legal, 66; social, 113
Consequentialism, 87, 99; and deontology, 80, 100; good-based, 27
Conservatism: conservatives, 93; pro-bigness, 201–2
Constitution: and Platonic myth of the Cave, 138; Chief Justice Marshall's conception of, 101; its presumed Lockean origins, 39; its unity of form and substance, 39; transcendental wholeness of its text, 138, 145; unwritten, 39, 59, 71, 101, 127, 144, 156
Constitutional: doctrine of double standard, 127–31, 154; image as the founding juridical myth, 146; penumbras, 99, 101; revolution of 1937, 70, 125–31, 154; tradition, 38–39, 64, 170, 203
Constitutional law. *See* Law
Constitutional rights. *See* Rights
Consumerism, 195; consumeristic mind 2–3
Contemplation, 44, 118, 192; and action, 86, 204. *See also* Meditation
Contract: triumph of, 59; freedom/right of, 61, 65, 68
Conventionalism, 45, 113–14
Cooperation, 86, 109; Brandeis on, 198; movement, 84–85
Coppage v. Kansas, 74 n.72
Corporations, 6, 10, 230
Courage, 25, 30, 95
Cover, R. M., 94
Credit: agencies, 11; economy, 11; information, 7, 10, 11
Critical Legal Studies, 66–68
Cruzan v. Director, Missouri Dept. of Health, 176–79
Cryptography, 9

Daly, H., 120 n.28
Darwinism, social, 61, 78, 191
Data: Data Protection Board, 229; Data Commissioner, 229–30; incorrectness of, 8; financial, 10; fiscal, 10
Data banks: fusion of private and public data banks, 7; governing principles, 226–28; networking of private and

public data banks as undermining the separation of powers, 15; of governmental bureaucracies, 10; riddled with errors, 14; *Whalen v. Roe*, 166–67
Dawson N. L., 189, 195
Death: and birth, 34, 163; and spiritual privacy, 176; euthanasia, 176–79; mystery of life and death, 163, 179
Defamation, 55
Delatte, Armand, 50 n.34
Deliberation: and public privacy, 105; definiton of, 105. *See also* Political deliberation
Democracy: demise of privacy as breaking down American democracy, 15; democratic potentialities of the Internet, 10; enlightened, 83; in Brandeis, 194–202; informational centralization as undermining it, 15; in Montesquieu, 64–65; Jeffersonian agrarian model, 62; oligarchy and democracy 2; spiritual, 200–202; totalitarian, 132
Democratic: participation, 128; party, 93
Deontology: and consequences, 114; and empiricism, 83; and liberalism, 28–29, 80, 141; deontological atomism, 23; rights-based, 27; formal/substantive, 79, 114
Descriptive, and prescriptive, 22, 105
Dialectics: cosmic, 93; dialectical holism, 129, 158, 172; identity of opposites, 63, 65, 94, 191; of privacy and cosmic responsibility, 39; liberal-empirical type of, 45
Dialogue: and community, 38; value of, 93
Dickinson, Emily, 190
Doe v. Bolton, 138–39, 156, 174
Double standard. *See* Constitutional, doctrine of double standard
Douglas, Justice William, 25, 38, 129, 134, 172, 174; and Bigness, 134–35, 188; and Black, 135, 158; and Brandeis, 134–35, 158; and Mill, 209–10; and political-economic Brandeisianism, 136, 208; and minorities, 135; and Native Americans, 135, 211; and New Deal, 132; anti-Establishment, 134–35; *Doe v. Bolton*, 208–10; Douglas/Goldberg approach, 145–47, 153; data banks, 166–67; esoteric and exoteric sides of his *Griswold* opinion, 138–39; freedom of speech, 210; implicit rights, peripheral and foundational, 137–39, 144; in *California Bankers*, 166; natural law and formal/substantive due process, 134, 136, 174; capitalism as totalitarian, 135; *Griswold v. Connecticut*, 135–47; natural law/rights, 130, 136, 138, 209–12; naturalist and environmentalist, 134, 149 n.30, 210–11; on democracy, 135; on Fourteenth Amendment's incorporation and double standard, 126–31; on personality, 208–9; on property rights, 154–55, 208; on technological invasions of privacy, 153, 180 n.4; privacy as implicit fundamental right, 134, 208; privacy as the most fundamental right, 147, 208–12; *Roe v. Wade*, 207; siding with anti-Vietnam War movement, 135; theory of rights, 130, 136, 138, 208–12; theory of penumbras, 134–39; to be let alone vs. expression, 212; transpersonalist, 209–11
Dreams, 43, 178, 234
Dualism: of class interests, 77; of descriptive and prescriptive, 22; of legal and moral, 91; of spirit and matter in Aristotelianism and Thomism, 32–33; of spheres, 66; of subject and object, 103, 234; of theorethical and practical in Aristotelianism, 34; of public and private, self and other, 98, 141, 169–70, 174–75, 234; social, 232–35. *See also* Private and public
Due process: 60, 134, 137, 139, 145, 197; formal/substantive, 147, 155, 156, 196–98; procedural, 205. *See also* Substantive due process
Duplex Printing Press Co. v. Deering, 203
Duties, 65; identity of rights and, 94
Dworkin, Ronald, 29, 49 nn.20, 21, 150 n.56; and Harlan, Jr., 142

Eavesdropping, 57–58
Ecological transpersonalism. *See* Transpersonalism, ecological
Ecology. *See* Environmentalism
Economy: centralization of, 132; credit economy, 11–12; information economy, 228, 230; market economy, 3–4; global capitalistic economy, 3–4; nonprofit, 232; unlimited growth, 11, 14, 85, 165, 201; steady-state, 84–85
Education, 96, 122 n.64; 233–34; as prevention of crime, 97; educational interference, 91
Ely, John, 25, 128–29, 156, 157, 162; and the utilitarian tradition, 181 n.22
Emerson, Ralph Waldo, 25, 38–39, 187, 188; and Brandeis, 188, 190–95; and Douglas, 210; and Greek thought, 190; dialectical identity of private and public, 191–92; father of American environmentalism, 194; history, 191; holographic conception of language, 206; meditation and prayer, 192; living property, 205; Reason vs. Understanding, 193; self-reliance, 192; spiritual human nature, 191; universal mind, 191
Empiricism, 67, 83, 86, 188, 231; and liberalism, 27; its current predominance, 45; its political theory, 25, 46
Environment: and privacy, 5; and productive/consumptive choices, 113–14; and meat overconsumption, 114
Environmentalism: Brandeis's environmental ideas, 194–95; earth as mother, 159; ecological and transpersonal project, 16, 84–85; ecological responsibility, 110; Emerson and Thoreau its American fathers, 194; green economy, 233
Equality: abstract, 65, 69; democratic, 128; equal protection clause, 130; paradox of equality/inequality, 41, 44
Error, 93, 96; learning through, 94, 111; right to, 175
Essence, 37–38, 40, 44, 94, 104, 118; human, 80
Essential/Existential, 26, 40, 41, 203, 206

Essential/existential/empirical, 44, 84
Ethics: categorical imperative, 36, 42; definition of, 42; ethical action, 44; ethical development, 80, 88, 94, 98, 234; ethical habituation, 37; ethical relativism, 78–79, 91; ethical-spiritual interiority and privacy, 8, 10, 24, 162; golden rule, 42, 81; liberal ethical relativism, 31–32
Euripides, 189
Euthanasia, 176–79
Evil: and matter, 33; as absolutization of partness, 94
Existence, 40, 44; existential limits and interdependence, 42, 94, 159
Existential awareness, 103, 104, 119, 212
Existential harm. *See* Principle of existential harm
Existential self-destruction. *See* Self-destruction, existential
Existential selfhood, principle of, 98, 104–5, 160
Expression: and human interiority, 13, 209; and participation, 2. *See also* Freedom, of expression

Family, 111, 156; and euthanasia, 176–79; and violence, 111, 143; childrearing and parental caring, 160–62; contraception, 133–34, 156; marital privacy, 143–44, 156, 173; marriage and procreation, 130, 156, 173; right of, 137, 209; natural contraception, 182 n.34
Fear, 95, 103
Federal Bureau of Investigation (FBI), 8
Feminism, 160–63, 167; feminist criticism of abortion decisions, 168; on childbirth over abortion, 172
Field, Justice, 60
Fifth Amendment, 15, 71, 99, 101, 104, 135, 145, 203, 226; and computer matching, 14; and right to privacy, 138–47, 153; emptied by universal and preventive attack on informational privacy, 9; in *Boyd*, 58–59
First Amendment, 15, 104, 210, 226; and freedom of expression, 13, 210; and right to privacy, 138–47, 153, 179;

Index

emptied by the generalized attack on formational privacy, 12–13; firstness of, 126–31, 145, 179, 204; right to knowledge, 137
Flaherty, David, 226–27, 228
Footnote four. *See U.S. v. Carolene Products Co.*
Form: and language, 46; substantive form, 36, 43. *See also* Platonic forms
Formal/substantive, 44, 66, 139; due process, 139, 147, 155, 174, 196–98, 204; formal/substantive unity of Bill of Rights, 39; *See also* Judicial Review
Founding Era, 39, 64; Founding Fathers, 13, 102
Fourteenth Amendment, 60, 61, 126, 130, 135, 137, 145, 226; theories of incorporation, 126–31. *See also* Equality, equal protection clause
Fourth Amendment, 15, 71, 99, 101, 103, 185 n.63, 203, 226; and computer matching, 14; and right to privacy, 138–47, 153; emptied by preventive and universal attack on informational privacy, 9; in *Boyd*, 58–59
Frank, Jerome, 121 n.59, 135
Frankfurter, Justice: on Brandeis, 192, 204; on double standard, preferred freedoms, balancing test, 131, 133; theory of incorporation, 126–27
Frankfurt School, 2
Freedom: and responsibility, 43–44, 65; decisional, 111; intellectual, 34; of expression, 13, 78–79, 117, 154, 204, 209–10; of choice, 21, 115, 160, 171, 174–76, 207; of contract, 60, 65; of minorities, 78; of religion, 211; of speech, 90, 94–97, 210; preferred freedoms, doctrine of, 125–31. *See also* Liberty
Fried, Charles, 175

Gandhi, 86
Garfield, Helen, 128, 130, 205; undue fusion of Brandeis's and Harlan's constitutional theories, 139–44; on abortion, 157
Gavison, Ruth, 48 n.6

General interest, 6, 66; dissolution of its distinction from particular interests, 15; utilitarian, 68
General will, 36, 43, 96, 197; as public interiority, 37, 47; vs. will of all, 35, 64
Genetics: genetic privacy and genetic ideology, 5–6
Gilbert v. Minnesota, 93, 94
Glancy, Dorothy, 71 n.3, 190, 209
God: in Brandeis, 189–90; in Douglas, 211; in religious communitarianism, 34–35
Goethe, J. W., 10; 83; realm of the Mothers, 43; and Brandeis, 189–90, 196; and Emerson, 190
Goldberg, Justice, 136, 137; concurring opinion in *Griswold*, 144–47
Goldmark, Alice, 192
Good, 66, 68; and Buddha-nature, 27; and Tao, 40; good-based consequentialism, 27; good life, 160, 170, 207; good man and good citizen, 37
Gossip, 4, 13, 231; in Warren's and Brandeis's article, 54; market of, 13–14
Government: and privacy, 1–17, 165–66; authority, 63, 68; Big Brother, 166; ends, 70; its power to interfere, 62, 66, 67, 69, 78, 116, 170; of wealth, 110, 230
Greek thought, 164, 189, 190
Griswold v. Connecticut, 129, 135–47, 156, 162, 168, 174
Grey, Thomas, 122 n.60, 158

Habeas corpus, 1, 111. *See also* Privacy, physical
Habeas mentem, 16, 112. *See also* Privacy, formational
Habits, 112, 209
Happiness: and goodness, 170; and liberty as end, 95; and utility, 80–81; pursuit of, 102
Harlan, Justice J. M., 67–68, 128
Harlan, Justice, Jr., 133, 137, 174; and Frankfurter, 139–40; traditionalist constitutional theory, 139–44; theory of privacy and rights, 139–44

Harm: omissive, 69; to self, 67–68, 160; to others, 111, 159
Harm principle, 29, 67, 68, 100, 160; in *Lochner*, 67; natural law understanding of, 67, 69. *See also* Principle of existential harm
Harrington, James, 39, 64
Harris v. MacRae, 168
Hart, H.L.A., 158
Hate, and group discrimination, 167–68
Health: and privacy, 5–6, 209; and power of pharmaceutical industry, 5; and genetic engineering, 5–6; State's power to protect it, 62, 66
Hegel, G.W.F.: and bad vs. true infinity, 3–4; and heart centred faith religion, 35; and *Notrecht*, 122 n.65
Heisenberg's principle, 48 n.3
Heracleitus, 93
Heroism: and spirited-emotional soul, 30; patriotic, as a communitarian value, 35; heroic individuals, 200; self-sacrifice, 107
Hierarchy of rights. *See* Rights
Hinduism, 211
History: and conscience, 126; and tradition test, 173; historical evolution, 102
Hobbes, Thomas, 74 n.61, 122 n.65
Hobbies, 112–13, 209
Holism, 2, 144, 170–71; dialectical, 129, 132, 172; transpersonal, 93
Holmes, Justice, 60, 65, 77–78, 91–92, 93, 94, 98, 132, 173, 193
Holographic paradigm, 48 nn.3, 7, 51 n.38; holographic analysis of the concept of privacy, 23–25; holographic identity, 41
Homeorhetic. *See* Natural Law, homeorhetic
Homosexuality, 143, 172–76
Horwitz, Morton, 59
Human dignity, 176–79. *See also* Rights, natural
Humanism: secular, 42; spiritual, 190
Huxley, Aldous, 5, 14

Identity: and diversity, 167–68; atomistic, 23, holographic, 41, 115

Independence: and universal standpoint, 42, 191; non-separate independence, 36, 40, 93–119, 202–6
Independence/interdependence, 27, 40, 191, 200
Individualism: acquisitive, 28; ethical-spiritual, 17, 39, 135, 176; liberal, 174; romantic, 187; selfish, 118
Individuality: communitarian conception of, 174–75; free individuality and liberalism, 17; planetary, 233; transpersonal conception of, 83, 135, 176
Inequality, paradox of equality/inequality, 41
Infinity: bad vs. true infinity, 3–4; spiritual, 27; within and without, 194
Information: centralization of, 8, 15, 166–67, 231; computer information flawed, 6; credit, 10–11; ends of private information gathering, 4; inferential relational retrieval, 7–8; Information Age, 228, 230; maximization of, 230; medical, 6; personal information for psychographic profiles, 12; transactional information and signatures, 9
In re Conroy, 178
In re Quinlan, 176
Intellect: intellectual understanding, 42; pleasures of, 80
Interdependence, 27, 40, 159, 188, 191; and existential limits, 42, 94; cosmic, 194
Interference: Mill's notion of, 67; only in emergencies, 98; with self-harmful actions, 67–68; coercive interference, 106, 111, 112, 113, 118, 203; maieutical, 115
Interiority: and contemplation, 44; privacy as interiority, 2, 208, 211–12, 231; ethical and spiritual, 12, 37; its expression, 208; its spiritual quality and foundational value, 13; in the abortion situation, 162–65; its intrinsic value, 80
Internet, 6, 13, 233–35; Internet revolution and its positive potentialities, 10, 233

Index

Intimacy, 21, 23, 100, 143; and associational privacy, 167–68; as other directed personality, 209; sexual, 111
Introspection, 46, 118, 190

James, Henry, 53–54
Jefferson, Thomas, 97, 102; influence on the Constitution, 39; agrarian model of democracy, 62, 194
Jesus, 81, 84, 86, 211
Judgement: as opposed to choice, 177; substituted, 176–79
Judges: and Data Board, 229; their spiritual privacy, 141, 162, 196; the new post-*Roe* generation of, 158, 170–72, 174–75, 206–7
Judicial: supervision, 178–79; restraint, 70, 127, 131, 132, 136, 176, 196
Judicial review: formal/substantive, 66, 139; natural law conception of, 137, 196
Jurisprudence: constitutional, 170; "ex facto oritus jus," 22; Roman and Brandeisian, 22
Justice, 66, 100; as inner ordering of the soul, 37; essence of community, 37; implicit principles of, 60, 127; inherent in the facts, 188

Kant, Immanuel, 43, 84
Karst, K. L., 184 n.48
Katz v. United States, 153, 166, 173, 207
Kennedy, David, *Critical Legal Studies* movement, 66–68, 74 n. 65
Kennedy, Justice A., 170
Kovacs v. Cooper, 130

Language: and Forms, 46; its limits, 45–46
Lasch, Christopher, 18 n.7, 181 n.25
Laski, Harold, 78, 202
Law: and liberalism, 31–32; American constitutional law, 38–39; and morality, 59, 106, 108, 116; and privacy, 43–44, 47; and revolution, 39; and spirituality, 39; and the mind, 44; corruption of, 63; criminal, 154, 180 nn.3, 7; higher, 64, 101, 195; interiority its limits, 43; its essential moral character, 62, 195; its holistic and transpersonal essence, 39, 174; ontological, 138, 195
Lawyers: and political life, 63; corporate, 61–63; holistic legal education, 63
Leadership: righteous, 189; transpersonal notion of, 199–202
Legal Formalism, 32, 59–71, 99, 132, 170, 196; its liberal-utilitarian legal theory, 67–71
Legal literalism, 99, 134, 169
Legal positivism. *See* Positivism
Legal Realism, 101, 135
Legal tests: balancing, 66, 132, 140; clear and present danger, 78, 93, 96, 111, 113, 130, 133, 203–5, 210, 235; compelling interest of State, 156–65, 169, 208; ends and means analysis, 58–59, 66, 70; history and tradition, 173; probable cause, 133, 166; rational basis, 128; sliding scale, 226; substituted judgment vs. best interest in euthanasia, 176–79; undue burden on the abortion choice, 171–72
Legislation: Bank Secrecy Act, 165–66; Loyal and Security Program, 132
Liberalism: and community debate, 113; and communitarianism, 142–43; and the law, 31–32; and the spirited-emotional soul, 30–31; as antiheroic, 30; as privatism, 23–25, 43, 46, 90, 174; as the dualistic version of empiricism, 27; as voluntarism, 29, 174–75; contemporary, 106; dualistic, 27, 78, 141, 158, 170; Harlan Jr. and , 141; in Justice Blackmun, 158, 206–7; its dialectic with utilitarianism, 16, 67, 207, 231; its definition and the philosophy of privacy, 27–32; liberal atomism, 67; liberal dialectics, 45; liberal formalism, 170; liberal personality and free choice, 30, 174, 225, 232; liberal relativism, 31, 234; liberal tradition, 95; liberal-utilitarian legal theory, 59–71; "liberalism plus" of the pro-privacy post-*Roe* judges, 172, 207; post-Millian, 202; pro-bigness, 201–2; Rawlsian liberalism and primary goods, 31. *See also* Mill, John Stuart

Liberty: and authority, 65; as an end and as a means, 95; negative, 65; of doing as we like, 90; of thought, 90, 126, 204; right to, 60, 61; vs. law and morality, 91. See also Freedom
Life: as function of the soul, 164; right to, 54, 60; spiritual, 160; worth living vs. as such, 160, 179
Life/death, 47; mystery of life and death, 163, 179
Ligget v. Lee, 199
Linowes, David, 6–9
Lochner Era, 58–71; Lochnerism, 61, 125, 129, 154, 197
Lochner v. New York, 58, 65, 125, 136; Harlan's dissent, 68–71
Lockean tradition, 25, 154
Locke, John, 27–29, 50 n.24, 154; his constitutional thought, 64–65
Logic: formalistic, 63; logic of facts, 61–62, 65, 71
Logos, 40, 63, 193
Lord Byron v. Johnston, 57
Love, 25; and family life in relation to liberal personality, 30; in the abortion situation, 161
Lynch v. Household Finance Corp., 154–55, 208

McCarthyism, 132–34; Loyalty and Security Program, 132
MacIntyre, Alasdair, 32–33
MacKinnon, C., 168
MacPherson, C. B., 85
Macrocosm/Microcosm, 40, 93, 146
Maieutics, 106, 115, 118, 122 n.64; maieutical leadership, 201
Majority: majoritarianism, 37, 156, 162; opinion, 78; powers, 92. See also Will, majoritarian
Mapp v. Ohio, 133
Marcus Aurelius, 86
Market, 68; market economy and capitalism, 3; market researchers, 4; marketplace of ideas, 78, 92, 93
Marketing, 9; micromarketing, 12; telemarketing, 12
Marshall, Chief Justice, 101, 122 n.61

Marshall, Justice Thurgood, 154, 158, 168, 176, 206
Mason, A. T., 116, 192, 201
Mass society, and culture 2, 11
Matter: and existence, 40; and mind, 22; and sense, 26; and spirit, 32–33
Meat, 114
Mediation: dualistic a posteriori, 83, 141, 174, 207
Medical ethics, 6
Meditation, 50 n.32, 192; in the pregnancy/abortion choice, 162. See also Contemplation
Meiklejohn, A., 149 n.37, 214–17
Melvin v. Reid, 56, 72 n.16
Metaphysics: a priori/a posteriori, 101; as myth, 39; in Plato, 39–40; of privacy, 45–48; transpersonal, 39–45
Meyer v. Nebraska, 128, 136
Mill, John Stuart, 25, 154, 158; and alcohol consumption, 115–16; and capitalism, 84–85; and Millianism, 91, 100, 154, 158, 209; and privacy, 87; competition and value of work, 120 n.26; contradictory dialectics, 79, 81, 82, 86; dualistic mediation a posteriori, 79, 83, 91; enlightened democracy, 83; harm principle, 29, 67, 79, 88, 91; his reintroduction of liberal dualism into utilitarian monism, 78, 80; legal positivist, 91; love of money, power, fame, 82; marketplace of ideas, 78–79; notion of the philosopher, 87; on Plato and Socrates, 120 n.19; possessive egoism, 81–86; principle of liberty, 88–92; relativism, 78; self-regarding sphere/actions, 82, 88–92; slavery, 84; steady state economics, 84–85; supererogatory virtue, 84; theory of liberty, 77–92; tyranny of the majority, 2–3, 83; transpersonalist, 83–84, 90, 92; utilitarianism vs. Platonism, 80; vs. Bentham, 80; virtue and utility, 81
Miller, Arthur, 7
Mind: and matter, 22, 41, 44, 63; and soul, 24; as Nous, 40; Cosmic Mind, 40, 191; dualistic, 94; habeas mentem, 16, 112; its invasion from TV and me-

dia, 12, 231; liberty of, 126, 129, 231; life of, 34 , 203; mental handicap, 178; mental illness, 118; mental pleasures, 80; mind invaders, 13; of enlightenment, 118; over body, 82, 127, 179; peace of, 55, 131; transformation of, 4; unconscious, 178
Minorities, 78–79; enlightened, 201
Miranda v. Arizona, 154, 180 nn.3, 7
Mistakes. *See* Error
Money: money making and its use, 10; as a mode of self-consciousness, 24–25; love of, 81
Montesquieu, 64–65, 200
Moore, Barrington, 48 n.1
Moral: autonomy, 22, 23, 42, 98, 105, 115, 200; dualism of legal and, 91, 141; habituation, 87; interference, 62, 66, 68, 91; judgment, 141; persuasion, 91
Morality: as the non separately independent essence of the law, 59, 108, 189; conventional, 113–14; essence of nature, 195; inherent in facts, 188; forum internum and forum externum, 141; moral law, 62, 189, 195; State's power to protect it, 62, 66, 68, 159; traditional, 37, 86, 113–14, 170, 174–75; *See also* Ethics
Muller v. Oregon, 61–62, 68
Murdoch, Iris, 51 n.41
Murphy, Justice: and due process, 139; on Fourteenth Amendment's incorporation and double standard, 126–31
Mysticism, 33, 86, 211
Myth, 118, 234; and metaphysics, 39; philosophical, 46

N.A.A.C.P. v. Alabama, 148 n.25
Nation, 34–35
National Security Agency (NSA), 9
Natural law: American tradition of, 59, 66, 68, 101; ancient and medieval natural lawyers, 64, 74 n.53, 196, 209; during the Lochner Era, 58–71; genuine, 60–61, 66; homeorhetic, 63, 68, 73 n.51, 101, 126, 132, 138, 188, 195–96; precepts, 209; theory of implied limitations of government, 63–64. *See also* Substantive due process
Natural Rights. *See* Rights
Nature: as anima mundi, 18 n.6; as symbol of spirit, 193, 235; human, 80; individual presocial, 46, 194; moral character of, 195; solitude in, 53, 194
Needs, 109
New Deal, 125, 132, 194; Brandeis and, 194, 197; Douglas's criticism of, 132; for the Information Age, 235
New York Central v. Winfield, 198
New York State Ice Co. v. Liebmann, 197
Ninth Amendment, 101; and right to privacy, 138–47; and unwritten Constitution, 144
Non-self-destruction: principle of, 93, 97, 202–6; as a general implicit constitutional principle, 97, 103–4; articulated into privacy, personality, property, 97–98, 103, 107, 202–6; definition of, 104
Non-separate independence. *See* Independence
Nous, 40; noetic reflexivity, 118

O'Connor, Justice Sandra, 170–72
Olmstead v. United States, 58, 98–103, 117, 153, 173, 179, 202, 207
Olsen v. Nebraska, 135
One: Absolute One and Cosmic One, 40, 191; and the Many, 39; as most primordial reality, 40; as Matter and Spirit, 41; One-Absence, 44
Opinion. *See* Freedom
Orwell, George, 5, 14

Pacifism, 93–94
Palko v. Connecticut, 126
Panopticon, 7, 10; post-modern Panopticon with many all-seeing centers, 10
Pantheism, 187
Paradox: of equality/inequality, 41
Parent, W. A., 22, 48 n.4
Paris Adult Theatre v. Slaton, 159, 210
Participation: as a communitarian value, 32–37, 232; democratic, 128, 200; political, 35
Paternalism, 158

Patriotism, 35
Pavesich v. New England Life Insurance Inc., 56–57, 72 n.13
Peckam, Justice, 65–70
Perfectionism, 80
Person: as a sacred icon, 227; individual and collective, 37, 47; respect for, 97
Personality: and addiction, 115; and self-reproduction, 209; and violence, 97; as the intermediate dimension of love/family and taste/self-care, 30, 45, 143, 209; habeas mentem, 112; inviolate, 55; legal, 65; other-directed and self-directed, 111, 208; rights of, 1, 55, 208–9. *See also* rights
Philosophy: and the concept of privacy, 21, 23–25; perennial, 83, 85; philosophical traditions, 25
Pierce v. Society of Sisters, 128, 136
Planned Parenthood of Southeastern Pennsylvania v. Casey, 170–72
Plato, 86, 120 n.19; and abortion, 182 n.31; and Emerson, 190; Guardians, 30; his metaphysical views, 39–40; justice as inner ordering of the soul, 37; myth of Er, 86–87; Meno, 122 n.64; Parmenides, 51 n.36; Phaedo, 51 n.44; philosopher kings, 86; Republic, 37; Symposium, 50 n.32; spirited-emotional soul, 31; tripartition of money/body/soul, 24–25; the band of thieves, 37
Platonic Forms, 33, 36, 40, 45; as "realm of the Mothers," 43
Platonism, 25, 27, 32, 37, 49 n.8, 50 n.32, 80, 202; and the American founding, 39, 64; and the Gods, 34; as western wisdom tradition, 38; emanationism, 32; Platonic politics, 37, 96, 187
Pleasure: maximization of, 25–27, 78–80; higher, 80; spiritual significance of, 158
Poe v. Ulmann, 133–34, 136, 141, 146
Police, 7, 8, 99, 228
Political deliberation, 95–96, 114, 117, 204; and art, 113; as essence of State, 97

Politics: and spirituality, 38; interest group, 96, 132; Plato and collective political souls, 37; romantic, 187. sociopolitical impulse and life, 209; transformational and transpersonal, 37–38, 187–202
Popper, Karl, 234
Popular sovereignty: as general will and foundation of the separation of powers, 64; social control and the overturning of, 15
Pornography, 13, 159, 210, 227, 235
Positivism: legal, 45, 91, 134, 162; utilitarian, 25, 27
Posner, Richard, 13, 48 n.5; and gossip's educational value, 14, 231; vs. Bloustein, 22
Possessivism, 23, 25, 82–85
Powe, L. A., 211
Pregnancy, 156–65; informed consent, 162; inseparability of mother and fetus, 160
Prescriptive, and descriptive, 22, 47
Press: copyright, 55, 94–97, 210; newspapers, 53–54
Pribram, Karl, 51 n.38
Prince Albert v. Strange, 55–56
Principle of existential harm, 47, 97, 202–6; as involving the unity of harm to self and to others, 104; in the abortion situation, 159–60
Principle of integrity, 23–25
Principle of privacy: as distinct from the right, 21, 47, 138, 208; as implied in all rights, 46–47, 109, 208, 212; as foundational constitutional principle, 138–47, 153, 226
Principles: common law, 58–59; implicit constitutional, 59, 103–4; of privacy, 230
Privacy: a post-materialistic issue, 230; and abortion, 153–65, 168–72; and common law, 53–58; and computer matching, 14; and environmental pollution, 5; and genetic engineering, 5–6; and habeas corpus, 1; and health, 5, 112, 228; and hobbies, 112–13; and inferential relational retrieval, 7–8; and

Index

life/death issues, 34, 47; and marketing, 9, 12; and responsibility, 8; and technology, 5, 53, 131, 153; and telephone, 9; and the workplace, 6–7; and TV/advertising, 2, 12, 46, 103, 113, 231; and unemployment, 7; as a function of public life in communitarianism, 33; as a general constitutional principle, 58; as being left alone, 2, 22, 104, 147, 202; as communion, 43; as essence of property, 101, 202; as ethical-spiritual, 24; as inclusive of community, 24; as interiority, 2, 47, 208; as involving solitude and introspection, 21; as locus of human spiritual nature, 33, 42; as multilayered yet unitary, 21; as ''private sphere,'' 47; as related to intimacy and family life, 139–44, 173–75; as spatial-decisional, 179, 206–7; as spiritual self-reliance, 4; as withdrawal/forthcoming, 24, 42–43, 46, 104, 179, 202; associational, 35, 167–8; bodily, 153, 179, 111–12; circle of privacy protection, 231; concept of, 23–25, 38–48; contemplative, 102; death of, 2; decisional privacy, 1, 179, 206–7, 225; economic reductionism of, 26; empirical/existential/essential, 46–48; essential, as the paradox of inner cosmic communion, 46, 162; existential, as a bridge to essential privacy, 46, 218–19; family's privacy, 34, 111, 130, 143, 155–56, 173, 228; feminist criticism of privacy semantics, 168; financial and fiscal, 165–66, 228; Form of, or in itself, 45; formational, 2, 4, 10, 153, 225–35, 231; four categories of privacy, 1–2; governmental invasions of, 99–103; holistic conception of, 2; home, 93, 143, 153; informational privacy, 1–2, 10–11, 225–35; in Mill, 87; its distinctiveness and coherence, 21; its invasion as an economic good, 13–14; its demise breaking down American democracy, 15; medical, 6, 156, 166–67; mental/noetic privacy, 33–34, 112–13, 118, 131, 153, 204, 208; metaphysics of, 45–48; normative reductionism of, 22; of conscience, 78, 153; new post-Roe privacy paradigm, 158–59; 170–72, 174–75, 206–7; of the accused, 153; of the judge, 141, 162, 196; paradigms, 23–25, 174–5, 206–7; physical, 1, 99, 109, 225; political/public, 2, 35, 47, 105, 218; primacy of, 43, 93, 98, 198, 202, 211, 232; Privacy Amendment, 225–26; public and private invasions, 58; reductionistic conception of 2, 26, 98, 103, 173; revolution of, 235; tort, 56; self-directed and other-directed, 105, 117–19, 202–19; sexual/reproductive, 33, 155–65, 168–72, 209; spatial, 179, 206–7; spiritual, 33, 37, 41, 50 n.32, 71, 105, 118, 146, 162, 179, 198, 203–4, 235; transpersonal conception of, 38–48, 135, 232; vicious circle of privacy and circle of vicious privacy, 8–10. *See also* Philosophy, and the concept of privacy; Principle of privacy; Right to privacy

Private: autonomy, 68; consumption, 4; opinion, 77–79

Private and public: their empiricist dialectics in Weinstein, 45; liberal dualism of, 28, 65, 90, 141; communitarian dualism, 33–37; feminist criticism of dualism, 168; fusion of 2, 7; 9, 15, 228, 230; utilitarian monism of, 67; their dialectical unity, 190–92

Private sphere, 46, 69, 82, 91, 98, 130; and liberalism, 16, 23, 30, 31, 65

Privatism (liberal), 23–25, 43, 46, 90, 174

Prohibition, 99, 116

Property: right to, 1, 23, 46, 77, 205–6; and self-preservation, 107–10, 206, 209; as a shield of personality and privacy, 59, 154–55, 205–6, 208; as the most external dimension of rights, 45; destruction of, 97, 107; over intangibles, 54, 99, 103; intellectual, 55; personal, small 165–66, 199; private property, 109, 205; self-directed and other-directed, 107, 110, 208. *See also* Rights; Right to property

Prosser, William J., 25, 72 n.15; his criticism of Warren & Brandeis, 56–58
Public: discussion, 95; duty, 95; life, 34; privacy as its function in communitarianism, 34–36
Public Interest. *See* Common good
Publicity, 54; right to, 57
Punishment, 97; for destruction of other-directed property, 107
Pythagorean tradition, 39, 50 n.34, 86

Quantum physics, 48 n.3

Racism, 118, 167–68, 210
Raines, J. C., 42, 51 n.39
Rationalism: and secular communitarianism, 33–34; unity of real and rational, 22, 63
Rawls, John, 49 n.21, 154; Rawlsian liberalism and primary goods, 31
Reason: eternal, 83, 193; holistic, 62; inherent in human soul, 177; inherent in things, or logic of facts, 61–63, 139, 196; judicial, 63, 196
Reasonableness, test of, 58, 62, 71
Redlich, N., 146–47, 150 n.64
Reflection, 43, 105; in the abortion situation, 160–65, 172
Rehnquist, Chief Justice, 159, 173; false communitarianism of, 170
Rehnquist Court: and abortion, 168–72; and euthanasia, 176–79
Relations, impersonal vs. personal, 111
Religion, 42, 189; and abortion, 164–65; eastern and western, 38, 211; freedom of, 126, 211; religious individual, 42
Repression. *See* Interference
Republicanism, 96; republican element in liberal and utilitarian thought, 17
Republican Party, 93
Responsibility: and freedom, 43–44, 65; as the great developer, 95, 200; cosmic/universal, 39, 83, 94; ecological, 110, 211; loss of responsibility due to computerization of management-workers relation, 7; loss of responsibility and the "vicious circle of privacy," 8; reproductive, 161

Revolution: its definition, 38; of the concept of privacy, 38–48
Rifkin, Jeremy, 122 n.68, 232
Rights: against self-incrimination, 101, 180 n.3, 203; and duties, 65, 94; as shields for the private individual, 46; associational, 167–68; deontology, 27; dialiminal absolutism of, 133, 203; fundamental, 98, 126, 144; formalism of, 170; *Griswold-Roe* rights revolution, 1; general conception of, 37, 41, 202–6; of citizens, 63, 68; of free choice, 25, 171, 174–75; of free speech and assembly, 97–98, 126, 204, 210; of religion, 126, 211; of reproductive autonomy, 130, 156, 209; scheme of rights, 213, 212–19; to access and correction of data, 227; to appeal, 204; to choice of profession, 204; to counsel, 180 n.3; to die, 176–79; to education, 204; to locomotion, 204; to silence, 130, 180 n.3, 211; to knowledge, 137; protection of, 68
Rights, constitutional: and incorporation, 60, 125–31; implicit, 127; in Justice Harlan, 70
Rights, hierarchical tripartition of rights, 30, 45, 47, 105, 202–6, 208–12; as articulated into six levels, 106, 202–6
Rights, mental/spiritual: and double standard, 127–31, 133; and euthanasia, 178–79
Rights, natural, 23, 66, 67, 69, 179, 209; their liberal-utilitarian understanding, 59–71; natural rights-utilitarians, 67–71, 77
Rights, sexual/reproductive, 209; abortion, 155–65; contraception, 133–34
Rights of personality, 1, 103, 127, 173, 202–6, 208–9; and self-reproduction, 209; as the intermediate dimension of rights, 45, 202–6; reduction of privacy to, 173; their reduction to property rights inside the liberal-utilitarian framework, 31
Rights of property, 60, 154; as fundamental, 205–6; as the most external dimension of rights, 45, 202–6

Index

Right to privacy, 1, 22, 25, 37; and common law, 53–58; as implied into personality and property rights, 46, 202; as "a priori" yet concrete natural right 22–23; as right to be let alone, 54, 58, 102, 147, 173, 202; as the quintessential right, 46–47, 147; as a general constitutional principle, 138–47, 153; constitutionalization of, 130, 133, 134; defined, 212; distinguished from personality rights, 203–4; most comprehensive of rights, and most valued by civilized men, 102–3, 146, 198, 202; right to associational privacy, 133; Warren's & Brandeis's 1890 article, 54–58

Right to property: as proprietary privacy, 46, 205–6; as right to wealth, 31; fundamental and non-fundamental, 205–6; in the *Lynch* case, 154–55; primacy of, 154; privacy as property over personal information, 23. *See also* Property

Right to wealth, 23, 31, 110

Robbins, John, 122 n.68

Roberts v. United States Jaycees, 183–84, n.48

Roe v. Wade, 154, 155–65, 168–72, 174–75, 207

Roosevelt, President, 125, 132, 190, 197

Rosenblum, Nancy, 48 n.1

Rothfeder, Jeffrey, 6, 12, 13, 14

Rousseau, Jean Jacques: compassion, 188; envious comparison, 103, 195; general will vs. will of all, 35, 64, 74 n.54; human perfectibility, 199

Rule, James, 230–32

Ruppert v. Caffey, 116

Rutledge, Justice: and due process, 139; on Fourteenth Amendment's incorporation and double standard, 126–31

Saia v. New York, 131

Sandel, Michael, 32, 34, 143; on the pre-*Roe* and post-*Roe* privacy paradigms, 174–75

Scalia, Justice A., 170

Schafer v. U.S., 196

Schenck v. United States, 78

Schiller, Friedrich, 83

Schoeman, Ferdinand, 2, 48 nn.1, 2; his communitarian pitfall, 34–35; his definition of privacy, 22

Science: Heisenberg's principle, 48 n.3; holographic, 51 n.38

Scoglio, Stefano, 49 nn.9, 18

Searches and seizures, 1, 57, 103, 185 n.63, 203; habeas corpus, 1; electronic universal and preventive search as emptying Fourth and Fifth Amendments, 9

Self: and crime, 107–8; and interdependence, 27; and other, 65, 118; appetitive, 11; awareness of, 42; communitarian conception of, 174–75; egoistic, 96; empiricist notion of, 67, 106; essential universal self, 42, 106, 119, 165, 178, 211; fantasizing, 233; holographic, 41, 160; in the abortion situation, 159–60; lower, 3, 4, 233; noetic, 88; no-self in Buddhism, 50 n.32; perfection/realization, 80, 187–88; personal, 23; possessive-consumeristic, 4; principle of selfhood, 212; transpersonal conception of, 27, 41, 187–88, 211. *See also* Existential selfhood

Self-destruction: and self-harm, 111; as addiction, 115–16; existential, 84, 97, 111, 178, 204; vs. physical destruction, 107. *See also* Non-self-destruction

Self-direction, 88, 89, 98, 104; its priority over other-direction, 105, 212; self-directed actions, 89

Self-preservation, 107–10, 206; and alcoholism, 115; as a natural right, 108, 209; included in the right of privacy, 109

Self-regarding sphere/actions. *See* Mill, John Stuart, self-regarding sphere actions

Self-reliance, 96, 103; resilient, 115; spiritual, 189

Self-sufficiency, 83; as part of right to property, 108

Sense, and matter, 25–27

Separation of powers, 64; breakdown of, 15; dualistic understanding of, 64–65

Seventh Amendment, 126
Sex: and privacy in communitarianism, 33; sexism, 118; sexual education, 163; sexual intimacy, 111, 209; sodomy, 173–76; virtual, 235
Shakespeare, William, 190
Shklar, Judith, 30, 121 n.59
Sidis v. F. R. Publish. Corp., 56, 72 n.17
Silence, 44, 130, 233–34
Sixth Amendment, 126
Skinner v. Oklahoma, 130
Slander and libel. *See* Tort
Slaughter-House cases, 60
Slavery: in Locke, 28–29; in Mill, 84; voluntary, 107, 227
Smith, Adam, 154, 191
Smith, Jeff H., 229
Socrates, 38, 48 n.8, 50 n.32, 51 n.44, 62, 80, 81, 83, 84,120 n.18; and Emerson, 190; and maieutics, 106
Solitude, 21, 47, 53, 190
Soul, 42, 46, 164; acquisitive soul and utilitarianism, 24–27; and time, 25; Emerson's Over-Soul, 191; its "eternity," 48 n.8; its Platonic tripartition, 24–25; its inherent reason, 177; justice as its inner ordering, 37; spirited-emotional soul and liberalism, 30–31; spirited-emotional soul and communitarianism, 35–36; transpersonal, 35
Souter, Justice D., 170
Speech, 79; deliberative, 117; freedom of, 90, 94–97, 210; racist, 210
Spencer, Herbert, 61, 66, 77
Spirit, 3, 32, 118, 179, 193; and nature, 193–4; as the One, 41, 191; liberty of, 129
Spiritual: depths, 3, development, 88, 94; ethical-spiritual privacy, 24; life, 33; happiness as, 102; human nature, 33, 43, 98, 102, 179, 189, 191, 210; individualism, 39, 176; native American tradition, 211; politics (Davidson & McLaughlin), 50 n.29; self-realization, 43, 70, 209, 231; self-reliance, 189, 190; traditions, 164, vs. intellectual,

moral, 193–94; *See also* Privacy, spiritual
Spretnak, Charlene, 50 n.30
Stanley v. Georgia, 173
State, 33; and capitalism,1–17, 165–66; and privacy, 1–17; and Society, 64–65, 231–32; compelling interest of, 156–65, 208; its educational function, 96; end of, 94, 95; *See also* Government
State of the World, 122 n.68
Stealing, difference between greedy, petty and needy, 108
Stevens, Justice, 164, 166; beyond the spatial-decisional conception of privay of the new post-*Roe* paradigm, 179, 206–7; on abortion, 169–72; on euthanasia, 178–79
Stewart, Justice, 134, 154–55
Stoics, 80, 81, 84, 86, 187, 190, 195, 196
Stone, Justice, 127–31
Strossen, N., 211
Strum, Philippa, 189, 199
Sublime, 35
Substantive due process, 128, 162; and family rights, 130; and implict principles of justice, 60, 127; economic, 61; natural law understanding of, 68, 127, 137; non-economic, 128, 135, 136, 155
Substantive form. *See* Forms
Symbol, symbolic expressions, 43.
Taft, Chief Justice, 99–100
Taste, 112–15, 207, 209; and personality, 30, 209
Technology, 5, 53, 131, 153, 194–95, 230
Telephone, 53, 194; and pen register, 9
Television (TV), 46, 103, 231; impact on people's minds, 2, 234–35, TV and advertising, 2, 12, 113, 194, 231, 233
Thomas, Justice C., 170
Thomas Aquinas, Saint, 32–33
Thoreau, Henry D., 25, 38, 53, 190, 210; master of contemplation in nature, 194
Thornburg v. American College of Obstetricians, 175, 183 n.35
Thought, 79; as inherently self-directed, 88, 118; its priority over action, 43–44,

Index

88, 202–6, 211–12. *See also* Liberty, of thought
Tilly, Charles, 17–18 n.5
Time, and soul, 25
Tort: of privacy, 56; of slander and libel, 55
Totalitarianism: as a result of the misdirected absolute-impulse, 4ff.; Bigness as, 4; capitalism as totalitarianism of souls, 16–17, 234; of TV mass culture, 233; totalitarian "vicious circle of privacy," 8–10; utilitarian, 83
Totality: human quest for totality, 3–4
Tradition: and history test, 173; traditionalism, 37, 86, 113–14, 139–44, 156, 170
Transformation: social, cultural and spiritual, 12, 160–65, 230–31; transformational politics, 37
Transpersonal: dialectics, 63; conception of privacy, 45–48; metaphysics, 39–45; political theory, 38, 43, 85, 188, 194–202; transpersonal and humanistic psychology, 187; tradition, 63, 100, 188–90, 202
Transpersonalism, 24, 25, 27, 37, 232; and abortion, 160–65; and euthanasia, 176–79; and instincts, 158; ecological, 37–38, 194, 210–12; dialectically monistic, 63, 90; Platonic, 80; spiritual democracy, 199–202
Trespass, 57–58, 153
Tribe, Laurence, 60, 61, 94, 157, 166; on associational privacy, 167
Tripartition of privacy, personality, property. *See* Privacy; Personality; Property
Truman, President, 132
Truth: and opinion, 78–79; and error, 93; and wholeness, 94; attainability and discovery, 79, 95; morality as, 189
TWR, 9, 11

Unger, Roberto (*Critical Legal Studies*), 66, 74 n.65
Universality: in communitarianism, 32–37; perspective, 105; universal standpoint, 42
Urofsky, M., 189

U.S. v. Carolene Products Co., 127–29
Utilitarianism: and Ely J., 181 n.22; and fear, 95; and social darwinism, 61; as defined by "pleasure-through-wealth" maximization, 17; as possessivism, 23–25, 158; Benthamite, 25, 67; greatest good of the greatest number, 77; its dialectic with liberalism, 16, 67, 207, 231; sense-reductionism and the utilitarian principle, 26; liberal-utilitarian legal theory, 59–71; monistic, 23–25, 78, 90; rule-utilitarianism, 81; wealth maximizing, 198, 225
Utility: and virtue, 81–86; as ultimate value, 80; criteria of, 92

Van Alstyne, W. W., 154–55
Vedas, 86
Village of Belle Terre v. Boraas, 167, 182 n.27
Vinson Court, 131–34
Virtue, 31, 81, 90, 95; and utility, 81–86; despiritualization of, 86; love of, 82; supererogatory, 84
Volstead Act, 116–17
Von Humboldt, Wilhelm, 83, 95

Wallerstein, Immanuel, 17 n.5
Warren, Chief Justice Earl, 133, 137
Warren, Samuel, 190; 1890 article "The Right to Privacy," 54–58
Warren Court, 154
Watts, Alan, 211
Wealth: and self-reliance, 110; oligarchic distribution of, 2; maximization of, 3, 23, 26, 67, 68, 84, 198, 205, 225, 230; social and ecological uses of, 110. *See also* Right to wealth
Webster v. Reproductive Health Services, 164, 168–70
Weinstein, W., 45
Weiss, Paul, 48 n.1
Welfare: and computer matching, 14; demise of, 232; government's power to protect it, 62, 66; State, 66, 132, 165
West Coast Hotel v. Parrish, 125
Westin, Alan, 17 n.1, 57, 72 n.25

West Virginia Board of Education v. Barnette, 130
Whalen v. Roe, 166–67
White, Justice, 134, 154, 170; opinion in *Bowers*, 173
Whitehead, N., 122 n.64
Whitney v. California, 94–96, 104, 106, 117
Wholeness: and partness, 51 n.38, 63, 94; as end, 83, 94; inner, 83; its liberal denial, 32; limited whole, 145–46; perspective, 94; private, 95
Whole of Wholes, 36, 41, 44, 63, 64, 66, 104, 133, 145; and personal choices, 113; as the centre of transpersonal political theory, 43, 188; in Brandeis, 95, 197, 200; in Cardozo, 126–27
Wilber, Ken, 48 n.3
Will: subjective, 83, 105; majoritarian, 45, 92, 95, 156, 140; traditional, 45, 156. *See also* General will
Wiretapping, 57–58, 99–103
Wisdom: and leadership, 201, Ageless, 38; inner, 87; in government, 93, 228
Wolin, Sheldon, 2
Wordsworth, William, 187
Work: end of, 232; privacy in the workplace, 6–7

About the Author

STEFANO SCOGLIO is a Research Assistant at the University of Urbino, Italy. He is the founder and president of a successful health food company.

ISBN 0-275-95607-5

HARDCOVER BAR CODE